Contents

List of figures and tables   *page* vii
List of contributors   ix
Acknowledgements   xv
Abbreviations   xvii
Map of Kaliningrad region   xix

1 Introduction: adapting to European integration? Kaliningrad,
   Russia and the European Union   1
   Stefan Gänzle and Guido Müntel

Part I Analytical framework

2 Conceptualising Europeanisation in Eastern Europe:
   EU impact in 'likely' and 'unlikely' member states   31
   Christoph Knill, Diana Pitschel and Michael W. Bauer

3 How do enclaves adjust to changes in the external
   environment? A theory of enclaves and the case of Kaliningrad 51
   Evgeny Vinokurov

4 EU–Russia–Kaliningrad relations – a case of soft
   securitisation?   68
   Holger Moroff

**Part II The policy framework: Kaliningrad in its domestic and
international context**

5 Multi-level governance and centralisation in Russia:
   implications for EU–Russia relations   89
   Joan DeBardeleben

6 Federalism in Russia: opportunity or constraint for
   Kaliningrad?   108
   Stefan Meister

7 Social identity and regionalisation: the case of Kaliningrad 124
   Anna M. Karpenko

8 Kaliningrad in its neighbourhood – regional cooperation with
   Poland and Lithuania   132
   Silke Schielberg

9 Regional organisations in the Northern Dimension area and
   Kaliningrad   147
   Tobias Etzold

Part III **Empirical evidence: Kaliningrad and policy adaptation
          vis-à-vis the EU**

10 Economic policy   169
    Evgeny Vinokurov

11 European principles in a Russian context: the transformation
    of social policy?   183
    Vyacheslav Dykhanov

12 Environmental governance in Kaliningrad: lost
    opportunities   195
    Guido Müntel

13 Public health policy: how does Kaliningrad adapt to the EU?   209
    Alexandre Berlin and Greg Mestdag

14 Higher education in Kaliningrad   222
    Stefan Gänzle, Stefan Meister and Conrad King

15 Integrated management of the EU-Russia common
    border: the Kaliningrad perspective   236
    Alexey Ignatyev, Konstantin Shopin and Pyotr Shopin

Part IV **Conclusions**

16 Summary: Kaliningrad and Europeanisation '*à la carte*'   249
    Stefan Gänzle and Guido Müntel

17 Russia: a case for revising the concept of Europeanisation   255
    Gabriella Meloni

    Postscript: Coping with Stalin's legacy and Putin's autocracy –
    Kaliningrad between post-Soviet Russia and the European
    Union   269
    Helmut Hubel

    Index   273

Figures and tables

Figures

1.1 Factors of change and constraints to adaptation in
   Kaliningrad   *page* 17
2.1 EU regulatory policies and domestic institutional change   44
10.1 What market do you judge to be the most promising for
   Kaliningrad goods?   179

Tables

1.1 Economic performance of Kaliningrad (Kal) and Russia (RUS):
   annual change of GRP   7
1.2 Directions of change in analytical concepts applied   14
1.3 Adapting to European integration? Expected impact on policy
   areas in Kaliningrad   19
3.1 Incomes per capita in nominal terms in the enclave in
   comparison with the mainland's average and their correlation
   with the economic regime   61
3.2 Incomes relative to M and S   62
11.1 Distribution of competences of public authorities in social
   protection   185
11.2 Distribution of competences of public authorities in
   social-labour relations (pre-2007)   186
16.1 Adapting to European integration? Policy areas in Kaliningrad 251

CONTRIBUTORS

Michael W. Bauer has been Assistant Professor at the Department of Politics and Management of the University of Konstanz since 2004. He holds a Ph.D. from the European University Institute in Florence. Bauer is the author of *A Creeping Transformation? The European Commission and the Management of EU Structural Funds in Germany*, Dordrecht, Kluwer Academic Publishers, 2001. He is the editor (with Christoph Knill) of *Management Reforms in International Organisations*, Baden-Baden, Nomos, 2007.

Alexandre Berlin is Honorary Director of the European Commission and Associate at the Institute for European Studies, University of British Columbia as well as European Director of the Canadian Students Study Tours to the European Institutions. He received his Ph.D. in chemistry from the University of Washington (Seattle, USA) in 1960 and carried out post-doctoral research at New York University. Berlin held various positions at the European Commission, including that of the Head of Public Health. He is currently adviser to WHO and the Council of Europe on health matters in relation to south-eastern Europe and Member of the Executive Task Force of the South-Eastern Europe Stability Pact-Health Network.

Joan DeBardeleben is Professor of Political Science and of European and Russian Studies at Carleton University, Ottawa (Canada). She is Director of the Centre for European Studies, Associate Director of the Institute of European and Russian Studies and Co-Director of the East–West Project, which houses research on Russian social, economic, and political developments. She received her Ph.D. from the University of Wisconsin-Madison in 1979 and taught at McGill University prior to going to Carleton University in 1991. She is the author of several books and articles dealing with Russian politics, public opinion, labour relations and privatisation, and elections. She also maintains a research interest in environmental issues and policies in the post-communist world.

Vyacheslav Dykhanov is Assistant Professor at the Chair of Politology and Sociology at 'Immanuel Kant' Russian State University, Kaliningrad. He received his Ph.D. in historical sciences from Kiev National University 'Taras Shevchenko', Ukraine in 1999. He also holds a diploma in finance and credit. He was Assistant Lecturer at the National Academy of Public Administration in Odessa, Ukraine. Furthermore, he worked for the Odessa Branch of the Ukrainian Academy of Public Administration at the President's Office between 1999 and 2001. Since 2000, he has been engaged as an expert in various projects dealing with the issue of regional development, some of them relating to the Kaliningrad oblast.

Tobias Etzold is currently a Ph.D. student in Politics at Manchester Metropolitan University, UK, where he conducts the research project: 'The Council of the Baltic Sea States, Nordic Council and the Nordic Council of Ministers in a theoretical perspective: Continued existence and future options in light of the EU enlargement of 2004.' From October 2003 to February 2005, he was research assistant at the Schleswig Holstein Institute for Peace Research (SHIP) at the University of Kiel, and here he was mainly occupied with EU–Russia/Kaliningrad relations and Kaliningrad-related policies of international organisations and countries. He graduated from the University of Nijmegen in 2000. He worked as Project Assistant at the Secretariat of the CBSS in Stockholm in 2001.

Stefan Gänzle is Visiting Assistant Professor (DAAD) at the Institute for European Studies and the Department of Political Science at the University of British Columbia. He has been a research fellow at the University of Jena, the European University Institute and a researcher-in-residence at the OSCE. He is the author of *Die Europäische Union als außenpolitischer Akteur: Eine Fallstudie am Beispiel der EU-Politik gegenüber den baltischen Staaten und Russland* [The European Union's Foreign Policy in the Making: The Case of the Baltic States and Russia], Baden-Baden, Nomos, 2007 and the editor (with Allen G. Sens) of *The Changing Politics of European Security: Europe Alone?*, London, Palgrave, 2007.

Helmut Hubel is a Professor of Political Science. He held the Chair of Foreign Policy and International Relations at the 'Friedrich Schiller' University, Jena (Germany) from 1998 until 2007. Now living in England, he continues teaching in Jena. He received his doctorate from the 'Philipps' University of Marburg/Lahn in 1978 with a study on arms control policy in the Baltic Sea area during the East–West conflict. Hubel received his *Habilitation* from the University of Bonn in 1993 with a study on the end of the East–West conflict in the Orient. His studies focus on the EU as a foreign policy actor, on EU–Russia relations, US foreign policy, and regional conflicts. Among his major publications is *EU Enlargement and Beyond: The Baltic States and Russia*, Berlin, A. Spitz Verlag, 2002 (with Aino Bannwart and Stefan Gänzle).

Alexey Ignatyev holds the position as Head of the Centre for European Partnership in Kaliningrad. He graduated from the Kaliningrad Technical Institute and has continued his education in the Russian State Academy of

Public Administration. For more than twenty years, he has been working in the spheres of international relations, regional planning and development, public administration, investment promotion and also support to development of small and medium business. Ignatyev is a Member of the Board of Directors of the Regional Economic Development Agency (Kaliningrad), the Founder and the President of the Association of International Experts on the Development of the Kaliningrad Region (AIKE) and also a Member of the Advisory Board under the Interdepartmental Working Group on the development of the Kaliningrad Region established under the Administration of the Russian President in 2004.

Anna Karpenko is a Ph.D. candidate as well as Senior Lecturer at the Department of Political Science and Sociology of 'Immanuel Kant' Russian State University, Kaliningrad. She received her M.A. in Political Science with distinction from Manchester University in 2007. In her thesis, she is occupied with the discourses on the regional identity of Kaliningraders.

Conrad King received his M.A. from the Institute of European Studies at the University of British Columbia, with a thesis on the Bologna Process and higher education governance. With prior degrees in Education and European History, the latter with high distinction from the University of Toronto, King has lectured in the education departments at universities in Spain and Korea. He has conducted research on Canada–EU teacher exchange programmes as well as the trans-Atlantic impact of the Bologna Process.

Christoph Knill holds the Chair of Comparative Public Policy and Administration at the University of Konstanz. He specialises in European governance, Europeanisation and its impact on national administrations as well as environmental policy. He is the author (with Duncan Liefferink) of *Environmental Politics in the European Union: Policy-Making, Implementation and Patterns of Multi-Level Governance*, Manchester, Manchester University Press, 2007.

Stefan Meister is a research assistant at the German Council on Foreign Relations in Berlin (Russia/Eurasia Programme). For his Ph.D. he researched the topic of 'Russian universities between global and national change'. Before this positon he was Research Assistant at the University of Jena, and he has been a short term election observer for the OSCE and the German Foreign Office since 2004. His professional experience also includes a Researcher position at the Centre for International Relations, Warsaw, Poland. His research focuses on Russian regions, Russian Foreign Policy, Russian Education Policy and Polish and EU Eastern Policy towards Belarus and Ukraine.

Gabriella Meloni holds a Ph.D. from the European University Institute (EUI) of Florence, with a thesis focused on the analysis of the mechanisms which have allowed the EU to promote legislative approximation in Russia and in Ukraine. Meloni has previously worked at the University of Rome 'La Sapienza', as well as in many research projects in transition countries and in institutions like the Russian European Centre for Economic Policy (RECEP). Meloni is the editor (with Marisa Cremona) of *The European Neighbourhood Policy. A Framework for Modernisation?*, EU Working Paper Law 2007/21.

Greg Mestdag received his Masters in Political Sciences/International Relations from the Université Libre de Bruxelles in 2005, the title of his thesis being 'Kaliningrad, une région modèle pour la collaboration russo-européenne?'. He then conducted research in Kaliningrad during 2006 in scope of the present volume. He later worked for Member of European Parliament, Danute Budreikaite, Vice-Chairwoman of the Committee on Development of the European Parliament and is currently on the Trade Projects and Support team for the Bank of New York Mellon.

Holger Moroff is Lecturer in International Relations at Friedrich Schiller University, Jena. He was Research Fellow at the Institute for European Politics in Berlin and is a postdoctoral fellow in the European Foreign and Security Policy Studies programme. His research activities focus on European integration, foreign policy of the EU, political corruption, theories of International Relations and security and theories of political representation. He is the editor of the book *European Soft Security Policies*, Helsinki and Berlin, Finnish Institute of International Affairs, 2002, and has published numerous articles on EU–Russia relations.

Guido Müntel works at the German Foreign Office. Prior to this he conducted research to obtain a Ph.D. at the Queen's University, Belfast, UK. During that time (2003–2006), he also lectured at the 'Friedrich Schiller' University, Jena, Germany, and the 'Immanuel Kant' Russian State University in Kaliningrad. He received his M.A. in Political Science in 2002 from the University of Jena. His primary research interest is the development of the Kaliningrad exclave in the context of its international and European relations. Publications in journals and edited volumes include articles on the Europeanisation of Kaliningrad, the Kaliningrad transit problem, elections and election observation in Russia and Russian foreign policy. His contributions to this volume are the result of his doctoral research and they reflect exclusively the individual perspective of the author, not the German Foreign Office.

Diana Pitschel is currently Research Associate at the Chair of Policy Analysis and Public Administration, University of Constance, Germany. Here she works for the project 'EU Convention Debate and Regional Mobilization' granted by the Elite Research Programme of the State Foundation of Baden-Württemberg. She studied Political Science, Intercultural Business Communication and English Language Studies at the University of Jena, Germany. She holds a scholarship of the State Foundation (Landesstiftung) of Baden-Württemberg, Germany and is a member of the Centre for Junior Research Fellows, University of Constance, Germany.

Silke Schielberg has been engaged at the Schleswig Holstein Institute for Peace Research (SHIP) in Kiel, Germany, as Research Associate in the subject area of Cooperation and Conflict Prevention since 2002. Moreover, she is a Ph.D. candidate at the Institute of Political Science, Justus Liebig University of Gießen, Germany. Between 1994 and 2001, she studied Political Science, East-European History and Slavistics at the University of Kiel. In her Ph.D. thesis she examines regional cooperation between Kaliningrad, Poland and Lithuania.

Konstantin Shopin is the Head of the Customer Relations Division at the Raiffeisen Bank, Kaliningrad. He participated in a number of research projects related to EU–Russia cooperation and Kaliningrad. His latest publication (with A. Zernov) is *Kaliningrad Transit of Goods: in Need for a Strategic Approach to Problem-Solving*, Kaliningrad, East–West Institute, 2005.

Pyotr Shopin is a Project Manager with the Kaliningrad Regional Economic Development Agency. With some years experience in implementation of projects within the framework of EU–Russia cooperation programmes, he has taken part in research projects on Kaliningrad-related issues.

Evgeny Vinokurov is currently Head of the Economic Analysis Unit at the Strategy and Research Department of the Eurasian Development Bank. He was a postdoctoral researcher at the Institute for World Economy and International Relations at the Russian Academy of Science in Moscow. He received his Ph.D. in Economics from University Pierre Mendès-France (Grenoble II) and the degree of *kandidat nauk* from Moscow State Pedagogical University. He also holds a *Magister iuris* (Göttingen University) and a Lawyer's Diploma (Kaliningrad State University). His main research interests comprise post-Soviet integration, Russian economy and EU enlargement. Among his publications are *Kaliningrad: Enclaves and Economic Integration* (CEPS, Brussels, 2007), *A Theory of Enclaves* (Lexington Books, Lanham, MD, 2007), and (with Katlijn Malfliet and Lien Verpoest) *The CIS, the EU, and Russia: The Challenges of Integration*, London, Palgrave Macmillan, 2007.

Acknowledgements

This book is the result of a multi-annual academic cooperation between the Institute for Political Science at the 'Friedrich Schiller' University of Jena and the Political Science Department at the 'Immanuel Kant' Russian State University (2003–6). In addition to the core research teams based in Jena, Moscow and Kaliningrad, we have been lucky to find additional scholarly support to bring this research project to a successful end. As with all collaborative projects, this volume would not have been possible without the assistance of many organisations and individuals.

We are more than grateful to acknowledge the generous support of the German Academic Exchange Service (DAAD) and the Swiss Foundation '*Avec et pour les autres*' for funding cooperation between the Jena and Kaliningrad universities in 2004–6. During this period, a number of contributors visited the respective partner institution, to jointly develop this research project. In particular, we would like to acknowledge a research and conference grant from the Fritz Thyssen Foundation (Germany), which enabled us to convene a workshop on 28–30 April 2006 in Jena. Furthermore, we would like to express our gratitude to the Institute for European Studies (IES) and the Department of Political Science at the University of British Columbia for providing the intellectual atmosphere to discuss the results of this project.

Many individuals have offered input on various drafts of the chapters. We also wish to thank particularly Clive Archer (Manchester Metropolitan University), David Phinnemore (Queen's University of Belfast), Klaus Dicke (University of Jena), Gennady M. Fedorov ('Immanuel Kant' Russian State University, Kaliningrad), Tarvo Kungla (European Parliament), Alexander Sergounin (Nizhny Novgorod State Linguistic University), Olga Potemkina (Institute of Europe, Russian Academy of Science, Moscow), Georgii Dykhanov (Consulting Centre 'Business Experts', Kaliningrad), Helmut Hubel (University of Jena), Vladimir Krivosheev ('Immanuel Kant' Russian State University), and Alexander Salenko ('Immanuel Kant' Russian State University). We have benefited greatly from their insights during the conference in Jena. We are very indebted to Matthias Heise for helping to organise the conference and to Holger Obbarius (Jena), for his sound management of the administrative and technical tasks throughout the years. Conrad King, a graduate student from the IES Masters programme was helpful in bringing the style into line with the publisher's requirements. Ole J. Heggen, a cartographer at the Department of Geography, University of Victoria, expertly designed the map. Most of all, however, we are grateful to our authors, who were always supportive of our quest to produce a coherent volume.

We would like to dedicate this book to our academic teacher, Prof. Dr Helmut Hubel. His support from the very first idea until the conclusion of this project has been of great importance.

Stefan Gänzle, *Vancouver*
Guido Müntel, *Berlin*
Evgeny Vinokurov, *Almaty*

Abbreviations

AC	Arctic Council
AIDS	acquired immuno-deficiency syndrome
BEAC	Barents Euro-Arctic Council
BEN	Baltic Euro-regional Network
BSR	Baltic Sea region
BSSSC	Baltic Sea States Sub-regional Cooperation
CBC	cross-border cooperation
CBSS	Council of the Baltic Sea States
CEES	Common European Economic Space (EU–Russia)
CIS	Commonwealth of Independent States
CS	EU 1999 Common Strategy on Russia
CSFSJ	Common Space of Freedom, Security and Justice (EU–Russia)
ENP	European Neighbourhood Policy
EU	European Union
FTP	Federal Target Programme
GDP	gross domestic product
GRP	gross regional product
HIV	human immunodeficiency virus
HLG	High Level Group
IBM	integrated border management
Interreg	EU interregional cooperation programme
KSU	Kaliningrad State University (former name of RSU)
NATO	North Atlantic Treaty Organization
NC	Nordic Council
NCM	Nordic Council of Ministers
ND	Northern Dimension (EU)
NDAP	Northern Dimension Action Plan (EU)
NDEP	Northern Dimension Environmental Partnership (EU)
NDIS	Northern Dimension Information System (EU)
NGO	non-governmental organisation
OECD	Organisation for Economic Cooperation and Development
OMC	open method of coordination (EU)
PCA	Partnership and Cooperation Agreement
PHARE	Poland and Hungary: Assistance for Restructuring their Economies programme (EU)
RECEP	Russian European Center for Economic Policy

RF	Russian Federation
RSFSR	Russian Soviet Federative Socialist Republic
RSU	Russian State University 'Immanuel Kant' (formerly KSU)
SEZ	Special Economic Zone
STAKES	Finnish National Research and Development Centre for Welfare and Health
TACIS	Technical Assistance for the Commonwealth of Independent States (EU)
TB	tuberculosis
Tempus	Trans-European mobility scheme for university studies (EU)
UBC	Union of Baltic Cities
UNESCO	United Nations Educational, Scientific and Cultural Organisation
WHO	World Health Organization
WTO	World Trade Organization

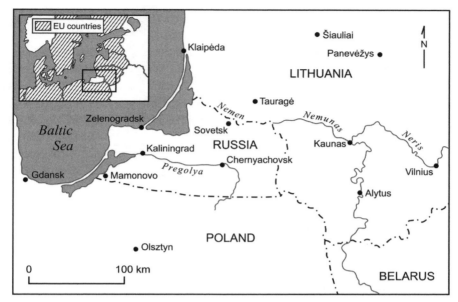

Map of Kaliningrad region

Stefan Gänzle and Guido Müntel

1

Introduction: adapting to European integration? Kaliningrad, Russia and the European Union

The Kaliningrad oblast[1] is one of the few regions where some traces of the old East–West conflict can still be perceived. Following Lithuania's independence and the subsequent dismantlement of the Soviet Union in 1991, the region is now – as an integral part of the Russian Federation – 'wedged' between Poland and Lithuania, thus geographically detached from the mainland and technically an exclave. At the same time, security-related perceptions and concerns *vis-à-vis* this region have changed. During the Cold War, Kaliningrad – the Soviet Union's most western territory – served as a military outpost of high strategic importance in the Baltic Sea. Yet since the early 1990s, various problems pertaining to Kaliningrad's social, economic and political transformation, its military conversion as well as its exclave-specific character have been perceived as threats to security and stability in north-east Europe (see Wellmann 1994; Lachowski 1998; Joenniemi *et al.* 2000; Sergounin 2001; Averre 2002). Any development of this region has at least an indirect impact on the Baltic Sea area and other parts of Europe. Therefore, Kaliningrad still lies at the heart of contemporary security issues in the region, though by and large these issues have switched from 'hard' to 'soft' (see Moroff 2002). Moreover, the region can be identified as the core of a 'security complex'.[2] From this perspective, Kaliningrad provides a focal point of security and threat perceptions in Russia, Poland, Lithuania and the European Union. However, as much as Kaliningrad can be framed as a potential 'threat' to regional security, it also displays numerous opportunities to actually foster interaction and cooperation between Europe's key regional powers, the EU and Russia. Kaliningrad has the potential to serve as a 'pilot' or 'model region'[3] for strengthening their relationship and as a nucleus for forms of integration of Russia *with* the European Union.

Hence, our motivation for composing this volume derives from Kaliningrad's role as a perceived security problem in the Baltic Sea region as well as its potential to serve as Russia's main opening to the EU (and *vice versa*) and a 'pilot region' for their mutual cooperation and integration. We are interested in studying how interaction between Russia and Kaliningrad on the one side, and their European partners on the other side, contribute to the development of the exclave. Instead of taking the more obvious International Relations/security approach to formulate our research questions, we address this topic as an instance of 'Europeanisation': How do EU–Russia relations 'feed back' into Kaliningrad's domestic arena, or, put differently, is Kaliningrad becoming 'Europeanised' – at least to some extent? In particular, do EU standards and norms impact on the exclave and in what ways?

We will analyse the framework conditions for such externally-driven changes. First of all, a set of exogenous variables is paramount, referring to forms, content and the conduct of interaction between the European and Russian partners. Besides this, we assume a number of endogenous variables to be critically important, such as the domestic constraints imposed by post-Soviet transformation and the relations with the federal centre. Finally, exclave-related factors like the region's economic dependency on neighbouring countries or its social identity appear to be highly relevant for the region's development and externally-induced changes.

With this set of variables in mind, we seek to apply (and eventually modify) the concept of Europeanisation *vis-à-vis* third countries (or, as in our case, a part of a third country). Europeanisation, increasingly a buzzword of European integration and EU studies, has been developed over the last decade on the basis of research on domestic changes in EU member states as well as candidate countries (see Featherstone and Radaelli 2003; Schimmelfennig and Sedelmeier 2005; Schimmelfennig 2007; Graziano and Vink 2007). Does the concept of Europeanisation equip us with a useful toolkit to understand externally-driven change in a third state, or a part of a third state, that is not seeking to acquire EU membership? Although we are not going to examine the European impact on Russia in general, we claim that singling out Kaliningrad as a test case will provide insights and explanations that will shape future research on the Russian Federation in relation to Europe.

Kaliningrad: the background[4]

In the aftermath of the Second World War, the Soviet Union annexed the city of Königsberg together with the northern part of the formerly German province of East Prussia. Not only was the region renamed Kaliningrad oblast but it was also transformed into a military outpost in the Baltic Sea. From 1946 to 1991, due to its strategic importance as the Soviet Union's most western territory, access to Kaliningrad was highly restricted. This was only one aspect to change in the wake of domestic reforms and global transformation that started in the era of Mikhail Gorbachev. Indeed, Kaliningrad was one of many places in post-communist Europe to face the same opportunities and challenges of a process of triple transition – in terms of democratic, economic and societal change. In comparison with other countries in Central and Eastern Europe as well as with other Russian regions, Kaliningrad has been peculiar in its geo-political situation since the dismantlement of the Soviet Union in 1991. The exclave is more than 500 km away from the territory of the Russian mainland and borders Poland and Lithuania, which have since become EU and NATO member states.

Exclavity has had a significant impact on post-communist transition processes. A number of specific issues are intrinsically connected to the region's enclave and exclave status, including 'double peripherality' to both mainland Russia and the EU (Joenniemi et al. 2000; Vinokurov 2007). However, as we will see in this book, Kaliningrad has been, in fact, treated as a rather normal oblast of the Russian Federation despite the rhetoric of Kaliningrad being a 'pilot region' in EU–Russia relations. One of the pertinent consequences of Russia's federal design is that the regional competences are limited. In fact, this exclave region surrounded by foreign states is not supposed to possess any independent foreign policy of its own. Thus, the role and the interests of the Russian federal government are central in determining Kaliningrad's political and economic course.

In political terms, the transition process in the Kaliningrad region – as in Russia as a whole – remains an unfinished project, and prospects are dim. Democratic institutions formally exist, but the concentration of power in the executive and the 'hollowing out' of democratic control mechanisms have led to a kind of authoritarianism. As a consequence of Putin's efforts at centralisation, one can observe a congruence across the Russian regions as regards the structures and habits of their governments, legislatures, party systems and increasingly, civil society (see Slider 2001). Nevertheless, cross-regional comparisons on the 'level of democracy' in Russia showed different and even somewhat encouraging results for Kaliningrad.[5]

Up until 2008, Kaliningrad has had four governors (the head of the regional executive), a succession that has aptly illustrated the ups and downs of politics in Kaliningrad and Russia. From the dismantlement of the Soviet Union in 1991 until 1996, Yury Matochkin, a liberal, market-minded politician, was governor of the oblast. The 1996 regional elections replaced him with Leonid Gorbenko, a former head of Kaliningrad's fishery port and 'krepky khozyaystvennik' – a term used in the 1990s to describe high-level managers, usually with a strong Soviet pedigree, who were supposed to curtail the chaos of reform and bring stability and prosperity to Russian regions. Gorbenko, however, proved to be a less than able governor, his reign notorious for a financial scandal that nearly bankrupted Kaliningrad. Vladimir Egorov, the former Commander-in-Chief of the Baltic Fleet, won the elections of 2000, with evident backing from President Putin. He was criticised for his lack of charisma, and his governorship was marred by mismanagement and several corruption scandals.[6] Nevertheless, it was during his mandate that Kaliningrad started to recover economically. Since 2004, regional governors are nominated by the federal president and only need approval from the regional Duma (legislative body). In practice, they are *de facto* appointed by the president. As the five-year term of Vladimir Egorov ended in November 2005, his successor, Georgii Boos, was 'parachuted' in from Moscow.

The omnipotent role of the head of the executive exists at the federal as well as the regional level of governance in Russia. Parliaments and political parties have had a rather declaratory and ceremonial function in policy-making. The Russian Constitution as well as the 'basic law' (*ustav*) of Kaliningrad have ensured the supremacy of the executive.[7] A key factor continues to be the regional leaders' basis of legitimacy; the direct election of Kaliningrad's regional governor in 1996 and 2000 provided the governor with enhanced legitimacy and independence from the regional legislature. Yet what is more, informal processes and structures have intensified this. The influence of regional parties and parliament has been circumscribed by federal support for particular candidates in gubernatorial elections (like in the case of Egorov in 2000). The appointment of Governor Boos in 2005 has clearly further strengthened the links between the executive powers in Kaliningrad and Moscow, and lowered executive accountability *vis-à-vis* the regional parliament. In view of the executive's dominance, the business or political careers of deputies have benefited when they have withheld potentially conflicting perspectives. And finally, fragmentation and instability of political parties have contributed to the weakness and lack of influence of the regional parliament.[8]

The role of political parties is rather weak in Russia and Kaliningrad, hampered by a lack of development 'from below' as actors representing the general public. During the 1990s, the founding of regional parties, which was possible until the reform of the federal party law in 2001 and 2004, resulted in party pluralism and instability. Parties have since been unable to attract a larger clientele for electoral support and often lack charismatic leadership, both necessary for a firm power basis in parliament and regional politics (Ross 2002: 92–121). The new party law has aimed at transforming the party system to be less fragmented and with fewer parties. This, taken with reform of election laws at both federal and regional level, which have set high standards for representation in the legislature, appears to have achieved the desired result: in Kaliningrad's parliament, United Russia enjoyed a clear majority (twenty-six of forty seats), while the Communist Party (four seats) and the remaining independent deputies played only a marginal role.[9] However, cleavage structures of party affiliation along traditional lines have been absent, which has resulted in rather volatile voter support and a general lack of trust in political parties. This has been further exacerbated by the practice of 'installing' presidential parties at the federal centre in Moscow, leaving the evolution of a stable party system in Russia rather uncertain.

Actors from 'civil society'[10] and non-governmental organisations (NGOs) in Russia have had an even more difficult process in firmly establishing themselves as players in the political life of post-Soviet Russia. Nevertheless, they have appeared more successful; in a 2000 study on civil society in Kaliningrad, NGOs were surprisingly well established, whereas there was little evidence of the main characteristics of civil society, i.e. self-organised and autonomous forms of interest formulation and representation, within political parties (and media) (Birckenbach and Wellmann 2000: 34–7). There are more than 2,000 NGOs registered in the oblast, 250 of which focus on social services (Zverev 2007: 18), and this despite difficult conditions for the development of NGOs during the transition process in Russia. The pre-eminent occupation of people, whether they would be passive supporters or active volunteers for NGOs, has been for their own immediate well-being and advancement, i.e. work and income. This has posed a serious challenge to the material as well as personal resources of NGOs. Additionally, the subtle attempts at regulation and control of NGO activities under President Putin has occurred mainly through economic mechanisms like taxation and the control of grants. The perceived concept of 'civil society' in the country's leadership is that its organisations are allowed to subsist but only under conditions agreeable to the state; NGOs can engage in the collective development of politics unless this engagement becomes unfavourable or even contradictory to the leadership's interests. At the same time, the state has not established institutional channels of influence for civil society actors.[11] In Kaliningrad, the 'Regional Public Chamber' was established in 2001 to represent local and regional NGOs and to consult with the regional government – but it could not really have any success. Thus, only by using direct personal contacts to policy-makers in administration or parliament can NGOs occasionally acquire some influence on single legislative projects. Generally, the political system remains closed for the representation of civil society's interests.

In the context of economic development and performance, Kaliningrad's transition has been complicated by various factors: Soviet heritage, conditions of exclavity and enclavity as well as a number of external economic challenges to which the region has had to adjust. The Soviet legacy of a planned economy has had a more pervasive dimension in Kaliningrad, as the former dominance of military aspects over civilian life was especially visible in the economic sector. The regional economy and labour market were highly dependent on the military, so that the disarmament of the region after 1991 required a simultaneous conversion from military to civilian-oriented industry (Zverev 1998).

Kaliningrad's second distinctive feature is that it is of small size with a population of less than one million. The region has only a limited domestic market (and incidentally, a limited resource base) which does not allow local industries to achieve economies of scale. These constraints create a significant asymmetry between domestic production and consumption, where economic connections with neighbouring countries, and thus a favourable trade regime, become vital for successful economic development. Yet trade with mainland Russian regions also plays an extremely important role in Kaliningrad's economy. As an integral part of the Russian Federation, Kaliningrad's close economic ties with mainland Russia have become even stronger in the twenty-first century, owing to the increase of import substitution as well as Russian state and private investments in the region.

The third distinctive feature of Kaliningrad is that it is an enclave, where external factors naturally acquire an exceptionally high importance. The issue of transit, which has been temporarily solved by an EU–Russian agreement, is vital (Müntel 2003; Vinokurov 2006b). As Kaliningrad is situated at a double periphery between Russia and the EU, the oblast is vulnerable to changes in the economic environment on two fronts: on the one hand, EU enlargement and changes in Russia–EU relations play an enormous role in the economic life of the region; on the other, Russia's quest for integration into the world economy (illustrated by Russia's bid for WTO membership) is also extremely important. These processes and their consequences for trade regimes could represent serious risks as well as new opportunities for Kaliningrad's small and vulnerable economy.

However, when assessing the economic performance over the past fifteen years, one can see that the greatest crises of the 1990s have been overcome. Instead of suffering a deep fall in productivity and growth, Kaliningrad now displays an annual average gross regional product (GRP) growth of approximately 10 per cent; a growth rate that has continuously exceeded the rate of the Russian Federation (see Table 1.1). While Kaliningrad's designation as a 'Special Economic Zone' (SEZ) has been subject to much discussion,[12] there has been less debate about the 1998 financial crisis in Russia that devalued the currency and resulted in higher demand for regional and domestic products. Consequently, regional production and trade with the Russian mainland increased, as did both foreign and Russian investment in the oblast. However, foreign capital still does 'not play a vital role in Kaliningrad's economy' (Zverev 2007: 15). Growing oil production and the installation of a gas-run power plant strengthened the economic independence of the region and even extended its assortment and size of exports. Oil and refined products are by far the most exported goods, followed by ships and machinery. Finally, the region's geographic location and its potential as a transport hub for Russia's trade with the West has been increasingly utilised.

Despite continuous growth, the economic prospects of Kaliningrad are opaque. Its future prospects might be determined by several recent and fundamental changes. The impact of EU enlargement has been unique for Kaliningrad, as it has transformed the region into an EU enclave. More importantly, Kaliningrad's dependence on the customs privileges provided by the SEZ regime is notorious, as this regime influenced the region's sustain-

Table 1.1 Economic performance of Kaliningrad (Kal) and Russia (RUS): annual change of GRP (in %, 1995–2006)

	1995	1996	1997	1998	1999	2000	2001	2002	2003	2004	2005	2006
RUS	−4.1	−3.4	0.9	−1.9	5.4	9.0	5.0	5.6	7.3	7.1	6.4	6.7
Kal	−16.2	−14.2	−4.5	−9.5	6.8	14.4	6.0	9.5	11.5	12.3	13.0	12.0

Source: Various reports compiled by the Centre of Markets in Transition of Helsinki School of Economics, Economic Monitoring of Northwest Russia, available on the Internet at www.economicmonitoring.com (accessed 24 August, 2007).

ability in terms of economic development. The new 'Law on the Special Economic Zone in Kaliningrad' in force since 1 April 2006 has the potential to bring about significant change to the economic orientation of the oblast by granting SEZ status for twenty-five years.[13] The next decade will see further reforms and developments that are likely to have a sizeable impact on Kaliningrad, one of which will most likely be Russia's accession to the WTO. Other developments may be the result of progress (such as the establishment of the Russia–EU Common European Economic Space (CEES)) or stalemates in EU–Russia relations.

The making of an 'issue': Kaliningrad in EU–Russia relations

Kaliningrad faces two types of problems today. The first type, as demonstrated, is 'home-made' and is the result of post-Soviet legacies and poor governance in terms of domestic and federal policies concerning the Russian exclave. The second type is related to its character as a Russian exclave *and* EU enclave, or 'semi-enclave' (see chapter 3 in this volume), with a considerable burden of responsibility put on at least two EU member states and the EU in general. It is important to note that the EU has not refrained from assuming its share of responsibility for Kaliningrad. This was clear from a statement by Richard Wright, then Head of the Moscow-based European Commission Delegation to Russia:[14]

> Finally I should like to assure [...] the citizens of Kaliningrad that the EU [...] is doing its utmost to ensure that Kaliningrad, as an integral part of the Russian Federation, will have a prosperous future in the context of an enlarged EU. I do not subscribe to the notions that Kaliningrad will be 'surrounded' or an 'enclave, cut off from Russia.' The EU has no intention whatsoever to separate Kaliningrad from the rest of Russia.

As early as 1993, the European Parliament had commissioned a report on the political, social and economic situation of Kaliningrad, thus demonstrating a keen interest in the region's future (Hoff and Timmermann 1993). Financial and technical assistance has been provided by the EU from the earliest stages, i.e. the inception of the TACIS programme in 1991/92. Until 2003, approximately €50 million was committed to Kaliningrad, and then at the time of EU enlargement, an additional €25 million was allocated to the region between 2004 and 2006 for projects covering administrative reform, energy, transport, enterprise restructuring, management training and environment (see Commission 2006).

Thus, while one can speak of a rather 'low profile' EU engagement during the 1990s, matters changed after 1999, when Kaliningrad developed into a major issue. With the looming EU enlargement, it became clear that Kaliningrad would be an EU enclave in the foreseeable future. In the aftermath of the Council's decision in December 1999 in Helsinki to pursue membership talks with all Eastern European candidate states – including Lithuania and Latvia – Kaliningrad was catapulted to the forefront of EU–Russia relations. The first European Commission Communication on Kaliningrad was published at the beginning of 2001, and was entitled 'The EU and Kaliningrad' (Commission 2001). In this, the Commission did not yet recognise the necessity for special arrangements for the movement of people in and out of the Kaliningrad region. The Commission believed that to ensure a smooth transition to the new visa regimes, it could be sufficient to examine such issues as the cost of passports and visas, the efficiency of border crossings, the adequacy of consular offices and rules for small border traffic. Assessing the economic situation of the region, the Commission stressed the positive impact of EU enlargement on the regional economy (like better opportunities for exports because of lower tariffs in the new member states), while leaving aside potential negative aspects. Such a strategy of stressing the beneficial effects while ignoring the negative consequences has been characterised as the EU's 'fair weather strategy' towards Russia (Haukkala 2000; van Elsuwege 2002).

The situation changed considerably in 2002, when Kaliningrad became a highly politicised topic in Russia. Presumably, the most important reason for this was the strong intention of Moscow to secure Kaliningrad as an integral part of Russia in the face of EU and NATO enlargement. This is also evident in the choice of priority issues for negotiations with the Union, i.e. passenger and cargo transit. Until then, transit had been somewhat artificially singled out of the whole range of economic, political, and institutional issues. Suddenly, Kaliningrad became an issue that was framed as a rather classical security threat – the transit issue loomed over the EU–Russia relationship, resulting in a major deadlock. However, as pressures – both Russian and internal – mounted on the EU, the Commission had to respond and handle the difficult situation. In September of 2002, the Commission issued a Communication to the Council entitled 'Kaliningrad: Transit' (Commission 2002a) that paved the way to the tenth EU–Russia Summit in November 2002 and its 'Joint Statement on Transit between the Kaliningrad Region and the Rest of the Russian Federation' (Commission 2002b). Here, the parties acknowledged 'the unique situation of the Kaliningrad Region as part of the

Russian Federation but separated from the rest of the Federation by other states' and agreed to pursue a comprehensive package of measures to facilitate the easy passage of borders, and in particular to create a 'Facilitated Transit Document' scheme, in force since 1 July 2003. Moreover, trilateral negotiations between Russia, Lithuania and the EU – a new format within the EU–Russia dialogue – took place on the basis of decisions at the Summit to conclude a set of decisions for the implementation of facilitated transit schemes. The Facilitated Transit Document and Facilitated Railway Transit Document schemes have been functioning rather smoothly.[15]

Following the EU accession of Poland and Lithuania in 2004 and the 750th anniversary of the city of Königsberg/Kaliningrad in 2005, the EU's attention towards the Russian exclave has become less 'politicised' – or, using the terms of the Copenhagen School, 'de-securitised' (see chapter 4 in this volume). That, with regards to Kaliningrad, the EU–Russia relationship has rarely encountered major stumbling blocks can be attributed primarily to three factors. First, due to the increased presence and gradual expansion of the EU into the Baltic Sea region and the corresponding ramifications for trans-national cooperation, Kaliningrad has a firm place on the European Commission's agenda. Since the inception of the Council of the Baltic Sea States (CBSS) in 1992[16], the European Union and the Commission were involved in various aspects of Baltic Sea cooperation, following an initiative by Germany and Denmark (Hubel and Gänzle 2002). In 1995, Sweden and Finland joined the EU and Finland launched its Northern Dimension (ND) Initiative in 1997 to raise the profile of Northern Europe within the EU, with Kaliningrad being one beneficiary of these ND projects. In 1998, Poland and Estonia began accession negotiations with the EU, and in 2000, Lithuania and Latvia followed suit. These north-east European states finally became members of the EU in 2004, comprising half of all new member states from Eastern Europe.

The second reason Kaliningrad has not been a major stumbling block to EU–Russia relations is due to EU member states governments – in particular Germany – strictly refraining from individually addressing issues pertaining to Kaliningrad through a bilateral framework with Russia. In principle, Germany assured both Russia and Poland that it would not infringe upon its international commitments by supporting secessionist movements in Kaliningrad. German political contacts with Kaliningrad's authorities are not high profile, allowing some of its federal *länder*, such as Schleswig-Holstein and Brandenburg, to assume leadership roles. Instead, there is a tacit, cross-party agreement to allow the European Union a central role in steering the process of Kaliningrad's path towards Europe.

The third reason, and the most important one, is that the political leadership of the Russian Federation and Kaliningrad itself were both willing to embrace the idea of forging closer links between Kaliningrad and the EU. By proposing to develop the oblast into a 'pilot region' for EU–Russia relations,

President Putin ultimately subscribed to similar suggestions that had been voiced previously by Russian government officials. Yet neither the EU nor Russia has elaborated what a 'pilot region' in EU–Russia would ultimately entail. Most often it is perceived as an intention to intensify dialogue on the exclave, and to implement Western standards and regulations for the economy and modernisation of the region (Smorodinskaya 2001).

While the EU and Russia have described their mutual relationship as a 'strategic partnership', neither of them has yet made any bold effort to define the long term perspective of this particular relationship. Bilateral relations have evolved significantly since the early 1990s. In 1994, both the EU and Russia signed the Partnership and Cooperation Agreement (PCA) that established a wide range of opportunities to cooperate in economic, political, security and cultural matters. In 2005, this was reinforced by the prospective creation of four Common Spaces in the economic sphere, the area of research and education, with external security as well as justice and home affairs. These 'integrated' areas would be based on common goals and aims, coordinated policies, and compatible rules and regulations. In 2006, Russia and the EU further agreed to renegotiate a new agreement because the PCA (which entered into force in 1997 for a period of ten years) was soon to expire. However, because of Polish and Lithuanian resistance, the German EU Council Presidency of 2007 failed to broker a mandate to start negotiations for a new EU–Russia agreement.

The main assumption of the PCA is that Russian legislation would, by and large, converge towards EU norms and standards. While the PCA, in principle, aims at 'Europeanising' Russia, the wording of the Common Spaces is much fuzzier. In an enlargement-like mode of governance, the EU developed an inclusionary approach *vis-à-vis* Russia (Gänzle 2002; 2007a; Lavenex 2004), yet the key question is whether Russian administrative norms and policies are being aligned with EU legislation. Article 55(2) of the PCA stipulates that Russia align its legislation with the EU's *acquis communautaire* in the field of economy and related areas, like business law, competition, taxation, transport, social standards, environment, etc. In this regard, Kaliningrad has provided a particularly interesting test case through which the question of facilitation of, or resistance to, harmonisation and adaptation of EU norms may be explored.

Methodological framework

Literature and research on Kaliningrad and EU–Russia relations

Building on traditional perceptions of security, early studies on post-Cold War Kaliningrad provided rather brief accounts of the region's development, the heritage of Soviet rule, the size and potential threat of the military based in the region and the conversion of the military-industrial complex (Hoff and

Timmermann 1993; Wellmann 1994; Zverev 1998). From the late 1990s onwards, the interest shifted away from the traditional security focus, such that general and descriptive accounts on the region's development have dominated (Joenniemi *et al.* 2000; Krickus 2002). Other studies have more specifically addressed a variety of themes around domestic transition and external environment (Baxendale *et al.* 2000; Birckenbach and Wellmann 2003), or put emphasis on Kaliningrad's economic development (Fedorov 1998; Kivikari 1998; Samson *et al.* 2003; Vinokurov 2004b). Other central themes are the region's relations with federal authorities in Moscow (Leshukov 2000; Karabeshkin and Wellmann 2004), or the debate on regional identity (Brinks 1998; Oldberg 2000). Finally, the European context is generally well covered in the literature; the discourses and policies of the region's direct neighbours are analysed (Lachowski 1998; Janusauskas 2001; RDA 2005), as are specific questions related to the context of EU–Russia relations and the EU's eastern enlargement (Fairlie 1999; Stanyte-Tolockiene 2001; Huisman 2002; Holtom 2005).

Although the academic literature on Kaliningrad is extensive, our volume offers additional insights and a new approach. First, it provides a thorough analysis of the region's institutional structures, actors' interaction and decision-making, and the resulting policy-output within the selected fields. Second, as there are few studies on political transition processes in the region, we will draw conclusions on the general situation and character of institutional structures and decision-making processes in Kaliningrad. Third, while attention has been given to the variety of relations between Kaliningrad and foreign partners, a specific and detailed enquiry into their conduct and the implementation of projects is unavailable. Fourth, while contributing to the literature on domestic developments as well as on the international context of Kaliningrad, it is the overlap and linkages between these two spheres that we think to be of crucial importance. This has been more extensively analysed in the case of the EU member states and accession countries. The influence of external factors on regional governance in Russia, however, has hardly yet been studied using the analytical lens of 'Europeanisation' research. In this volume, we approach Kaliningrad – and implicitly, EU–Russia relations – from such an angle. Did Kaliningrad adapt to European integration? If so, to what extent did it become 'Europeanised'? What is different about the EU–Russia relationship in regards to Kaliningrad? How does the Kaliningrad oblast participate in the processes of cooperation and integration with its European neighbours, and thus reconcile the pressures of adaptation to European modes of governance with its status as an integral part of the Russian Federation?

Towards the research question
Throughout the 1990s, the process of enlargement placed the European Union in a rule-shaping position *vis-à-vis* its neighbourhood. Conditionality for EU membership and the transposition and implementation of the *acquis communautaire* not only contributed to a further strengthening of democracy and the market economy in the post-communist societies in Central and Eastern Europe, but also led to an adaptation of candidates' polities, politics and policies towards the EU (Linden 2002; Schimmelfennig and Sedelmeier 2005). Moreover, European integration (see below for further explanation) can even affect those countries that are outside the EU and not on their way to membership. Third countries often pursue an agenda of intensified cooperation with the European Union, with the possible result that their institutional structures, decision-making processes, and underlying norms and principles are significantly influenced by the EU (Mattli 1999; Kux and Sverdrup 2000).

This raises the question of whether the Russian Federation also faces comparable adaptive influences and pressures on its domestic structures. The region of Kaliningrad, with its unique situation as an enclave within the widened EU, appears particularly receptive to externally induced change and adaptation. Although adaptive pressures resulting from EU membership obligations obviously do not and will not exist, forms of intensified cooperation or integration (in the more general sense) with the EU and other European actors are perceptible and create exogenous pressures or incentives for domestic change. First, Russia's partnership with the EU creates 'quasi-obligatory' requirements. Formal agreements, joint projects and mutual declarations, such as the Partnership and Cooperation Agreement, or most recently the project of the four Common Spaces, contain provisions to enhance cooperation and integration (also with particular reference to Kaliningrad). Moreover, the country's membership in sub-regional organisations (for example, the Council of the Baltic Sea States, where the Kaliningrad exclave is a particular region of attention) generates further commitments with regard to the oblast. Second, numerous projects of financial and technical assistance are implemented in Kaliningrad together with, or at least sponsored by, foreign partners. Here, the EU (mainly through its TACIS programme) or its member states (mostly Germany, Sweden, Denmark, Poland and Lithuania) provide not only resources, but also expertise and advice to partners in the exclave. Both public authorities and non-governmental organisations in the region are the recipients and beneficiaries. Third, beyond the assistance projects, institutionalised bilateral relationships and networks encompassing political-administrative bodies or societal interest groups with international partners create the forum for exchange of views and interests, but also a framework for the transfer of ideas and approaches.

Furthermore, rather endogenous pressures and framework conditions exist that result from Kaliningrad's unique geographical situation and circumstances of post-Soviet domestic transition. These, too, might facilitate such interaction and subsequent domestic changes: exclaves are often highly dependent on external influence, especially in the economic sphere (Vinokurov 2006a; 2007). The region's cross-border trade and heavy economic reliance on its European partners might require compliance with their standards and regulations, not only in the economic but also in the educational and environmental spheres. In addition, Kaliningrad maintains various historic and societal links with its neighbourhood which facilitate the emergence of a 'regional identity' that is open to intensified interaction with and adaptation to European partners (Oldberg 2000). Finally, the continuing process of post-Soviet political, social and economic transformation in Kaliningrad, and Russia in general, provides an advantageous framework of 'openness' to alternative and external modes of governance (Lavenex 2004; Gänzle 2007b).

Therefore, incentives and/or pressures for such change and adaptation can arise either direct-coercively through obligations from bilateral treaties or membership in an international organisation, indirect-coercively due to functional interdependencies (for example, in the economy, technology, and environment), or voluntarily due to changed identities and perceptions of more appropriate, legitimate, or, simply 'better' solutions. In this context, we argue that Kaliningrad presents Russia's main opening to the EU. Consequently, we query whether any political structure, process or policy-outcome in the Kaliningrad oblast has become increasingly susceptible to the influence of the region's European neighbours and the European Union itself. Hence we pose the following central question: *To what extent has the Russian region of Kaliningrad been affected by and especially adapted to the 'widened EU'?* On the one hand, this would answer how the exclave participates in the processes of cooperation and integration with its European neighbours, and thus reconciles the pressures of adaptation to European modes of governance with its status as an integral part of the Russian Federation. On the other hand – and from a more European perspective – this ponders the EU's potential and ability to shape norms and regulations outside its borders.

Analytical framework
To answer our research question, there are further and subordinate questions developed from an analytical framework containing contextual factors and variables related to externally-induced domestic change. The analyses in this volume apply or closely relate to existing analytical concepts of 'policy transfer' (Dolowitz and Marsh 1996), 'policy diffusion' (Tews 2002), 'policy convergence' (Bennett 1991), 'lesson-drawing' (Rose 1991), and in particular 'Europeanisation' (Olsen 2002; Featherstone and Radaelli 2003; Graziano and Vink 2007). Despite their terminological variety and different specific analytical angles and methodology, these concepts refer to processes in which institutional structures, patterns of decision-making, knowledge and ideas,

and policy approaches and outputs applied within one political entity are transferred to, and applied in, another political entity over time. Here, top-down approaches (such as policy convergence) often exist separately from analyses with a perspective of sideway directions (e.g. policy learning, policy diffusion, policy transfer and lesson-drawing), or of bottom-up ways as strategic choices for policy promotion or 'national projection'[17] (see Table 1.2).

Table 1.2 Directions of change in analytical concepts applied

Top-down	Policy convergence
Top-down and vertical ('sideways')	Policy learning, policy diffusion, policy transfer, lesson-drawing
Bottom-up and vertical ('sideways')	Policy projection
Bottom-up	Policy promotion

Source: Wong 2005: 140.

Also related to these concepts is the literature on 'Europeanisation' (Olsen 2002). This approach, which influences the analytical framework that guides the analysis in this volume, has 'skyrocketed' in terms of academic attention over the past decade.[18] It directs its attention particularly to the European integration process as the driving factor for change in the domestic settings of EU member states, candidates and third countries. Despite a variety of definitions and even basic understandings of the term 'Europeanisation', it is generally accepted that it denotes

> [p]rocesses of a) construction, b) diffusion, and c) institutionalization of formal and informal rules, procedures, policy paradigms, styles, 'ways of doing things', and shared beliefs and norms which are first defined and consolidated in the making of EU public policy and politics and then incorporated in the logic of domestic discourse, identities, political structures and public policies. (Radaelli 2003: 30)

Whereas merely conceptual accounts of the concept of 'Europeanisation' have succeeded in combining the interactive and dialectic processes of top-down, bottom-up and horizontal transfer (e.g. Radaelli 2003; Howell 2004; Simanska 2004), empirical studies have hardly focused on this. The reason is that such an endeavour obscures the differentiation between 'cause' and 'consequence' of certain processes and results, and it poses limits to the positivist perspective in social science to isolate, alter and measure independent and dependent variables of analysis (Howell 2004: 10–11).

However, we argue that in the case of third countries, all three directions can matter, depending on the degree of symmetry or asymmetry in the relationship with their partner. Policy promotion can be seen when third countries manage to impose their agenda within the context of EU negotiations, although this is not dissimilar to EU member states that use foreign policy negotiations at the European level to project their national objectives. Clearly, we assume that these efforts occur in institutional contexts which are more open to third country participation, such as the Russia-oriented partnership approach of the Northern Dimension conferences or the Bologna format of pan-European cooperation in higher education.

This volume seeks to add a case study to this Europeanisation research by analysing Kaliningrad as another example of third country adaptation, or to be more precise, of a sub-national entity of a third country. To clarify again, we are not going to examine the EU's impact on Russia in general, but we claim nevertheless that singling out Kaliningrad as a test case will provide insights and explanations that may shape future research on Russia's relation to, and integration with, Europe. Also, this can provide several further innovations and possibilities to test the hypotheses and explanations suggested by the literature so far. First, sub-national units of third countries have not yet been studied independently from the national context. Second, this is the first analysis of adaptation in a (part of a) post-communist transitional country that has not acceded to the EU nor is preparing for accession.

Applying this framework is based on the assumption that Europeanisation processes are the result of processes of integration in Europe. Integration is to be defined less narrowly and state-centrically, but in a sense of combining more formal types of integration where the deliberate political sanction of states is involved, with rather informal and societal interaction and interdependencies where authoritative intervention is absent. In a nutshell, integration in Europe is not solely caused by the institutions and decisions of the European Union and does not exclusively affect EU member states or aspirants. First, and as already outlined, the EU has engaged in processes of formal and informal cooperation and integration with outside countries where domestic adaptation processes can be observed as well. Second, the EU is not a single monolithic entity but comprised of individual member states, sub-national administrative units at regional and municipal levels, and numerous non-state actors. They autonomously pursue their cooperative relations and policies towards outside partners, and therefore can serve as agents of institutional and policy transfer as well. Third, other international organisations and networks exist in Europe that promote cooperation and integration, whether at the level of the sub-regional (e.g. Council of Baltic Sea States, Nordic Council) or sub-national (e.g. Euroregions, Union of Baltic Cities). Therefore, it would be misleading to limit the analysis of Europeanisation solely to the EU and its current and aspirant member states. Instead, one should consider 'Europe' in a more general understanding, with its 'many faces' and 'fuzzy borders' as an agent for processes of domestic adaptation. Thus, we seek to elucidate and at the same time modify the concept of Europeanisation. The steps of analysis throughout this study are informed by this analytical framework. Similar to the main thrust of these studies, we emphasise and confirm the relevance of both the exogenous inputs of cooperation as adaptive pressures, and the endogenous/domestic conditions as intervening variables for change and adaptation.

What is more, Europeanisation studies often employ the analytical framework of 'new institutionalism' (March and Olsen 1984; 1989; Peters 1999). Herein, institutions are broadly defined as formal and informal structures that shape and determine the individual or collective decisions and actions taken by the actors embedded in them. Two distinguishable logics of behaviour, based on ontologically different assumptions, can be discerned: first, rational actors follow the 'logic of consequentiality' based on cost–benefit calculations; second, actors may subscribe to a more cognitive 'logic of appropriateness' and are guided by collective understandings about appropriate behaviour according to established rules and norms (March and Olsen 1996). However, analyses of Europeanisation tend to combine these different logics, which inform and determine the assumptions of the mechanisms of Europeanisation (e.g. Knill and Lehmkuhl 1999; Héritier 2001; Börzel and Risse 2003). Moreover, they also include a 'historical institutionalist' argument, describing the existence and possible persistence of a 'misfit' of structures, processes, interests or ideas between the European and the domestic setting (Steinmo *et al.* 1992; Mahoney 2000).

More specific and applicable to our case study of Kaliningrad and its involvement in forms of cooperation and integration in Europe, there are several observable mechanisms of influence and change. The provision of external assistance and financial support can result in a change of the incentive structure and the interests of rationally behaving domestic actors, whether state administrative bodies or NGOs. Also possible is a redistribution of actors' resources that alters the opportunity structures within the domestic setting and thus allows single actors to increase their influence in the political decision-making processes.[19] On the other hand, there can be frequent interaction in organisational bodies and networks for consultation and joint decision-making that facilitates cognitive change and adaptation through exchanges of views and perceptions, arguing, persuasion and mutual learning. A redefinition of ideas and actors' behaviour might occur, possibly leading to a socialisation towards European values and approaches. Finally, the context of political, economic and societal transformation in post-Soviet Russia and Kaliningrad might facilitate processes of change and adaptation towards European ideas and models, because one can expect a general openness to alter (pre-)existing modes of governance. At the same time, organisational and behavioural patterns exercised over a period of several decades might cast their 'shadow of the past' and obstruct the introduction of innovation.

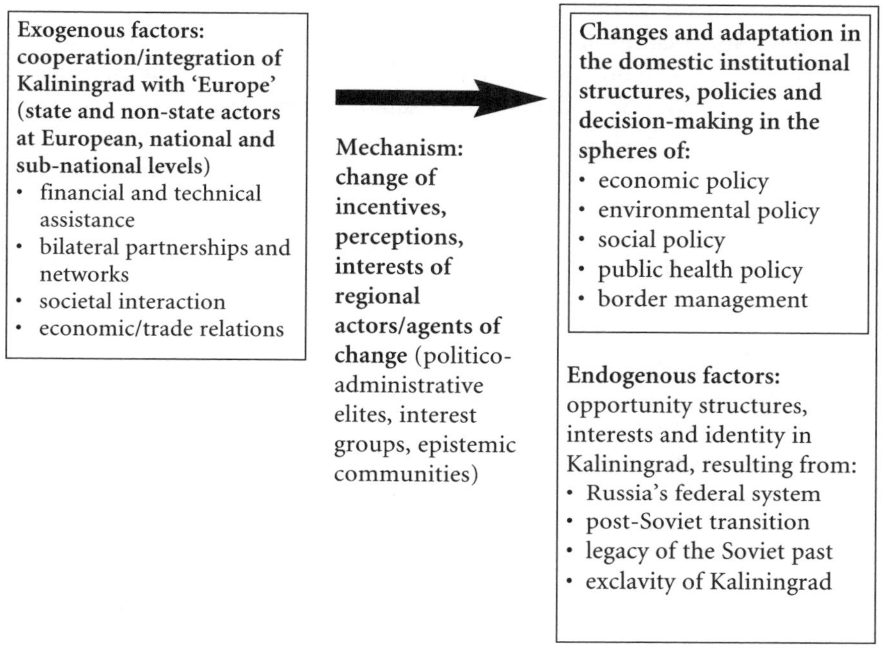

| Exogenous factors: cooperation/integration of Kaliningrad with 'Europe' (state and non-state actors at European, national and sub-national levels) • financial and technical assistance • bilateral partnerships and networks • societal interaction • economic/trade relations | Mechanism: change of incentives, perceptions, interests of regional actors/agents of change (politico-administrative elites, interest groups, epistemic communities) | Changes and adaptation in the domestic institutional structures, policies and decision-making in the spheres of: • economic policy • environmental policy • social policy • public health policy • border management

Endogenous factors: opportunity structures, interests and identity in Kaliningrad, resulting from: • Russia's federal system • post-Soviet transition • legacy of the Soviet past • exclavity of Kaliningrad |

Figure 1.1 Factors of change and constraints to adaptation in Kaliningrad

This framework allows for expanding the research question we posed above, i.e. to what extent the Kaliningrad region has become subject to pressures of externally induced change and of adaptation to European modes of governance (in other words, undergone processes of Europeanisation)? In particular, we pose the following questions:

- What changes have taken place in the legislative output, institutional structure and policy-making processes of Kaliningrad during the years of post-Soviet transformation and intensifying interaction with European partners, starting in 1991?
- To what extent do these changes reflect an adaptation towards European norms or structures and patterns of political decision-making? Does Kaliningrad converge to Europe?
- Which factors were relevant for inducing those changes – endogenous and/or exogenous?
- Among the exogenous factors for change, what is the importance of the European input – in other words, the degree and content of cooperation with, and integration of, Kaliningrad/Russia within 'Europe' that create pressures for change and adaptation?
- What is the impact of structures and processes established during the Soviet era on current processes of change (for example, the effects of the

'shadow of the past')? Are there path-dependent processes that hinder change and adaptation?

• Does the Russian phenotype of 'federalism' allow the regional authorities in Kaliningrad to act independently and thus create flexible arrangements in view of the specific needs of the exclave?

• What are the mechanisms of adaptation and transfer between 'Europe' and Kaliningrad/Russia, i.e. what logic of behaviour is underlying the processes of change?

• Does the academic concept of Europeanisation provide a useful 'toolkit' to understand externally driven change in Kaliningrad?

We seek to answer these questions by analysing and comparing several policy areas of the Kaliningrad region with the institutional structures, processes of decision-making (*politics*) as well as policy-outputs (*policy*) therein. This aims at exploring in detail possible mechanisms and evidence of adaptation to European norms and standards. Our analysis will encompass the following policy areas: economic policy; higher education; environmental policy; social policy; public health policy; integrated border management and economic policy.

The selection of case studies is based on the different degrees of interaction with international (primarily European) partners and of regional competence for their management (legislation, administration and implementation). Within economic and environmental policy, as well as higher education and integrated border management, cooperation between Kaliningrad/Russia and European partners is comparatively developed. In these policy areas, a high number of contacts with international partners exist at various levels, such as: technical and financial assistance from the EU and Western European countries; partnerships and networks of state authorities and societal interest groups across the Baltic Sea; exchange programmes between educational institutions; and trade relations. In contrast, cases in which cooperation is admittedly less developed are social policy and public health policy. Therefore, we consider these two variables – of interaction with international partners and of regional competence – as highly important for the degree and mechanisms of Europeanisation to be expected and observed. They are not, however, of sole explanatory character.

Towards this background, we have formulated the following hypotheses: (1) If Russian authorities – whether federal or regional – allow the Kaliningrad region to assume a 'pilot region' role in terms of closer cooperation with the EU, its member states and adjacent regions, we would expect to see some form of Europeanisation. (2) Furthermore, we assume greater adaptation to European integration in policy areas which are characterised by relatively higher regional autonomy and dense cooperation with the EU. Hence, we would expect Europeanisation to be rather pronounced in the area of environmental policy where the region disposes of competencies and international cooperation. In turn, a policy area with few devolved competences and very little cooperation with European partners, like the field of public health, is unlikely to adapt to European norms and standards. Where one of the two variables has a positive value while the other variable has not, we can expect a modest impact of Europeanisation on the domestic setting.

Table 1.3 Adapting to European integration? Expected impact on policy areas in Kaliningrad

Policy area	International cooperation	Regional autonomy	Expected impact
Economic policy	high	low	modest
Social policy	low	high	modest
Environmental policy	high	high	high
Public health policy	low	low	none
Border management	high	low	modest
Education policy	high	low	modest

Overview of chapters

The chapters of this volume are organised into three parts. In the first part, three chapters complement our theoretical framework: Christoph Knill, Diana Pitschel and Michael W. Bauer design a framework for analysing EU-driven change which is, in principle, applicable to both EU candidate countries and neighbouring states. They propose a policy-analytical framework that combines actor-centred and institutionalist models as explanatory factors arguing that the potential for change at the domestic level depends on the distinct governance patterns – compliance, competition and communication – inherent to EU regulatory policies. Additionally, the EU's capability to apply regulatory pressure upon a third country is determined by this country's ambition to become a member of the EU. In the next chapter, Evgeny Vinokurov asks what the changes are to which an enclave needs to adjust. Building upon a theory of exclaves, he provides a perspective which takes into account the specific domestic conditions of enclavity. He argues that EU enlargement to encompass Poland and Lithuania can be conceived in terms of a challenge for the Russian exclave of Kaliningrad. After an analysis of the economic and political features responsive to exogenous processes and, more specifically, shocks, he examines various types of integration as well as options for the mainland's policy concerning its exclave and applies his theoretical findings to the case of Kaliningrad. Finally, Holger Moroff links the issue of Kaliningrad to the contemporary debate in International Relations about securitisation and de-securitisation. He uses the concept of 'soft-securitisation' in order to describe a process of putting essentially domestic soft security threats in third countries with a potential cross-border impact on the external policy agenda.

The second section of the volume studies the framework conditions that determine the potential exposure of Kaliningrad to Europeanisation. The framework conditions are first, the exogenous input for change – in other words, the policy approaches of the EU and other European partners towards the Kaliningrad region and Russia in general; and second, the endogenous conditions that might foster or obstruct processes of (externally induced) change including the interest of domestic actors and institutional structures – in particular, the question of whether general opportunities exist for regions like Kaliningrad within the federal system of Russia to develop contacts and modes of cooperation with foreign actors independent of Moscow. Joan DeBardeleben analyses the limits of the EU's governance approach in dealing with Russia. She acknowledges that Russian authorities are extremely resistant to matching any EU policy which may imply raising the profile of its regional entities and elites. Vladimir Putin has made a great effort to ensure the loyalty of the regions. She assumes that new opportunities to shift loyalty may arise for regional elites in the wake of the upcoming presidential elections. Complimentarily, Stefan Meister provides an assessment of the development of Russian federalism since 1993. He thoroughly studies the repercussions of Putin's 're-centralisation approach' in regards to Kaliningrad and maintains that Moscow is still the key to the level of Kaliningrad's interaction with outside partners. Anna Karpenko assesses to what extent residents of Kaliningrad feel 'European' and whether they have developed a genuine regional identity. Then, Silke Schielberg and Tobias Etzold dissect the net of sub-regional cooperation connecting the oblast with neighbouring regions from Poland and Lithuania as well as from the Baltic Sea area.

The third section of this volume focuses on the analysis of the potential for change and adaptation in our selected policy areas. In order to increase the comparative edge of the results, the following questions have provided further guidance throughout the single cases: Is there an impact of structures and processes (path-dependency) established during the Soviet era that might hinder current processes of change and adaptation? Does the federal system of governance in Russia allow the regional level autonomous change and adaptation to European norms and standards in this specific policy area? What changes have taken place in Kaliningrad's legislation, institutional structures, and policy-making processes within the policy areas since 1991? Which factors were relevant for inducing those changes – endogenous and/or exogenous? Among the exogenous factors for change, what is the importance of the European input – in other words, the degree and content of cooperation with, and integration of, Kaliningrad/Russia within 'Europe' that creates pressures for change and adaptation? What are the mechanisms of adaptation and transfer between 'Europe' and Kaliningrad/Russia? Six case studies aim at answering these questions in their respective policy fields. Evgeny Vinokurov takes on economic policy. Vyacheslav Dykhanov provides an overview on social policy, including the most recent developments in 2005–6. Guido Müntel investigates the nascent environmental policy. Alexandre Berlin and Greg Mestdag report the results of their research on public health. Stefan Gänzle, Stefan Meister and Conrad King assess the influences resulting from cooperation in the domain of higher education. Alexey Ignatyev, Konstantin Shopin and Pyotr Shopin study integrated border management on Kaliningrad's border with Poland and Lithuania.

Following a chapter by Stefan Gänzle and Guido Müntel summarising the main findings of section three, Gabriella Meloni extends the analysis of Europeanisation processes to Russia in general. Her empirical findings and her conclusions of more general character confirm the evidence received from the preceding case studies, in that processes of change and adaptation in Kaliningrad caused by cooperation with European partners can be discerned only to some extent. Nevertheless, she argues that the EU has promoted a process of socialisation of Russia, ultimately initiating a mechanism of soft coordination which has some elements recalling the open method of coordination (OMC).[20]

Conclusion

Although we are cautious in completely subscribing our research and analysis under the rubric of Europeanisation, we demonstrate that over time the EU has tried to exert influence on Russia through bargaining about conditions and rewards and through the promotion of a strategy of persuasion and limited conditionality. We argue that this takes the form of Europeanisation 'à la carte' or 'selected adaptation'. Against the backdrop of Europeanisation research, the Russian Federation does not unilaterally embrace EU standards and norms, but instead seeks to choose and influence policy-making at the European level to ensure that its concerns are taken into account, which can be seen as policy promotion. Hence, we are witnessing the making of a special form of 'partial' and 'deliberative' Europeanisation 'à la carte', as Russia attempts to influence the EU's institutional core and policy-making process as much as possible.[21]

Ultimately, our findings also raise important questions about the extent to which the EU should be obligated to assist neighbouring states and regions, especially in areas that have an impact on the interests of its own member states; whether Europeanisation is in fact a 'good thing' as the usage of the term implicitly suggests. The analyses also pose questions for the future of EU–Russian relations. If Kaliningrad and other border regions were to undergo Europeanisation processes, and Russia agrees to adopt European norms or even legislation resulting from the PCA, where does Europe end?

Notes

1   In this book, the terms Kaliningrad, Kaliningrad region, and Kaliningrad oblast are used interchangeably as synonyms, unless there is an explicit reference to the city of Kaliningrad.
2   Barry Buzan defines a security complex 'as a group of states whose primary security concerns link together sufficiently closely that their national securities cannot realistically be considered apart from one another' (Buzan 1991: 190).
3   The concept of a 'pilot region' is mentioned for the first time in the 'Medium-term Strategy for Development of Relations between the Russian Federation and the European Union (2000–2010)', available on the Internet at http://ec.europa.eu /external_relations/russia/russian_medium_term_strategy/index.htm (accessed 7 November 2007).
4   The authors are grateful to Evgeny Vinokurov for his help and advice on this section.
5   Although it is dubious that these comparisons provide a clear picture of democratic standards, at least they allow a comparative assessment within Russia. Accordingly, Marsh (2004) put Kaliningrad thirty-first of seventy-eight regions on the basis of electoral participation and political competitiveness from data of executive elections in 2000. For Petrov (2004), Kaliningrad was twelve out of eighty-eight, based on expert evaluations. McMann and Petrov (2000) placed Kaliningrad sixth among fifty-seven regions, based on qualitative surveys among regional elites on their broader understanding of democracy.
6   For instance, see 'Court acquits ex-Kaliningrad governor of abuse of office', press release of Interfax, 14 September 2006.
7   The actual exercise of legal competences by the executive is also dependent on the personality of the leader – President Putin has taken more advantage of it than his predecessors.
8   Until 2006, only five of thirty-two deputies in Kaliningrad's Duma were proportionally elected via party lists. Therefore, rather loose and unstable parliamentary factions independent of political parties existed. It has been the rise of the party United Russia (favourable to the Kremlin and the regional governor) that has led to the domination of parliament by a single party. With the March 2006 elections in Kaliningrad, half of the forty seats in the Duma were proportionally distributed.
9   In the March 2006 elections, United Russia won this clear majority in the regional Duma through the aforementioned legal changes as well as because of some legitimate popularity, but also through 'electoral management' secured through the use of administrative and vast financial resources (Meister and Müntel 2006).
10 While not elaborated on in this volume, a discussion on the appropriateness of using a Western academic and political understanding of the concept of 'civil society' in the context of post-Soviet Russia and Kaliningrad can be found in McFaul and Treyger (2004: 136–42).
11 On the rare occasion the state has established these channels, like when they formed the federal Civic Forum in 2001, it was generally those NGOs aligned with federal policy that were admitted.
12 The SEZ was first set up in 1991 by the federal government under the name *Yantar* ('Amber'). However, the law effectively establishing a 'Free Economic Zone' was subsequently ignored and never properly applied. On 22 January 1996 a new law 'On the Special Economic Zone in Kaliningrad Oblast' was adopted, which exempted goods produced in the oblast from customs duties. It was most recently renewed in 2006 in order to foster Kaliningrad's foreign trade and to attract foreign investment to the region. For an opposing view on its impact on the growth of GDP/GRD, see Fedorov 1998 or Smorodinskaya 2005.

13 The revised SEZ regime no longer provides customs exemptions, but rather offers tax breaks and privileges to larger investors, including foreign ones (Zverev 2007: 11).

14 From an interview with Richard Wright, Head of EC Delegation in Russia, in *Dvornik* (a newspaper in Kaliningrad), available on the Internet at www.delrus.cec.eu .int/en/cis_8.htm (accessed 8 August 2006).

15 For a detailed description of how the new regimes function in practice, see Vinokurov (2004a; 2004b).

16 The Council of the Baltic Sea States (CBSS) was established as an intergovernmental body in Copenhagen on 5–6 March 1992. Its members are: Denmark, Estonia, Finland, Germany, Iceland, Latvia, Lithuania, Norway, Poland, Russia, Sweden and the European Commission.

17 Torreblanca (2001: 1, 3) describes this dimension of Europeanisation in the area of EU foreign policy as 'projection'.

18 For overviews and conceptual clarification, see Featherstone and Radaelli (2003) and Olsen (2002).

19 On 'political opportunity structures', see McAdam (1996: 26–9).

20 The open method of coordination (OMC) has been an instrument of the Lisbon strategy of 2000. The OMC provides a relatively new framework for cooperation between the member states, whose national policies can thus be directed towards certain common objectives. With the Commission's role being limited to surveillance (and the European Parliament and Court of Justice virtually playing no role), member states are evaluated by one another. In principle, this intergovernmental method, using peer pressure, takes place in areas which fall within the competence of the member states, such as employment, social protection, social inclusion, education, youth and training.

21 Two main Russian foreign policy strategies pursuing this particular objective have been identified. The first aims at the establishment of a unique form of 'strategic partnership' between the Russian Federation and the EU. Since the end of the 1990s, Russia has increasingly resisted the EU's attempt to lump it together with other states from Eastern Europe, in particular Ukraine and Moldova, under the umbrella of the European Neighbourhood Policy (ENP). Instead, the Russian government puts its trust in generating a *sui generis* relationship with the European Union. Second, Russia aims to mobilise its 'special partners' in the EU – in particular Germany, but also France, Italy and Great Britain – in order to implement a 'Russia-first' policy, taking into account special concerns by countries which have historically embraced the idea of a genuine relationship with Russia.

References

Averre, D. L. (2002), 'Security Perception among Local Elites and Prospects for Cooperation across Russia's North-Western Borders', Working Paper 16, Zürich, ETH.

Baxendale, J., S. Dewar and D. Gowan, eds (2000), *The EU & Kaliningrad: Kaliningrad and the Impact of EU Enlargement*, London, Federal Trust.

Bennett, C. J. (1991), 'What Is Policy Convergence and What Causes It?', *British Journal of Political Science*, 21(2): 215–33.

Birkenbach, H. M., and C. Wellmann (2000), *Zivilgesellschaft in Kaliningrad. Eine Explorationsstudie zur Förderung partnerschaftlicher Zusammenarbeit erstellt im Auftrag des Schleswig-Holsteinischen Landtages [Civil society in Kaliningrad: an exploratory study in support of cooperative partnership, conducted for the State Parliament of Schleswig-Holstein]*, Kiel, Schleswig-Holsteinisches Institut für Friedenswissenschaften.

Birckenbach, H. M. and C. Wellmann, eds (2003), *The Kaliningrad Challenge: Options and Recommendations*, Münster, Hamburg, London, LIT.

Börzel, T. A. and T. Risse (2003), 'Conceptualizing the Domestic Impact of Europe', in *The Politics of Europeanization*, ed. K. Featherstone and C. M. Radaelli, Oxford, Oxford University Press: 57–80.

Brinks, J. H. (1998), 'The Miraculous Resurrection of Immanuel Kant: Germany's Breakthrough to Former East Prussia', *Political Geography*, 17(5): 611–15.

Buzan, Barry (1991), *People, States and Fear: An Agenda for International Security Studies in the Post-Cold War Era*, London, Harvester Wheatsheaf.

Commission (2001), 'The EU and Kaliningrad', Communication from Commission to the Council on 17 January, Brussels, COM 26 final, available on the Internet at http://europa.eu.int/comm/external_relations/north_dim/doc/com2001_0026en01.pdf (accessed 12 December 2007).

Commission (2002a), 'Kaliningrad: Transit', Communication from Commission to the Council on 18 September, Brussels, COM 510 final, available on the Internet at http://europa.eu.int/comm/external_relations/north_dim/doc/com02_510.pdf (accessed 12 December 2007).

Commission (2002b), 'Joint Statement on Transit between the Kaliningrad Region and the Rest of the Russian Federation', Brussels, concluded on 11 November 2002, available on the Internet at http://ec.europa.eu/external_relations/russia/summit_11_02/js_kalin.htm (accessed 12 December 2007).

Commission (2006), 'The Northern Dimension: EU Support to Kaliningrad', available on the Internet at http://ec.europa.eu/comm/external_relations/north_dim/kalin/index.htm (accessed 13 August 2006).

Dolowitz, D. and D. Marsh (1996), 'Who Learns What from Whom: a Review of the Policy Transfer Literature', *Political Studies*, 44(2): 343–57.

Fairlie, L. D. (1999), 'Will the EU use the Northern Dimension to solve its Kaliningrad Dilemma?', Working Paper 21, Copenhagen, Copenhagen Peace Research Institute.

Featherstone, K. and C. M. Radaelli, eds (2003), *The Politics of Europeanisation*, Oxford, Oxford University Press.

Fedorov, G. (1998), 'The Social and Economic Development of Kaliningrad', in *Kaliningrad: The European Amber Region*, ed. P. Joenniemi and J. Prawitz, Aldershot, Ashgate: 32–56.

Gänzle, S. (2002), 'Presence and Actorness of the EU in the Baltic Sea Area: Multilevel Governance Beyond the External Borders of the European Union', in *EU Enlargement and Beyond: The Baltic States and Russia*, ed. H. Hubel (with the assistance of A. Bannwart and S. Gänzle), Berlin, A. Spitz Verlag: 73–103.

Gänzle, S. (2007a), 'EU–Russia Relations and the Repercussions on the "In-betweens"', in *Europe's Last Frontier? Belarus, Moldova, and Ukraine between Russia and the European Union*, ed. O. Schmidtke and S. Yekelchyk, London, Palgrave: 195–229.

Gänzle, S. (2007b), 'Externalizing Governance and Europeanization in EU-Russian Relations', in *The Boundaries of EU Enlargement: Finding a Place for the Neighbors*, ed. J. DeBardeleben, London, Palgrave: 53–69.

Graziano, P. and M. Vink, eds (2007), *Europeanization: New Research Agenda*, Houndsmills, Palgrave Macmillan.

Haukkala, H. (2000), 'The Making of the European Union's Common Strategy on Russia', UPI Working Papers 28.

Héritier, A. (2001), 'Differential Europe: National Administrative Responses to Community Policies', in *Europeanisation and Domestic Change*, ed. J. Caporaso, M. Green Cowles and T. Risse, Ithaca, Cornell University Press: 1–21.

Hoff, M. and H. Timmermann (1993), *Kaliningrad: Russia's Future Gateway to Europe?*, RFE/RL Research Report, 2(36): 37–43.

Holtom, P. (2005), 'The Kaliningrad Test in Russian–EU Relations', *Perspectives on European Politics and Society*, 6(1): 31–54.

Howell, K. E. (2004), *Developing Conceptualisations of Europeanization: Synthesising Methodological Approaches*, Belfast, Queen's University Belfast (Queen's Papers on Europeanisation, 3/2004).

Hubel, H. and S. Gänzle (2002), 'The Council of the Baltic Sea States (CBSS) as a Sub-regional Policy Response to Soft Security Risks in the Baltic Sea Area', in *European Soft Security Risks. The Northern Dimension*, ed. Holger Moroff, Helsinki and Berlin, Kauhava: 251–80.

Huisman, S. (2002), *A New European Union Policy for Kaliningrad*, Paris, EU Institute for Security Studies (Occasional Papers, 33).

Janusauskas, R. (2001), *Four Tales on the King's Hill. The 'Kaliningrad Puzzle' in Lithuanian, Polish, Russian and Western Political Discourses*, Warsaw, ISP Pan.

Joenniemi, P., S. Dewar and L.D. Fairlie (2000), *The Kaliningrad Puzzle: A Russian Region within the European Union*, Karlkrona (Sweden), Baltic Institute and the Åland Islands Peace Institute.

Karabeshkin, L. and C. Wellmann (2004), *The Russian Domestic Debate on Kaliningrad: Integrity, Identity and Economy*, Münster, Lit-Verlag.

Kivikari, U. (1998), 'The Application of Growth Triangle as a Means of Development for the Kaliningrad Region', in *The External Economic Relations of the Kaliningrad Region*, ed. U. Kivikari, M. Lindström and K. Liuhto, Turku, Institute for East–West Trade: 1–27.

Knill, C. and D. Lehmkuhl (1999), 'How Europe Matters: Different Mechanisms of Europeanization', *European Integration Online Papers*, 3(7).

Krickus, R. J. (2002), *The Kaliningrad Question*, Lanham (MD), Rowman & Littlefield.

Kux, S. and U. Sverdrup (2000), 'Fuzzy Borders and Adaptive Outsiders: Norway, Switzerland and the EU', *Journal of European Integration*, 22(3): 237–70.

Lachowski, Z. (1998), 'Kaliningrad as a Security Issue: An Expert View from Poland', in *Kaliningrad: The European Amber Region*, ed. P. Joenniemi and J. Prawitz, Aldershot, Ashgate: 130–48.

Lavenex, S. (2004), 'EU External Governance in "Wider Europe"', *Journal of European Public Policy*, 11(4): 680–700.

Leshukov, I. (2000), 'The Regional-Centre Divide: The Compatibility Conundrum', in *The EU & Kaliningrad: Kaliningrad and the Impact of EU Enlargement*, ed. J. Baxendale, S. Dewar and D. Gowan, London, Federal Trust: 127–39.

Linden, R. H. ed. (2002), *Norms and Nannies: The Impact of International Organizations on the Central and East European States*, Lanham (MD), Rowman & Littlefield.

Mahoney, J. (2000), 'Path-dependency in Historical Sociology', *Theory and Society*, 29(4): 507–48.

March, J. G. and J. P. Olsen (1984), 'The New Institutionalism: Organizational Factors in Political Life', *American Political Science Review*, 78(3): 734–49

March, J. G. and J. P. Olsen (1989), *Rediscovering Institutions: The Organizational Basis of Politics*, New York, Free Press.

March, J. G. and J. P. Olsen (1996), 'Institutional Perspectives on Political Institutions', *Governance*, 9(3): 247–64.

Marsh, C. (2004), 'Measuring and Explaining Variations in Russian Regional Democratisation', in *Russian Politics Under Putin*, ed. C. Ross, Manchester, Manchester University Press: 176–97.

Mattli, W. (1999), *The Logic of Regional Integration: Europe and Beyond*, Cambridge, Cambridge University Press.

McAdam, D. (1996), 'Conceptual Origins, Current Problems, Future Directions', in *Comparative Perspectives on Social Movements. Political Opportunities, Mobilizing*

Structures, and Cultural Framings, ed. D. McAdam, J. McCarthy and M. Zald, Cambridge, Cambridge University Press: 23–40.

McFaul, M. and E. Treyger (2004), 'Civil Society', in *Between Dictatorship and Democracy: Russian Post-Communist Political Reform*, ed. M. McFaul, N. Petrov and A. Riabov, Washington DC, Carnegie Endowment for International Peace: 135–73.

McMann, K. M. and N. V. Petrov (2000), 'A Survey of Democracy in Russia's Regions', *Post-Soviet Geography and Economics*, 41(3): 155–82.

Meister, S. and G. Müntel (2006), 'Regionalwahlen in Russland – Ein Gradmesser für die demokratische Entwicklung?' ['Regional elections in Russia – an indicator for democratic development?'], *Russlandanalysen*, 106: 11–13.

Moroff, H. (2002), 'Introduction', in *European Soft Security Policies: The Northern Dimension*, ed. H. Moroff, Helsinki and Berlin, Kauhava: 12–36.

Müntel, G. (2003), 'Kaliningrads Weg aus der Isolation? Eine Analyse des Transitkompromisses zwischen der EU und Russland' ['Kaliningrad's way out of isolation? An analysis of the transit compromise between the EU and Russia'], *Osteuropa*, 53(2–3): 249–61

Oldberg, I. (2000), 'The Emergence of a Regional Identity in the Kaliningrad Oblast', *Cooperation and Conflict*, 35(3): 269–88.

Olsen, J. P. (2002), 'The Many Faces of Europeanization', *Journal of Common Market Studies*, 40(5): 921–2.

Peters, B. G. (1999), *Institutional Theory in Political Science. The 'New Institutionalism'*, London and New York, Continuum.

Petrov, N. (2004), 'Regional Models of Democratic Development', in *Between Dictatorship and Democracy: Russian Post-Communist Political Reform*, ed. M. McFaul, N. Petrov and A. Riabov, Washington DC, Carnegie Endowment for International Peace: 239–67.

Radaelli, C. M. (2003), 'The Europeanization of Public Policy', in *The Politics of Europeanisation*, ed. K. Featherstone and C.M. Radaelli, Oxford, Oxford University Press: 27–56.

RDA (2005), *Regional Policies in the Border Areas of Poland and Lithuania: Purposes, Mechanisms and Opportunities to Use Their Experience in the Kaliningrad Region*, Kaliningrad, Regional Development Agency.

Rose, R. (1991), 'What is Lesson-drawing?', *Journal of Public Policy*, 11(1): 3–30.

Ross, C. (2002), *Federalism and Democratisation in Russia*, Manchester and New York, Manchester University Press.

Samson, I., V. Lamande, I. Elisseeva, N. Burova and G. Fedorov (2003), *A New Look at Kaliningrad Region*, Grenoble, Université Pierre Mendès-France.

Schimmelfennig, F. (2007), 'Europeanization Beyond Europe', *Living Reviews in European Governance*, 2(1), available on the Internet at www.livingreviews.org/lreg-2007–1 (accessed 23 August 2007).

Schimmelfennig, F. and U. Sedelmeier, eds (2005), *The Europeanization of Central and Eastern Europe*, Ithaca, Cornell University Press.

Sergounin, A. (2001), 'EU Enlargement and Kaliningrad: The Russian Perspective', in *Are Borders Barriers? EU Enlargement and the Russian Region of Kaliningrad*, ed. L. D. Fairlie and A. Sergounin, Helsinki and Berlin, The Finnish Institute of International Affairs and The Institute for European Politics: 139–90.

Simanska, B. (2004), 'Europeanization of the Regulatory Arrangements in Central and Eastern Europe (Conceptualization)', paper for the second pan-European conference 'Standing Group on EU Politics', Bologna, 24–26 June 2004.

Slider, D. (2001), 'Politics in the Regions', in *Developments in Russian Politics 5*, ed. S. White, Z. Gitelman and R. Sakwa, Houndmills, Palgrave: 147–68.

Smorodinskaya, N. (2001), 'Kaliningrad Exclave: Prospects for Transformation into a Pilot Region', unpublished manuscript, Moscow, East–West Institute.

Smorodinskaya, N. (2005), 'Kaliningrad's Economic Growth Problem', in *Russia and the European Union: Prospects for a New Relationship*, ed. O. Antonenko and K. Pinnick, London and New York, Routledge, 263–81.

Stanyte-Tolockiene, I. (2001), 'Kaliningrad Oblast in the context of EU Enlargement', in *Lithuanian Political Science Yearbook 2000*, ed. A. Jankauskas, Vilnius, Vilnius University Press: 217–50.

Steinmo, S., K. Thelen and F. Longstreth, eds (1992), *Structuring politics: Historical Institutionalism in Comparative Analysis*, Cambridge, Cambridge University Press.

Tews, K. (2002), *Der Diffusionsansatz für die Vergleichende Policy-Analyse. Wurzeln und Potentiale eines Konzepts. Eine Literaturstudie* [*Diffusion as a concept in comparative policy analysis: Its origins and potentials*], FU Berlin, Forschungsstelle für Umweltpolitik, FFU-Report 2002–02.

Torreblanca, J. I. (2001), 'Ideas, Preferences and Institutions: Explaining the Europeanization of Spanish Foreign Policy', ARENA Working Paper 01/26, Oslo, available on the Internet at www.arena.uio.no/publications/wp01_26.htm (accessed 12 December 2007).

van Elsuwege, P. (2002), 'EU Enlargement and its Consequences for EU–Russia Relations: The Limits of a "Fair Weather Strategy"', Leuven, Chair Interbrew-Baillet Latour Working Papers (October): 10–11.

Vinokurov, E. (2004a), 'Kaliningrad's Borders and Transit: Practicalities and Remaining Bottlenecks', CEPS Commentary, available on the Internet at www.ceps.be/Article .php?article_id=264 (accessed 12 December 2007).

Vinokurov, E. (2004b), *Economic Prospects for Kaliningrad: Between EU Enlargement and Russia's Integration into the World Economy*, Brussels, CEPS Working Document 201.

Vinokurov, E. (2006a), 'Enclaves and Exclaves of the World: Setting the Framework for a Theory of Enclaves', ZDES Working Paper, Bielefeld University and St Petersburg State University, available on the Internet at www.zdes.spb.ru (accessed 12 December 2007).

Vinokurov, E. (2006b), 'Kaliningrad transit and visa issues revisited', Brussels, CEPS Commentary.

Vinokurov, E. (2007), *Kaliningrad: Enclaves and Economic Integration*, Brussels, CEPS.

Wellmann, C. (1994), *Market Place or Garrison? On the Future of the Kaliningrad Region*, Kiel, Projektverbund Friedenswissenschaften.

Wong, R. (2005), 'The Europeanization of Foreign Policy', in *International Relations of the European Union*, ed. C. Hill and M. Smith, Oxford, Oxford University Press: 134–53.

Zverev, Y. M. (1998), 'The Kaliningrad Defence Industry: Problems of Conversion', *Defence and Peace Economics*, 9(4): 395–406.

Zverev, Y. M. (2007), 'Kaliningrad: Problems and Paths of Development', *Problems of Post-Communism*, 54(2): 9–25.

PART I

Analytical framework

CHRISTOPH KNILL, DIANA PITSCHEL AND
MICHAEL W. BAUER

2

Conceptualising Europeanisation in Eastern Europe: EU impact in 'likely' and 'unlikely' member states

Introduction

The enormous progress European integration has made over the last decades has raised the question of how it impacts on EU member states. Hence, under the label of Europeanisation, processes of domestic institutional and policy changes supposedly triggered by 'Europe' increasingly have become a focal point of scholarly attention. Recently, even explanations of the dynamics of the EU enlargement process base their arguments on Europeanisation approaches. The application of the concept of Europeanisation is thus no longer restricted to political changes in 'official' member states of the European Union. Rather it is used to describe processes of domestic change in candidate as well as in applicant or neighbour countries (Hix and Goetz 2000; Schimmelfennig 2004; 2007; Bauer and Pitschel 2006). This raises concerns about the applicability of explanatory approaches developed within Europeanisation research and their potential to cope with domestic changes in non-member states.

Within the field of Europeanisation research, several analytical frameworks have been developed to explain the varying impact of European integration on domestic structures. Basically, those approaches can be distinguished by their differential analytical starting point. A first approach identifies the misfit between European and domestic institutional structures as the key catalyst for domestic change (Duina 1997; Héritier *et al.* 1996). Secondly, a number of studies emphasise European leverage on changed opportunity structures and the potential reorganisation of actor constellations at the national level (Marks and McAdam 1996; Harmsen and Wilson 2000; Schneider 2001). A third explanatory approach combines issues of institutional compatibility and modifications of domestic opportunity structures (Börzel and Risse 2000; 2003; Green Cowles and Risse 2001; Knill 2001). Fourthly, a constructivist based explanatory framework points out the distinctive character of European discourse (Checkel 1999; Lavenex 2001; Jacquot and Woll 2003; Radaelli 2004; Risse 2004).

This article focuses on the policy-analytical model as an explanatory framework that synthesises actor-centred and institutionalist elements (Knill and Lenschow 1998; 2005; Knill and Lehmkuhl 2002). The policy-analytical model regards regulatory measures as the central element in the policy-making process, and national administrations as key actors in the implementation of EU regulatory policy. It does not contravene other approaches but clarifies the scope conditions in which either interests, institutions or ideas unfold maximum explanatory power. Its central argument is that the potential for change at the domestic level varies with respect to distinct governance patterns – compliance, competition and communication – underlying EU regulatory policies (Knill and Lenschow 2005: 584).

Tackling the question of applicability of Europeanisation approaches, we argue that the policy-analytic framework is best suited to explain domestic institutional change also in states that are not formally members of the European Union. Indeed, with the help of the policy-analytical approach we can conceptualise EU impact as it reaches far beyond the borders of the Union (M. Smith 1996; Friis and Murphy 1999; Commission 2003; Schimmelfennig 2004; Archer 2005; Schimmelfennig and Sedelmeier 2005a; K. E. Smith 2005). The European Neighbourhood Policy (ENP), involvement in post-communist transformation processes in Central and Eastern Europe, engaging with the initiative in a 'wider Europe',[1] as well as numerous political and economic cooperations with non-member states (e.g. in the European Free Trade Association), all suggest that the EU is gradually expanding its sphere of influence beyond the circle of member states (Lavenex 2004, Lavenex and Uçarer 2004; Sedelmeier 2006). Hence, it is plausible to assume that the European Union's policies also impact 'abroad' in one way or another.

On the basis of this assumption, we extend the governance-based approach that was developed in view of the EU-15 to the EU of 27 member states and beyond. Adapting the policy-analytical framework we aim at generating theoretical propositions about the potential of regulatory EU policies to trigger domestic institutional and policy change in non-EU states. We expect the impact of EU regulatory policies to vary with different governance patterns also in non-member states. In addition to the governance mode we assume a second factor to play a crucial role, namely the ambition of the country to become a member of the EU. In cases where countries have high ambitions to obtain membership status, the EU is in the position to apply pressure by making use of the coercive tool of conditionality. Conditionality is based upon a logic of 'reinforcement by reward' (Schimmelfennig and Sedelmeier 2004: 662), i.e. the EU announces that it will reward those states which implement its measures with EU membership (and all advantages bound to it).

We argue that the potential of the EU to exert influence on processes of domestic change can be expected to be higher in countries that have already reached candidate status and have good membership prospects (labelled here as 'likely members') than in states that have no hope of joining in the foreseeable future (labelled here as 'unlikely members').

The chapter is structured as follows: it introduces each governance pattern found in EU regulatory policies – compliance, competition and communication. Elaborating on those aspects that are likely to determine the behaviour of domestic administrations, we successively develop hypotheses about the potential impact of different policies on processes of domestic change in member states, candidate countries and other non-member states.

Impact of EU governance patterns on bureaucratic adaptation processes: compliance, competition and communication

Regulatory intervention is the crucial tool to influence – and in a number of cases even to authoritatively prescribe – desired behaviour of public and private actors. The EU relies heavily on this steering device, not least in order to establish and to run the Common Market as the centrepiece of European integration. However, the EU usually uses distinct modes of regulatory intervention. Three different steering mechanisms can be distinguished – compliance, competition and communication – each of which is tied to particular institutional conditions and relies on different requirements or incentives for member states to adapt their policies and institutions. National administrations, which act as key players in the implementation process, tend to react to these stimuli according to certain logics that in turn impact on the occurrence and the scope of domestic institutional change (Knill and Lenschow 2005: 585).

Compliance

Governance by compliance presupposes the existence of legally binding and common European rules that have to be implemented at the domestic level, conceding national bureaucracies only marginal levels of discretion to national implementers. Compliance-based regulations typically appear in policies of positive integration, i.e. they are aimed at establishing a sound environment for the participants of the European Common Market. They impose constraints on national actors in order to safeguard certain standards for the protection of workers, consumers and the environment as well as cultural assets.

On first sight, it may appear paradoxical that member states are willing to hand over regulatory power to the EU since – once it has gained this power – the EU can create coercive regulations, which put them under enormous implementation pressure. Furthermore, in cases of non-compliance the member states have to reckon with possible sanctions. Compliance measures normally have a far-reaching impact on the national institutional system, its organisation and its working practices. They can oblige bureaucracies to establish new regulatory instances, to centralise their regulatory procedures or to introduce structures of horizontal coordination. Legally binding European rules additionally challenge domestic bureaucratic styles, since they demand adjustments in modes of state intervention or administrative interest mediation.

Scrutinising which rationality determines national administrations' response to compliance measures displays that they follow a persistence-driven logic. They try to meet the EU requirements formally, but at the same time they attempt to minimise institutional adaptation costs. Even though they are bound to adjust to the prescriptive rules by European law, they are free to decide how to implement the requirements in the domestic system. The mechanism of compliance sets its priorities on the formal implementation of EU rules in due time. Aspects of bureaucratic efficiency, however, are of subordinate importance and are not explicitly demanded by the EU. The adjustment efforts of national administrations frequently follow patterns of administrative self-adaptation and are accompanied by gradual and successive modifications of working styles and routines (March and Olsen 1989). Taking into account the significance of institutional persistence and continuity for national bureaucracies, it does not astonish that adaptation efforts are restricted to absolutely necessary measures that merely suffice to fulfil the requirements of the EU. Hence, in member states, institutional and policy change evoked by compliance measures is moderate and proceeds rather gradually (Knill and Lenschow 1998; Knill 2001).

This point can be plausibly illustrated with reference to numerous empirical examples from the field of environmental policy. The environmental impact assessment (EIA) directive, for instance, obliges persons or agencies in charge of specified kinds of public or private projects to inform the designated public about the environmental impact of their projects (Council 1985). The environmental impact assessment has to be taken into consideration by those public authorities that decide on the approval of the respective project. The adequate implementation of the EIA directive would entail the concentration of horizontal integration of administrative control responsibilities. Considering that the assessment includes the impact of the respective project on water, air and soil as well as its potential threats to flora, fauna and human health, the designated public authority should be capable of evaluating the impacts comprehensively. The cross-country study of the implementation results revealed, however, that the efforts of national bureaucracies are unambiguously persistence-driven. For example in Germany, the national administration resisted the adoption of the integrated approach. In order to secure existing administrative structures they confined themselves to the implementation of the EIA in existing authorisation procedures and continue to base the authorisation practice on a single media approach (Knill and Lenschow 2005: 592).

Analysing the potential impact of compliance-based policies on non-EU states, the obligatory nature of the respective policy is a decisive aspect. In order for regulatory policies to have a definite effect, the EU must have legislative authority in the respective country, i.e. it must be able to enforce its rules and should have tools at its disposal to sanction non-compliance. With the candidate countries this precondition is given. The EU has set out the implementation of the *acquis communautaire*, a compilation of about 90,000 pages of legislation, as a condition for EU membership. The candidate countries have to adopt all existing EU laws and norms – thus, as regards legal obligations, they are on a par with member states and face the same compliance pressures (Grabbe 2003: 312).[2] However, we suggest that the rationality underlying candidates' reactions to compliance will deviate from that of member states due to their applicant status and the power asymmetry between the EU and the applicants. Rather than being oriented towards securing domestic institutional models they are driven by what Schimmelfennig and Sedelmeier (2004: 669) have termed '*acquis* conditionality', namely the ambition to achieve full EU membership. The EU, however, grants this reward only if the applicant almost fully complies with its rules; in cases of non-compliance the gain of membership can be either deferred or completely denied, so respective countries are under considerable strain to adhere to the regulations set out by the EU. In order not to put their membership prospects at stake, national administrations demonstrate their willingness to adhere to EU rules and even implement unpopular measures (Lavenex 2004: 694). However, in this context it should be acknowledged that eventually their implementation capacity is largely dependent on the bureaucratic effectiveness of domestic administrations (Knill and Hille 2006).

Within the phase of candidacy the responses of states to compliance measures may vary due to the status of their application. At the very beginning of the application process applicants make great efforts to prove their maturity to become full members and adhere to even very restrictive EU measures. This may change rapidly as the accession negotiations proceed. As soon as the accession date is set and the exclusion from EU entry becomes unlikely, national bureaucracies may exhibit fatigue or even resistance to the implementation of EU-created rules. This is especially the case when the adjustment of EU norms is attached to high adaptive costs (Schimmelfennig and Sedelmeier 2005b: 216) or when they run the danger of losing popularity (Steunenberg and Dimitrova 2007). This trend could be observed in Bulgaria and Romania shortly before the EU finally made a decision on their membership. Although their accession was scheduled for January 2007, a monitoring report by the European Commission published in early 2006 revealed that efforts in both countries to enforce law reforms and to combat corruption were insufficient and did not meet European standards (Commission 2006). Despite the still existing shortcomings, the final decision to accept both countries as EU members was only made in October 2006. As Steunenberg and Dimitrova (2007) pointed out, the diminishing effectiveness of conditionality may be explained by the fact that the EU can no longer rely on conditionality as accession comes closer. Furthermore, the Commission may intentionally abstain from enforcing an increased number of conditions within the candidate countries in order to be able to give a justifiable recommendation for the admission of the new members in the Council of Ministers and the European Parliament.

However, credible prospects of and expected benefits from membership remain the major driving forces determining candidate countries' response to EU compliance measures (Sedelmeier 2006).[3] They outweigh concerns of national bureaucracies on potential adaptation costs and their immanent reflex to preserve existing domestic institutional structures and policies (Schimmelfennig and Sedelmeier 2005b: 215). These tendencies can be observed, for example, in the adaptation of the EU's equal opportunities legislation in the former Central and Eastern European candidate countries. Whereas this policy field played virtually no role before the accession process, '[t]he European Union's attractive offer of EU membership joined to its well-developed gender equity legislation brought about dramatic change in legislation dealing with gender equity [in Central and Eastern Europe]' (Seppanen Anderson 2006: 109). Both the Czech Republic and Poland adapted their national legislation to the eight directives of chapter thirteen of the *acquis communautaire* in the late 1990s and early 2000s since the European Union made it unmistakably clear that accession, amongst other aspects, is also bound to the enforcement of equal rights for women (*ibid.*). The Czech Republic, Hungary and Poland comprehensively adapted their secondary legislation in the field of social policy (health, safety in the workplace, social protection programmes) to European standards irrespective of high adaptation costs (Sissenich 2005; Kaufman 2007). Equally, the Central and Eastern European member states rapidly adapted the migration *acquis* and their asylum and migration legislation to the standards of their Western neighbours (Lavenex and Uçarer 2004). Taking those aspects into consideration, we hypothesise that EU regulatory policies based on the governance pattern of compliance have a high potential to stimulate political and institutional adaptation processes within the candidate countries.

In the third group of states, which have either no membership ambition or a medium-term admittance perspective, the situation is completely different. Due to their status as neither members nor candidates they are not part of the common regulatory system of the European Union. The EU has no legal claim to impose obligatory regulations on them or to prescribe certain institutional models and procedures. Furthermore, it lacks the possibility of using conditionality as a coercive tool. Consequently, non-members with no interest in or chance of joining the EU lack reasons to initiate any adjustment processes. Instead, they will preserve the existing institutional structures. Hence, we expect compliance-driven EU regulatory policies to have no effect on processes and outcomes of domestic change in those countries. If those countries voluntarily decide to comply with restrictive EU measures, internal factors or potential benefits (like the hope of achieving candidate status in the long term) are supposed to play the decisive role. In those cases the adaptation of EU legislation is rather piecemeal and selective (Sedelmeier 2006). Referring to the example of EU gender equity legislation, Russia or Ukraine (for instance) have no inducement to adapt laws as long as they are not rewarded with the advantages that EU membership or the credible prospect of membership brings about.

Competition
The second major governance pattern applied in EU regulatory policy is competition between national administrative systems to achieve EU requirements. Competition-based regulations aim to ensure the functioning of the Common Market by gradually abolishing distorting factors such as national regulatory barriers ('negative integration'). Member states are asked to adjust certain institutional arrangements within the domestic arena in order to achieve particular policy goals (for example, the improvement of the quotas of foreign direct investment), and to effectively raise member states' competitiveness (Oates and Schwab 1988; Vogel 1995; Murphy 2004).

Regulatory EU policies operating within the competition pattern are only partially binding for national implementers. They restrict themselves to the formulation of the so-called 'rules of the game' that are obligatory for the member states, yet they abstain from providing concrete models prescribing how member states have to adjust their institutional design and leave them broad discretion in accomplishing the common aim (Knill and Lehmkuhl 2002). Therefore, their impact on domestic institutional structures is less direct than is the case with compliance measures. Nevertheless, those measures of so-called 'negative integration' imply a number of challenges to national institutions.

The rationale behind institutional change in the context of competitive measures differs fundamentally from the compliance logic. Instead of self-preserving interests of bureaucracies, it is market competition that constitutes the driving mechanism for institutional and political adaptation. Thus, institutional change is stimulated by the perceived need to improve the functional effectiveness of member states' institutional arrangements in comparison to those of other participants within the Common Market. The institutional reflex to conserve existing structures is repelled, unless the preservation of existing arrangements would strengthen the domestic position in market competition. Instead, effects such as the impact of certain regulatory domestic measures on the competitive position of national economies within the Common Market are the central aspect under consideration. The performance-governed logic of institutional change is based on system competition. It is the nature of competition that member states turn out to be winners or losers of the competitive arrangement depending on their performance in regard to national regulatory institutions and practices. This aspect becomes obvious, for example, when examining the effects different taxation systems of member states have on the movement of capital and national economic performance.

Adapting domestic institutional structures to competitive requirements, national administrations are in most cases not able to act on their own authority. Given that the consequences of national competitive performance have a decisive impact on the domestic political and economic system as a whole, it becomes more likely that societal and political actors intervene and promote institutional change. In those situations, the preserving self-interests of administrations are of secondary importance depending on the power of societal and political groups and their ability to enforce their preferences. Under those prevailing circumstances, national administrations play an instrumental role; their potential of being transformed 'from outside', however, increases (Knight 1994; Knill 2001).

In consideration of those aspects it can be stated that regulatory EU policies stimulating competition between national systems have the potential to trigger comprehensive institutional changes within member states. Bureaucracies can only push through their persistence-driven approach when the competitive performance of existing institutional structures is considered as being at a satisfactory level. Only in those cases will we find periods of institutional persistence or incremental forms of bureaucratic self-adaptation. However, if the discussion about potential advantages or disadvantages for the national economy enters the political agenda, decisions about the form and scope of institutional adjustment are opened up for the interference of all kinds of societal and political actors.

Reactions to competition-stimulating measures are well demonstrated with reference to the example of road haulage policy that regulates the operation of non-resident hauliers in domestic markets. This policy is aimed at the creation of a deregulated transport market within the Community. It has established legally binding guidelines for the abolition of national regulations protecting their domestic transport markets. Member states have to follow these general principles; how they implement them into their national system is at their own discretion. Road haulage policy had a challenging impact on domestic institutional regulations. It opened up new opportunities, especially for users of hauliers' services, whereas it restricted the available options for other groups of actors, such as domestic transport companies. Furthermore, member states were exposed to the pressures of international regulatory competition to abolish the regulatory obstacles of a free market. Evaluating the processes triggered by EU policy within distinct member states, it turns out that adjustment measures were clearly performance-driven and led by the claim to support the competitiveness of the domestic transport industry (Héritier *et al.* 2001). It is especially the German and Italian cases that demonstrate that existing regulation patterns were subject to far-reaching adjustments liberalising the transport market and abolishing protecting regulations like price controls or licensing schemes (Kerwer 2001; Teutsch 2001).

Considering the obligatory character of regulations based on a competitive approach, their potential impact on domestic change in non-member states first and foremost depends on the EU's capability to enforce its regulation on those states. Apart from that, a second factor is of major importance: the interest of the non-member states in participating in the Common Market and the potential gains they expect from their participation.

Candidate countries are (at least partly) involved in the Common Market long before they accede to the EU. On the one hand, they are subject to market-related conditionality. They have to ensure that their institutional structures fit the requirements of the market system of the EU and that they adopt the provisions set up for the Single Market. In this context it seems likely that candidates far from actual accession will increase their efforts in order to improve their accession prospects. On the other hand, they have to prove their competitiveness to other market participants (Schimmelfennig 2004). Striving to improve their competitive position in the Common Market, they can make use of their special status as candidates. By accepting the conditions set out in the *acquis*, they are, in the long run, obliged to implement market-regulatory rules set out by the EU. However, they have broad discretion to develop their own approaches in converting to the legal guidelines. They have negotiated transitional periods for the implementation of certain rules, which enable them to focus on the adoption of regulations that are prioritised by the EU or that are most profitable for them. This aspect is depicted with reference to EU structural policy, in particular with the required introduction of the statistical sub-state units (NUTS II). All Central and Eastern European candidate states rapidly established NUTS II units expecting large-scale monetary aid from the EU and long term profit for the economic and social development of the region (Brusis 2002; Hughes *et al.* 2004; Ferry and McMaster 2005). The implementation of rules that are of subordinate importance or that are less attractive to them, however, is likely to be postponed. Hence, we assume that by adapting their domestic institutional structures to the Common Market, candidate countries are mainly driven by a performance-oriented rationality. Yet, we also acknowledge that conditionality considerations are at work. In consideration of those aspects, we hypothesise that in the medium term, competitive measures set up by the EU are likely to foster gradual change in candidate countries.

The EU lacks the competence to issue market regulations with regard to states with no accession prospects or ambitions. Notwithstanding, some third countries presumably are highly interested in participating in the Common Market (Bulmer and Padgett 2005). This ambition is likely to be conditioned by economic considerations. However, the adoption of EU market regulation rules would take place on a voluntary basis. Hence, the countries are free to selectively adopt those regulations which are most useful for them in an economic sense. Rules that may restrict them in their economic activities or have a negative impact on their competitiveness are likely to be rejected. Such tendencies can be observed with the creation of a Common Economic Space – one major goal codified in the 'Roadmap' commonly agreed on by the EU and Russia (Commission 2005). Although Russia expressed its willingness to cooperate with the European Union in principle, it does not accept measures that would impair its economic freedom. Emphasising its status as an equal partner, it does not agree to change its protectionist policy in regard to its 'flagship industries' (metallurgy and chemicals), or to negotiate about free trade since its exports of gas and oil to the EU are mainly tariff-free (Emerson 2005). Another illustrative example for the selective adaptation to EU legislation is the Ukrainian energy policy. Although Ukraine agreed to open up its electricity and gas market and strengthen its regulatory authorities, its overall assessment is so far only shallow and declarative (Wolczuk 2003; Hofer 2007). While Ukraine has made much effort in adapting its electricity to the European networks of the Union for the Coordination of Transmission of Electricity (UCTE),[4] it is consciously lagging behind in the liberalisation of the gas market for geo-strategic reasons (Hofer 2007). Consequently, competitive EU policies can be expected to induce less significant change of domestic structures in third countries from a long term perspective.

Communication

This pattern of governance refers to the communication among national regulatory agents grouped together in EU legal or institutional networks. Applying the governance approach of communication, the EU stimulates information exchange and mutual learning between national policy-makers. Furthermore, it aims to promote the development of innovative forms and models of problem-solving that can be integrated into the member states' regulatory systems. Communication-based measures abstain from setting legally binding rules. Instead they are designed to support national policy-makers looking for regulatory models and concepts to tackle policy problems (Knill and Lehmkuhl 2002).

Originally, the communication approach was practised in international organisations such as the OECD before it was adopted by the European Union. It is marked by its openness and its emphasis on the voluntary participation of actors. Communication-based measures give national actors broad discretion to interpret suggestions from the EU and to decide how to adjust domestic conditions adequately. Concepts that are successfully applied in certain countries are promoted via policy transfer rather than competitive selection (Dolowitz and Marsh 2000). The basic idea is to encourage domestic actors to draw lessons from the evaluation of their own approaches to certain policy problems in comparison with other concepts (Rose 1991; Tews 2002).

The rationality that underlies communicative approaches is to secure and increase the legitimacy of particular institutional models within European discourse. National actors aspire to demonstrate that they were involved in the development of a broadly accepted policy model or, at least, they adhere to it in order to legitimise its existence. Emphasising the aspect of legitimacy, the rationality underlying this approach diverges both from the persistence-driven logic as well as from the logic of competition since it is primarily focused on the response to European discourse rather than on minimising domestic institutional change. Rapid changes and comprehensive reforms of domestic institutional structures are accepted by national bureaucracies as long as they serve the goal of protecting a legitimate institution (Knill and Lenschow 2005: 589).

Explanations of the legitimacy-based reasoning are to be found in the specific characteristics of European network structures that integrate national political actors and administrators. In those networks, actors observe each other. That implies that not only do they have the opportunity to watch how others solve similar problems and learn from their example; rather they must convince their counterparts of the quality and legitimacy of their concepts. Hence, institutional change evoked by communication measures is a product of legitimising the requirements that confront national administrations. Additionally, factors such as time pressures (Bennett 1991: 223), considerations to save costs (Tews 2002: 180) or constellations of high uncertainty (DiMaggio and Powell, 1991: 70) put national bureaucracies under pressure to adjust their institutions to commonly accepted models. Therefore, institutional change in member states induced by communication-based EU policies is moderate or even high, especially in those cases where a certain policy model has proved to be a kind of leading model.

An illustrative example of governance by communication from the literature on member states is the open method of coordination (OMC). It is applied in policy areas such as education, employment and research and development, and flanks those measures that build a more complete economic union. The OMC involves the fixation guidelines for the Union and timetables for the achievement of common goals, the development of indicators and benchmarks as tools for identification of best practice, the translation of European guidelines into national reform plans as well as monitoring, evaluation and peer review. The concrete measures taken vary between different policy fields. The OMC is directed to move national administrations from a persistence-driven to a responsive mode of behaviour.

Committing national administrations to develop national action plans, they are compelled to adjust intra- and interdepartmental structures to this procedure. Cross-national peer review demands that bureaucracies justify domestic institutional structures and working procedures and demonstrate that they are communicable and attractive to peers (Knill and Lenschow 2005: 599). The considerable impact of communication-based measures can be observed in the field of employment policy. The EU's focus on the employment rate of women and active labour market policies challenged those member states of the southern welfare state-type or with a corporatist background to rethink their models (De la Porte 2002).

As pointed out above, the EU aims to promote mutual learning and information exchange in EU legal or institutional frameworks by applying a communicative governance approach. However, to fully grasp the impact of communication-driven EU policies on non-member states, one should consider that member states communicate with third states within the framework of numerous associations, partnership agreements and other platforms. Within those structures the EU does not exert pressure on national actors to comply with certain standards; rather, as we have suggested above, it is the legitimacy-driven response of the network participants that fosters domestic institutional adaptation processes. Since both candidate countries and other non-members are involved in network relationships with the European Union, regulatory EU policy based on a communication approach is likely to have impacts on both groups of states.

Through accession negotiations, candidate countries are tightly embedded in the European network. Due to conditionality they are subject to consistent demands to review and to legitimise their policy approaches. The European Commission sets up benchmarks in particular policy areas and provides examples of best practice (Hodson and Maher 2001: 725; Grabbe 2003: 314). Consequently, the indirect pressure to adjust their approaches to commonly accepted models is tangible. Hence, we expect EU regulatory policies based on the communication approach to evoke moderate domestic institutional change in applicant countries in the medium term.

An illustrative example of the impact of communication-based measures on candidate countries is the administrative Twinning Programme launched by the EU. Although there are no binding EU regulations prescribing a certain model for public administration systems, the EU set up a benchmarking system expressing European Union values and principles in public administration (Verheijen 2004). The Twinning Programme was designed to meet those benchmarks and to support candidate countries establishing an efficient administration that is capable of applying the *acquis* (Papadimitriou and Phinnemore 2004: 624). With this Programme being carried out by experienced administration experts from member states, the EU hopes to make unwieldy and centralised bureaucracies in Central and Eastern European compatible to modern Western European standards. For example, in the field of visas, asylum, migration and border control, the EU is very active in the countries of former Yugoslavia, offering technical and administrative assistance, like training measures for domestic staff or improving the efficiency of the institutions (Lavenex and Uçarer 2004).

Also with regard to communication-oriented measures, the impact on countries far away from membership is supposedly greater. Unlike the so-called 'front-runners', these countries feel compelled to prove their trustworthiness as future members of the Union and therefore demonstrate their openness to EU measures and models. Furthermore, it is especially those states in a transitional phase and lacking a stable institutional structure that appreciate the guidelines, benchmarks and evaluation schemes set out by the EU to structure their domestic adaptation processes (Grabbe 1999).

Responding to increasing interdependence with its neighbour states to tackle common policy problems including issues of defence, justice and home affairs as well as issues of environmental protection and energy supply, the EU seeks to establish communicative networks with those neighbouring countries (Lavenex 2004). The installation of such networks requires that neighbours perceive a need to cooperate. Only if this cooperation is achieved, do the respective counterparts face the need to legitimise their approaches and, if necessary, adhere to a common set of values and harmonise their policies. So far, the EU has established a number of communication platforms involving actors from third countries. Within several Partnership and Cooperation Agreements (PCA) with Russia, Ukraine and Moldova, the EU has together with its partners agreed on common strategies and action plans in migration policies. However, as long as discrepancies between the partners occur, e.g. in the case of transit visas which allow Russian citizens to cross Lithuania to the Russian enclave of Kaliningrad, the prospects for successful policy transfer remain limited (Lavenex and Uçarer 2004: 433; see also Moshes 2003). Another example refers to the energy dialogue with Russia which probes the possibilities of cooperation in the energy sector (Commission 2000). Within the initiative to establish a Common Space of Research, Education and Culture, the EU and Russia agreed to work on Russia's adjustment to European educational standards (see chapter 14 in this volume). However, it is recognised that this project demands a broad time frame since '[i]t will doubtless take a generation or two for Russia and the EU to genuinely converge in terms of mindsets and political values perceived across society as a whole' (Emerson 2005). Taking those developments into consideration, we suppose that within those structures EU policies based on the communication approach might have a limited impact on domestic institutional change in non-member states in the long term.

	Member states	Candidate countries ('likely members')	Other non-members ('unlikely members')
Compliance	Moderate change (persistence driven)	Significant change (conditionality driven)	No effect (persistence driven)
Competition	Significant change (performance driven)	Moderate change in medium term (performance driven)	Slight change in long term (performance driven)
Communication	Moderate to significant change in medium term (legitimacy driven)	Moderate change in medium term (legitimacy driven)	Slight change in long term (legitimacy driven)

(Vertical columns between the sets of data are labelled "Transitional period".)

Figure 2.1 EU regulatory policies and domestic institutional change

Conclusion and perspectives

Recently, Europeanisation has been used as an explanatory concept for domestic change in states that are not formal members of the European Union (Schimmelfennig 2007). This raises questions about the applicability and the explanatory power of existing analytical frameworks within the non-member state context. In this chapter we have investigated the potential of the policy-analytical approach in this respect. We have demonstrated that the policy-analytical toolkit can indeed serve for hypotheses development and thus constitutes a sound basis for a structured analysis of the impact of Europeanisation on domestic change beyond the circle of present EU member states.

The policy-analytical approach systematically analyses the impact of different patterns of EU governance on the process and outcome of national institutional and policy change. Compliance, communication and competition each have specific potential to trigger national adjustments, depending on the rationality underlying domestic actors' behaviour. Applying the governance approach to non-member states, we assume that two aspects are of major importance. First of all, we hypothesise that varying impacts of different patterns of governance can be observed in non-member states. Second, we regard a country's ambition to receive membership status as a decisive factor determining the potential effects of EU regulatory policy. Therefore we analytically distinguish between candidate countries with accession prospects and other non-member states with no membership prospects in the foreseeable future. Based on those assumptions we develop hypotheses about EU-induced change in member states, candidate countries and other non-member states and establish a framework for systematic empirical analysis.

However, if scholars take the governance approach as basis for empirical analysis, they have to meet several challenges. First of all, they have to consider that the policy-analytical approach operates with ideal types of governance. In political reality it might turn out to be challenging to assign certain policy measures to precisely one specific form of governance and to formulate unambiguous expectations about its potential to trigger domestic change. Nevertheless, the existence of 'hybrid forms' does not contradict the general argument. It rather points to the need for careful analysis of the complexities behind EU policies.

Second, it will be necessary to clarify which changes of domestic institutional structures are induced by European policies and which are conditioned by other intervening factors. Domestic change can be stimulated by a range of internal or external factors that are not related to Europeanisation pressures. It may, for example, be attributed to globalisation and the increasing internationalisation of finances and markets or to party political struggles in the national arena (Treib 2003; Lenschow 2006: 60). In order to tackle this problem, several methodological strategies can be applied. At first, Europeanisation studies would benefit from increasing variation of the independent variable. By including non EU-related control groups it becomes feasible to control the differential effects of Europeanisation on domestic institutional arrangements (Haverland 2005). Furthermore, Europeanisation studies could extend their explanatory power by making more efforts in process tracing (Lenschow 2006). It makes sense to precisely track the chronology of distinct stimuli and domestic change in order to assure that European policies are actually the causal factor for domestic change.

Finally, one should be aware that the outlined model constitutes only a first step towards improving the analytical basis for tackling these thorny methodological and conceptual issues. However, it provides researchers, who are primarily interested in empirical research, with a tool to better orient and fit their individual work into the joint endeavour of accumulating knowledge and producing candidate explanations that can be used to advance the necessary debate. In particular, our model will help to systematically derive competing hypotheses to inform empirical research, thereby encouraging scholars to engage, first and foremost, in careful comparative investigation (George 1979; George and Bennett 2005). This is a research strategy that, as we have argued throughout this chapter, bears by far the greatest potential for identifying and explaining EU-induced change in third countries.

Notes

1   With this initiative the Commission reacted to the increasing interdependencies with its neighbouring states in the south and east. It aims to promote trans-national economic relations, common shared values and cooperation combating security threats. The initiative refers to Algeria, Egypt, Israel, Jordan, Lebanon, Libya, Morocco, Palestine Territories, Syria and Tunisia as well as Belarus, Moldova, Russia and Ukraine (Commission 2003).
2   It has to be considered that the candidate countries do not have to transpose all EU regulations immediately. Transitional periods have been conceded to them, leaving them room to implement the regulations within a certain negotiated timeframe.
3   According to Schimmelfennig (2004: 254), credible membership prospects require a credible assurance of accession (candidates must be sure that they will be affiliated when they fulfil the conditions), a credible threat of exclusion (candidates must be sure that they will not be accepted if they fail to comply with the conditions) and a concrete definition of the accession conditions and the existing deficits.
4   The UCTE is responsible for the coordination and the enlargement and represents thirty-four net operators from twenty-two Western and Eastern European countries.

References

Archer, C. (2005), *Norway Outside the European Union*, London, Routledge.
Bauer, M. and D. Pitschel (2006), 'Europäisierung als Konzept zur Erklärung von Dezentralisierung und Regionalisierung in Mittel – und Osteuropa – Mehr Fragen als Antworten' ['Europeanisation as an explanatory concept for decentralisation and regionalisation in Central and Eastern Europe: More questions than answers'], in *Jahrbuch des Föderalismus*, Baden-Baden, Nomos: 44–56.
Bennett, C. J. (1991), 'What Is Policy Convergence and What Causes It?', *British Journal of Political Science*, 21(2): 215–33.
Börzel, T. A. and T. Risse (2000), 'When Europe Hits Home: Europeanization and Domestic Change', *European Integration online Papers*, 4(15), available on the Internet at http://eiop.or.at/eiop/texte/2000–015a.htm (accessed 30 November 2006).
Börzel, T. A. and T. Risse (2003), 'Conceptualizing the Domestic Impact of Europe', in *The Politics of Europeanization*, eds K. Featherstone and C. M. Radaelli, Oxford, Oxford University Press: 57–80.
Brusis, M. (2002), 'Between EU Requirements, Competitive Politics, and National Traditions: Re-creating Regions in the Accession Countries of Central and Eastern Europe', *Governance*, 15(4): 531–59.
Bulmer, S. and S. A. Padgett (2005), 'Policy Transfer in the European Union: An Institutionalist Perspective', *British Journal of Political Science*, 35(1): 103–26.
Checkel, J. T. (1999), 'Social Construction and Integration', *Journal of European Public Policy*, 6(4): 545–60.
Commission (2000), 'European Union–Russia Energy Dialogue: Joint Declaration', available on the Internet at http://europa.eu.int/comm/external_relations/russia /summit_30_10_00/statement_en.htm (accessed 3 April 2006).
Commission (2003), 'Wider Europe Neighbourhood: A New Framework for Relations with our Eastern and Southern Neighbours', Brussels, COM 104 final, available on the Internet at www.europa.eu.int/comm/world/enp/pdf/com03_104_en.pdf (accessed 27 April 2006).
Commission (2005), 'Roadmap for the Common Economic Space: Building Blocks for

Sustained Economic Growth', available on the Internet at http://eu2005.lu/en/actualites/documents_travail/2005/05/10–4spaces/4spaces.pdf (accessed 11 May 2006).

Commission (2006), 'Monitoring Report on the State of Preparedness for EU membership of Bulgaria and Romania', Brussels, COM 214 final.

Council (1985), 'Council Directive of 27 June 1985 on the Assessment of the Effects of Certain Public and Private Projects on the Environment', 85/337/EEC, Official Journal L 175, 5 July 1985: 0040–8.

De la Porte, C. (2002), 'Is the Open Method of Coordination Appropriate for Organising Activities at European Level in Sensitive Policy Areas?', European Law Journal, 8(1): 38–58.

DiMaggio, P. J. and W. W. Powell (1991), 'The Iron Cage Revisited: Institutionalized Isomorphism and Collective Rationality in Organizational Fields', in The New Institutionalism in Organizational Analysis, ed. P. J. DiMaggio and W. W. Powell, Chicago, University of Chicago Press: 63–82.

Dolowitz, D. P. and D. Marsh (2000), 'Learning from Abroad: The Role of Policy Transfer in Contemporary Policy-Making', Governance, 13(1): 5–23.

Duina, F. (1997), 'Explaining Legal Implementation in the European Union', International Journal of the Sociology of Law, 25(2): 155–80.

Emerson, M. (2005), 'EU–Russia: Four Common Spaces and the Proliferation of the Fuzzy', CEPS Policy Brief, 71.

Ferry, M. and I. McMaster (2005), 'Implementing Structural Funds in Polish and Czech Regions: Convergence, Variation, Empowerment?', Regional and Federal Studies, 15(1): 19–39.

Friis, L. and A. Murphy (1999), 'The European Union and Central and Eastern Europe: Governance and Boundaries', Journal of Common Market Studies, 37(2): 211–32.

George, A. L. (1979), 'Case Studies and Theory Development: The Method of Structured, Focused Comparison', in Diplomacy: New Approaches in History, Theory, and Policy, ed. P. G. Lauren, New York, Free Press: 43–68.

George, A. L. and A. Bennett (2005), Case Studies and Theory Development in Social Sciences, Cambridge (MA), MIT.

Grabbe, H. (1999), 'A Partnership for Accession? The Implications of EU Conditionality for the Central and East European Applicants', Robert Schuman Centre Working Paper 12/99, San Domenico di Fiesole, European University Institute.

Grabbe, H. (2003), 'Europeanization Goes East: Power and Uncertainty in the EU Accession Process', in The Politics of Europeanization, ed. K. Featherstone and C. M. Radaelli, Oxford, Oxford University Press: 303–27.

Green Cowles, M. and T. Risse (2001), 'Europeanisation and Domestic Change: Conclusions', in Transforming Europe: Europeanisation and Domestic Change, ed. M. Green Cowles, J. Caporaso and T. Risse, Oxford, Oxford University Press: 217–37.

Harmsen, R. and T. M. Wilson (2000), 'Introduction: Approaches to Europeanization', in Europeanization: Institutions, Identities and Citizenship, ed. R. Harmsen and T. M. Wilson, Amsterdam, Editions Rodopi: 13–26.

Haverland, M. (2005), 'Does the EU Cause Domestic Developments? The Problem of Case Selection in Europeanization Research', West European Politics, 29(1): 134–46.

Héritier, A., C. Knill and S. Mingers (1996), Ringing the Changes in Europe: Regulatory Competition and the Transformation of the State, Berlin, De Gruyter.

Héritier, A., D. Kerwer, C. Knill, D. Lehmkuhl, M. Teutsch and A. Douillet, eds (2001), Differential Europe: New Opportunities and Restrictions for Policy-Making in the Member States, Lanham (MD), Rowman & Littlefield.

Hix, S. and K. H. Goetz (2000), Europeanised Politics? European Integration and National Political Systems, London, Frank Cass.

Hodson, D. and I. Maher (2001), 'The Open Method as a New Mode of Governance: The Case of Soft Economic Policy Co-ordination', *Journal of Common Market Studies*, 39(4): 719–46.

Hofer, S. (2007) 'Die Europäische Union als Regelexporteur. Die Europäisierung der Energiepolitik in Bulgarien, Serbien und der Ukraine' ['The European Union as exporter of rules: Europeanising energy policy in Bulgaria, Serbia and Ukraine'], Draft for the International Relations Conference of the German Association for Political Science (Deutsche Vereinigung für Politische Wissenschaft) 13–14 July 2007, available on the Internet at www.politikwissenschaft.tudarmstadt.de/fileadmin/pg/Sektionstagung_IB/Darmstadt_HOFER.pdf (accessed 18 September 2007).

Hughes, J., G. Sasse and C. Gordon (2004), 'Conditionality and Compliance in the EU's Eastward Enlargement: Regional Policy and the Reform of Sub-national Government', *Journal of Common Market Studies*, 42(3): 523–51.

Jacquot, S. and C. Woll (2003), 'Usage of European Integration: Europeanisation from a Sociological Perspective', *European Integration Online Papers*, 7:12, available on the Internet at http://eiop.or.at/eiop/texte/2003–012a.htm (accessed 14 February 2006).

Kaufman, R. (2007), 'Market Reform and Social Protection: Lessons from the Czech Republic, Hungary, and Poland', *East European Politics and Societies*, 21(1): 111–25.

Kerwer, D. (2001), 'Going Through the Motions: The Modest Impact of Europe Italian Transport Policy', in *Differential Europe: New Opportunities and Restrictions for Policy-Making in the Member States*, ed. A. Héritier, D. Kerwer, C. Knill, D. Lehmkuhl, M. Teutsch and A. Douillet, Lanham (MD), Rowman & Littlefield: 23–56.

Knight, J. (1994), *Institutions and Social Conflict*, Cambridge, Cambridge University Press.

Knill, C. (2001), *The Europeanisation of National Administrations: Patterns of Institutional Change and Persistence*, Cambridge, Cambridge University Press.

Knill, C. and P. Hille (2006), '"It's the Bureaucracy, Stupid": The Implementation of the Acquis Communautaire in EU Candidate Countries 1999–2003', *European Union Politics*, 7(4): 531–52.

Knill, C. and D. Lehmkuhl (2002), 'The National Impact of European Union Regulatory Policy: Three Europeanization Mechanisms', *European Journal of Political Research*, 41(2): 255–80.

Knill, C. and A. Lenschow (1998), 'Coping with Europe: The Impact of British and German Administrations on the Implementation of EU Environmental Policy', *Journal of European Public Policy*, 5(4): 595–615.

Knill, C. and A. Lenschow (2005), 'Coercion, Competition and Communication: Different Approaches of European Governance and their Impact on National Institutions', *Journal of Common Market Studies*, 43(3): 581–604.

Lavenex, S. (2001), 'The Europeanisation of Refugee Policies: Normative Challenges and Institutional Legacies', *Journal of Common Market Studies*, 39(5): 851–74.

Lavenex, S. (2004), 'EU External Governance in "Wider Europe"', *Journal of European Public Policy*, 11(4): 680–700.

Lavenex, S. and E. Uçarer (2004), 'The External Dimension of Europeanization: The Case of Immigration Policies', *Cooperation and Conflict*, 39(4): 417–43.

Lenschow, A. (2006), 'Europeanisation of Public Policy', in *European Union: Power and Policy-making*, 3rd edn, ed. J. J. Richardson, Abingdon, Routledge: 55–71.

March, J. G. and J. P. Olsen (1989), *Rediscovering Institutions: The Organizational Basis in Politics*, New York, Free Press.

Marks, G. and D. McAdam (1996), 'Social Movements and the Changing Structure of Political Opportunity in the European Union', *West European Politics*, 19: 249–78.

Moshes, A. (2003), 'Kaliningrad: Challenges Between Russia and Europe', in *Prospects and Risks Beyond EU Enlargement. Eastern Europe: Challenges of a Pan-European Policy*, ed. I. Kempe, Opladen, Leske and Budrich: 177–94.

Murphy, D. (2004), *The Structure of Regulatory Competition*, Oxford, Oxford University Press.

Oates, W. E. and R. Schwab (1988), 'Economic Competition Among Jurisdictions: Efficiency Enhancing or Distortion Inducing', *Journal of Public Economics*, 35: 333–54.

Papadimitriou, D. and D. Phinnemore (2004), 'Europeanisation, Conditionality and Domestic Change: The Twinning Exercise and Administrative Reform in Romania', *Journal of Common Market Studies*, 42(3): 619–39.

Radaelli, C. M. (2004), 'Europeanisation: Solution or Problem?', *European Integration Online Papers*, 8:16, available on the Internet at http://eiop.or.at/eiop/texte /2004–016a.htm (accessed 30 November 2006).

Risse, T. (2004), 'Social Constructivism and European Integration', in *European Integration Theory*, ed. A. Wiener and T. Diez, Oxford, Oxford University Press: 159–76.

Rose, R. (1991), 'What is Lesson-Drawing?', *Journal of Public Policy*, 11(1): 3–30.

Schimmelfennig, F. (2004), 'Starke Anreize, ambivalente Wirkungen: Die Europäisierung Mittel- und Osteuropas' ['Strong incentives, ambivalent effects: The Europeanisation of Central and Eastern Europe'], *Leviathan*, 32: 250–68.

Schimmelfennig, F. (2007), 'Europeanization Beyond Europe', *Living Reviews in European Governance* 2:1, available on the Internet at www.livingreviews.org/lreg-2007–1 (accessed 20 September 2007).

Schimmelfennig, F. and U. Sedelmeier (2004), 'Governance by Conditionality: EU Rule Transfer to the Candidate Countries of Central and Eastern Europe', *Journal of European Public Policy*, 11(4): 661–79.

Schimmelfennig, F. and U. Sedelmeier (2005a), 'Introduction: Conceptualizing the Europeanization of Central and Eastern Europe', in *The Europeanization of Central and Eastern Europe*, ed. F. Schimmelfennig and U. Sedelmeier, Ithaca, Cornell University Press: 1–28.

Schimmelfennig, F. and U. Sedelmeier (2005b), 'Conclusions: The Impact of the EU on the Accession Countries', in *The Europeanization of Central and Eastern Europe*, ed. F. Schimmelfennig and U. Sedelmeier, Ithaca, Cornell University Press: 210–28.

Schneider, V. (2001), 'Europeanization and the Redimensionalization of the Public Sector: Telecommunication in Germany, France and Italy', in *Transforming Europe. Europeanisation and Domestic Change*, ed. M. Green Cowles, J. Caporaso and T. Risse, Oxford, Oxford University Press: 60–78.

Sedelmeier, U. (2006), 'Europeanisation in New Member and Candidate States', *Living Reviews in European Governance*, 3:1, available on the Internet at http://europeangovernance.livingreviews.org/Articles/lreg-2006–3/ (accessed 18 September 2007).

Seppanen Anderson, L. (2006), 'European Union Gender Regulations in the East: The Czech and Polish Accession Process', *East European Politics and Societies*, 20(1): 101–25.

Sissenich, B. (2005), 'The Transfer of EU Social Policy to Poland and Hungary', in *The Europeanisation of Central and Eastern Europe*, ed. F. Schimmelfennig and U. Sedelmeier, Ithaca, Cornell University Press: 156–77.

Smith, K. E. (2005), 'The Outsiders: The European Neighbourhood Policy', *International Affairs*, 81(4): 757–73.

Smith, M. (1996), 'The European Union and a Changing Europe: Establishing the Boundaries of Order', *Journal of Common Market Studies*, 34(1): 5–28.

Steunenberg, B. and A. Dimitrova (2007), 'Compliance in the EU Enlargement Process: The Limits of Conditionality', *European Integration Online Papers*, 11(5), available on the Internet at http://eiop.or.at/eiop/texte/2007–005a.htm (accessed 18 September 2007).

Teutsch, M. (2001), 'Regulatory Reforms in the German Transport Sector: How to Overcome Multiple Veto Points', in *Differential Europe: New Opportunities and Restrictions for Policy-Making in the Member States*, ed. A. Héritier, D. Kerwer, C. Knill, D. Lehmkuhl, M. Teutsch and A. Douillet, Lanham (MD), Rowman & Littlefield: 133–72.

Tews, K. (2002), *Der Diffusionsansatz für die Vergleichende Policy-Analyse. Wurzeln und Potentiale eines Konzepts. Eine Literaturstudie* [*Diffusion as a concept in comparative policy analysis: Its origins and potentials*], FU Berlin, Forschungsstelle für Umweltpolitik, FFU-Report 2002–02.

Treib, O. (2003), 'Die Umsetzung von EU-Richtlinien im Zeichen der Parteipolitik: Eine akteurszentrierte Antwort auf die Misfit-These' ['Party politics and the implementation of EU directives: an actor-centered response to the hypothesis of misfit'], *Politische Vierteljahresschrift*, 44: 506–28.

Verheijen, T. (2004), 'Administrative Transformation and the Accession Agenda', *Zeitschrift für Staats- und Europawissenschaften*, 2(3): 372–92.

Vogel, D. (1995), *Trading Up: Consumer and Environmental Regulation in a Global Economy*, Cambridge (MA), Harvard University Press.

Wolczuk, K. (2003), 'Ukraine's Policy towards the European Union: A Case of "Declarative Europeanization"', Robert Schuman Centre for Advanced Studies and Centre for Russian and East European Studies, University of Birmingham, available on the Internet at http://batory.org.pl/ftp/program/forum/eu_ukraine/ ukraine_eu_policy .pdf (accessed 18 September 2007).

Évgeny Vinokurov

3

How do enclaves adjust to changes in the external environment? A theory of enclaves and the case of Kaliningrad

Introduction

There are more than 280 enclaves and exclaves[1] in the world with a total population of approximately 2.7 million.[2] They range from micro-enclaves, such as the Spanish Llivia or the German Büsingen, to large enclave complexes, such as Cooch Behar at the border of India and Bangladesh, and large individual enclaves, such as Kaliningrad. Even more of them existed in the past. A finer typology of enclaves includes, first, *true enclaves*, i.e. the parts of a state entirely enclosed in another state; second, *semi-* (or *coastal*) *enclaves*, i.e. the parts of a state enclosed within the land territory of another state, yet in possession of a sea border (that is, not fully surrounded); and, third, *pene-enclaves*, i.e. territories that are, although not separated from the mainland, practically accessible only through the territory of another state. In addition, there are so-called *mere exclaves*, which represent regions that, while being isolated from their mainland, are surrounded by more than one state. Thus, they are not enclaves in relation to other states but merely exclaves in relation to the mainland.

Kaliningrad is an interesting case in this respect. It can be technically described as a mere exclave since it borders two states, Poland and Lithuania. On the other hand, both states are members of the European Union so it is possible to say that Kaliningrad is a semi-enclave of the EU. This view is reinforced by the fact that the enclave-specific issues of the movement of goods and people lie within the competence of the EU. In general, this term is logically cogent when looking from the mainland's side.

What are the changes to which an enclave has to adjust? To begin with, a region has to cope with the major challenge of becoming an enclave. Then, in the course of its existence, an enclave has to adapt to numerous changes in the political and economic environment, which often take the form of a shock. The vital feature is that the source of changes may lie both in the mainland state and in the surrounding state. Finally, a region has to adapt itself to changes in the political and economic framework in the case of disenclavement.

This chapter occupies itself with the adjustment to changes and, more specifically, to exogenous processes. Relative to Kaliningrad, the EU eastern enlargement is an exogenous process that has exerted a significant and enclave-specific impact on the oblast since 2002, even before the official accession in 2004. Other instances of exogenous processes have been the disruption of economic continuity as a consequence of the break-up of the Soviet Union (1990–92), the 1998 Russian monetary and financial crisis, and Russia's WTO accession.

This chapter addresses two main issues. First, it examines the way enclaves adjust to exogenous processes, assessing the specific features that distinguish enclaves and exclaves from 'typical' non-enclave regions of the same state in the way they react to shocks. The mechanisms and conditions to reduce the scale of shocks and to alleviate the burden of adjustment represent the second matter of investigation. We try to determine the main components and preconditions of a more stable and healthy economic and political framework in which enclaves might operate.

Enclaves and exclaves are an under-researched area. The available scientific literature occupies itself mostly with studying separate enclave regions. A comprehensive review of literature on enclaves and exclaves is provided in Vinokurov (2006; 2007b). Attempts to engage in comparative studies include Robinson (1959), Catudal (1979), Whyte (2002), Zverev (2003), Klemeshev (2005), and Vinokurov (2002; 2006; 2007b). The issue of adaptation to shocks has not been treated in the literature *per se*, although it was examined implicitly in various individual case studies, such as Gold (2000) on Ceuta and Melilla, Gold (2005) on Gibraltar, Whyte (2002) on Cooch Behar, and Whyte (2004) on Baarle.

The chapter proceeds as follows: the next section elaborates enclaves' economic and political features relative to the issue of adjustment to exogenous processes and, more specifically, to shocks. Section three analyses various types of integration as well as options for the mainland's policy concerning its exclave. Section four sets the benchmarks on whether economic success depends on openness and/or economic orientation. Finally, in section five, the theoretical findings are applied to the case of Kaliningrad.

Economic and political features of enclaves

The two powers that have most to do with an enclave are the mainland state and the surrounding state. These two sides and an enclave itself compose the mainland-enclave-surrounding state (MES) 'triangle' (Vinokurov 2006: 46–62; 2007b). The sides of the triangle are: first, mainland-enclave relations (M-E); second, enclave-surrounding state relations (E-S); third, mainland-surrounding state relations on general issues (M-S). In addition, there is the influence of mainland-surrounding state relations on the enclave issue (M-S-E). The impacts are not necessarily of equal strength. The decisive impact is the pressure that the mainland exerts upon enclaves. Likewise, the general context of the mainland-surrounding state relations is *the* context in which an enclave must find its place and to which it should adapt its vital activities. Further, the impact of the surrounding state's economy and politics is immeasurably larger than the reverse (Vinokurov 2007b: 71–86). The asymmetry of size and power of an enclave in comparison to both the mainland and the surrounding state evokes its vulnerability to exogenous processes. In some instances, it makes enclaves prone to shocks.

Enclaves demonstrate a number of specific features, which condition both the specific character of enclave shocks and the specific character of enclaves' response to a shock. Among these features there are enclavity (understood as embeddedness into the surrounding state), exclavity (understood as detachedness from the mainland), both possibly enhanced to a 'double periphericity', smallness of local production and consumption base, increased vulnerability and consequent typical overreaction to shocks, as well as insufficient competences to respond directly to exogenous challenges.

Enclavity, exclavity and resulting vulnerability

The vulnerability of enclaves stems from a variety of factors. The principal ones are, first, the vulnerability of mainland-exclave access, second, small size, and, third, the high exposure to economic and political shocks particularly in the context of M-S relations (Vinokurov 2005; 2007b).

The problem of mainland-exclave communication, also referred to as the problem of access or transit, is the central issue in the mainland-exclave vector of the MES triangle. It is deeply rooted in the nature of an enclave, since the embeddedness in the surrounding state and its detachedness from the mainland makes an enclave/exclave what it is. The communication has three vital components: first, the movement of goods and services; second, the movement of people; and third, the movement of military and police forces as well as state officials.

As soon as an enclave emerges, it faces the problem of communication with the mainland. If appropriate arrangements are made by the mainland and the surrounding state, problems can be dealt with and mitigated at an early stage, otherwise they can be severe from the very beginning if an enclave is involved in the turmoil of international politics, tensions, and military conflicts. Communication problems can act as an additional shock and impede the prospects of economic and societal recovery. To give an example, one of the many metaphors for West Berlin from 1945 to 1990 was that of a 'seismograph' (Hörning 1992: viii), indicating its vulnerability and responsiveness to even minor tensions of the Cold War.

From an economic perspective, enclavity and exclavity become apparent in vital matters, such as higher transportation costs in trade with the mainland or tariff and non-tariff barriers impeding access to the proximate market. The problems of access and the related issue of disproportionately high transportation costs are typically quite high on an enclave's agenda. Interregional trade within the state is obstructed by the exclave's remoteness. Shipment costs often make supply and reception of processed goods, but especially raw and partially-refined materials, more expensive and economically inefficient. Kaliningrad is a convincing example of this, being separated from the central regions of Russia by more than 1,000 km, three borders and two countries. Its industries have had to cope with the disruption of Soviet-era trade patterns in the new conditions of territorial dividedness and increased market prices for transportation services.

Is the problem of access and disproportionate transportation costs less severe in semi-enclaves like Kaliningrad than in true enclaves, which are fully embedded into the surrounding state? Kaliningrad has convenient access to the Baltic Sea to the west and a variety of ways to ensure communication with mainland Russia, such as land routes via Lithuania and Belarus, via Lithuania and Latvia, via Poland and Belarus; air transportation; and the maritime route to St Petersburg. Under normal circumstances, economic expediency narrows the choice to the Kaliningrad–Lithuania–Belarus–Russia route. All major railways and roads as well as pipelines and power lines were routed through Lithuania during the Soviet era, so that access through Poland is no longer economically justified. The possibility of sea connection with St Petersburg is largely devalued by economic considerations as well. 80–90 per cent of imports come from Central Russia (Moscow), the Volga region, and Siberia, while 80 per cent of Kaliningrad's exports go to Central Russia. St Petersburg and north-west Russia are minor trade partners for Kaliningrad. In December of 2002, a ferry service from Kaliningrad to St Petersburg was opened due to political considerations, but it has been unprofitable and must be subsidised by the state. Businesses do not use it because existing direct land links through Lithuania and Belarus are less expensive. It should be noted that there are normal and extraordinary conditions. Under normal conditions, economic considerations are salient and cost calculations often narrow the choice of options. However, under extraordinary conditions – such a military conflict or a blockade – then other possibilities may be considered despite the costs.

Furthermore, tariff and non-tariff barriers have considerable influence on the economies of many enclaves. There is a trend towards the gradual diminishment of custom borders within the frameworks of the WTO, free trade associations and the European Union, which may have a special meaning for enclaves. As an effect of the agreements on lowering tariff barriers and removing non-tariff barriers in international trade, enclaves often have an opportunity to considerably raise volumes of trade. Not only international trade is intended in this, but also the trade that an enclave has with other regions of the same state. The latter form of trade would be eased because the obstacles to transit trade have also decreased. Such changes may also naturally lead to processes of import and export re-orientation, like switching from trade with the mainland to trade with surrounding states, thus changing the structure of a region's economic relationships and its trade balance. In general, the process of lowering the level of tariff barriers and removing non-tariff barriers has a positive influence on the economies of enclaves. Examples are the smaller enclaves inside the EU in which economic life is significantly eased by European integration, and Alaska, under the conditions of the North American Free Trade Agreement (NAFTA). However, as we shall see, a negative impact is also possible.

Double periphericity

The notion of double periphericity is not uncommon for enclaves. For example, Kaliningrad was justly epitomised as the 'double periphericity' (Joenniemi *et al.* 2000) and 'overlapping periphery' (Emerson *et al.* 2001: 31–2) of Russia and the EU. Beside its periphericity to Central Russia, it is also located on the periphery of the EU. The immediate neighbours of the region are underdeveloped and suffer from acute economic problems. Along Kaliningrad's border, the Warmińsko-Mazurskie voivodship is the least developed Polish region, and the developed industrial areas of Lithuania (Vilnius and Kaunas) are quite distant. Enclaves are typically located in remote areas, far from the industrial and commercial centres. Hence it seems that double periphericity is a natural consequence of an enclave's geographical location relative to the economic geography of both the mainland and the surrounding state.

Small size

Most enclaves are rather small (although some exceptions do exist) and consist of relatively compact territories with a small population. Enclave-based enterprises have to contend with the capacity of internal markets being insufficient for a viable home base. The local markets do not suffice to serve as a basis for an effective large-scale production of many types of goods and services, especially those in high-tech industries. This can have very important consequences for their economic policies, in particular an aversion to import substitution, and conversely, to the acceptance and preference of distinctive export orientation.

The small size of enclave economies and an insufficient range of products may lead to a considerable asymmetry between the structures of domestic consumption and domestic production. Imports constitute a disproportionately large part of internal consumption. The enclaves, at least the economically successful ones, are deeply integrated in the world economy.

They are, however, subject to serious dangers of influence of external sources of instability, like protectionist moves from their main trade partners or exogenous shocks in the global economy. The impossibility of considerably widening the range of produced goods deprives these territories – not only sovereign states but non-sovereign exclaves – of one of the opportunities to defend themselves against the pronounced negative influence of such external factors.

Insufficient competences for direct policy response

An enclave, unlike an enclaved state, has less room in determining its own economic policies. Usually, an enclave has no right to develop its external relations and forge international contacts, which is a competence of the federal centre. Besides, it is not uncommon that the mainland would look suspiciously at an enclave's attempts to communicate with the outside world directly, as this could undermine its authority and sovereignty over the enclave. This sensitive issue in mainland-enclave relations is caused by the enclave's detachedness. In contrast, an enclaved state is generally not bound by such constraints. It can develop its independent external policies, albeit with regard to the position of the surrounding state. This point is vividly illustrated by the development of tourism. Enclaves have to deal with numerous constraints regarding their attempts to forge international alliances and implement policies to attract larger numbers of foreign tourists. Enclaved states have much more flexibility and are usually more successful in increasing their attractiveness. As Robinson (1959: 295) noted, 'the exclave shares most of the disabilities of isolation with the enclaved state but can reap few of the rewards that can compensate for it, because these rewards depend on the exercise of some degree of sovereignty, which the enclave normally does not have'. In sum, an enclave is typically a passive policy-taker with limited opportunities to provide feedback and insufficient competences to respond directly to specific challenges put forward by the enclave situation.

'Washing out' enclavity by means of integration and liberal economic regime

Since the impact of enclavity on a region is typically negative, it is crucial to understand how enclavity can be diluted. It is normal for an exclave to be tied to the home country not only politically but economically as well. An opposite strategy is also possible, wherein an enclave becomes economically assimilated to its neighbour. That may mean inclusion of the exclave into the customs territory of the surrounding state as well as the use of the neighbour's currency. The direct taxes continue to go to the mainland while indirect taxes are paid to the surrounding state. For much of the twentieth century, the Austrian enclaves of Kleines Walsertal and Jungholz were subject to a very nineteenth-century convention, with their customs and currency under German control (made largely superfluous by European integration). However, options for an enclave's economic regime are not limited to being tied to the mainland or being assimilated by the surrounding state, nor are these options necessarily superior to others. There are four basic possibilities to handle a region's enclavity in a decisive fashion:

1   Strengthening M-E economic ties as a means of binding an enclave to its mainland and ensuring comparable levels of economic development;
2   M-S integration as an overarching scenario that may effectively 'wash out' the enclavity and solve most of the enclave-specific problems;
3   Economic inclusion of an enclave into the surrounding state;
4   Economic openness of the enclave to the outside world.

Strengthening economic ties with the mainland appears as a natural option that can be justified primarily by political reasoning. By ensuring smooth M-E communication and by promoting M-E economic ties, the task of making the enclave increasingly dependent on the mainland for economic survival is fulfilled. Therefore, the enclave is firmly tied up to the mainland, and any separatism attempts are curtailed. A second possibility is M-S integration, as can be observed for many enclaves inside the EU. Enclave-specific problems are solved automatically as a by-product of integration. In the absence of M-S integration, two options could be available: economic inclusion of an enclave into the surrounding state (without transfer of sovereignty) or establishing a regime of economic openness of an enclave to the outside world.

On the level of the mainland's policy towards the enclave, these options are materialised in two choices. The first choice is either to strengthen the ties with the mainland or to liberalise the enclave towards the outside world. The second choice, if the mainland selects a policy of economic openness for the enclave, is whether to allow for integration specifically with the surrounding state or to liberalise the enclave towards the whole world not making any explicit preferences for the surrounding state.

There have been a variety of special measures, economic regimes and economic support measures applied in enclaves, ranging from offshore or special economic zone regimes, to special assistance programmes and heavy allowances to promote the public sector. In several cases (Büsingen, Ceuta, Melilla, Jungholz, Kleines Walsertal, and others) an enclave has been excluded from the mainland state's customs territory. In the case of Büsingen, it was followed by the inclusion of the enclave in the surrounding state's customs territory. Some enclaves (Gibraltar, Ceuta, Melilla, Livigno) have been excluded from value-added tax requirements. As another option, a special currency regime allowing for the circulation of the surrounding state's currency can be introduced (Vinokurov 2006).

The majority of the world's enclaves, however, do not possess a special economic regime. The economic regimes of such enclaves do not differ from the standard economic regime applied to the other regions and administrative entities of the mainland state, with the exception of special rules for transit that can sometimes be agreed on to ensure an efficient M-E communication.

Economic incapability combined with increased vulnerability explains why special economic regimes are established so often in enclaves. A special economic regime can make an enclave viable in a situation where its natural assets do not suffice to survive. Two approaches can be employed: the compensatory approach establishes a special regime to compensate for detachment from the mainland; alternatively, the mainland may choose to liberalise the enclave towards the surrounding state and the rest of the world, thus mitigating the enclave's isolation.

Compensatory approach

For the economic policy of the mainland, a compensatory approach is inferior to a liberalisation approach. Nevertheless it is often employed, fuelled by an unwillingness to liberalise an enclave for various political reasons. With the compensatory approach, the mainland offers compensations for increased costs of transit (i.e. cargo, passenger, post), subsidies for industrial development, or subsidies for utilities. This approach is evident, for example, in Spanish Ceuta and Melilla. Compensatory policies prove costly to the mainland's budget yet reach their ultimate goal – comparable levels of economic development and personal incomes – only partially. Despite all possible measures of support, the purchasing power of the enclave's residents remains inferior to the purchasing power of mainland residents. One of the important typical elements of the compensatory approach is the existence of a large public sector paid for by the mainland. This is used as a measure of indirect economic support, and typical examples include Ceuta, Melilla, Gibraltar, and West Berlin. The share of the public sector is also well above average in Kaliningrad where the public government alone employs 7.2 per cent of the workforce, up from 3 per cent in 1990 (Kaliningrad Regional Committee for Statistics 2004).

Liberalisation approach

Two policies of liberalisation can be applied: an enclave can be economically integrated with the surrounding state; or a policy of economic openness to the outside world can be pursued. In the first approach, European small and pene-enclaves have proven to be the most advanced in terms of economic integration with the surrounding state. The most convincing example is the 'Büsingen model' of integration. Briefly, it consists of inclusion of an enclave into the surrounding state's customs territory and partial application of the surrounding state's legislation, supplemented by the free movement of people. Economic inclusion of an enclave into the surrounding state supposedly works only with small entities and is not readily applicable to larger enclaves. Besides, such inclusion is only possible if the M-S relations are characterised by trust and confidence. The second approach is general economic openness to the outside world. While the first policy is more readily applicable to small and micro-enclaves, land-locked within the surrounding state, the second policy suits the larger coastal enclaves and exclaves. Just as the 'Büsingen model' is exemplary for the first policy, a 'Hong Kong model' is a textbook example of the second. With this approach, the enclave is supplied with a broad mandate of economic self-government that lets it determine its own economic policy and react to changes in the external environment with a sufficiently high degree of autonomy.

Due to economic considerations (i.e. higher conventional and non-conventional trade costs with the mainland), enclaves are bound to pursue an outward orientation. In fact, it would remain the only economically viable option for an enclave in the absence of the special regulations explicitly supporting economic connection to the mainland. Yet such policies are not supported by economic but rather political considerations. The enclaves, just like small states, cannot obtain high levels of economic development and economies of scale without accepting a profound integration into the international division of labour. The geographical position of an enclave, its detachedness from the mainland and proximity to foreign markets (especially the market of the surrounding state), dictates the necessity for outward economic orientation. This openness increases vulnerability by exposing an enclave to the outside world. However, on the whole, the enclave-specific vulnerability actually decreases for two reasons. First, an enclave becomes less dependent on the mainland for market and economic assistance. Second, the issues of mainland-enclave communication and transit through the surrounding state cease to be critical for the enclave's life subsistence and economic survival. And ultimately, an enclave obtains an opportunity for dynamic economic growth.

Economic theory does not provide a definite answer to the question of the effects of integration on border regions, allowing for only vague conclusions about the spatial effects of integration. Depending on the specific circumstances, border regions might benefit, lose out, or not be affected by integration (Niebuhr and Stiller 2002). However, our conclusion for the enclaves is anything but vague. Economic integration – regardless of whether this is with the surrounding state or on a non-discriminating basis – has significant positive effects on enclaves. This can be explained by the notion of exclavity. Despite being located at the periphery, a typical border region is nevertheless well-connected to other regions of the same state. It can profit from the economy of scale in the internal market. An enclave, unlike the typical border region, faces the problems of isolation, higher transportation costs, and enclave-specific vulnerability caused by detachedness from the mainland and inclusion into the territory of the surrounding state. Integration in any form causes the dilution of enclavity and exclavity, thus effectively removing or at least mitigating the enclave-specific problems of economic development.

Openness as the precondition for economic well-being

The following list is a comprehensive sample of existing and former enclaves and enclave complexes that will be the reference for the data in this section. Although this list was conditioned by the availability of data, it comprises more than 90 per cent of currently existing enclaves (in population terms) as well as the most important historical cases.[3] Each enclave is followed, in brackets, by its mainland:

True enclaves:
Baarle enclave complex (Belgium, Netherlands), Barak (Kyrgyzstan), Büsingen (Germany), Campione (Italy), Dzhangail (Uzbekistan), Cooch Behar (India, Bangladesh), Jungholz (Austria), Llivia (Spain), Vennbahn enclaves (Germany), St. Pierre and Miquelon (France), West Berlin (Germany)

Coastal enclaves:
Alaska (USA), Ceuta (Spain), Melilla (Spain), Gibraltar (UK), Hong Kong (UK), Macau/Aomen (Portugal), Oecussi-Ambeno (East Timor)

Mere exclaves:
Kaliningrad (Russia), Nakhichevan (Azerbaijan), East Pakistan (Pakistan), East Prussia (Germany)

Pene-enclaves:
Kleinwalsertal (Austria), Livigno (Italy), Point Roberts (USA),
Os de Civis (Spain)

Only four enclaves out of the twenty-six in this sample enjoy or have enjoyed per capita incomes higher than their mainland's average. These are the contemporary West European enclaves of Llivia and Campione and the historical cases of Hong Kong and Macau. In these cases, there has been only a slightly superior level (for instance, incomes in Campione are comparable to Italy's most prosperous regions in the northern part of the country). At the same time, eleven enclaves (40.7 per cent) possess incomes per capita roughly comparable to the mainland's average. Twelve enclaves (44.4 per cent) have an inferior level to their respective mainlands. Therefore, the occurrence of a higher per capita income in an enclave respective to its mainland is rather an exception.

Open and closed economic regimes are understood primarily in terms of openness to the outside world in general and the surrounding state in particular; in terms of the movement of people, goods and services. There is a clear correlation between income per capita and the presence or absence of economic openness within a regime. All enclaves with incomes either higher or equal to the mainland's average enjoy a regime of economic openness towards the outside world. The majority of enclaves with incomes inferior to the mainland's average are closed to the outside world. In four cases, in which an enclave is poorer than its mainland despite having relatively open economies (Ceuta, Melilla, Gibraltar, St Pierre and Miquelon), the liberal economic regime appears to provide a cushion against even lower income levels.

Table 3.1 Incomes per capita in nominal terms in the enclave in comparison with the mainland's average and their correlation with the economic regime

Nominal income per capita in enclave:	Superior to mainland	Equal to mainland	Inferior to mainland
Number of enclaves	4	10	12
Economically open (special preferences and/or low barriers)	4 (Llivia, Campione, Hong Kong, Macau)	10 (Baarle, Büsingen, Jungholz, Vennbahn, Alaska, Kaliningrad, Kleinwalsertal, Livigno, Point Roberts, Os de Civis)	4 (Ceuta, Gibraltar, Melilla, West Berlin)
Economically closed (no special regime, high barriers)	0	0	8 (Barak, Cooch Behar, Dzhangail, St Pierre and Miquelon, Oecussi-Ambeno, Nakhichevan, East Pakistan, East Prussia

Source: Vinokurov (2007b: 288).

In examining incomes per capita in comparison with *both* the mainland and the surrounding state, successful economic development may be defined by comparing incomes per capita in an enclave with those of the mainland and the surrounding states. In other words, we look at the quality of life relative to both M and S. Five groups are singled out: first, the one with superior incomes to both M and S; second, with superior incomes to either one, while equal to another one; third, with incomes equal to both M and S; fourth, a group of enclaves with the incomes per capita in between the figures for M and S; and fifth, enclaves with incomes inferior to both M and S (i.e. apparent economic failures).

Table 3.2 Incomes relative to M and S.

Groups according to income per capita relative to M and S:	True enclave	Coastal enclaves	Mere exclaves	Pene-enclaves	Total in sample
Superior to both M and S	0	2 (Hong Kong, Macau)	0	0	2
Superior to either M or S while equal to another	2 (Llivia, Campione)	0	0	0	2
Equal to both M and S	2 (Büsingen, Vennhahn)	1 (Alaska)	0	4 (Jungholz, Os de Civis, Klein-walsertal, Point Roberts)	7
Intermediary group	1 (West Berlin)	3 (Ceuta, Gibraltar, Melilla)	2 (East Prussia, Kaliningrad)	0	6
Economic failure	4 (Barak, Dzhangail, St Pierre and Miquelon, Cooch Behar)	1 (Oecussi-Ambeno)	2 (Nakhichevan, East Pakistan)	0	7

Historically, there have only been two cases in which an enclave exceeded both the mainland and the surrounding state in terms of income per capita. These were Hong Kong and Macau in the 1980s and 1990s. Even with these enclaves, this was true only for the last two decades of their existence (1980s–90s); before that, both enclaves on the Chinese coast were inferior to their respective mainlands. Two other enclaves, Llivia and Campione, fall into the second group: their incomes per capita are comparable to the richer surrounding state, while exceeding somewhat the average mainland level. The largest group consists of enclaves that coincide with both M and S (that is, full economic equality exists in the MES triangle). The M>E>S ratio is the most typical for the intermediary group (currently in Gibraltar, Ceuta and Melilla as well as in historical West Berlin (1949–89) and East Prussia (1920–39)). Therefore, Kaliningrad is currently an exception, as its income level is comparable to the mainland while inferior to the surrounding states (an M=E<S ratio). Finally, seven enclaves in the sample, or 25 per cent, represent an economic failure, their incomes per capita being inferior to both M and S, regardless of the difference between the two.

An enclave can develop an economic orientation towards the mainland, the surrounding state (the most common case), or towards the rest of the world. It can also tend to be self-sufficient or combine several orientation vectors. Self-sufficiency is a consequence of isolation, a closed economic regime, and an underdeveloped economy. For instance, it is characteristic of the Fergana Valley enclaves in Central Asia. As Central Asian states began asserting their statehood, there was an apparent negative impact on the enclaves. The previously smooth trade connections were broken during that period, and the enclaves were forced into a more self-sufficient economy, with a lower standard of living as an immediate consequence of the imposed isolation.

Successful enclaves tend to develop a multi-vectored orientation avoiding concentration of trade and economic connection with the mainland only. The dynamic economies and economic growth appear to be conditioned by the liberal and open economic regimes. Multi-vectored economic connections with the surrounding state and with the rest of the world are natural consequences of an open economy. To put it another way, although an enclave's prosperity correlates positively with an economic orientation towards the surrounding state and the rest of the world, the economic success of an enclave depends not on its economic orientation but rather on whether it enjoys a state of economic openness towards the outside world.

An enclave's economic and political openness towards both the mainland and the surrounding state is the precondition for the achievement of political stability and economic prosperity. Openness is the normal case in relations with the mainland as the enclave represents an integral part of the state. So, in referring to openness on the M-E axis, we usually discuss whether there exists a smooth and undisturbed flow of people, goods, services, capital, political participation, and ideas; with the issues of transit brought to the foreground. Despite geographical proximity, openness is much more difficult to obtain in relations with the surrounding state. Here, the issues of a visa-free regime, facilitated trade in goods and services, and border regimes come to the fore.

Conclusion: Kaliningrad's adjustment to successive changes from 1990 to 2004 and beyond

As demonstrated earlier, enclaves possess a number of features which condition their specific response to changes in their external environment. Among these features are enclavity (understood as embeddedness into the surrounding state), exclavity (understood as detachedness from the mainland), smallness of local consumption and production base, increased vulnerability and consequent typical overreaction to change, as well as insufficient competences to respond directly to exogenous challenges. On the whole, these features determine an enclave's typical overreaction to changes in the external environment. A combination of exclavity, enclavity, an enclave's geographic and economic smallness as well as its passive policy-taker position is primarily responsible for enclaves' overreactions to such events compared with 'typical' regions on the mainland. The uniqueness of an enclave relative to a typical region is likely to be highly visible in those fields where enclavity and exclavity factors play a decisive role, such as economic policy. At the same time, it might be less visible in the sectors where more homogeneity exists, such as education or health care.

The issue of Kaliningrad's economic development has to be viewed in the framework of EU–Russian relations, because its most salient feature is that it finds itself in the condition of integration into the European economy due to geographical position and the enclavity factor. Kaliningrad-related integration processes are thus specific and differ in many respects from the Russian regions on the mainland. The pivotal actors, which exercise decisive influence on Kaliningrad's economy, are Russia (more exactly, Russia's federal centre) and the EU. If obliged to choose *the* actor for Kaliningrad, this would definitely be Russia's federal centre. There is no doubt that, despite the region's detachedness from the mainland, Moscow defines the course that Kaliningrad will follow. This is done in multiple ways. One example is the federal legislation on a Special Economic Zone (SEZ) that contains specific provisions for the region. Another tool is the federal centre's financial and economic policies, including financial transfers and the Federal Target Programme (FTP). Beginning in 2005, with governors now nominated by the president, the direct policy influence of Moscow on the regional level has become even greater.

Still, for its part, the European Union can also influence Kaliningrad's affairs in several ways. First, EU–Russia agreements on Kaliningrad-related matters such as passenger and cargo transit are pivotal for the enclave. Second, the EU provides direct economic assistance to the region. Third, its member states, notably Denmark, Sweden, and Germany, conduct independent programmes of cooperation with the region. And fourth, the policies of the adjacent countries, Poland and Lithuania, are central to the border cooperation and border economics.

As Russia and the EU are decisive powers for Kaliningrad, EU–Russia economic and political relations are the framework with which we must view the prospective development of the region. This view corresponds fully to the principal framework of the mainland-enclave-surrounding state triangle, which underpins the theory of enclaves. Much of Kaliningrad's prosperity depends on the general state of Russia–EU relations, demonstrated by the Kaliningrad transit crisis in 2002. The crisis began because of deficiencies in these relations, until both sides managed to find and implement a decision for passenger transit, which, despite its drawbacks, alleviated some of the most difficult consequences of EU enlargement for the Kaliningrad region. On the whole, compared with other changes (particularly the introduction of the SEZ regime and the 1998 crisis), the EU eastern enlargement has so far had a relatively minor impact on Kaliningrad (Vinokurov 2005; 2006; 2007a) partially thanks to the agreement reached between the EU, Lithuania and Russia on the most urgent matter of passenger transit.

In the long run, EU–Russia integration within the Common Spaces has the potential to mitigate many of Kaliningrad's enclave-specific problems, and hence to effectively 'wash out' its enclavity. For example, movement towards the visa-free regime may effectively solve the problem of passenger transit through Lithuania altogether, while regulatory convergence and trade facilitation have the potential to mitigate the issue of transit in goods. Furthermore, EU–Russia free trade would diminish Kaliningrad's economic enclavity in relation to the EU market, and integration of infrastructure would reduce the oblast's vulnerability stemming from issues of electricity and gas supplies.

As long as EU–Russia integration remains a long term prospect, Russia's policy towards the enclave remains the primary means to ensure Kaliningrad's durability to exogenous processes. An enclave's economic and political openness towards both the mainland and the surrounding state has been the primary precondition for the achievement of political stability and economic prosperity. All enclaves with incomes either higher than or equal to the mainland's average enjoy a regime of economic openness towards the outside world. Generally, special economic regimes – either of economic integration with the surrounding state or those that make an enclave an organic part of the global economy – are necessary for an enclave to be economically viable.

The mainland can employ two approaches in its policy towards the enclave. The compensatory approach is employed when a special regime is introduced to compensate for detachment from the mainland. Alternatively, the mainland may choose to liberalise the enclave *vis-à-vis* the surrounding state and the rest of the world, thus mitigating the enclave's isolation. The core content of the Kaliningrad SEZ, created in the 1990s, aimed at liberalisation of the region's foreign trade. However, the rhetoric underlying the SEZ was following the lines of the compensatory approach, i.e. introducing special regulations in order to compensate the region for its detachedness, for longer and more expensive transport routes, and for the comprehensive de-militarisation during the 1990s when the number of military personnel stationed in the region was reduced from 100,000 to 25–30,000 within only a few years (Vinokurov 2007a). The later Federal Target Programme (2002–10) implicitly followed the lines of the compensatory approach, as the emphasis was put on projects ensuring the economic security of the region, such as the new thermoelectric gas-power station, and strengthening its ties with the Russian mainland (Vinokurov 2007a: 88–9). However, from the point of view of economic development and better adjustment to multiple challenges, the compensatory approach is inferior to the liberalisation approach, as the latter results in a healthier economic structure, which is more sustainable in the long run.

Notes

1   An enclave is a part of the territory of a state that is enclosed within the territory of another state. Conversely, an exclave is a detached part of a state that is surrounded by the territory of another state or states. An exclave can possess access to sea. It can also be surrounded by more than one state. The decisive criterion is its separation from the respective mainland. It is crucial to understand that any enclave is simultaneously an exclave, but not every exclave is an enclave since it can be surrounded by more than one state as Nakhichevan or Kaliningrad are. For the state that surrounds an enclave/exclave, the term 'surrounding state' will be used. The state of which an enclave/exclave makes a part is called a 'mainland state'.
2   Not including the Palestinian territories and Nagorno Karabakh (see Vinokurov 2006: 43–6; 2007b).
3   For a complete list of enclaves see Vinokurov (2007a; 2007b) or the supplementary materials to the latter book available on the Internet at www.vinokurov .info/enclaves.htm.

References

Catudal, H. M. (1979), *The Exclave Problem of Western Europe*, Tuscaloosa, University of Alabama Press.

Emerson, M., N. Tocci, M. Vahl and N. Whyte (2001), *The Elephant and the Bear: The European Union, Russia, and Their Near Abroads*, Brussels, Centre for European Policy Studies.

Gold, P. (2000), *Europe or Africa? A Contemporary Study of the Spanish North African Enclaves of Ceuta and Melilla*, Liverpool, Liverpool University Press.

Gold, P. (2005), *Gibraltar: British or Spanish?*, Oxford and New York, Routledge.

Hörning, E. M. (1992), *Zwischen den Fronten. Berliner Grenzgänger und Grenzhändler 1948–1961* [*Between the lines. The border commuters and border traders of Berlin*], Köln, Weimar and Wien, Böhlau Verlag.

Joenniemi, P., S. Dewar and L. D. Fairlie (2000), *The Kaliningrad Puzzle: A Russian Region within the European Union*, Karlkrona (Sweden), The Baltic Institute and the Åland Islands Peace Institute.

Kaliningrad Regional Committee for Statistics (2004), *Kaliningradskaya oblast v cifrach*

2004 [*Kaliningrad in numbers 2004*], Kaliningrad.

Klemeshev, A. (2005), *Problema eksklavnosti v kontekste globalizacii* [*The problem of exclavity in the context of globalisation*], St Petersburg, St Petersburg University Press.

Niebuhr, A. and S. Stiller (2002), *Integration Effect in Border Regions: A Survey of Economic Theory and Empirical Studies*, HWWA Discussion Paper 179.

Robinson, G. W. S. (1959), 'Exclaves', *Annals of the Association of American Geographers*, 49 (September): 283–95.

Vinokurov, E. (2002), 'Anklavy v mirovoy economike i politike' ['Enclaves in world economy and politics'], *Mezhdunarodnaya economica i mezhdunarodnye otnosheniya* [*World economy and international relations*], 9: 83–8.

Vinokurov, E. (2005), 'The Enclave-Specific Vulnerability of Kaliningrad', in *Kaliningrad 2020: Its Future Competitiveness and Role in the Baltic Sea Economic Region*, ed. Kari Liuhto, Turku, Pan-European Institute: 56–74, available on the Internet at www.kaliningradexpert.org/publications/ (accessed 15 August 2007).

Vinokurov, E. (2006), 'Enclaves and Exclaves of the World: Setting the Framework for a Theory of Enclaves', ZDES Working Paper, University of Bielefeld and St Petersburg State University, available on the Internet at www.zdes.spb.ru (accessed 15 August 2007).

Vinokurov, E. (2007a), *Kaliningrad: Enclaves and Economic Integration*, Brussels, CEPS.

Vinokurov, E. (2007b), *A Theory of Enclaves*, Lanham (MD), Lexington Books.

Whyte, B. (2002), 'Waiting for the Esquimo: An Historical and Documentary Study of the Cooch Behar Enclaves of India and Bangladesh', PhD thesis, Research Paper 8, School of Anthropology, Geography and Environmental Studies at the University of Melbourne.

Whyte, B. (2004), '"En Territoire Belge et à Quarante Centimètres de la Frontière", An Historical and Documentary Study of the Belgian and Dutch Enclave of Baarle-Hertog and Baarle-Nassau', Research Paper 19, School of Anthropology, Geography and Environmental Studies at the University of Melbourne.

Zverev, Y. M. (2003), *Kaliningradskaya oblast v klassifikacii anklavnykh (eksklavnykh) territories of the world* [*The Kaliningrad Oblast in the classification of enclave (exclave) territories of the world*], Kaliningrad, Kaliningrad State University Press.

Holger Moroff

4

EU–Russia–Kaliningrad relations – a case of soft securitisation?

Why does the EU want Kaliningrad to change? The assumption that it wants and has to do so is as ubiquitous as it is unquestioned. Most studies want to capture factors of change and constraints to adaptation in Kaliningrad, focusing on exogenous inputs and endogenous obstacles to, or catalysts for, change.

This normative assumption in favour of change is neither self-evident nor equally applied to all neighbours of the EU. Let us draw a comparison between two political islands in the 'EU sea': Kaliningrad and Switzerland. Of course, one is an exclave cut off from its motherland and the other is a sovereign, self-contained state. However, both are EU neighbours and both are encircled by the EU. Why do EU policies towards and discourses on these two entities differ so much? One could argue that it is the final aim of the EU to turn Kaliningrad into a kind of Switzerland. Or as Chris Patten, then EU Commissioner for external relations, put it, 'into the Hong-Kong of the Baltic Sea' (Patten 2001).

The difference lies in perception and framing as much as in the real, substantive conditions. There are far more proceeds of international organised crime laundered or deposited in Switzerland and Lichtenstein than are generated in Kaliningrad. However, when the EU talks about Switzerland or Lichtenstein, it talks about economics, business and the Common Market. It sees the countries as commercial opportunities and wants to achieve legal harmonisation in economic affairs;[1] whereas Kaliningrad is viewed as a security risk, struck with poverty, pollution, communicable diseases and crime (Fairlie and Sergounin 2001; Pursiainen 2001; Moroff 2002a; Moshes 2003). The aim of EU policy is therefore societal stabilisation in order to prevent internal risks from spilling over into the surrounding area, i.e. into the EU. The EU approach to Switzerland resembles trade policies towards a partner of equal societal and economic standards; their approach to Kaliningrad resembles development policies towards a partner with very different standards and outlooks. Both policies are equally aimed at making the 'encircled' entities more similar to the EU, the former focusing on commercial gain, the latter revolving around soft security gains. However, it is much less obvious what constitutes a benefit in the realm of soft security than that of economics. The discourse is therefore more complex than a simple balance sheet and it is based on a broad discourse of threat perceptions as much as on the attempts of political actors to gain new remits for action and self-legitimisation.

This chapter tries to develop a framework of analysis on how the EU addresses those security and development concerns in its neighbourhood, taking Kaliningrad as a case in point and as a geographic as well as mental outpost of the EU's most important neighbour – Russia. Thus it can serve as a touchstone for EU–Russia relations at large.

Soft securitisation, a conceptual grid

Soft securitisation introduces problem-solving governance modes into the foreign policy field of soft security. Soft security comprises non-military and non-strategic issues with a potential cross-border impact, like international crime, pollution, nuclear safety, communicable diseases and illegal migration. It can also refer to anything that destabilises a country in such a way that it becomes a threat to its neighbours or other third countries, such as extreme asymmetries in living standards, weak rule of law, and the things that flow from that, i.e. corruption, crime and refugees.[2] Thus security issues in external policy are being framed as domestic security problems because of their cross-border impact, and then they are approached in a cooperative, low politics-focused and problem-solving manner rather than being instrumentalised in a confrontational power game of trying to increase influence over a third country in general. Soft securitisation thus works through persuasion, not through coercion – the means usually chosen in the wake of hard securitisation. It uses engagement and mutual deliberation through policy networks of experts on solving a given problem, not through exclusion, divide-and-rule or *realpolitik* by experts on power politics, a task that usually falls to diplomats. This form of soft securitisation is in contrast to the Copenhagen School's concept of securitisation (Buzan *et al.* 1998).[3] This refers to a political process in which a government or other securitising actors are framing normal policy issues as exceptional security issues and thus justifying exceptional measures, circumventing the normal form of democratic governance or justifying 'actions outside the normal bounds of political procedure' (*ibid.*: 24; see also Waever 1995; Buzan and Waever 2003). In this sense securitisation is viewed as a kind of state failure, since the state's political rules are being transgressed. In contrast, through soft securitisation, a political actor poses a security issue as essential but not existential. On the scale from low to high politics it ranks among the technical and functional low politics issues. Three degrees of issue securitisation can thus be distinguished:

1   Technical, soft securitisation: applying soft power and abiding by the rules of normal politics;
2   Politicised securitisation: using confrontational public diplomacy and changing the rules;
3   Hard securitisation: building on strategic hard power and transgressing rules.

In this chapter, soft securitisation is treated as a process of putting a third country's essentially domestic soft security threats with a potential cross-border impact onto one's external policy agenda. It is thus a foreign policy tool of those potentially affected by that impact. They are interested in having their security concerns recognised by the third country in question, which might mean changing the third country's threat and security perceptions. For the EU, which has relatively high soft security standards (i.e. on individual, human and societal security), interacting with neighbours who have much lower standards means changing their thinking about them. One could call this kind of Europeanisation 'ideational' or 'perceptional'.[4] Soft securitisation implies first creating similar problem consciousness and sufficient awareness abroad. Thus it is similar to the Copenhagen School's concept of desecuritisation[5] but differs in a significant way: whereas desecuritisation refers to turning a securitised, high politics issue back into a low politics issue, soft securitisation tries to keep issues on a low politics plane in the first place, while still framing them as security – albeit *soft* security – issues. Although issues can move up the politicisation ladder and become hard security issues, soft securitisation aims at keeping them at or pulling them down to a problem-solving policy plane. While hard securitisation frames an issue as an exceptional, extraordinary emergency and instrumentalises it by using the problem, soft securitisation keeps it in the realm of the ordinary management of security-related problems.

However, the EU as foreign policy actor does not only want to solve a given or framed soft security problem (i.e. Europeanisation of policy content), but it also tries to solve it in a manner similar to its own ways of domestic policy-making (i.e. Europeanisation of politics or governance). When applied to issues that have undergone soft securitisation, this means they are being treated like normal domestic soft security problems. In the EU case, that is through an inclusive, deliberative and multi-level policy process (see Kohler-Koch and Jachtenfuchs 1995; Wallace *et al.* 2005; Jachtenfuchs and Kohler-Koch 2006).

The reason for this may be seen in the way the main actor in these soft security fields, the European Commission, evolved and now operates. The Commission began as a strong actor in the fields of the Common Market and in the Union's internal 'development' (i.e. regional and structural policy).

Since the Commission has only certain policy-making tools at its disposal, it has to frame problems – also those in the EU neighbourhood – in a way to which these instruments can be applied.[6] A strong policy-making mechanism that evolved internally is the inclusive, deliberative, multi-level policy-making mode. This has also become an essential feature of the EU's and especially the Commission's 'actorness' quality in foreign policy. This is due to the fact that the Commission, and the EU at large, is not able to act effectively and coherently on highly politicised and securitised issues, since it has neither the mandate nor the mechanisms to do so.

In order to apply this kind of domestic policy-making abroad, the EU needs partners on various levels as well as the input of civil society and experts.[7] By implication, if not by design, the EU thus induces the creation of such partners. In order to cooperate with the EU, the countries concerned create the necessary counterparts for interaction. This kind of Europeanisation can be conceptualised as involuntary institutional spillover; not in the sense of strict downloading but rather a flexible adaptation of third parties for meaningful interaction with the EU, thus resembling Europeanisation of their polity.

However, not only do actors adapt to EU institutional requirements, but also their policies and, what is more, their policy-making process. Thus the EU might introduce its own kind of deliberative, multi-level governance to its neighbours (Europeanisation of politics). Soft securitisation is a means of achieving just that in the field of soft security. This chapter will initially demonstrate how the EU became a dominant actor through soft securitisation of issues such as migration, organised crime, pollution, environmental degradation, nuclear safety, communicable diseases and poverty in its neighbourhood; and secondly, how the neighbourhood or parts thereof such as Kaliningrad responded to this.

Olav Knudsen might be right in rejecting soft security as a 'serious academic concept' (Knudsen 1998: 47–8) and giving preference to the concept of cooperative security defined as cooperation on security issues between putative opponents that, if successful, might lead to a true security community (*ibid.*: 4). However, it is precisely the aim of a soft security approach to deconstruct such putative oppositional attitudes and find or construct a common ground of mutual interests upon which to act jointly. It is thus that the label of soft security serves to give a broader non-military meaning to security.

Clive Archer (2001: 188) has suggested adding the dimension of ease of achievement to the concepts of hard and soft security. Archer provides the example of the ease with which the Baltic states and Russia became partner countries of the Northern Dimension but their difficulty in acceding to the EU. Conversely, in the realm of hard security, that it is easy for the Baltic countries to participate in KFOR (the NATO-led Kosovo Force) but hard to join NATO. This analysis seems to focus on the straightforwardness with which states attain regime membership rather than the ease of achieving the aims and tasks of these regimes. Again, as is true for the cooperative security concept, it concentrates more on structures and institutions rather than on the kind of threats with which they are engaged.

Soft security has the connotation that if only agreement can be reached on content, institutional form becomes of secondary concern. As the traditional functionalist Mitrany would put it, form follows function.[8] Both cooperative security and the ease of becoming a member of an organisation or regime puts the emphasis on states, whereas from a governmental actor perspective, soft security analysis focuses on specific problems. It takes an issues-oriented problem-solving perspective, which at later stages spills over into the realm of policy-making, that is, the interplay between politics and polity.

EU–Kaliningrad–Russia: what kind of relationship?

How to establish a cooperative soft security relationship with Kaliningrad under conditions of asymmetrical bi-polarity between the EU and Russia in Europe and in the shadow of strong Russian state centrism? This is the central theme in the EU and its member states' policies towards the Russian exclave. The question needs to be answered against the background of an EU–Russia relationship, which is essentially characterised by a double asymmetry with a strong and unified economic power on the EU side and a strong and unified strategic actor on the Russian side. The former has been an ascending and expanding but diffuse governance system (with variable collective decision-making and implementing regimes in varying policy fields); the latter has been in decline through the 1990s but has become an increasingly unitary power.

Why use the term soft security relationship? A study of EU documents on its 'neighbourhood policy' since the early 1990s shows one concern dominating all others: namely fear of instability and conflict at the external borders of the Union, with a potential for spillover into the Union proper (in the form of refugees, illegal migration, crime, communicable diseases, pollution, nuclear waste and contamination, etc.). Thus the EU strove for a preventive non-military security strategy. To that end, its main foreign policy instruments have been conditional association agreements, granting market access and assistance. Beyond enlargement these same instruments have been used, though on a much smaller scale. They have usually been directed towards state entities. For example, the Northern Dimension – a regional policy directed towards the littoral states of the Baltic Sea as well as Norway and Iceland – has for the first time included in an institutional way non-state actors and sub-state entities as partners for dialogue and targets for assistance beyond EU borders (Moroff 2002a: 150–8).

Soft security questions hinge on the perception of interdependence and the ability to steer that interdependence (Keohane and Nye 1977). From this perspective, soft securitisation is not necessarily linked to objective external threats but is the outcome of framing processes in political discourses and practices by which an issue becomes defined as a security problem, requiring political action according to public and elite opinions (Moroff 2002b: 12–36).[9]

Securitisation in the Copenhagen School's sense can be viewed as functionalism in reverse. Where functionalism leads through spillover from low politics integration to high politics integration (also in the original sense that form follows function, that is polity follows policy), securitisation means the state or other actors (re)claim low politics issues (such as health or environmental policy) as their domain for extraordinary action by turning them into a high politics security threat. But that is not the case for the soft security issues taken up by the EU. Here the concept of soft securitisation can be fruitfully applied: first, because when the EU acts a multitude of actors are involved, and not just one hierarchical unitary state actor or a single securitising non-state actor; second, it is a low politics problem-solving approach in order to tackle those issues where the state might act as facilitator but not the sole actor as would be the case in military security matters. Soft security issues require a problem-solving approach, though the sectors they deal with might stretch beyond the areas where states traditionally invoke a prerogative for action. However, the mechanisms typically applied in these new fields of external action are very different from the old ones; they are mainly collective problem-solving approaches. The threat does not usually emanate from other states as such but from parts of their societal activities (pollution, health, crime, poverty, etc.), so these are common problems and call for joint action. EU action on soft security matters via soft securitisation might be a means of desecuritisation, and hence, foreign policy becomes a problem-solving external policy.

How does the EU view Kaliningrad and its neighbourhood at large?

In its 1999 study of possible scenarios on how Europe might look in the year 2010, the forward studies unit of the Commission (Commission 1999: 45–52) developed one particularly bleak outlook in its chapter entitled 'Turbulent Neighbourhoods'. This chapter referred to a siege mentality as an expression of the fear Europeans might then feel towards the world beyond their borders, a world beset with ethnic tensions, a gradually disintegrating Russia, environmental degradation, epidemics and proliferating international crime all inextricably interlinked and leading occasionally to terrorist incidents inside the EU. With its methodology of anticipating hindsight (looking back at the EU in the 1990s from an imaginary vantage point in 2010) they note, 'In its state of general languor, the European public did not notice all the new military and soft security threats on the Union's doorstep' (*ibid.*: 46). Future historians would then describe EU policy reactions as a failed attempt to implement an effective *cordon sanitaire* strategy against the uncontrollable deluge of migrants and refugees from neighbouring regions.

The current EU policy on the external frontier is dominated by justice and home affairs (JHA) considerations, giving apparent credibility to the image of a 'fortress Europe'. However, a general uncertainty about the definitive external limits of the EU and the attraction of the EU from within neighbouring states has the effect of giving the external frontier aspects which are more analogous to old imperial frontiers than those of a nation-state.

> In very general terms Member States have certain basic principles in common (rule of law, parliamentary democracy, respect for human rights, private property as the basis of market economies). The significance of the external frontier is different according to the degree to which the neighbouring state adheres to these principles. For example, the external frontier with Switzerland and Norway is viewed differently from that with Morocco and Russia. (Anderson 2000: xiii)

Consequently, the EU's policy towards its direct neighbourhood is one of projecting those basic principles shared by the EU's member states. Thus the Partnership and Cooperation Agreement (PCA) with Russia calls explicitly for legal approximation, meaning Russian alignment with the *acquis communautaire* in those fields where Russia wants to interact and trade with the EU. It is, whether consciously or not, an attempt at making its proximate vicinity more similar to itself, creating and reproducing a socio-political landscape of centre/periphery. This, in relation to Russia or Kaliningrad, does not only have to do with the great economic asymmetries in the EU's favour (Vahl 2001: 7–8), but also with a strong path dependency as a result of the painstakingly negotiated *acquis communautaire* in various policy fields, which, for reasons of internal rigidity and inertia, cannot be changed easily even if the negotiating partner is of equal or even larger economic size.[10]

Some of the Commission officials[11] who had produced the dreadful scenario of turbulent neighbourhoods were also contributing to the Commission's communication on conflict prevention of mid-2001 and its dossier on 'Wider Europe' of March 2003. These proposed a neighbourhood policy for the coming decade, and it appears to have provided the negative backdrop before which a whole array of soft security measures were summoned up to confront and avert such appalling prospects. Soft security issues loom large in the Commission's conflict prevention concept and its new European Neighbourhood Policy (ENP), as well as in its Security Strategy of December 2003 and in the Commission's communication on 'Security Research – the next step' of September 2004, which comprise virtually all soft security fields. Among other things, the Commission (2001a: 4–6) calls for action against environmental degradation, the spread of communicable diseases, population flows and human trafficking as well as support for democracy, the rule of law and civil society. The explicit aim is to project stability into the Union's direct neighbourhood. It is noteworthy that the first and foremost means of pursuing this goal, according to the Commission paper, is through the 'strengthening of regional-cooperation in a wider context', thus indirectly according a pilot function to the Northern Dimension policy frame, whereas the new ENP in itself is a clear bilateral instrument between the EU and every single participating country.[12]

However, it is revealing that Javier Solana, the EU High Representative for Common Foreign and Security Policy, used the term 'soft security' in a speech on 'The EU–Russia Strategic Partnership' delivered in Stockholm on 13 October 1999 (Solana 1999). Not only is one overriding concern of the EU's Northern Dimension policy approach – which is the Union's soft security policy *par excellence* – the integration of Russia and its north-western parts into some sort of regional cooperation to ensure the safe and stable neighbourhood of an enlarged EU, but it is also telling that Solana stressed those soft security aspects which subsequently were to evolve into the main areas of the Northern Dimension Action Plan for Kaliningrad as well. This Action Plan provides the overarching framework for the EU's soft security policy in Europe's north-east at large (Moroff 2002a). With a view to the post-Cold War international situation, Solana notes:

> It is a long time since security was thought of only in terms of military force. We all know that security is far broader today, that it includes economic, environmental, and social issues. Indeed, non-military threats to security loom much larger in the mind of most people … [speaking explicitly of soft security he states] … But non-military aspects of security are not soft options. For these non-military security threats are not adequately dealt with by any of our international institutions … Although NATO is evolving and takes a wider range of functions, those will hardly cover organized crime, insecure borders, ecological security, ethnic migration and a score of other threats to people living peaceful lives. This is where the European Union must take up the challenge. And nowhere is this going to be more important than in our partnership with Russia. (Solana 1999: 1)

The European Union and Russia

If the normative difference in EU–Russia relations lies in the predominance of a geopolitical zero-sum game approach to foreign policy on the Russian side and an integrationist positive-sum game approach on the EU side (Vahl 2001: 7–12; Emerson 2001: 10), then the soft security concept seems to partly bridge this divide by focusing on societal and not strategic cooperation. Whereas cooperative security focuses mainly on defence matters and describes the governmental interaction patterns more accurately, soft security begins by defining the source of common security threats. It is predicated on a joint risk assessment and leaves the manner of treating those risks to the most pragmatic and efficient implementation mechanisms at hand. This does not mean that confronting soft security problems successfully is easy to achieve; on the contrary, many of these problems will never be solved completely (for example, when we think of pollution, nuclear safety, crime, illegal immigration and corruption). They can only be minimised to tolerable – and that means necessarily subjective, time and place dependent – levels. Threats are not necessarily self-evident; they are in good part a result of social construction and contingent upon changing perception patterns. For the Baltic republics it has been demonstrated that hard security questions are seen as most important for the present and the immediate future, whereas soft security problems are perceived to constitute by far the major risks in the longer term future (Prantl 2000: 17–18). However, perceptions can change quickly with the flux of current events.[13]

Russia seems to be particularly cooperation-prone where it can be an active player (that is in the security field and on high politics issues), thus leading to an intrinsic politicisation, if not securitisation, of its external relations. Meanwhile, the EU is mainly interested in expanding its regulatory regimes into the neighbourhood as a precondition for internal market access and aid with the aim of fostering societal security.[14] Thus the EU is rather interested in depoliticisation and thus desecuritisation. There are also numerous institutional reasons for this discrepancy. The EU can act best in technical terrain without high political or media salience. The EU creates security without talking about security as a matter of survival, i.e. without hard securitisation. Because the EU proffers a system of diffuse power-sharing with a consensual rather than a confrontational and politically-charged discourse, it cannot handle nor sustain such a discourse since it has no such strong political mandates. For the EU, it is thus extremely difficult to obtain a clear political mandate from its member states for pro-active international behaviour on high politics issues. In contrast, Russia is characterised by a highly (re-)centralised and hierarchical political leadership, which makes for the very opposite of diffusely-pooled sovereignty and power-sharing. Its foreign policy is geared towards gaining or retaining power and influence, relying on realist precepts and behaving like a modern Westphalian state (Moroff 2007a).

The European Union and Kaliningrad

The EU and some of its (mainly northern) member states pursue a foreign policy of solving problems and making a foreign entity – like Kaliningrad – more compatible with its own system of governance in order to ensure meaningful interaction. It is a half-conscious attempt at expanding its grid of governance, and it is an essentially post-modern and post-Westphalian method of foreign policy-making.

It remains to be seen whether this implies hard securitisation of formerly normal domestic policy issues or whether it means soft securitisation by internationalising domestic policy processes of problem-solving and deliberation, thus counterbalancing the view – dominant in Moscow – that international politics is in essence a strategic zero-sum power game. For that matter, hard or soft securitisation are processes and discursive practices, constructing a problem as pertaining either to an exceptionally sensitive security policy realm, usually generating exceptional executive privileges, or to normal politics, calling for a transparent, deliberative, problem-solving management with broad participation and democratic legitimation. The latter resembles EU practices and thinking. Convincing third parties like Russia to act and interact in the aforementioned policy fields as they pertain to Kaliningrad is a process of policy diffusion and thus Europeanisation beyond arguing and bargaining.[15] It is policy adaptation through policy practice and interaction patterns, by example and emulation, by standard setting, role conceptions and living up to expectations of other actors (Moroff 2007b). It is a patient persuasion by action for new kinds of policies and policy processes. Tempus-TACIS money might not be much, but how and for what it is used might very well be more important than the amount.[16]

One indicator of such policy and governance diffusion can be seen in the 'Nida initiative' of Russia and Lithuania (Usakas 2000). Here we find the many soft security threats emanating from Kaliningrad being taken up in a problem-solving manner of multi-level external governance. Thus not only do we find ideational spillover, manifested in the delineation of a common ground for cross-border problem-solving, but also behavioural spillover. It can be identified in the way that both Russia – with considerable input from Kaliningrad – and Lithuania interacted in drawing up this joint initiative within the framework of the Northern Dimension.[17] Thus participation in an inclusive, deliberative, multi-level governance system can also alleviate the policy-taker problem, since third countries or regions have a voice and can provide input, which also creates a sense of policy ownership. This is something which is required and strengthened through both parties' financial commitments in the co-financing schemes common to most EU assistance programmes.[18]

The European Commission (Commission 2001b) identified five arenas for joint action with Russia on Kaliningrad. First, economic development is mentioned, as the Commission noted that the region's standard of living is only about 80 per cent of the Russian average and that poverty and unemployment had increased dramatically in the late 1990s. However, it rejected setting up a special fund for Kaliningrad, being wary of giving any signal that Kaliningrad was singled out for special support. Instead, the Commission referred to its TACIS programme and placed Kaliningrad well within the Russian north-west for which it held a special TACIS window. Secondly, it wanted to promote good governance and the rule of law through EU projects for public administration, judicial reform and training programmes for local civil servants. Third, the fight against organised crime is mentioned as the Commission recognised that crime is very likely to affect neighbouring EU member states. It wanted to tackle it through the Task Force on Organised Crime in the Baltic Sea region and through twinning programmes for magistrates. Fourth, environmental challenges were listed, highlighting in particular the problem of water pollution and the disposal of nuclear waste. Fifth, health was recognised as a major concern as the spread of communicable diseases is a serious problem in Kaliningrad. Through TACIS, the EU supported initiatives dealing with HIV and tuberculosis. All of these soft security issues were agreed to be a basis for action by the EU Council and much of it was echoed again during the official visit of the EU's external relations commissioner, Benito Ferrero-Waldner, to Kaliningrad on 28 February 2006, putting special emphasis on the Northern Dimension Environmental Partnership (NDEP).[19]

As it evolved from 1998 onward, the Northern Dimension has offered the Russian side partnership and voting rights in regional soft security plans, thus giving it a first taste of EU decision-making. It provides for dialogue and cooperation between the Commission, member states, the northern countries associated with the EU (Norway and Iceland) and the Russian Federation. Implementation is carried out within the framework of the PCA with Russia, thus influencing such financial instruments as TACIS and the EU interregional cooperation programme (Interreg). The policy-making process is characterised by subsidiarity with active participation of all stakeholders in the north, including regional organisations, local and regional authorities, the academic and business communities, and civil society. They are mustered in confronting those soft security challenges mentioned by the Commission. It is first and foremost about avoiding the emergence of new dividing lines in Europe in the wake of EU enlargement, recognising the wide disparities in standards of living, environmental challenges such as nuclear waste and waste water management, public health and insufficient transport and border crossing facilities. According to the EU–Russia summit of 24 November 2006, the biggest change will come about during 2008 when the Northern Dimension policy will not only be a part of external policies of the EU, but a common policy of four equal partners: the EU, Iceland, Norway and Russia, with special efforts towards Kaliningrad and north-west Russia.

As of 2006, the NDEP has leveraged investments of more than €1.5 billion for environmental projects, pooling for the first time the joint resources of international financial institutions operating in the region, i.e. the European Bank for Reconstruction and Development, the European Investment Bank, the Northern Investment Bank and the World Bank. The coordination of these financial institutions is provided by a steering group, which orients its lending very closely on the priorities identified in the Northern Dimension

Action Plans (NDAPs). It is especially noteworthy that in 2001, the European Investment Bank – which is essentially EU-funded – received for the first time a mandate for lending €100 million to Russia for projects within the NDEP in the Baltic Sea basin of Russia, notably St Petersburg and Kaliningrad. This mandate was renewed for an additional €500 million in 2006 for projects in the sectors of environment as well as transport, telecommunications and energy. While most of that money went to the St Petersburg region, Kaliningrad was second, receiving €22 million for district heating rehabilitation and a further €49.2 million slated for a solid waste management project.[20]

A potential depoliticisation and thus soft securitisation of the targeted policy issues is likely to be facilitated by involving such international financial institutions that focus on the technical aspects of concrete projects and policy outcomes. Beyond that, a local TACIS office for regional development opened in Kaliningrad in 2001, and a Euro-Faculty sponsored by the Council of Baltic Sea States with EU support opened at Kaliningrad State University, thus providing further education and training to Kaliningraders, especially in law and economics.

Of course, interaction and cooperation in soft security policy fields points to a neo-functionalist project (Barrera and Haas 1969), counting on spillover effects that then eventually reach into hard security realms. This assumption comes with two caveats though. Positive interdependence such as in economic relations means a kind of burden sharing and division of labour that does not lead to one-sided developments within any of the participating countries. That would be the case if a certain kind of economic interdependence resembling mercantilist systems were to evolve, for example, between Russia and the EU, whereby the former sells raw materials and energy supplies in return for the latter's finished products. This is likely to lead to greater state monopolistic structures in Russia rather than to an open and diversified market economy. Although functionalism has been influential, it has not swept all before it and its assumption that stability and peace will grow in step with cross-border interaction might not materialise all the time. A certain tyranny of harmony comes about because 'the more you cooperate, the more you have in common, and therefore the more you can quarrel about' (Mouritzen 1998: 56). One might add that this risk will increase as the larger the surface of potential friction grows. Suffice to say, this is a caution against an idealistic view of interdependence, for it can have negative as well as positive expressions.

Conclusion

Two scenarios for the future of Kaliningrad seem possible. The bleak one would place it in the double periphery at the far end of the economic and political centres of both the EU and Russia, with Russia using it as a bargaining chip on visa, military transit and other high politics questions. Or the brighter version might see such geo-political manoeuvring being supplanted by geo-economic incentives and a joint focus on soft security problems.

The EU is certainly not interested in fuelling secessionist tendencies in Russia by granting special privileges to Kaliningrad. Why does the EU want to induce change in Kaliningrad in the first place? To ameliorate soft security threats is one reason; the other is its sense of mission on a wider value scale, which goes beyond problem-solving and aims at showing how problems should generally be solved in a democracy with sufficient civic virtues and societal involvement. However, threat perceptions (and thus pressure to act) can and do differ between Russia and Kaliningrad on the one side and the EU on the other (for example in matters of nuclear safety, pollution, communicable diseases, migration and crime). What is more, in the realist tradition, problems are not only there to be solved but they might be used as bargaining chips or instrumentalised for other purposes. Many offers by the EU to enhance the economic situation in Kaliningrad were officially turned down by Moscow for fear of increasing separatist tendencies. However, this response might also be a tool of public diplomacy, keeping Kaliningrad an island of poverty inside an EU sea of affluence. Thus, the Russian government would be able to demonstrate dramatically the negative impact of EU enlargement and EU disregard for Russia in general. Or it has attempted to use Kaliningrad as the thin end of a wedge cracking the hard shell of the Schengen *acquis* by trying to secure visa-free travel for all Russians through the back door. This would eventually have been the consequence of granting visa-free travel to Kaliningraders.[21]

These are two cases in point where problems are kept on the back burner for later use, whenever the international situation provides a window of opportunity for bargaining over – or showing off – with certain problems. This is the same logic that applies to many other frozen conflicts the Russian Federation is involved in as well, especially in Transnistria, Georgia, and Chechnya. Thus it remains an open question whether Kaliningrad becomes a case of soft securitisation within EU–Russia relations. Possibilities of turning it into such a case are abundant even though the political will might be lacking.

Notes

1   This is not surprising, given that Switzerland is the fourth largest trading partner of the EU.   See   http://trade.ec.europa.eu/doclib/docs/2006/september/tradoc_113450.pdf (accessed 20 November 2006).

2   Especially after the end of the Cold War, security studies started to expand and diversify. Several new conceptions of security evolved, e.g. human security and soft security. Human security – a term first used in the 1994 UNDP Human Development

Report (UNDP 1994) – consists of several dimensions (the UNDP introduced seven: economic, food, health, environmental, personal, community and political security). Critical to this concept is a change in the object of security from states to human beings. Some of the key texts are: United Nations Development Programme 1994; Owen 2004; Glasius and Kaldor 2005; Krause 2005. For a critical analysis see Paris 2001. On soft security see Heininen and Lasinantti 1999; Moroff 2002b; Tassinari 2003; Aldis and Herd 2005. Moroff (2002b: 13) defines soft security issues as: 'security matters of a non-military nature that do not involve inter-state violence'.

3   For the Copenhagen School security is about survival, i.e. a security issue has to pose an existential threat to a referent object. Because of this quality, it legitimises emergency measures (Buzan *et al.* 1998: 23f). An issue becomes securitised when it is presented as an existential threat that makes emergency measures necessary and moreover justifies 'actions outside the normal bounds of political procedure', that 'break the normal political rules of the game' (*ibid.*: 24). The presentation of an issue as an existential threat is the *securitising move*, yet for successful securitisation to take place the audience has to accept this securitising move. Securitisation is the 'inter-subjective establishment of an existential threat' (*ibid.*: 25). Security is considered as a negative, as a failure to deal with an issue in a normal way. Soft securitisation means framing a security concern as essential but not existential. It therefore promotes a cooperative problem-solving policy-making mode, it does not need exceptional, extraordinary measures.

4   For a discussion of various Europeanisation concepts see Olsen 2002; 2004.

5   Desecuritisation can be defined as the endeavour 'to move [issues] out of this threat-defense sequence and into the ordinary public sphere' (Buzan *et al.* 1998: 29).

6   This is, of course, similar to the 'trash-bin' or 'garbage-can' model of bureaucratic politics where solutions search for their problems (See Cohen *et al.* 1972). I would qualify this, however, because the EU does not actively search, it rather shapes the perception of certain problems in a way that its instruments (or policy solutions) can be applied.

7   Internally, the Commission needs regional entities in EU structural policies even in highly centralised, unitary member states, or in its Interreg III programme, covering also non-members around the Baltic Sea. It also needs experts and civil society for its comitology processes, from which it derives legitimacy by talking to all interested parties and stake holders before proposing an initiative.

8   This also means that there might be a sequence of Europeanisation: policies (content and issues) spilling over into politics (policy-making, governance), having finally an impact on polity (structures and set of actors).

9   The origin of the expanding security agenda lies in the nuclear stalemate of strategic symmetry from the early 1970s, the result of which was a *rapprochement* between the two superpowers through the Conference on Security and Cooperation (CSCE) in Europe .When problems of hard security become insolvable, challenges to soft security may take their place on the current affairs agenda. It was, however, the renewed weapons race and the Russian intervention in Afghanistan during the early 1980s that reinforced the prominence of hard or military questions on the security agenda.

10   A case in point is provided by the Uruguay Round negotiations between the EU and the USA, where it was virtually impossible to go back to the EU to again open up a number of positions which had been agreed on by all member states for the Commission's negotiating mandate.

11   Interviews with Commission officials and Policy Unit officials in Brussels, March 2003.

12   ENP Individual Action Plans, e.g. EU–Moldova Action Plan, available on the Internet at http://ec.europa.eu/world/enp/pdf/action_plans/moldova_enp_ap_final_en.pdf.

13 For example, during the fight for independence the environmental threat posed by Soviet nuclear power stations and mining fields in Lithuania and Estonia was perceived to be very great. Soviet industry and technology was framed as poisoning the homeland. Once independence was gained both countries were very reluctant to close down those installations when asked by the EU. Their economic value was now perceived to be greater than their environmental threat.

14 For the concepts of societal, soft and human security see Moroff (2002b: 24–8).

15 In contrast to Risse's argument that it is already a high politics game as it involves arguing about general norms and standards of behaviour (Risse 2000), the persuasion game in soft securitisation is about identifying common problems and then solving them jointly.

16 TACIS provides assistance for economic and social reforms in the republics of the former Soviet Union and Mongolia, excluding Central and Eastern Europe (see http://ec.europa.eu/comm/europeaid/projects/tacis/index_en.htm, accessed 22 November 2006). Tempus has been a trans-European programme for higher education cooperation, and under TACIS it operates as an EU aid scheme for the restructuring of higher education systems in the former Soviet republics (see http://ec.europa.eu/education/programmes/programmes_en.html, accessed 17 July 2007).

17 The precise wording of the initiative can be found as Annex III to the Northern Dimension Action Plan, available on the Internet at http://europa.eu.int /comm/external_relations/north_dim/doc/comm1998_0589m.pdf (accessed 22 November 2006). The context of its development is explained in detail by the then Vice-Foreign Minister of Lithuania (Usakas 2000).

18 Given that the EU can use its resources only by complementing and adding to precisely defined priorities by Russia (Patten 2000), it is all the more important to see where those Russian priorities shift. We can detect a small conceptual spillover in the Russian discourse on and with the EU. Is such linguistic adoption just a disguise? Ideational and linguistic spillover is a form of widening (or limiting) the 'space of communication', and as shown for EU enlargement, rhetorical action (Schimmelfennig 2001) can entrap the speaker – he might be forced to act on rhetoric some time in the future. Thus, producing a text is producing a reality of sorts; even a comment on 'reality' might change this reality. Other documents showing a change in Russian foreign policy thinking can be identified. Here are three: National Security Concept January 2000 (available on the Internet at www.russiaeurope.mid.ru/russiastrat2000.html); Foreign Policy 4th Concept June 2000 (an excerpt available on the Internet at www.bits.de/NRANEU/US-Russia/A%20Official%20Docs/RussForeignPolConc_towardsUS.html); and the Defence White Paper October 2003. Soft threats mentioned in these documents are: criminal organisations linked to the political sphere (both legislative and executive); public health (alcohol consumption, drug use, low birth rates); trans-national organised crime; illegal trafficking in drugs and weapons (the most important task being to combat international terrorism and collaborate with other states purposefully); and the minority rights of the Russian-speaking population in Latvia and Estonia. Not only do we find soft security issues looming large in Russian foreign policy and strategic documents, they also become more important over time. Furthermore, Russia is concerned with many of these issues in its sub-regional activities in the Black Sea Cooperation Group, the Council of Baltic Sea States, the Barents Euro-Arctic Council, and last but not least the Northern Dimension, all of which address soft security questions if not in a problem-solving manner, then at least in a confidence-building one.

19 For an analysis of the emergence of the NDEP, see Moroff (2002a: 202–6). Current projects and funding details available on the Internet at http://ec.europa .eu/external_relations/north_dim/ndep/index.htm (accessed 22 November 2006).

20 Information on funding by international financial institutions available on the Internet at www.ndep.org/projects.asp?type=nh&cont=prjh&pageid=4 (accessed 27 July 2007).

21 The recent success in granting facilitated visas to certain groups in Russia (students, researchers, businessmen, etc.) would most likely not have been possible without having the visa question continuously on the agenda through the Kaliningrad transit problem (see Müntel 2003).

References

Aldis, A. and G. P. Herd, eds (2005), *Soft Security Threats and Europe*, London, Routledge.

Anderson, M. (2000), 'Frontiers of the European Union', in *Advancing the Union: Report by the Independent Commission for the Reform of the Institutions and Procedures of the Union*, London, ICRI.

Archer, C. (2001), 'The Northern Dimension as a Soft-Soft Option for the Baltic States' Security', in *The Northern Dimension: Fuel for the EU?*, ed. Hanna Ojanen, Helsinki, The Finish Institute for International Affairs & Institut für Europäische Politik: 188–209.

Barrera, M. and E. B. Haas (1969), 'The Operationalization of Some Variables Related to Regional Integration: A Research Note', *International Organization* 23(1):150–60.

Buzan, B., O. Waever and J. Wilde (1998), *Security: A New Framework for Analysis*, Boulder (CO) and London, Lynne Rienner.

Buzan, B. and O. Waever (2003), *Regions and Powers: The Structure of International Security*, Cambridge, Cambridge University Press (Cambridge Studies in International Relations, 91).

Cohen, M., J. G. March, and J. P. Olsen (1972), 'A Garbage Can Model of Organizational Choice', *Administrative Science Quarterly*, 17(1): 1–25.

Commission (1999), Forward Studies Unit, 'Scenarios Europe 2010: Five Possible Futures for Europe', Working Paper, Brussels.

Commission (2001a), 'Communication from the Commission on Conflict Prevention', Brussels, COM 211.

Commission (2001b), 'The EU and Kaliningrad', Communication from Commission to the Council on 17 January, Brussels, COM 26 final, available on the Internet at http://europa.eu.int/comm/external_relations/north_dim/doc/com2001_0026en01.pdf (accessed 22 November 2006).

Emerson, M. (2001), *The Elephant and the Bear: The European Union, Russia and their Near Abroads*, Brussels, CEPS Paperbacks.

Fairlie, L. F. and A. Sergounin (2001), *Are Borders Barriers? EU Enlargement and the Russian Region of Kaliningrad*, Helsinki and Berlin, The Finnish Institute of International Affairs and Institut für Europäische Politik (Programme on the Northern Dimension of the CFSP, Vol. 13).

Glasius, M. and M. Kaldor (2005), 'Individuals First: A Human Security Strategy for the European Union', *Internationale Politik und Gesellschaft*, 1: 62–83.

Heininen, L. and G. Lassinantti, eds (1999) *Security in the European North: From 'Hard' to 'Soft'*, Rovaniemi (Finland), Arctic Centre, University of Lapland (Arktisen Keskuksen tiedotteita, 32).

Jachtenfuchs, M. and B. Kohler-Koch (2006), *Europäische Integration* [*European integration*], reprint of the 2nd edn, Wiesbaden, VS Verl. F. Sozialwissenschaften.

Keohane, R. O. and J. S. Nye (1977), *Power and Interdependence: World Politics in Transition*, Boston, Little, Brown and Co.

Knudsen, O. (1998), *Cooperative Security in the Baltic Sea Region*, Paris, WEU Institute for

Security Studies, Challiot Paper 33.

Kohler-Koch, B. and M. Jachtenfuchs (1995), *Regieren im dynamischen Mehrebenensystem* [*The system of multi-level governance*], Working Paper AB III, No. 12, Mannheim, Mannheimer Zentrum für Europäische Sozialforschung.

Krause, K. (2005), 'Human Security: An idea whose time has come?', *Sicherheit + Frieden*, 23(1): 1–6.

Moroff, H. ed. (2002a), *European Soft Security Policies: The Northern Dimension*, Helsinki, Ulkopoliittinen Inst. (Programme on the Northern Dimension of the CFSP, 17).

Moroff, H. (2002b), 'Introduction and Theoretical Considerations' in *European Soft Security Policies: The Northern Dimension*, ed. H. Moroff, Berlin and Helsinki, Finnish Institute of International Affairs: 12–36.

Moroff, H. (2007a), 'Russia, the CIS and the EU: Secondary Integration by Association?', in *The CIS and the EU: Compatibility of Integration Options for the Post-Soviet Space*, ed. K. Malfliet, L. Verpoest and E. Vinokurov, Hampshire, Palgrave Macmillan: 95–120.

Moroff, H. (2007b), 'Kohärenz in der Vielfalt? – Die Politik der EU gegenüber Russland' ['Coherence in diversity? EU policy towards Russia'] in *Kollektive Außenpolitik – Die Europäische Union als internationaler Akteur* [*Collective foreign policy: The EU as an international actor*], ed. M. Jopp and P. S. Peter, Baden-Baden, Nomos: 179–210.

Moshes, A. (2003), 'Kaliningrad: Challenges Between Russia and Europe', in *Prospects and Risks Beyond EU Enlargement. Eastern Europe: Challenges of a Pan-European Policy*, ed. I. Kempe, Opladen, Leske and Budrich: 177–94.

Mouritzen, H. (1998), 'Fragmented North: Comment', in *Approaching the Northern Dimension of CFSP*, ed. M. Jopp and R. Warjovaara, Ulkopoliittinen instituutti & Institut für Europäische Politik.

Müntel, G. (2003), 'Kooperationsfelder von heute und morgen – Kaliningrads Weg aus der Isolation? Eine Analyse des Transit-Kompromisses zwischen der EU und Russland' ['Areas for cooperation from today until tomorrow: Does Kaliningrad leave isolation? An analysis of the transit deal between the EU and Russia'], *Osteuropa*, 53(2–3): 249–61.

Olsen, J. P. (2002), 'The Many Faces of Europeanization', *Journal of Common Market Studies*, 40(5): 921–2.

Olsen, J. P. (2004), 'Europeanization' in *European Union Politics*, 2nd reprint, ed. M. Cini, Oxford, Oxford University Press: 333–48.

Owen, T. (2004), 'Human Security – Conflict, Critique and Consensus: Colloquium Remarks and a Proposal for a Threshold-Based Definition', *Security Dialogue*, 35(3): 373–87.

Paris, R. (2001), 'Human Security: Paradigm Shift or Hot Air?', *International Security*, 26(2): 87–102.

Patten, C. (2000), 'Speech at the European Parliament, 12 December 2000', available on the Internet at http://europa.eu.int/comm/external_relations/news/patten/russia_report .htm (accessed 22 November 2006).

Patten, C. (2001), 'Northern Dimension and Co-operation in the Baltic Sea Area', Speech at the Overseas Club and 'Pro Baltica' with Hamburg Mayor O. Runde and Finnish Foreign Minister E. Tuomioja, Dresdner Bank Hamburg, 6 June 2001, available on the Internet at http://ec.europa.eu/comm/external_relations/news/patten/sp01_260.htm (accessed 5 May 2008).

Prantl, J. (2000), *Security and Stability in Northern Europe: A Threat Assessment*, Helsinki, UPI Working Paper.

Pursiainen, C. (with the assistance of P. Haavisto and N. Lomagin) (2001), *Soft Security Problems in Northwest Russia and their Implications for the Outside World: A Framework for Analysis and Action*, Helsinki, Finnish Institute of International Affairs, UPI Working Papers.

Risse, T. (2000), '"Let's argue!" Communicative Action in World Politics', *International Organization*, 54(1): 1–39.

Schimmelfennig, F. (2001), 'The Community Trap: Liberal Norms, Rhetorical Action, and the Eastern Enlargement of the European Union', *International Organization* 55(1): 47–80.

Solana, J. (1999), 'The EU–Russia Strategic Partnership', speech by the High Representative of the European Union for the Common Foreign and Security Policy given on 13 October 1999 in Stockholm, available on the Internet at www.ue.eu.int/newsroom (accessed 5 May 2008).

Tassinari, F., ed. (2003), *The Baltic Sea Region in the European Union: Reflections on Identity, Soft Security and Marginality*, Gdańsk, Wydawn. Uniw. Gdańskiego (The Baltic Sea Area Studies, Vol. 8).

United Nations Development Programme (1994), *Human Development Report 1994 (New Dimensions of Human Security)*, New York, Oxford University Press.

Usakas, V. (2000), 'Lithuania and Russia: Knowing the Past, Building Genuine Partnership for the Future', *Lithuanian Foreign Policy Review*, 2: 9–26.

Vahl, M. (2001), '"Just good friends?" The EU–Russian "Strategic Partnership" and the Northern Dimension', Brussels, CEPS Working Paper 166.

Waever, O. (1995), 'Securitisation and Desecuritisation', in *On Security*, ed. R. D. Lipschutz, New York, Columbia University Press: 46–86.

Wallace, H., W. Wallace and M. A. Pollack, eds (2005), *Policy-making in the European Union*, 5th edn, Oxford, Oxford University Press (The New European Union Series).

PART II

The policy framework: Kaliningrad in its domestic and international context

Joan DeBardeleben

5

Multi-level governance and centralisation in Russia: implications for EU–Russia relations

Introduction

Recent political reforms in Russia have reinforced centralising tendencies and have raised questions about the democratic credentials of the evolving Russian political system. At the same time, EU enlargement has extended Russia's border with the European Union, including new frontiers with the Baltic States and Poland. While the Russian system is moving away from the federalist structure put in place by the 1993 Russian Constitution under Boris Yeltsin's guidance, some neighbouring states are becoming integrated into more complex multi-tiered governance structures. While these states are not themselves federal systems, EU regional policies and cross-border initiatives provide an impetus for activation of regional actors. Thus, Putin's re-centralisation approach appears to place Russia at increasing loggerheads with some fundamental precepts of the EU, just when the two entities stand face to face across lengthier shared borders. The EU nonetheless continues to pursue an active policy of Europeanisation in regard to Russia, while the effectiveness of conditionality as a tool in its policy towards Russia has been challenged by Russia's rising self-assertion and increased economic might (DeBardeleben 2007).

This chapter explores the potential implications of these developments, with special attention to the Kaliningrad oblast, where the dilemma is posed in particularly poignant form. Kaliningrad is not a typical border region; its location poses both exceptional opportunities and potential risks for Russia in its relations with the EU. Kaliningrad thus may represent a limiting case in analysing the implications of Putin's reforms for border relations. In this chapter we argue that the example of Kaliningrad supports the hypothesis that the thrust of Putin's centralising reforms, which involved the installation of loyal regional elites within a centralised patronage structure, can be made compatible with cross-border economic cooperation efforts with the EU on a regional level; however, the structure of incentives affecting Russian regional leaders works to avoid spillover of cooperation into governance questions. Thus the goal of promoting EU–Russian cooperation that is consistent with the Russian understanding of state sovereignty is made compatible with centralising domestic reforms. This situation, in turn, is less likely to facilitate political Europeanisation.

The first portion of the chapter analyses the nature of Putin's centralising reforms. The second part examines some general factors that may affect the nature of cross-border cooperation between the EU and neighbouring regions. The next section takes into consideration the incentives and interests affecting regional elites, in the context of central policy. In the final section, specific aspects of the Kaliningrad context are examined.

Russia's centralising reforms: formation of a national patronage system

While few doubt that Putin's recent reforms have a centralising impetus, more controversial is whether this form of centralisation is facilitative or inhibitory to the development of constructive relationships with neighbouring countries. Upon Putin's election as president in 2000, reforms to the political party and federal systems were almost immediately and simultaneously placed on the agenda, governed by the notion of the 'vertical of power', which can be understood to mean the establishment of a unified system of executive authority. Designed to counteract the extreme decentralisation of the Yeltsin period, the reforms were presented as reinforcing a clear definition of authority between the various levels of government. Early vehicles to implement these reforms included the creation of seven federal districts to oversee federal bodies in the eighty-nine (by early 2008 reduced to eighty-five[1]) units of the Russian Federation, a process of harmonisation of federal and regional laws, and the removal of governors from the Federation Council. The primary discourse surrounding these reforms has involved concepts such as rule of law, state capacity and efficiency.

A related reform involved the adoption of a new law on local self-government. A controversial initiative, this law was heralded by some as clarifying the areas of jurisdiction of the various levels of government (federal, regional, local), and by others as reducing the scope of local autonomy (Lankina 2005: 145–77). The measure is widely interpreted as granting increased leverage to regional authorities over localities, a concession for loss of autonomy of the regions themselves. Responsibilities of lower bodies in some policy areas are weakened (education, medical care), while financial resources to carry out others are considered by many to be inadequate. In late 2004, while discussing the Beslan hostage-taking, Putin implicated inadequate discipline at the regional level and weaknesses in the system of unified executive power throughout the country (Putin 2004). This interpretation of the crisis provided a pretext for the next round of centralising measures, this time involving the elimination of direct election of regional executives, to be replaced by a process involving presidential nomination and approval by the regional legislative body. The reform was passed into law in December 2004 and over time the new process of gubernatorial selection has been implemented across the country. A queue of governors requested reappointment before their normal terms of office expired, and in only a few cases have incumbent governors been rejected in favour of new figures. While Putin's earlier measures saw only minimal opposition, this reform did elicit an outcry in certain circles, including opposition political parties. A court case brought to contest the decision was unsuccessful.

These formal changes were accompanied by Putin's exercise of soft power, namely the strengthening of patron–client dependencies between central authorities and the regional executives. This was evidenced in the minimal protest from governors, even as their power and independence were progressively undermined. Similarly, Putin's gubernatorial nominees have generally been approved by regional legislatures with an unusually high level of unanimity. This use of administrative pressure to gain acquiescence if not compliance in pursuing a particular reform design reinforces a personalistic, clientelistic system of political power. The personalistic patronage-based system in the past extended to governors' regional networks, making them attractive allies in assuring delivery of votes and loyalty to incumbent figures in the central government. Accordingly, political, in addition to legal, processes have been very important in defining the evolving character of Russian federalism. Through these appointment processes, political dependence on the goodwill of the president takes on a self-perpetuating and formal character. The next stage in the process could involve the appointment of mayors by regional executives (Coalson 2005). A step in that direction in some regions (including Kaliningrad oblast) has involved the appointment of city managers, who might take over some important functions from the mayor (Dmitriyev 2007). Appointment of mayors, were it to be adopted, would involve a concession to regional leaders that would extend the patronage chain further.

The 1999 Duma election saw the rapid ascent of the Unity Party, later to become United Russia after the merger with the other establishment centrist formation, Fatherland/All-Russia. United Russia has become the main vehicle of the patronage machine. Governors jumped on the Putin bandwagon to be on the winning side, sometimes appearing on party lists for United Russia even when they were not party members. Regional leaders may believe that such acquiescence is the surest means to assure political survival.

Political party and electoral reforms also serve to nationalise politics, reducing possibilities for the establishment of regional political parties or of semi-autonomous regional political machines. In addition, small parties have a harder time meeting the new proportional representation threshold of seven per cent that took effect with the December 2007 Duma elections. Given requirements for party registration (increased from 10,000 to 50,000 signatures in December 2004), marginal parties have difficulty qualifying. In this system, regional politicians can enter the national legislative body either through appointment by the regional executive or regional legislature (for the Federation Council) or by being included on the party list of one of the large national parties (for the Duma). Thus inclusion in a national patronage network, exercised in part by the dominant political party, is increasingly the key vehicle for upward career mobility. Additional features of the new electoral law are the numerous conditions that may permit the electoral commission to reject inclusion of a party on the party list ballot. Such complex requirements create the possibility of selective enforcement, since nearly every party will have arguably violated one or another of the requirements.

The net effect of these combined changes is to develop a nationally based patronage system, in which regional political figures are promoted primarily through their association with the dominant national party (or parties) and/or support from the President. While this might counteract regional fragmentation, it shifts lines of political accountability upwards rather than downwards to the public. Patronage networks have strong political lineage in Russia, forming the most important dynamic for political recruitment and promotion during the Soviet era. As such, clientelistic relations are a familiar and understandable phenomenon to most Russians, not just the elite. In the Yeltsin period, bribes took on a more prominent role, supplementing the more subtle and nuanced character of patronage ties. Putin's putative attack on corruption meant a greater effort to institutionalise the more subtle forms of dependence involved in network politics. Recent indications from Moscow suggest that once the patronage network is in place, regional officials may be entrusted with more authority to carry out policies in line with central priorities. Elections in which leadership succession is at stake (as in the 2008 presidential election) may test the patronage system if members of the political elite try to establish alternative patronage structures and thus destabilise existing relations between the regional and central elites (Hale 2005).

Russian regions and the EU

Differing governance systems and regional incentives

This centralising and clientelistic nature of political relationships in Russia stands in marked contrast to multi-level governance structures emerging in the EU. From a theoretical perspective, multi-level governance depicts the complex and multi-layered sets of political interactions characterising the relations in and between constituent parts of the EU and its member states. Fallend *et al.* (2002: 565) see multi-level governance as being *sui generis* to the EU; it can be described as non-hierarchical, flexible and dynamic, with an important role for partnerships, political networks, interactive dependencies and exchange relations for problem-solving (Hooghe and Marks 2001). However, the networks and exchange relations in the EU are primarily institutional rather than personalistic, as in the Russian system. The notion of 'subsidiarity', defining the importance of devolving functions to the lowest level that can effectively carry them out, is a component of the EU's multi-level governance process, a concept hardly known in Russia. Along with multi-level governance, changing understandings of sovereignty in the EU (e.g., such as 'pooled' sovereignty) work to overcome the dichotomy between the nation-state as the exclusive location of state sovereignty and the transfer of certain power to the EU level (Barbato 2003). This notion also contrasts sharply with the centralisation of power occurring in Russia.

As part of multi-level governance, EU processes include a formalised role for sub-national units in the policy process (Bokajlo 2000: 348). Sub-national actors have participatory status, alongside national governments, in the development of cohesion policy (Hooghe 1996: 12). In some instances, such as the German case, this led to actual adaptation of domestic institutions to the new policy-making challenges (Börzel 2002). The ability of sub-national units to influence EU policy, as well as national outcomes, varies by country, but one important factor, Hooghe concludes, is the presence or absence of federalism (1996: 19). But even for unitary systems like Finland and the new member states of Central and Eastern Europe, EU accession has engendered the development of regional management structures which previously either did not exist or did not play the same role, required in order to access structural funds. Fallend *et al.* (2002) argue that these have become bargaining institutions as well as vehicles for information exchange. Poland's reforms, for example, give local voivodships the possibility of undertaking their own regional policy in cooperation with other European regions without the involvement of national level authorities (Bokajlo 2000: 348).

Relations between various levels of government or between various administrative levels in the European space are characterised by ambiguity and complexity. This contrasts sharply with Putin's federal reforms, which are driven by a desire for clarity and simplicity. The interface between these two differing types of governance systems has engendered speculation about its consequences. For example, Hubel (2005: 78–9) has suggested that 'the EU may challenge Russian leadership, both in Moscow and in its Western periphery, to develop a new, more flexible federal system that reconciles the interests of the regions on the EU borders with traditional Russian concepts of central state control'. On the other hand, Kaveshnikov and Potemkina (2003: 338–9) point out that while the asymmetric nature of EU–Russian relations may be 'an obstacle to the emergence of a strategic partnership', these asymmetries may also be used to further economic development on the basis of cross-border cooperation in particular sectors. Krok-Paszkowska and Zielonka (2005: 166) argue that as enlargement increases the complexity of the EU, 'this will make it easier rather than more difficult for Russia to integrate with the EU' in particular functional spheres, invoking the notion of spillover in particular areas of integration. This contrasts with Browning's view that in its external relations, the EU tends to behave like a typical unified state actor, concerned about distinctions between insiders/outsiders and security risks, rather than affirming the post-modernist multi-level governance approaches that are evident in internal EU relations (Browning 2001; 2002). In particular, Schengen border requirements illustrate this ambiguity and the challenge it poses for relations with Russia.

Geographic proximity and political influence

Geographic proximity may encourage cross-border economic and political influence. Kopstein and Reilly (2000) test theories of spatial location and conclude that proximity (or 'spatial stock') does have an independent influence but can be mitigated by factors such as openness to outside influences and incentives offered by neighbouring states to change. For the Central European states that acceded to the EU in May 2004, all factors worked in a positive direction to facilitate reforms consistent with EU norms. On the other hand, Kopstein and Reilly depict Russia as an exception to the clustering effects related to location factors, perhaps because the country's imperial history makes it less susceptible to outside influences. In particular, Russian regions' receptiveness to foreign contact may be strongly influenced by the nature of the regional political elite as well as by incentives offered by the federal centre (discussed below). Certain regions, such as Novgorod, have taken a proactive role in developing contacts with the European Union (Sergounin and Rykhtik 2002: 33).

Stefan Krätke, in his research on German–Polish border regions before enlargement, identifies economic factors that may affect susceptibility of border areas to reform or the ability of these regions to attract foreign investment, referring to the phenomenon of 'selective integration ... into the global economy' (Krätke 1999: 631–2). Border regions that do not have an economic structure capable of taking advantage of the benefits of proximity may take an asymmetric 'low road' of integration, i.e. with the less developed neighbouring state benefiting mainly due to low wages and production costs, or by becoming 'regional branch plant economies' (*ibid.*: 632). A further factor inhibiting effective economic integration in the immediate border areas can arise if the border area in the neighbouring EU country is itself peripheral and not well developed (*ibid.*: 659). Another possibility is the development of a 'bazaar economy', with informal cross-border speculative economic activities predominating. More beneficial forms of cross-border economic relations are available to regions with an innovative capacity due to the pre-existing industrial structure, and such features are often present in large urban centres that are not themselves border regions. This situation produces the possibility of 'cross-border cooperation between firms on a qualitatively high level'. An additional consideration has to do with proximity to markets, which may also draw foreign investment away from direct border regions that are less densely populated or have less market potential, as well as less innovative capacity (*ibid.*: 637).

Research on border relations on the EU's eastern perimeter before enlargement suggests another conclusion: good border relations have less impact on governance structures than on economic and human relations. Finnish–Russian experience indicates that while competence in particular policy areas may be developed through such cooperative efforts, this does not easily extend to governance issues. Rainer-Elk Anders (2003) uses the term 'border-spanners' to describe cross-border initiatives in the Karelian region. Working groups have been established directly at the regional level, a process assisted by strengthening of regional councils in Finland as part of EU membership requirements. Anders (*ibid.*: 323) refers to 'the emphasis on intergovernmental cooperation in the relationship between the EU and the Russian Federation. In the Russian case this emphasis is even greater' while the EU 'has allowed if not actively promoted processes of regionalisation, even on its territorial fringes'. Anders concludes that centralisation processes fashioned by Putin mean that 'the emergence of Russian regions as a site of governance in the relations with Finland and the EU is seen as a threat' (*ibid.*: 323).

Russian attitudes towards EU relations: central and regional perspectives

Incentives affecting regional elites
In considering responses to cross-border opportunities the regional elite may be influenced by several factors. Among these are the likely impacts on the population, perceived gains for regional economic actors and potential gains or threats to the elite's own position. These considerations may in turn be affected by incentives emanating from the federal centre. The priorities of federal policy themselves must therefore be considered since federal authorities may structure incentives to influence the behaviour of regional elites.

In general, Russia's centralising impetus reinforces accountability of regional elites upward rather than downward to the population. Since governors are no longer elected, but rather indirectly appointed by the president, they do not need to face judgment by the electorate. On the other hand, both personal career prospects and support for other regional priorities will depend in good measure on the goodwill of the president and his administration. This is not to say that the population's interests will necessarily be ignored, but rather that their influence may be filtered through other vehicles, including both federal policy and elections to the regional legislature (which must approve presidential appointees). Close links between the regional political elite and economic elites at either the national or regional level could also be important here, since Moscow's growing influence could give predominance to national over regional firms. An increase in insider–outsider economic disparities in relation to EU neighbours can also pose a problem for regional leaders even in the absence of electoral accountability.

Restrictions placed on regional leaders by federal authorities may overtly affect the ability of Russian regions to take advantage of European connections. With the 1998 passage of the federal 'Law on coordinating international and foreign economic relations of the members of the Russian Federation', the federal government restricted the ability of regional governments to develop independent relations with foreign governments. According to this law, regions are permitted to engage in cooperation only with regional or local governments of foreign states; they can deal with central authorities of foreign countries only via Moscow (Sergounin and Rykhtik 2002: 38). While such an approach is *de facto* often followed in other federal states, for example the United States and Canada (with some limited exceptions for Québec), the requirement seems to be more rigidly enforced in Russia through the creation of the federal districts and the presence of presidential envoys in the regions.

Russian state priorities and regional interests

The notion of state sovereignty plays an important role in the Russian position towards the EU as well as in federal relations with regional officials. Since 2000, any sharing of sovereignty with the regional governments has been resisted. The official Russian position defines EU–Russian relations as an equal 'strategic partnership', a notion articulated in the Medium-term Strategy for Development of Relations between the Russian Federation and the European Union (2000–2010)' (EU–Russia Strategy 1999). This document asserts that 'Russia must preserve freedom in defining and carrying out its internal and foreign policy, its status and advantages as a Eurasian state and the largest country of the CIS, the independence of its positions and activity in international organisations' (*ibid.*). The goal of the Strategy is defined as the 'ensuring of national interests and increasing the role and authority of Russia in Europe and the world' (*ibid.*).[2] The emphasis on 'national interests' places EU–Russian relations clearly in the neo-realist realm and depicts the EU as an equal state actor in the partnership, rather than as a complex and multi-layered international actor.

The Russian Strategy document designates trans-border cooperation as a goal of Russia's EU policy and also affirms that 'interested regions of Russia should have the possibility of actively participating in the development of partnership with the European Union in the economic and humanitarian spheres, and in the realisation of programs of cross-border cooperation' (*ibid.*). Euro-regions as well as arrangements for Kaliningrad and special inter-regional structures in the Baltic region are also mentioned, but clearly joint decision-making by regional partners, apart from the overall EU–Russia relationship, is not foreseen. The Strategy also poses the possibility of Kaliningrad serving as a 'pilot region' in EU–Russian relations. In 2003, Russia became a signatory of the 'European outline convention on trans-frontier cooperation between territorial communities or authorities' (Council of Europe 1981) and declarative statements by Russian officials indicate strong support for involvement of regional authorities in the process (Loshchinin 2005: 30–3). While changes have occurred in EU–Russia relations since the issuing of the 1999 policy document, the basic outlines of Russian state priorities remain fairly constant, with a strong emphasis on the potential benefits of economic cooperation, particularly maximising international investment. First Deputy Minister of Foreign Affairs Loshchinin stated that important priorities for regional governments would be the reduction of economic risk for investors and the establishment of a stable legal and political environment, along with appropriate financial incentives to attract outside capital (Loshchinin 2005).

To realise cross-border cooperation, the Russian federal authorities have established a set of institutions to assure coordination of regional and central policies. With the creation of an integrated executive structure and a national patronage system, central authorities may hope that regional authorities will not require or demand additional autonomy to optimise opportunities with EU partners. Putin may be willing to devolve certain arenas to loyal regional leaders, particularly as they relate to economic cooperation, rather than the creation of regional governance structures. However, some regional leaders have expressed discontent with the current parameters for regional involvement, along with demands for a clearer delineation of the areas of regional jurisdiction.

In 1994, a 'Consultative Council of Subjects of the Russian Federation for International and External Economic Links' was formed within the Ministry of Foreign Affairs (Council under the Ministry of Foreign Affairs 1994). The mandate of the body has been to improve coordinating mechanisms between the subjects of the Federation in order to assure a unified direction in Russia's relations with foreign countries and international organisations. At the fifteenth meeting of the group in April 2004, it recommended a more active role for Russian regions in international associations such as the Congress of Local and Regional Organs of Europe, the Assembly of Regions of Europe, and the Assembly of Border Regions of Europe, as well as measures to improve the investment climate in Russian regions (Kuz'min 2005). The sixteenth session of the Consultative Council dealt specifically with increasing the effectiveness of cross-border and inter-regional cooperation of Russian regions (Council under the Ministry of Foreign Affairs 2005a). In 2003, the president directed that an additional body be constituted, namely the Council of Heads of Subjects of the Russian Federation within the Foreign Ministry, to provide a forum for discussion of external political and foreign relations of the regions. The Council includes a rotation of seven regional heads (one from each federal district), and representatives of the presidential administration and of federal ministries and departments; its operation includes the formation of working groups.

The working groups have not, however, been silent in their concerns about the role of regions in cross-border cooperation. A particularly substantive and interesting report issued from a working group of the Council in January 2005. It is clear from this and other documents that the primary purpose of cross-border cooperation is defined as the solution of practical problems, such as stimulating economic development and job creation, attracting foreign investment, and nurturing trade relations. The working group document follows the official Russian government line in supporting the notion of strategic partnership and a relationship based primarily on interests, rather than values. While noting that the federal government encourages regional contacts, the document cites several key deficiencies from the perspective of regional governments. One of these issues is avoiding 'the development of contradictions between federal and regional interests', which will require the Ministry of Foreign Affairs to consider the interests of border regions in developing relations with neighbouring states. The report describes as counterproductive 'the current state of affairs, where regions of north-western Russia actively prepare themselves for participation in programs of the EU, at the same time that the federal centre does not express support for these initiatives' (Council under the Ministry of Foreign Affairs 2005b: 6). On a similar note, the working group proposes that representatives of executive organs of border regions should participate in the work of state commissions carrying out negotiations with Latvia and Estonia (*ibid.*: 13).

The report also notes that federal law is becoming more restrictive in terms of possibilities offered for regions to finance cross-border initiatives. Regional governments are not permitted to use their own resources to finance activities with counterparts abroad, and are limited to financing cross-border economic agreements. The authors complain that the Ministry does not provide the practical information required by regions to develop partnerships, that federal funds committed to projects are not always provided, and that regions often lack the resources needed to match EU funding commitments (*ibid.*: 26–7). Additional evidence of discontent of regional authorities appears elsewhere. Municipalities as well as regional leaders express frustration at overcoming the numerous obstacles involved in establishing relations with foreign partners and sometimes find back door methods of avoiding the requirement for federal approval (Sas 2002).

In addition, the Council of the Federation (the upper house of the Russian legislature) adopted a resolution in June 2005 bemoaning the inadequate legal basis for cross-border cooperation, particularly with

Commonwealth of Independent States (CIS) partners. The resolution calls on the government to take measures to fulfil its obligations in relation to the European framework convention on cross-border cooperation as well as other supportive international agreements, and also calls on the government to adhere to the second protocol of this convention which would broaden the legal foundation for participation of municipal formations in border cooperation (Parliamentary Newspaper 2005). The Council of the Federation also proposed a law, sent forward to the Duma for consideration, 'On cross-border cooperation in the Russian Federation', on 15 July 2004 (Federation Council 2004), which provides a clear delineation of the jurisdictions of federal, regional, and local organs in cross-border activities. The draft law did not receive the support of the government and the official government opinion asserted that 'organs of state power of the subjects of the Russian Federation have in their jurisdiction the right to undertake negotiations with foreign partners and also the consultation of agreements with them about realising international and external economic ties only with the agreement of the Government of the Russian Federation' (Zhukov 2004). The law was not dealt with further in 2005, although V. V. Loshchinin, First Deputy Minister of Foreign Affairs, affirmed in January 2005 that work would be done to produce a law in this area (Loshchinin 2005: 33). However, as of October 2007, nothing had been done to move the process along; the draft legislation was still indicated as included in the programme for decisions of the Duma in November 2007.[3]

This account suggests that regional leaders, who are often receptive and supportive of cross-border economic cooperation, are restricted in their ability to realise these opportunities due to legal restrictions and the demands of political loyalty to Moscow. In the case of the Kaliningrad oblast, from a federal perspective, both the risks and opportunities of cross-border cooperation are potentially higher than for most other regions, given Kaliningrad's potential isolation from the mainland and the possibility that increased regional interaction with international partners could generate spillover from the economic realm to the political (see also chapter 8 in this volume).

Kaliningrad: a special case?

In terms of its geographical location, Kaliningrad stands in the strongest position of any Russian region to maximise the benefits of EU cross-border cooperation. However, as noted above, other factors may reduce the locational advantage; these factors are both economic and political. Consistent with Krätke's findings, Kuz'min and Fazel'ianov point out that the most attractive Russian regions for foreign investors are industrially developed regions and those with rich natural resources. They also note that border regions, which are often economically depressed, fall into the group of regions least attractive to investors. In a typology of regions, the authors place Kaliningrad oblast in the second least attractive group, including regions that are 'export oriented, located near to international transport corridors with relatively developed market infrastructure' (Kuz'min and Fazel'ianov 2005: 50). This places Kaliningrad oblast in the same category with regions such as Stavropol krai, Krasnodar krai, Novgorod oblast, and Rostov oblast (*ibid.*). Creation of a Free Economic Zone and later a Special Economic Zone in Kaliningrad offered incentives to mitigate some of the region's economic disadvantages as a site for Western trade/investment, and the Russian federal government has generally been supportive of these efforts.

Political and economic factors affecting Kaliningrad's relations with the EU often cannot be clearly distinguished. Conflict between federal and regional authorities occurred in the 1990s over the degree of authority granted to the oblast in relation to custom and tax issues (Fairlie and Sergounin 2001: 152–4). Another intersection between the economic and the political has to do with cross-border disparities in the standard of living, for the latter may have economic roots with political implications. Therefore, while EU projects – such as several sponsored by TACIS – address these issues through efforts to improve the infrastructure, social and health policies, educational levels or environmental quality, they have a double-edged political side. First, they can help to stabilise the border environment and prevent popular discontent from accompanying increased awareness of relative disadvantage. On the other hand, cross-border regional cooperation can take on a life of its own. As contacts develop, they may serve to empower local civil society, as well as bringing economic benefits. In this way they may have the unintended consequence of strengthening coalitions to adjust internal power relations in Russia, or, at an extreme, to support secession of Kaliningrad from Russia. Fairlie and Sergounin (2001:140) note that 'Kaliningrad is currently perceived as the most pro-Western or cosmopolitan region in the country'. As a counter reaction, regional leaders may encourage and find fertile ground for what Joel Moses (2004: 108) calls populist xenophobia.

It is political factors that give the Russian government special concern that might lead it to be more restrictive in offering any autonomous role to regional officials in Kaliningrad than elsewhere. Because of the region's geographic separation from the rest of the country, it could more easily deviate from aspects of central policy, embodying all the risks that characterise border regions in general. This might include 'political uncertainty from its isolation, the economic dependency on its surrounding cross-national area, the social problems from its vulnerability, the ambiguity in the population's loyalty to and identity with Russia, and the leadership's populist xenophobia' (*ibid.*: 109), as well as some additional ones like separatist tendencies. The Russian government has kept a close eye on the oblast, retaining more significant political control and developing federal policies directed at the region (Fairlie and Sergounin 2001: 162–3; Kommersant 2001). Several authors raise the possibility that Kaliningrad could serve as a model for reshaping federal–regional relations in Russia, a perspective that Moscow would likely view with concern (Fairlie and Sergounin 2001: 141).

Motivations of local politicians and the Russian government could well diverge. Putin's efforts to institute a vertical alignment of power involve an effort to bring these interests into congruence. Actions under Putin's tenure indicated a desire to install a loyal political elite in the region that can take advantage of economic opportunities without risking political deviation. The defeat of Leonid Gorbenko in gubernatorial elections in 2000 apparently pleased Putin, and Gorbenko's replacement, Vladimir Egorov, expressed support for expanded European connections while working within the parameters of federal policy. Moses (2004: 127) credits Egorov's strategy with shifting Moscow's attitude towards Kaliningrad to 'an intent to accommodate rather than rule Kaliningrad'. Observers have variously interpreted the appointment, in July 2001, of a special deputy for Kaliningrad to oversee federal ministries and agencies. However, Evgeny Vinokurov (2004: 18) suggests a gradual transformation of Russian thinking after 2000, with Kaliningrad starting to be viewed as 'a connecting chain in the framework of EU–Russian dialogue' where 'geo-economic motivations push aside geopolitical considerations'. Similarily, Foreign Minister Sergei Lavrov (2005) stated it this way while in Kaliningrad on 27 May 2005: 'Reliable and strong borders are not an obstacle to the widest possible investment, trade, and economic cooperation.'

In 2005, Egorov did not request renewal as governor, and the Russian media speculated that Moscow did not favour Egorov because he was not a member of United Russia (Regnum 2006c). In September of 2005, Georgii Boos, a member of the presidium of the United Russia faction and deputy chair of the Duma at the federal level, was 'parachuted' in from Moscow to be governor of the region, even though local contenders would have been available and the media reported minimal support for him among the Kaliningrad elite (Regnum 2005). Boos has indicated his support for the integration of Russian business with the global economy, creating a two-way street on what is now a preferential window in Kaliningrad oblast for European business interests wishing to enter Russia (Rodin 2005). However, local business elites may be more concerned that his links to Moscow will mean benefits for Moscow-based business interests at the expense of local firms. Local firms might, in fact, have a greater interest in forging cross-border connections with EU partners than would their economically stronger Moscow rivals. At the same time, media commentary suggests that Boos and the United Russia faction are developing a loyal patronage structure within the regional legislature (Riabushev 2005). According to Regnum news agency, in March 2006 Boos evoked the danger of German-instigated separatist sentiments 'under the aegis of integrating processes' (Regnum 2006b). To place these developments within the context of our analysis of centre–regional relations, a relationship of clientelistic dependence between the Kaliningrad elite and

Moscow has been put in place to permit flexibility in economic matters while minimising political risks, including risks which could arise from efforts by loyal politicians to curry favour with electoral or other lobbying groups within the region. A side-effect might be to favour Russian interests from outside the region, which have Moscow linkages. At the same time, local observers have speculated that Boos' last-minute cancellation of a meeting with Lithuanian president Valdas Adamkus in February 2006 had less to do with reported ill health than with a call from Moscow (Regnum 2006a). If this interpretation is correct, even Boos apparently almost overstepped the bounds of acceptable independent action in this case.

Tools of soft control over the Kaliningrad Duma were evidenced in the March 2006 elections for that body. In that contest, competition was controlled in a manner congruent with electoral policies that have been emerging throughout the Federation since 2003. United Russia's dominance was assured not through overt electoral fraud, but through control of media and information, selective enforcement of the electoral law against opposition parties, and use of the 'administrative' resource, which involves distribution of selective incentives to stimulate political loyalty. The 16.5 per cent vote for 'against all' in the regional elections in Kaliningrad reflected a good deal of popular alienation from the process. Overall the elected legislature appears to be an ineffective tool of public accountability (Königsberger Express 2006). Non-traditional forms of protest, such as the road blockage by truck drivers[4] because of concern about changes introduced with the law on the Special Economic Zone in effect as of 1 April 2006 (Russian Gazette 2006), may be less easy to control with 'soft' power tools. However, when conflict goes to the street, this may be destabilising, potentially undermining efforts to increase the confidence of foreign partners and potential investors.

Conclusion

Russian federal authorities are resistant to multi-level governance within their own country, and insist on Russian state sovereignty in Russia's relations with the EU and other international actors. The EU has a more complex set of goals, some gravitating in the direction of opening borders, others concerned with limiting security risks. Putin made efforts to entrench a national patronage system that links regional elites to the federal government or presidential administration, and if eventually successful, then it may be possible for the president or his successor to accommodate sufficient regional autonomy within a vertical power structure to take advantage of opportunities offered by EU cross-border programmes. However, the very reason for creating this vertical alignment of executive power is rooted in the centripetal tendencies that are endemic to Russian political life. Kaliningrad is a textbook case, and therefore efforts by the presidential administration to embed the regional elite in the national patronage structure are hardly surprising. The speed with which regional loyalties switched to Putin, to United Russia and to the new centralising *modus vivendi* in Russian regional–federal relations that has unfolded since the year 2000 suggests that most regional leaders are pragmatic, responding to specific incentives in the environment. Thus, if regional leaders, with some degree of popular support, can fashion a mix of resources (including benefits of EU cooperation) to forge new regional power networks, they may well do so.

With the decline of 'conditionality' as a tool used by the EU in its relationship with Russia, it must rely increasingly on specifically fashioned 'carrots' to 'Europeanise' its neighbour. In turn, the problem that faces the Russian leadership and its 'carrot-and-stick' approach *vis-à-vis* the regions was that it might breed shallow roots of loyalty, and other carrots might be more enticing. With the leadership succession connected to the 2008 presidential election and the aftermath of it, the personalistic network established by Putin could come under challenge, producing new openings for regional elites to bargain new benefits. Whether a particular region grasps this opportunity may depend less on geographic location and more on the nature of regional elites and the opportunities they perceive, particularly their openness to outside linkages and their innovative responses to the varying incentive structures they face. The case of Kaliningrad may be a critical test case; not only scholars but Russian leaders will monitor it closely.

Notes

1 A series of mergers of autonomous okrugs into the oblasts or krais within which they are located have resulted in a gradual reduction in the number of federal units.

2 Translations by the author of this and other passages from documents where the Russian version of the document is cited.

3 This was indicated on the website of the State Duma, available on the Internet at http://asozd.duma.gov.ru/intranet (accessed 25 October 2007).

4 'A traffic jam 1 km long was arranged by Kaliningrad vans in protest against the law "On SEZ", March 29', according to reports of the Association of International Experts on the Development of the Kaliningrad Region, available on the Internet at http://kaliningradexpert.org/home. See also Riabushev 2006.

References

Anders, R.-E. (2003), 'Where Russia Meets the EU: Cooperation Across the Russian-Finnish Borderlands', in *New Frontiers of Europe: Opportunities and Challenges*, ed. I. M. Busygina, Moscow, Moscow State Institute of International Relations Russian (Russian Association of International Research): 295–329.

Barbato, M. (2003), *Souveränität im neuen Europa: Der Souveränitätsbegriff im Mehrebenensystem der Europäischen Union* [*Sovereignty in the new Europe: The concept of sovereignty and EU multi-level governance*], Hamburg, Verlag Dr. Kovac.

Bokajlo, W. (2000), 'Polen: Die neuen Woiwodschaften im Europa der Regionen' ['Poland and the new voivodships in the Europe of the regions'], in *Jahrbuch des Föderalismus 2000*, 1, Baden-Baden, Nomos Verlagsgesellschaft: 340–57.

Börzel, T. (2002), *States and Regions in the European Union: Institutional Adaptation in Germany and Spain*, Cambridge, Cambridge University Press.

Browning, C. (2001), 'The Construction of Europe in the Northern Dimension', working papers, *Columbia International Affairs On-line*, December, available on the Internet at www.ciaonet.org/wps/brc02/brc02.html (accessed 25 October 2007).

Browning, C. (2002), 'The Internal/External Security Paradox and the Reconstruction of Boundaries in the Baltic: The Case of Kaliningrad', working papers, *Columbia International Affairs Online*, July, available on the Internet at www.ciaonet .org/wps/brc04/brc04.html (accessed 25 October 2007).

Coalson, R. (2005), 'Mayoral Elections: Democracy's Last Stand?', *RFE/RL Russian Political Weekly*, 5 (4 March): 9.

Council of Europe (1981), 'European outline convention on transfrontier co-operation between territorial communities or authorities', available on the Internet at http://conventions.coe.int/treaty/Commun/QueVoulezVous.asp?NT=106&CM =1&CL=ENG (accessed 25 June 2007).

Council under the Ministry of Foreign Affairs (1994), 'O Konsul'tativnom Sovete sub"ektov Rossiskoi Federatisii po mezhdunarodnym i vneshnekonomicheskim sviaziam pri MID Rossii' ['Consultative Council of Subjects of the Russian Federation for International and External Economic Links, Ministry of Foreign Affairs of Russia'], available on the Internet at www.ln.mid.ru/nsdipecon.nsf/0/43256a0c0033bf7a43256d82003d83e1?OpenDocument (accessed 25 June 2007).

Council under the Ministry of Foreign Affairs (2005a), 'Rekomendatsii uchastnikov 16–ogo zasedaniia Konsul'tatinogo soveta sub"ektov Rossiiskoi Federatsii po mezh-dunarodnym i vneshneekonomicheskim sviaziam pri MID Rossii' ['Recommendations of the participants of the 16th session of the Advisory council of the subjects of the Russian Federation on international and foreign economic relations under the Russian Ministry of Foreign Affairs'], *Vneshneekonomicheskie sviazi [Foreign economic relations]*, April, available on the Internet at eer.ru/image/eer_magazine_16.pdf (accessed 25 October 2007).

Council under the Ministry of Foreign Affairs (2005b), Council of Heads of the Subjects of the Russian Federation, Ministry of Foreign Affairs of Russia, Report of the Working Group, 'O perspektivnykh napravelniiakh razvitiia mezhdunarodnykh i vneshneekonomicheskikh sviazei sub"ektov Rossisskoi Federtsiia s gosudarsrvami Evropeiskogo soiuza, Sovetom Evropy i ego strukturami' ['On prospective directions of international and foreign economic relations of the subjects of the Russian Federation with the EU member states, the Council of Europe and its structures'], 14 January, available on the Internet at www.ln.mid.ru/nsdipecon.nsf/0/fa4538b7cf4b0a12c3256f89002d5d1d?OpenDocument (accessed 15 June 2006, translated by the author).

DeBardeleben, J. (2007), 'Public Attitudes Toward EU–Russian Relations: Knowledge, Values, and Interests', in *The Boundaries of EU Enlargement: Finding a Place for Neighbours*, ed. Joan DeBardeleben, Houndsmill, Palgrave Macmillan: 70–91.

Dmitriyev, I. (2007), '"Mayors for Hire" Program Behind Kremlin Shake-up', *The Moscow News Weekly*, 21 June 2007, available on the Internet at http://mnweekly.rian .ru/politics/20070621/55258982.html (accessed 26 October 2007).

EU–Russia Strategy (1999), 'Strategiia razvitiia otnoshenii Rossiiskoi Federatsii s Evropeiskim Soiuzom na srednesrochnuiu perspektivy (2000–2010 gody)' ['Medium-term Strategy for Development of Relations between the Russian Federation and the European Union (2000–2010)'], available on the Internet at http://presidency .finland.fi/doc/liite/russiaru.rtf (accessed 25 October 2007).

Fairlie, L. D. and A. Sergounin (2001), *Are Borders Barriers? EU Enlargement and the Russian Region of Kaliningrad*, Helsinki, Finnish Institute of International Affairs.

Fallend, F., D. Aigner, and A. Mühlböck (2002), '"Europäisierung" der lokalen Politik? Der Einfluss der Europäischen Union auf Politiknetzwerke und Entscheidungsprozesses in der lokalen Wirtschaft, Beschäftigungs- and Arbeitsmarktpolitik in Österreich' ['"Europeanising" local politics? The EU's impact on policy networks and decision-making in Austria's local economy, employment and labour policy], in Europäisches Zentrum für Föderalismus-Forschung Tübingen, *Jahrbuch des Föderalismus 2002*, Baden-Baden, Nomos Verlagsgesellschaft.

Federation Council (2004) of the Federal Assembly of the Russian Federation, 'O proektefederal'nogo zakona, "O prigranichnom sotrudnichestve v Rossiiskoi Federatsii,"' ['Regulation of the Federaton Council "On the project of the Federal Law on the border cooperation in the Russian Federaton"'], available on the Internet at http://asozd.duma.gov.ru/intranet/kom16.nsf/I/ABC14EFFCE70A15AC3256F0000347900 ?OpenDocument (accessed 15 June 2006).

Hale, H. (2005), 'Regime Cycles: Democracy, Autocracy, and Revolution in Post-Soviet Eurasia', *World Politics*, 58(1): 133–65.

Hooghe, L. (1996), 'Introduction: Reconciling EU-wide Policy and National Diversity', in *Cohesion Policy and European Integration: Building Multi-Level Governance*, ed. L. Hooghe, Oxford, Oxford University Press: 1–26.

Hooghe, L. and G. Marks (2001), *Multi-Level Governance and European Integration*, Lanham, Boulder, New York, Oxford, Rowman & Littlefield Publishes, Inc.

Hubel, H. (2005), 'The European Union and Post-Soviet Russia as Direct Neighbours', in *Soft or Hard Borders? Managing the Divide in an Enlarged Europe*, ed. Joan DeBardeleben, Aldershot, Ashgate: 69–84.

Kaveshnikov, N. and O. Potemkina (2003), 'Rational Insight or Political Kitsch? Dividing Lines Existing or Imaginary, EU–Russia: Co-operation or …?', in *New Frontiers of Europe: Opportunities and Challenges*, ed. I. M. Busygina, Moscow, Moscow State Institute of International Relations (Russian Association of International Research): 330–49.

Kommersant (2001), 'Kontseptsiia federal'noi sotsial'no-ekonomicheskoi politiki v otnoshenii Kaliningradskoi oblasti' ['The concept of the federal social-economic policy concerning the Kaliningrad Region'], *Kommersant*, 20 March, available on the Internet at www.kommersant.ru/ documents.html?year=2001 (accessed 25 October 2007).

Königsberger Express (2006), 'Wahlsieg für "Einiges Russland" und "Gegen-Alle-Partei"' ['"United Russia" and "Against-all" party win elections'], *Königsberger Express*, 4 (April), available on the Internet at www.koenigsberger-express.com/main/show _artikel.php?id=631&kat=38 (accessed 25 October 2007).

Kopstein, J. and D. A. Reilly (2000), 'Geographic Diffusion and the Transformation of the Postcommunist World', *World Politics* 53(1): 1–37.

Krok-Paszkowska, A. and J. Zielonka (2005), 'The European Union's Policies Toward Russia', in *Russia's Engagement with the West: Transformation and Integration in the Twenty-First Century*, ed. A. J. Motyl, B. A. Ruble, and L. Shevtsova, Armonk (NY) and London, M. E. Sharpe: 151–69.

Krätke, S. (1999), 'Regional Integration or Fragmentation? The German–Polish Border Region in a New Europe', *Regional Studies*, 33(7): 631–41.

Kuz'min, V. I. (2005), 'Konsul'tativnyi sovet sub"ektov Rossiiskoi Federatsii po mezhdunarodnym i vneshneekonomicheskim sviaziam pri MID Rossii' ['Advisory council of the subjects of the Russian Federation on foreign economic relations under the Ministry of Foreign Affairs'], *Vneshnekonomicheskie sviazi* [*Foreign economic relations*], 4 (April): 36–7, available on the Internet at www.eer.ru/image/eer_magazine_16.pdf (accessed 15 June 2006).

Kuz'min V. I., and E. M. Fazel'ianov (2005), 'Vneshnie investitsionnye sviazi i regional'-noe razvitie: problemy i tendentsii' ['Foreign investment ties and regional development: problems and trends'], *Vneshnekonomicheskie sviazi* [*Foreign economic relations*], 8 (December): 50–3, available on the Internet at www.eer.ru/image /eer_magazine_16.pdf (accessed 15 June 2006).

Lankina, T. (2005), 'President Putin's Local Government Reforms', in *The Dynamics of Russian Politics, Volume 2: Putin's Reform of Federal-Regional Relations*, ed. P. Reddaway and R. W. Orrtung, Lanham (MD), Rowman & Littlefield.

Lavrov, S. (2005), 'Transcript of Remarks and Replies to Russian Media Questions by Minister of Foreign Affairs of the Russian Federation, Sergey Lavrov, Following Visit to Kaliningrad Region', Kaliningrad, 27 May, Association of International Experts on the Development of the Kaliningrad Region, available on the Internet at http://kaliningradexpert.org/news/kaliningrad?from=140 (accessed 15 June 2006).

Loshchinin, V. V. (2005), 'Rol' MID Rossii v razvitii mezhdunarodnykh i vneshneeko-nomicheskikh sviazei sub"ektov Rossiiskoi Federatsii' ['The role of the Ministry of foreign affairs in the development of international and foreign economic relations of the subjects of the Russian Federation'], *Vneshnekonomicheskie sviazi* [*Foreign economic relations*], 1 (January): 30–3, available on the Internet at www.eer.ru/image /eer_magazine_12.pdf (accessed 25 October 2007).

Moses, J. C. (2004), 'The Politics of Kaliningrad Oblast: A Borderland of the Russian Federation', *The Russian Review*, 63(1): 107–29.

Parliamentary Newspaper (2005), 'O nekotorykh problemakh realizatsii Kontsepsii prigranichnogo sotrudichestva v Rossiiskoi Federatsii' ['On the few problems in the realisation of the concept of border cooperation of the Russian Federation'], *Parliamentskaia gazeta* [*Parliamentary newspaper*], 7 (June): 17.

Putin, V. (2004), 'Vystuplenie na rashirennom zasedanii Pravitel'stva s uchastiem glav sub"ektov Rossiiskoi Federatsii' ['Speech on the enlarged session of the Government with the participation of the heads of Russian Federation's subjects'], Moscow, 13 September, available on the Internet at www.kremlin.ru/appears/2004/09/13 /1514_type63374type63378type82634_76651.shtml (accessed 25 October 2007).

Regnum (2005), 'Kaliningradskie deputaty ne khotiat "variaga" na post gubernatora: opros IA REGNUM' ['Kaliningrad's deputies do not want an outsider as the governor: opinion poll by IA REGNUM'], Regnum information agency, 19 August, available on the Internet at www.regnum.ru/news/499547.html (accessed 25 October 2007).

Regnum (2006a), 'Otmena vstrechi Georgiia Boosa s Baldasom Adamkusom: versii kalin-ingradskikh politologov' ['Cancelling the meeting of Georgii Boos and Valdas Adamkus: the versions of Kaliningrad politologists'], Regnum information agency, 13 February.

Regnum (2006b), 'Boos opasaetsia vnedreniia v umy kaliningradtsev separativskikh nastroenii so stronony FRG' ['Boos is afraid of the penetration of separatist attitudes into the minds of Kaliningraders inspired by the FRG'], Regnum information agency, 29 March, available on the Internet at www.regnum.ru/news/614198.html?forprint (accessed 25 October 2007).

Regnum (2006c), 'Kaliningradskuiu oblast vozglavit nepremenno edinoross?' ['Will the Kaliningrad region be led by the member of the United Russia?'], Regnum information agency, 25 August, available on the Internet at www.regnum.ru/news/502136.html (accessed 25 October 2007).

Riabushev, A. (2005), 'Bol'shoi Boos malen'koi territorii' ['The big Boos of the small terri-tory'], *Nezavisimaia gazeta* [*Independent newspaper*], 11 November, available on the Internet at www.ng.ru./printed/63550 (accessed 25 October 2007).

Riabushev, A. (2006), 'Dal'noboishchiki vziali Kaliningrad v kol'tso' ['Long-distance truck drivers have surrounded Kaliningrad'], *Nezavisimaia gazeta* [*Independent newspaper*],

30 March, available on the Internet at www.ng.ru/printed/66587 (accessed 25 October 2007).

Rodin, I. (2005), 'Boos zakroet okno v Evropy, no otkroet ulitsu' ['Boos will shut the window to Europe opening a street instead'], *Nezavisimaia gazeta* [*Independent newspaper*], 31 August, available on the Internet at www.ng.ru/printed/60990 (accessed 25 October 2007).

Russian Gazette (2006), 'Ob osoboi ekonomicheskoi zone v Kaliningradskoi oblasti i o vnesenii izmenenii v nekotorye zakonodatel'nye akty Rossiskoi Federatsii', ['On the Special Economic Zone in the Kaliningrad region and on the amendments in legislative acts of the Russian Federation'], Federal law of the Russian Federation from January 10, 2006, *Rossiiskaia gazeta* [*Russian Gazette*], 10 January.

Sas, I. (2002), 'Regiony khotiat sotrudnichat' s zarubezh'em bez kontroliia Moskvy' ['Regions want to cooperate with foreign partners without Moscow's controls'], *Nezavisimaia gazeta* [*Independent newspaper*], 4 July.

Sergounin, A. A. and M. I. Rykhtik (2002), 'Foreign and Security Policies as Legal Problems Between Centre and Regions', Working Paper 22 (March), Zürich, Center for Security Studies and Conflict Research, Eidgenössische Technische Hochschule.

Vinokurov, E. (2004), 'Kaliningrad in the Framework of EU–Russian Relations: Moving Toward Common Spaces', K. U. Leuven, Interbrew Baillet-Latour Working Paper 20 (March), available on the Internet at http://soc.kuleuven.be/iieb/ibl/docs_ibl /WP20–Vinokurov.pdf (accessed 25 October 2007).

Zhukov, A. (2004), 'Ofitsial'nyi otzyv na proekt federal'nogo zakona No 75537–4 "O prigranichnom sotrudnichestve v Rossiskoi Federatsii", vnesennyi Sovetom Federatsii Federal'nogo Sobraniia Rossiskoi Federatsii' ['Official response to the project of the Federal law no.75537–4, tabled by the Federation Council of the Federal Assembly of the Russian Federation'], 30 September, available on the Internet at http://asozd.duma.gov .ru/work/dz.nsf/ByID/835C98F73674666B432571BB005D77A9?OpenDocument (accessed 25 October 2007).

Stefan Meister

6

Federalism in Russia: opportunity or constraint for Kaliningrad?

Introduction

In the context of political and economic transformation, post-Soviet Russia has been shaped mainly through two processes. First, the disintegration of the Soviet Union was followed by the decentralisation and regionalisation of its successor state, the Russian Federation (RF). Through the 1990s, the weak central government was in conflict with increasingly powerful regions, as regional elites were becoming influential in both the domestic and foreign policy of the Russian Federation. Second, the end of the Soviet Union was often described as an economic, political and social defeat in the face of global competition. As a consequence of this opening up of the country, international processes and institutions were increasingly influential, and Russia became vulnerable to the external environment.

Internationalisation describes changes to the global environment of nation-states, as well as the increasing vulnerability of political and economic state systems to those changes (Schmidt 1995: 445). Interdependence between national economies, political decisions and societies is growing, yet the influence of internationalisation is filtered through national institutions that reflect historical experiences, political cultures and the preferences of domestic players (Keohane and Milner 1996: 10). To describe the effects of internationalisation (and Europeanisation) we have to analyse the influences of political preferences and institutions inside nation-states (*ibid.*: 15).

Both international and domestic processes have influenced the economic transformation, democratisation and institution-building of the post-1990 Russian state. The relations of centre and regions in post-Soviet Russia can be seen as the basic prism for these processes in the domestic context. Since the declaration of sovereignty of the Russian Socialist Federal Soviet Republic within the Soviet Union in 1990, there have been three main phases of centre–region relations in post-Soviet Russia (see Busygina 1998a: 1101). From the declaration of sovereignty in June 1990 to the presidential decree of the constitution in December 1993, there was a period of fragmentation of the common economic and legal space. From 1994 to 1999, durable conflicts between a weak federal centre and autonomous regions were characterised by a bilateral negotiation process and a lack of federal legislation. The result has been the strengthening of an 'asymmetric federalism'.[1] Since 2000, there has been a consolidation of presidential power resources and the integration of regional executive and legislative bodies in a central vertical alignment of power, followed by the standardisation of federal relations and the concentration of power by the president.

Federalism in Russia is far from being consolidated although it has reached some minimal standards like 'shared rule' and 'divided rule'. This is due to changing power constellations between centre and regions, problems of incomplete institution-building, and different attitudes of the players towards federal norms and legitimacy patterns. The balance of power between the centre and regions in post-Soviet Russia is determined by several factors, such as the capacity of the presidential regime and federal institutions; the economic, political and geographic resources of the regions; and the constitution of regional interests (Heinemann-Grüder 2004: 339). Ultimately, these factors define the space that the Russian regions[2] have for domestic and foreign policy, as well as offering a matrix for analysis.

The disintegration of the Soviet Union and the subsequent transformation of the Russian Federation have had a strong impact on the development of the Kaliningrad region. Kaliningrad's special situation as an exclave of the RF is directly connected with international and domestic processes. In 1991, the Baltic States became independent and in May 2004, along with Poland, they became members of the EU. In this 'hot phase' of the enlargement process (1999–2004), the small region of Kaliningrad became relevant for EU–Russia relations and a focus of political debate (Timmermann 2000).

This chapter analyses the development of Russian federalism, and the related domestic factors that influence the interaction of regions with the external environment. It will use the example of Kaliningrad as a special case of a Russian exclave inside the enlarged EU. The main questions to be answered are: What are the opportunities for the Kaliningrad oblast within the federal system to independently develop ties and modes of cooperation with foreign players? Which domestic processes, players, and institutions influence the scope of foreign cooperation and the attitudes of the regional elites?

Russian federalism from Yeltsin to Putin – setting the institutional patterns

The development of centre–region relations

The Russian Federation is a multi-ethnic state with huge regional disparities in socio-economic development, population density and natural resources. At the beginning of the 1990s, the federal republics played a major role in the processes of decentralisation and regionalisation. The Federation Treaty of 1992 fixed the different types of federal entities along ethnic lines and created an asymmetric federalism (Busygina 1998b: 242). The Constitution of December 1993 (designed by the presidential administration) was supposed to establish symmetric federal relations (Russian Federation 1993: Art. 5.1). President Yeltsin attempted to stop the fragmentation of the common economic and political space and to strengthen presidential power (Heinemann-Grüder 2000: 176). But the 'superpresidentialism'[3] of the Constitution did not reflect the real power situation at this time. In order to reduce the pressure of the regional elites, the presidential administration – in accordance with the Russian Constitution (Russian Federation 1993: Art. 11.3) – began negotiating bilateral treaties in February of 1994. These treaties arranged joint tasks between the centre and the regions, as well as delegating federal tasks to the states. Also during the mid-1990s, economic power (especially export-oriented industries and natural resources) began to play an increasing and decisive role in obtaining (tax) privileges.[4] The conflict between the centre and the regions – and between the regions themselves – became a conflict of economic distribution. When Vladimir Putin became president, these competing economic interests were a main reason for the regions' inability to build horizontal coalitions.

Putin came to power using the second war in Chechnya as a strong signal against separatism and disintegration (see Ortung 2000: 14). Consequently, his first steps as Russian president were federal reforms to strengthen his own position and that of federal institutions in the regions. He introduced seven federal districts led by presidential envoys, with their own bureaucracies. He changed the composition of the Federation Council, and eliminated the head of the regional executive and legislative from the second chamber. A new bill empowered him to remove the governors and presidents of the republics (*ibid.*: 15–16). Putin successfully subjugated the national media under state control, and by founding the new party Unity (later United Russia), the presidential administration consolidated control over the national legislature, and to a lesser degree, the regional parliaments. However, regional leaders still controlled administrative resources and the media within their regions, so United Russia was not successful everywhere (Chebankova 2005; Glosov 2005). Putin then abolished elections for the heads of the regional executives following the 2004 Beslan attack, further strengthening the vertical alignment of power.

These reforms helped to achieve the standardisation of a common political and economic space. The new envoys started to enact presidential policy in the regions, control the implementation of presidential decisions, impose staff policy in presidential interest, and inform the president about regional developments (Kryschtanowskaja 2005: 129). Changing the 'Law on the principles of the organisation of the legislative and executive state order' (July 2003) led to a clear limitation of joint tasks and a restriction of bilateral treaties (Heinemann-Grüder 2004: 353).

Responsibility for foreign policy – the constitutional background

According to the Constitution, the federal centre has sole responsibility in all relations with other states: for war and peace, foreign economic relations, defence and security policy, and the status and security of national borders (Russian Federation 1993: Art. 71). The centre and the regions have joint responsibility for the coordination of international and foreign economic relations of the federal entities and the fulfilment of international treaties (*ibid.*: Art. 72). The regions' sole responsibilities are those that are not either a federal or joint responsibility (*ibid.*: Art. 73). This general formulation in the Constitution, together with weak institutions, has created permanent centre–region conflicts.

In the mid-1990s, regional administrations were able to make decisions about national borders or foreign policy, normally prerogatives of a sovereign state (Kryschtanowskaja 2005: 124). The regions' interests in foreign relations focused on trade, direct investments, or ways to bring foreign capital into the region. Between 1991 and 1995, Russian regions signed more than 300 trade agreements with foreign countries. In its treaties with the regions, Moscow permitted seven federal republics and all the oblasts except Kaliningrad, Orenburg and Krasnodar to conduct some foreign economic relations (Schneider 2002: 19).[5] It was especially these border regions that were allowed less room for their own foreign relations because of the Kremlin's fear of disintegration. By strengthening the vertical alignment of power and federal institutions in the regions, Moscow was able to regain control of foreign relations in all parts of the country.

Kaliningrad in centre–region relations

Three groups of Russian regions are the most important sub-national actors in the international arena: export-oriented regions, ethnic republics and border regions. Their ability to develop international relations is dependent on the interest level of the regional elites,[6] along with their ability to bargain resources[7] towards the federal centre (see Makarychev 2000: 15–18).

Russia has forty-five border regions with sixteen neighbouring countries.

Both a border region and an exclave, Kaliningrad is a special case because it has no direct geographical connection to mainland Russia and is surrounded by EU member states (Vinokurov 2005: 56–74). The development of the region depends on the ability of regional and federal politics to form a strategy for integration in the Baltic Sea region without disintegration from Russia. Its main 'resource' is its geographic proximity to the EU and the interest of these neighbouring EU countries in modernising the infrastructure of the region and reducing differences in standards of living.

Federal policy towards Kaliningrad

Federal policy towards Kaliningrad is not so much a response to its exclave situation, but rather a result of Russian domestic networks and social attitudes. In the 1990s there was a Russia-wide political discourse on territorial integrity combined with issues of identity and Russia's place in the world (Karabeshkin and Wellmann 2004: 9–10). Until 1999, the federal government had little interest in developing Kaliningrad (Holtom 2002: 41–2). Moscow had no vision for the oblast, but at the same time, the federal government was afraid of separatist movements because of the region's economic and political decline.

In early 1996, Kaliningrad signed a power-sharing treaty with Moscow. This treaty confirmed trade and investment privileges (a Tax Free Zone) within the Special Economic Zone (SEZ) of Kaliningrad. Furthermore, the treaty allowed the regional administration to sign agreements with other Russian regions, federal ministries and institutions within their competence, although competence was not explicitly defined (Treaty 2002: Art. 3d). This short treaty only contained specific regulations describing the federal tax privileges. The regional administration is neither defined as a cooperation partner for federal policy, nor as an independent actor. The status of the region was regulated by the president and the federal government.[8] The federal government provided Kaliningrad with less room than other Russian regions for autonomous politics in the 1990s even though the federal government had no strategy to develop the exclave region.

From FEZ to SEZ – the absence of a consensus

Federal development policy was mainly intended to give Kaliningrad a special economic status. With the introduction of the Free Economic Zone (FEZ) 'Jantar' in 1991, Moscow wanted to support the transformation and economic reforms in the Kaliningrad region through privileges for foreign trade and federal investment. By 1996, the insurmountable conflict between regional and federal interests led Boris Yeltsin to abolish the FEZ and introduce a Special Economic Zone, formalised by federal law (Russian Federal Law 1996). Compared to the FEZ, federal limitations were stronger in the SEZ. The SEZ limited Kaliningrad's foreign policy, increased federal border control, and introduced licensing of key industries like amber mining, energy supply, transportation, the weapons industry and even the media.

With the new SEZ law, the only privilege for registered companies existed under the special customs regime. To bring Kaliningrad in line with the other regions of Russia, the federal government decided not to grant any special privileges concerning taxation, immigration, residence, or land ownership. However, implementing the legal framework of the new economic zone was problematic because federal ministries in Kaliningrad operated under their own laws in conflict with the SEZ. Such practices resulted in legal uncertainties about the SEZ and frequent changes in the rules that affected the investment environment (Barre 2005: 1). The SEZ regime was meant to alleviate the economic consequences of transformation for the region and the problems connected to its geographic location, yet the result was a pronounced structural deformation of the regional economy. The SEZ inadvertently rewarded trade and import activities over production and exports, resulting in currency speculation, tax evasion and customs fraud (Karabeshkin and Wellmann 2004: 49).

Once Vladimir Putin came to power, there was a long debate about the format of the SEZ, which ended with a reform draft in 2005 and a new law in April 2006 (Russian Federal Law 2006). The management of the new law is now divided into federal and regional parts. Appointed by the federal government, an 'authorised body' ensures that the SEZ is operating according to federal laws and coordinates communication between the Kaliningrad administration and the federal executive authorities. The administration of the SEZ is part of the oblast administration, although its head is appointed (and dismissed) by the governor only with the consent of the head of the authorised body (Russian Federal Law 2006: Chap. 1, Art. 3). The role of the authorised body is vaguely defined. To enjoy the privileges of the SEZ, a participant now has to invest at least 150 million roubles (approximately €4.4 million), which excludes small- and medium-sized businesses (*ibid.*: Chap. 2, Art. 10.4). The current Governor Georgii Boos considers it a success that the administration of the SEZ is not in the hands of Moscow but of regional officials (Königsberger Express 2006a: 4). A further innovation is the possibility of simplified travel and visa regulations for foreign participants of the SEZ (Russian Federal Law 2006: Chap. 5, Art. 19). With these regulations, the new SEZ law improves the existing legislation, but a better investment climate in the region will primarily result from clearer procedures and the reduction of numerous administrative barriers.

A new federal policy towards Kaliningrad

With the change of the presidency from Boris Yeltsin to Vladimir Putin, federal interest in the region has increased. In 2002, the power-sharing treaty from 1996 was abolished (Treaty 2002). Now only the relevant articles in the Constitution, the SEZ law and, since 2001 a Federal Target Programme, regulate the relationship and responsibilities between Moscow and the region. The region and the transit issue became a focus of presidential policy, especially in the context of EU enlargement. Putin's federal reforms increased the stability and homogeneity of the common political and economic space, as Kaliningrad became a part of Russia-wide discussion over strengthening the presidential vertical alignment of power and federal influence in the regions (Karabeshkin and Wellmann 2004: 27).

In September 2005, Vladimir Putin appointed Georgii Boos as governor. Boos is from the Moscow elite and had occupied the post of the vice-speaker in the State Duma and a key position in the pro-Kremlin United Russia party. This decision strengthened the federal influence on the regional elite and manifested a trend to bring problematic regions or regions of special interest under stronger federal control. With the introduction of seven federal districts in 2000, Kaliningrad joined the North West Federal District with St Petersburg as its capital. Kaliningrad received a special inspector from Moscow in March of 2006, Aleksander Dacyshin, who was responsible for the coordination of all federal power structures and the implementation of federal policy in the region.

From 2000, the Russian Federation developed its own Kaliningrad policy along with the EU–Russia dialogue. After a special meeting about Kaliningrad in the National Security Council, the Russian government adopted the 'Federal Target Programme on the Development of the Kaliningrad region up to 2010' in December of 2001. The programme set the priorities for the region in order to create conditions for sustainable socio-economic development and an attractive investment climate (see Federal Target Programme 2001). It proposed to modernise transport, telecommunications, and tourist infra-structure; to secure the independence of energy supply; to improve the ecological situation; and to extend the production and export potential of the region. The budget amounts to 93 billion roubles (approximately €2.5 billion) with only 8.4 per cent from the federal budget; the remainder from the regional budget, private enterprises, bank loans, and foreign investment (Joenniemi and Sergounin 2003: 101–2).

In the context of a stronger involvement of Kaliningrad in EU–Russia relations, the concept of Kaliningrad as a 'pilot region'[9] between Russia and the EU has been discussed. This concept was drafted by regional experts mostly from Kaliningrad State University 'Immanuel Kant' under the instruc-tion of the regional administration of Governor Vladimir Egorov. The goal of the regional administration was to identify Kaliningrad's position between the EU and Russia and to develop a regional strategy in the context of Russian, regional and international interests. The involvement of the EU or foreign players is part of this conceptual programme, but it emphasises the responsibility of federal and regional administrations. The programme main-tains that Kaliningrad should become a region with strong federal influence, a Special Economic Zone, and well-developed foreign relations (Klemeshev and Fedorov 2004: 41–61). To implement the concept, full integration of

Kaliningrad into the Russian economy and close coordination between the centre and the region is necessary. Although international relations of the Kaliningrad oblast depend on federal policy, regional players should be involved in discussions and meetings between the EU and Russia in order to achieve optimal solutions for the region. Therefore, the authors contend that as a 'region of cooperation', Kaliningrad should be integrated into both the Russian and Baltic/European economic spheres (*ibid.*: 62). In 2003, the regional administration adopted this concept as the 'Strategy for the socio-economic development of the Kaliningrad oblast as a region of cooperation up to 2010'. The Strategy never obtained relevance, because links with strategies and cooperation projects of the neighbouring states and the EU were missing. Moreover, the federal government showed no interest in using this concept, because it focused on the adoption of the new SEZ law (Gutnik and Klemeshev 2006: 347–8).

Since the new SEZ law has been in effect since 1 April 2006, the newly appointed governor and federal inspector for Kaliningrad have increased federal authority over the region. For instance, when Governor Boos travelled to Berlin at the end of January 2006 to promote the advantages of the new SEZ law for foreign investors, he was accompanied not only by his regional ministers, but also by President Putin's special representative to the EU, Sergej Jastrshembsky. The visit of the federal Deputy Minister for Foreign Affairs, Vladimir Titov, to the exclave in March 2006 offered another example of the permanent presence and interest of federal politicians in regional policy. In his speech, Titov declared that the region's relations towards the neighbouring EU countries would be ensured only by his ministry. Clearly, recent federal developments ensure that Kaliningrad's potential to foster its own exclusive international contacts will remain rather limited in scope. The regional administration's attempt to influence the negotiations between Moscow and the EU failed due to a lack of coordination at the federal and European levels.

Economic and political resources of the Kaliningrad region

Kaliningrad has less than one million inhabitants, a small territorial size and an extremely neglected infrastructure, so it is too small to become a commercial outlet or attract significant foreign investment.[10] With structural problems stemming from its former militarisation[11] and planned economy, Kaliningrad suffered an economic crisis during the 1990s that was intensified by its exclave characteristics.

At the beginning of the 1990s, the former strategic importance of Kaliningrad especially hampered the opening of the region to foreign investment. The federal government kept tight economic control of Kaliningrad, not fulfilling investment promises and constantly under-funding the region. Due to its location, the number of federal staff in Kaliningrad was larger than the regional administration, and used half of the staffing budget. The border situation resulted in the regional authorities owning only twelve per cent of public property, the majority belonging to the federal state (Oldberg 2002: 54). Kaliningrad's strategic location and the presence of the military did improve the region's bargaining position with the federal centre, resulting in additional inflows of federal budgetary resources for military and social needs.[12]

The region still maintains close links with the Russian economy and a low level of economic integration with neighbouring countries, so the instability of foreign investment in Kaliningrad is connected to its dependence on the federal economy. Nearly all foreign investments are oriented to the Russian market. Changes to the Russian economic situation or legal system influence foreign investors in Kaliningrad (Bunatjan 2005: 133). Nevertheless, the region is also highly dependent on neighbouring countries, particularly for imports of food, electronic products, and energy. Except for amber, the natural resources of the region are not considerable. There is some brown coal mining, peat harvesting, and oil production (the oil company LUKOIL being the biggest local tax donor), but these are only of regional importance (Knappe 2004: 17–20).[13] Governor Georgii Boos' idea of building an oil refinery in the region has been rejected by oil companies (LUKOIL, Sibneft, Rosneft) because of low profitability (Kaliningrad-aktuell 2006). The oblast's lack of integration, combined with the federal economic policy of the 1990s, has had an extremely negative impact on economic development. Kaliningrad has depended, and still depends, on federal allocations and federal decisions.

One of the main problems of Kaliningrad is energy supply. Approximately 90 per cent of the energy is transported through Lithuania, coming from Leningrad oblast or even Lithuania itself. Four possibilities for securing Kaliningrad's energy supply have been discussed: a new gas power station, a nuclear plant, modernising the energy supply through Lithuania and Belarus, or adopting EU electrification standards. The federal government decided to build a second gas power station (TEC 2), which is one of the most costly options; compared to the price of energy in central Russia, Kaliningrad will pay twice as much (Karabeshkin and Wellmann 2004: 65–6).

The notion of political resources refers to direct access of the regional political elite to the president and his power circle; loyalty to Moscow can be helpful in developing foreign economic relations. Following the difficult relations between the federal government and Leonid Gorbenko (governor from 1996 to 2000), the situation improved under his elected successor Vladimir Egorov. As a former admiral of the Baltic fleet, he was strongly supported by the presidential administration and had good relations with President Putin. Egorov was always part of official Russian delegations to Germany and Poland. Meanwhile, he lobbied intensively for Kaliningrad's interests in neighbouring countries and in Moscow (Moses 2004: 120). Georgii Boos, the current governor, also has excellent ties to the political and economic elites in Moscow. However, the question remains: does he promote Kaliningrad's interests in Moscow or Moscow's interests in Kaliningrad? He is opening up the regional economy, particularly to businesses from Moscow. To sum up, the regional economic resources are weak and the dependency on Moscow by investment in energy supply and infrastructure is high. The governor's good relations to the federal government is helpful for lobbying regional interests and can create some room to manoeuvre in foreign economic cooperation.

The fostering of regional economic interests

Despite the SEZ in the 1990s, foreign investment played only a limited role in the development of the regional economy. Between 1995 and 2001, average annual foreign direct investment never exceeded 10 per cent.[14] Since 2002, there has been a constant increase in foreign investment, similar to the rest of Russia (Bunatjan 2005: 133). While this is a positive development connected to a Russia-wide economic recovery, Kaliningrad ranks only thirty-second of thirty-four Russian regions in terms of foreign investment (*ibid.*: 134). In 2002, foreign direct investment was US$4.6 million. More than half of it came from Cyprus (US$2.9 million) and nearly one third from the Isle of Man (US$1.3 million), both typical destinations for Russian 'flight of capital'. Otherwise, Germany, Poland and Lithuania are the biggest 'real' foreign investors (Stein 2003: 362). The reason for these low direct foreign investments includes the instability of the SEZ law, but it is particularly due to the legal and political situation in the region.

During the privatisation process at the beginning of the 1990s, regional political and economic elites were not very interested in foreign investors. They wanted to control the distribution of the former Soviet economy by themselves. There was the typical post-Soviet symbiosis of regional politics and economy; business was interested in subventions and protectionism and the political elite wanted financial support for election campaigning (*ibid.*: 357). This led to uneven market access, corruption and a lack of transparency. With the first elected governor, corruption, authoritarian leadership, and protectionist policy increased and foreign investment decreased. Gorbenko established a protectionist policy for agricultural products. As the former director of the fishing port, he personally organised arrangements with foreign investors to take over port, oil and amber facilities (Moses 2004: 115). The influence of the regional oligarchs on his successor, Vladimir Egorov, was strong enough to preserve this protectionist policy, particularly for meat and paper production (Stein 2003: 363). Expectations that these policies would end with Governor Boos were not fulfilled. Instead, Boos integrated regional oligarchs into his administration, appointing Jurij Shalimov, the general director of a big agrarian company, as vice-premier, and Sergej Buchelnikov, who was responsible for the building sector in the old government as minister of construction (Government of Kaliningrad oblast 2007). A survey of foreign businessmen has demonstrated that the main obstacles for foreign investors are the instability of customs procedures and legal provisions, difficult bureaucratic procedures, the disinterest of regional bureaucrats, and the deficit of qualified personnel within the administration (Bunatjan 2005: 144–5).

The obstacles to democratic development

An analysis of the democratic development of the region demonstrates certain tendencies. In regional elections, the personality of a candidate tends to be more important than their party platform. Individuals have influenced regional politics since the beginning of the 1990s and even during Soviet times. Political elites have used their influence not for developing the welfare of the region, but for pursuing their own interests. The results are corruption, economic protectionism, populism, and control of and pressure on the media. In one example, Governor Gorbenko received special tax credits from the federal government to encourage the expansion of local enterprises. The enterprises partly repaid the money back to Gorbenko's administration, but he never repaid the federal government (Moses 2004: 114).

Popular response has been low election participation, protest voting, and increasing frustration with regional politics.[15] This situation is exacerbated by the lack of contribution from the current governor to the democratisation of regional politics. Prior to the Duma elections of March 2006, pressure was put on the management of the biggest regional newspaper *Kaliningradskaja Pravda*, as well as independent newspapers like *Kaskad*, *Dvornik* and *Novye Kolesa*. Igor Rostov, the president of the regional branch of the independent media company *Kaskad*, was first replaced and then taken to court. The editor-in-chief of *Kaliningradskaja Pravda*, Tamara Samjantina, also lost her job after she approved a critical article about Governor Boos's initiative to use the regional budget to finance flats for his ministers (Königsberger Express 2006b: 18). During the campaign for the regional Duma election in March of 2006, Boos and Mayor Juri Savenko used administrative resources to show support for the incumbent party United Russia.[16] The two main opponents of United Russia, *Rodina* (Motherland) and *Narodnaja partija* (Party of the People) were disqualified by the court (Nagornych 2006). United Russia now dominates the regional Duma – no real opposition exists any more. Finally, Russian NGOs are no longer allowed to observe elections and the Duma in Kaliningrad made a post-electoral decision to ban the media from its meetings. While strengthening the vertical alignment of power from the federal to the regional executives, the regional administration seems to be more dependent on the federal government than on its voters. The regional political elite are not interested in democratic participation and transparency; instead they ignore popular frustration and remove critical journalists and candidates.

Conclusion

After years of limited federal activity in Kaliningrad, Moscow's interest in the region has increased since Putin became president in 2000. First, the pressure from outside to solve the transit question as well as the social and economic problems in the context of EU enlargement brought Kaliningrad to the Kremlin's attention. Second, the new president's strategic policy to increase federal influence in the regions and to secure the common economic and political space changed Moscow's attitude towards Kaliningrad. However, this centralisation policy also limited the scope of regional elites for an independent domestic and foreign policy. There have been new federal institutions, like the presidential representative in the North West Federal District with a special inspector for Kaliningrad, along with changes to the departments of customs and the energy ministry. These have strengthened federal influence. Georgii Boos was appointed governor because he is loyal to Moscow and can reduce the influence of the regional cartel of elites.

There has been progress in the development of the Russian state, and in the integration of Russian regions within the common economic and legal space, as well as the modernising of infrastructure and administration. Yet augmenting the vertical alignment of power from above with limited control and feedback from local or regional levels is problematic for democratic participation. There will no longer be a state body willing and able to criticise politics at higher levels. Thus, it is vital that the regional executive and legislative can make decisions independent from Moscow that favour the region. As Klemeshev and Fedorov (2004) point out, the 'Federal development programme for Kaliningrad up to 2010' barely involves regional elites. There was neither a debate about this programme nor did regional experts participate in the preparation of the new SEZ; Moscow made the decision and the regional administration was charged with executing it. The programme should more closely match regional and local interests as well as consider the border and exclave situation (*ibid.*: 99).

The counter-productive policy of the regional elites and their attitude towards federal and international financial assistance has also been problematic. Regional elites need to become a real partner for interregional programmes, not merely recipients of federal and international support. A main task of the regional administration is to create a good climate for investment and competition. Throughout the 1990s, they did not use their proximity to the EU for modernising or developing the regional infrastructure and economy, being primarily interested in their own welfare. The inability of regional and federal authorities to develop a common strategy for Kaliningrad has its roots in the diverging interests of different groups, which varies from openness to isolation and protectionism (Averre 2002: 23).

The political elite in Moscow seems to be less concerned with developing Kaliningrad than emphasising Kaliningrad's integral inclusion in the Russian state. The focus on the integrity of the Russian state hinders the intensification of interregional cooperation with neighbouring states. Moscow does not yet have a long term strategy for the region. Implementation instruments have not been fixed and economically dubious projects, like the construction of a new gas power station and gas pipeline, reflect political expedience rather than the best option for regional development. Regulations that make visa entry easier for SEZ participants seem to be a change, but more needs to be done. It is vital that the administration ease travel and visa rules for tourism, improve conditions for investment, and develop stable and transparent legislation.

The regional elite's opportunities for independent interaction with the external environment are limited by the subordination of Kaliningrad to federal structures and stricter presidential control. The federal reforms implemented by President Putin limit the process of regionalisation as well as the space required for autonomous cross-border cooperation between Russian regions. Although Kaliningrad's particular location has generated special attention from the federal government, the result has been more control rather than more openness to foreign cooperation. Therefore, better coordination and strategic planning between Russia's central government and regional administrations are necessary. The future of Kaliningrad's interaction with its immediate neighbourhood depends on federal decision-making, the loyalty of the regional elites, and the personal contacts between Kaliningrad's governor and Moscow. Yet it also depends on the regional elite's attitude and determination to develop good governance and to be a real partner for Moscow and foreign partners.

Notes

1 Characteristic for the Russian state in the era of Boris Yeltsin was a large number of regions, differences of legal status between them, fundamental socio-economic differences, unqualified competences between centre and regions, and a lack of national political integration (Heinemann-Grüder 2001: 78–86).

2 In this paper the term 'region' will be used, in the same sense as Russian academic publications, concurrent with the term 'entity of the federation'. The current Russian state is divided into three levels: the federal (centre or national government), the regional and the local.

3 Yeltsin's constitution can be characterised by a concentration of executive power, a presidential administrative vertical alignment of power, direction and control claims of the president towards the regional administrations, and rule by decree (Heinemann-Grüder 2004: 340).

4 Chechnya is an exception because it is the only region that has not accepted its status as a part of the RF.

5 For more on regional foreign and security policy in the 1990s, see Schneider 2002; Perovic´ 2000.

6 Political interest in foreign relations can include proximity to foreign countries and cooperation along ethnic lines.

7   So-called 'bargaining resources' are raw materials, industrial potential, and ethnicity. They describe the ability of the regional political elite to enter into a bargaining process with the federal government on economic or political privileges like tax allowance, investment privileges, or political manoeuvrability in particular areas of regional politics.

8   Between 1991 and 1998, President Yeltsin and the federal government decided on fifteen normative acts of law for Kaliningrad, which is the highest number for Russian regions at this time (Sergounin 2001: 165).

9   The main idea of this concept is to use Kaliningrad as a testing ground for the modernisation of a Russian region, by adapting European standards and reproducing the results or using the experience for other parts of the RF. Developing new forms of economic cooperation and new principles of economic partnership between Russia and the EU is the medium term goal of the concept (Smorodinskaja 2001).

10   In 2000, Kaliningrad oblast contributed 0.55 per cent to the national industrial production and 0.65 per cent to agricultural production. It received 0.4 per cent of Russia-wide investment (Knappe 2004: 40).

11   This means a high concentration of military in the region and social problems with retired servicemen.

12   Still in 2006, the representative of President Putin in the North West Federal District, Ilja Klebanov, emphasised that the everyday life and the social situation of the military in the regions is of the highest federal interest.

13   Oil production but also the mining of amber and coal are topics of environmental discussions with neighbouring states. The main topic is the environmental threat of Kaliningrad, not its economy.

14   Poland, Latvia, and Estonia reached 20 to 25 per cent of foreign investment in the same period.

15   After the campaign for the Duma election in March of 2006, the voter participation reached only 37 per cent, with 17 per cent of voters selecting 'against all'. 'Against all' was second after the winner United Russia (34 per cent). Low electoral participation gives the new regional parliament limited legitimacy (Kommersant 2006).

16   Governor Georgii Boos and Mayor Juri Savenko promoted United Russia on billboards in the city.

References

Averre, D. L. (2002), 'Security Perception among Local Elites and Prospects for Cooperation across Russia's North-Western Borders', Working Paper 16, Zürich, ETH.

Barre, X. (2005), 'Analysis of the Draft Federal Law "On the Special Economic Zone of the Oblast of Kaliningrad"', Moscow, RECEP.

Bunatjan, G. Z., ed. (2005), *Kaliningradskaja Oblast: Novye Vyzovy, novye shansy. Mechanizmy Razvitija Unikal'nogo Regiona* [*The Kaliningrad region: new challenges, new chances. The development mechanisms for the unique region*], Moscow, IMEPI-RAN.

Busygina, I. M. (1998a), 'Die Regionen Russlands in den internationalen und außenwirtschaftlichen Beziehungen' ['Russia's regions in international and foreign economic relations'], *Osteuropa*, 11/12: 1101–9.

Busygina, I. M. (1998b), 'Der asymmetrische Föderalismus. Zur besonderen Rolle der Republiken in der Russischen Föderation ['Assymetrical federalism: The special role of the Russian republics'], *Osteuropa*, 7: 239–52.

Chebankova, E. A. (2005), 'The Limitations of Central Authority in the Regions and the Implication for the Evolution of Russia's Federal System', *Europe-Asia Studies*, 57(7): 933–49.

Federal Target Programme (2001), 'Federal'naja celevaja programma razvitija Kaliningradskoj oblasti na period do 2010 goda' ['Federal Target Programme for Development of Kaliningrad Region up to 2010'], available on the Internet at www.gov.kaliningrad.ru/index.php?idpage=563 (accessed 30 November 2006).

Glosov, G. (2005), 'What Went Wrong? Regional Electoral Politics and Impediments to the State Centralization in Russian, 2003–2004', *Ponars Policy Memo*, 337.

Government of Kaliningrad Oblast (2007), 'Structure of Government', available on the Internet at www.gov.kaliningrad.ru/index.php?idpage=69 (accessed 30 September 2007).

Gutnik, V. and A. Klemeshev (2006), *Baltiskij region kak poljus ekonomitscheskoj integracii Severo-Zapada Rosskijskoj Federacii i Evropejskogog sojuza* [*The Baltic region as the Russian north-west's pole of economic integration with the European Union*], Kaliningrad, BALTMION.

Heinemann-Grüder, A. (2000), *Der heterogene Staat. Föderalismus und regionale Vielfalt in Russland* [*The heterogenous state: Federalism and regional diversity in Russia*], Berlin, Arno Spitz.

Heinemann-Grüder, A. (2001), 'Der asymmetrische Föderalismus Russlands und die Rolle der Regionen' ['Russia's asymmetrical federalism and the role of the regions'], in *Russland unter neuer Führung*, ed. H.-H.Höhmann and H.-H. Schröder, Bonn, Agenda: 78–86.

Heinemann-Grüder, A. (2004), 'Putins Russland – Föderation ohne Föderalismus' ['Putin's Russia: Federation without federalism'], *Jahrbuch des Föderalismus*, Baden-Baden, Nomos: 339–55.

Holtom, P. (2002), 'Kaliningrad in 2001: From Periphery to Pilot Region', in *Russian Participation in Baltic Sea Region-Building: A Case Study of Kaliningrad*, ed. P. Holtom and F. Tassinari, Gdansk/Berlin, University Press Gdansk: 36–67.

Joenniemi, P. and A. Sergounin (2003), *Russia and the European Union's Northern Dimension. Encounter or Clash of Civilisations?*, Nishny Novgorod, Linguistic University Press.

Kaliningrad-aktuell (2006), 17 January, available on the Internet at www.kaliningrad.aktuell.ru/kaliningrad/wirtschaft/kaliningrad_lukoil_will_keine _clraffinerie_bauen_47.html (accessed 6 March 2007).

Karabeshkin, L. and C. Wellmann (2004), *The Russian Domestic Debate on Kaliningrad: Integrity, Identity and Economy*, Münster, Lit-Verlag.

Keohane, R. O. and H. V. Milner (1996), 'Introduction', in *Internationalisation and Domestic Politics*, ed. R. O. Keohane and H. V. Milner, Cambridge, Cambridge University Press: 3–24.

Klemeshev, A. P. ed. (2004), 'Region of Cooperation', *BALTMION*, Issue 9, Kaliningrad, Kaliningrad State University Press.

Klemeshev, A. P. and G. M. Fedorov (2004), *Ot izolirovannogo eksklava – k 'koridory pazvitiya'* [*From an isolated exclave to a 'corridor of development'*], *BALTMION*, Kaliningrad, Kaliningrad State University Press.

Knappe, E. (2004), *Kaliningrad aktuell, Leibnitz-Institut für Länderkunde* [*Kaliningrad now. Leibnitz Institute for Country Studies*], Leipzig, Selbstverlag IFL.

Kommersant (2006), 'Edinyj roseksamen' ['The common Russian exams'], *Kommersant*, 14 March.

Königsberger Express (2006a), 'Sonderwirtschaftszone soll Aufschwung bringen' ['Special Economic Zone set to launch prosperity'], *Königsberger Express*, 2: 4.

Königsberger Express (2006b), 'Lokale Presse im Aufruhr' ['Local press in rebellion'], *Königsberger Express*, 2: 18.

Kryschtanowskaja, O. (2005), *Anatomie der russischen Elite. Die Militarisierung Russlands unter Putin* [*Anatomy of the Russian elite: Russia's militarisation under Putin*], Köln,

Kiepenheuer & Witsch.

Makarychev, A. (2000), 'Islands of Globalization: Regional Russia and the Outside World', Working Paper 2, Zurich, ETH.

Moses, J. C. (2004), 'The Politics of Kaliningrad Oblast: A Borderland of the Russian Federation', *The Russian Review*, 63(1): 107–29.

Nagornych, I. (2006), 'Otvetsvennost za snjatie s vyborov vozloshili na partii' ['The responsibility for abolition of elections imposed on the parties'], *Kommersant*, 1 March.

Oldberg, I. (2002), 'Kaliningrad Between Moscow and Brussels', Working Paper 17, Zurich, ETH.

Ortung, R. (2000), 'Introduction', in *The Republics and Regions of the Russian Federation*, ed. R. W. Ortung, D. N. Lussier and A. Partskaya (East–West Institute), Armonk (NY), M. E. Sharp.

Perović, J. (2000), 'Internationalization of Russian Regions and the Consequences for Russian Foreign and Security Policy', Working Paper 1, Zürich, Centre for Security and Conflict Research.

Russian Federal Law (1996), 'Federalnoj zakon ob osoboj ekonomitcheskoj zone v Kaliningradskoj oblasti' ['Federal Law on the Special Economic Zone in Kaliningrad Region'], approved 22 January 1996, available on the Internet at www.gov.kaliningrad.ru (accessed 30 September 2007).

Russian Federal Law (2006), 'Federalnoj zakon ob osoboj ekonomitcheskoj zone v Kaliningradskoj oblasti i o venesenii izmenenij v nekotorye zakonodatelnye akty Rossijskoj Federacii' ['Federal Law on the Special Economic Zone in Kaliningrad Region and on Introduction of Amendment of some Acts of Law'], approved 10 January 2006, available on the Internet at http://document.kremlin .ru/doc.asp?ID=031902 (accessed 30 September 2007).

Russian Federation (1993), 'The Constitution of the Russian Federation', available on the Internet at www.constitution.ru/en/10003000–01.htm.

Schmidt, M. G. (1995), *Wörterbuch zur Politik* [*Dictionary of politics*], Stuttgart, Alfred Kröner Verlag.

Schneider, E. (2002), *Staatliche Akteure russischer Außenpolitik* [*State actors in Russian foreign policy*], Berlin, SWP-Studie 8.

Sergounin, A. (2001), 'The Russian Perspective', in *Are Borders Barriers? EU Enlargement and the Russian Region of Kaliningrad*, ed. L. D. Fairlie and A. Sergounin, Helsinki, UPI: 139–90.

Smorodinskaja, N. (2001), *Kaliningrad Exclave: Prospects for Transformation into a Pilot Region*, Moscow, East–West Institute.

Stein, S. (2003), 'Aufstieg, Fall und Neuanfang. Zehn Jahre Sonderwirtschaftszone Kaliningrad,' ['Rise, decline and new start. Kaliningrad's Special Economic Zone turns ten'], *Osteuropa*, 2/3: 353–67.

Timmermann, H. (2000), *Die russische Exklave Kaliningrad im Kontext regionaler Kooperation* [*The Russian exclave of Kaliningrad in the context of regional cooperation*], Bonn, BIOst, 20.

Treaty (2002), 'O Prekrashenii dejstvija dogovora o razgranitchenii predmetov v vedenija i polnomocij meshdu organami gosudarstvennoj vlasti Rossijskoj federacii i organami gosudarstvennoj vlasti Kaliningradskoj oblasti' ['On abolition of the treaty on delimitating the matters of control and powers between the bodies of state authority of the Russian Federation and the bodies of state authority of the Kaliningrad Region'], approved 31 May 2002, available on the Internet at http://faolex.fao.org/docs/texts /rus42740.doc (accessed 3 March 2005).

Vinokurov, E. (2005), 'The Enclave-Specific Vulnerability of Kaliningrad', in *Kaliningrad 2020: Its Future Competitiveness and Role in the Baltic Sea Economic Region*, ed. Kari Liuhto, Pan-European Institute, Turku: 56–74.

Anna M. Karpenko

7

Social identity and regionalisation: the case of Kaliningrad

Introduction

In the 1990s, some Russian regions found themselves involved in the process of cross-border region building in Europe. Kaliningrad was one of them, taking part in cooperation schemes in the Baltic Sea region as well as the Euro-regions programme. Since then, Russian elites have been ambiguous in their perceptions of regionalisation, showing both negative and positive attitudes towards it (Sergounin 2004: 17–33). The value of international cooperation is increasingly recognised. While the dynamic development of the Russian regions is usually perceived in terms of 'growth of investments', socio-cultural aspects of regionalisation, like identity-building, tend to remain underestimated and lacking in scholarship. In this chapter, the patterns of social identity in Kaliningrad – with a particular focus on ethnic and religious identifications – will be analysed: to what extent do the inhabitants of the exclave represent 'Western' or 'European' types of Russians?

In the first part of the chapter, there is a brief outline of the social and cultural aspects of European regionalisation. The second part is devoted to the development of social affiliations in the oblast during the Soviet period. In the third part, the contemporary 'identity situation' in the exclave is discussed.

Social identity and European region-building

Since the end of the Cold War, the role of regional actors in European and Russian political spaces has been changing. Regionalisation is not a new phenomenon in international relations; it already existed during the Cold War and was connected mostly with the domains of economic integration and security. In 'old' regionalism, a region is understood as created from 'above', i.e. as the result of a decision reached by heads of state. It is seen as a geographic area where states organise cooperation. 'New' regionalism instead focuses on another type of region created from below, in which states do not play a central role in cooperation and integration. New regionalism can be understood as a 'multidimensional form of integration which includes economic, political, social and cultural aspects and thus goes far beyond the goal of creating region-based free-trade regimes or security alliances' (Hettne 1999a: xvi). Such regions will attempt to become the subject of international politics (Lähteenmäki and Käkönen, 1999: 214). Regionalisation is a dynamic, multi-dimensional process. New regions are not defined *a priori* by states or military blocs; they rather evolve through a bottom-up process and define themselves in the making.

Scholars of the new regionalism describe the process of contemporary region-building in terms of five degrees of 'regionness', or 'regionality', understood to be the result or the current state of regionalisation. The first degree is referred to as a 'proto-region'; the region as a geographical unit. The second is the region as a social system, characterised by various types of cross-border relations between human groups, called a 'primitive' region. The third degree is termed a 'formal' or 'real' region with organised cooperation in cultural, economic, political or military fields. The fourth degree has the region as civil society, in which the organised forms of cooperation promote social communication and convergence of values between different cultural areas of a region – this level indicates a 'regional anarchical society'. The fifth has the region acting as a subject with a certain identity and legitimacy as well as capability and other qualities of an actor within international politics, defined as a 'region-state' (Hettne 1999b: 6–7).

New regionalism implies that successful regionalisation will depend on successful identity-building. This process is linked with the activity of a minority (elite) which seeks to construct and promote new identity as a means for group integration in order to achieve group interests. At the same time, successful communication of new ideas depends not only on their correspondence with rationally calculated and articulated group interests, but also with the attitudes and cultural patterns of the majority. New images should be able to establish emotional ties within a group. New region-building draws on a pluralistic model of identity which allows maximum room for inclusion of people from different backgrounds. A new European identity image is seen as being formed on the 'civic', rather than an antagonistic nationalist platform (van Ham 2000).

In social psychology, the term 'social identity' refers to the identity that people derive from their memberships in social groups. It is defined as 'that part of an individual self-concept which derives from his knowledge of his membership of a social group (or groups) together with the value and emotional significance attached to that membership' (Tajfel 1978: 63). It is the place a person has in the social world that is shared with other people, like gender, age, profession, ethnicity, lifestyle, etc. In modern societies, people have access to multiple shared places. Thus, there is the potential for various and partly overlapping – even conflicting – identities operating concurrently. Post-industrial network societies are being (re)defined and (re)created through multiple affiliations and various lifestyles of their members. For example, consuming practices, with their everyday simulation of multiple choices, continue to make a significant contribution to identity dynamics, causing changes in the behavioural style and attitudes of individuals.

Not all aspects of a person's social identity, or such multiple identifications, are equally salient at the same time. For most people, private (or core) identifications with small groups such as family, friends and colleagues are relatively stable and of the greater importance, which is also true for 50 to 80 per cent of respondents in contemporary Russia (Gorshkov and Tikhonova 2005: 77). The identifications that Russians make with larger groups tend to be labile and contextually dependent (Danilova and Yadov 2004: 27–30).

Social identity of Kaliningraders during the Soviet period

From 1945, when Königsberg became a part of the Soviet Union, it was set aside to turn into a new Soviet city in the former territory of East Prussia. Within a few years after the end of the Second World War, the German population was evicted from the region. The newcomers, many of whom arrived from parts of the Soviet Union that were devastated during German occupation, set out for a new life. For the new authorities, it was important to naturalise a connection from the former German territory with the Soviet Union as soon as possible. Yet this was a challenging task. If appealing to traditions and history is usually regarded as an important instrument during identity-building in a time of change (Hobsbawm 1992), then in the case of Kaliningrad, history was problematic. Russian historical connections to the region were quite limited, so the history of the oblast was allowed to appear in the official discourse beginning with the Second World War. After 1945, Kaliningrad became 'the most Western Soviet garrison', with a high proportion of the population constituted by military personnel, numbering up to 100,000 out of approximately 900,000 inhabitants by the end of the 1980s. In this respect, the war epic and heroism were also important to support the status of Kaliningrad as a military fortress and outpost (Browning and Joenniemi 2003: 70–3).

Despite this beginning, Kaliningrad ceased to become a reference model for a new 'truly Soviet' region, with various factors contributing to that failure. The first factor was the high level of migration, which was connected with the presence of military personnel and prevented people from making roots in the region and participating in identity-building. The second factor was that, despite their intentions and efforts, the Soviet authorities were never able to erase the past. The remnants of German architecture and material culture, archaeological findings, and the memories, myths and legends about Königsberg created a certain spirit of fascination and nostalgia for the imagined past of the destroyed town (Sezneva 2003: 80–5; Sezneva 2007). Forbidden Königsberg was bound to become a captivating phantom. Third, despite closed borders with the West and Poland, Kaliningraders had many contacts with its not fully 'Sovietised' neighbours: Lithuania, Latvia and Estonia. What is more, Kaliningrad used to be a large sea port, so that the impressions and consumer goods brought by seamen from their voyages contributed to a kind of distinct self-perception for Kaliningraders, who felt themselves a special community in the Soviet Union more open to the West, with privileged access to foreign goods and a sampling of Western culture, especially rock and pop music. Moreover, they were perceived by their fellow citizens as being closer to *Pribaltika* than to the other parts of Russia. Not only did a full Sovietisation of Königsberg/Kaliningrad fail, but instead there was openness to the West and Europe.

Ethnic and religious relations in Kaliningrad during the Soviet period were marked by a high degree of toleration and the absence of ethno-cultural conflicts. The ethnic composition of the population contributed to this peaceful setting: although there were 110 ethnic groups in the oblast by the end of the 1980s, the largest ethnic groups constituted Slavic peoples – Russians, Byelorussians and Ukrainians, who respectively constituted 78 per cent, 8.5 per cent, and 7.2 per cent of the population in 1989 (Dubova *et al.* 1998).

During the Soviet period of Kaliningrad's history, there was no religious tension, largely because there was no institutionalised religion until the 1980s. Religious activity was not encouraged by the atheist ideology of communism. The planned Sovietisation of the former German territory did not anticipate the construction of new churches, temples, mosques or synagogues. The requests of the post-war newcomers to establish an Orthodox parish were consequently denied by the local authorities (Gurov 2004: 48). Although there were small communities of Baptists, Adventists and Pentecostals, by the 1980s Kaliningrad had become a territory of successful 'atheistisation'. The situation started to change only with *perestroika*. The first orthodox congregation was registered in 1985, and in the early 1990s, the communities of Lutherans, Catholics, Muslims, Buddhists and others were institutionalised as well.

Social identity of Kaliningraders: the 'exclave' period

When the sense of collective identity within the Soviet state was lost and many previous national achievements were questioned, it became relatively easy to promote the image of ethnicity as something unchangeable during the chaotic post-Soviet period. However, after the break-up of the Soviet Union, ethno-religious tensions did not increase enormously. The patterns of toleration were sustainable enough to overcome the ideological breakdown of communism, especially in Kaliningrad. During the 1990s, it received a large influx of migrants from different parts of the former Soviet Union yet continued to prove its reputation as a non-xenophobic region. Our research, based on focus group interviews with local 'newcomers', demonstrated that Kaliningrad has been perceived as an open and hospitable place which is ready to welcome anybody who is really interested in starting a new life there.[1] The whole territory was settled by migrants, and therefore no ethnic group could seriously claim a dominant status on the historical grounds of being a more rooted or traditional community, certainly contributing to the remarkable tolerance of Kaliningraders. Since 1991, ethnic composition has not changed significantly: according to the 2002 Census, more than 92 per cent of the regions' population of 955,000 is represented by the Slavic ethnic groups (82 per cent Russian, 5 per cent Byelorussian and almost the same proportion of Ukrainians). The other relatively large ethnic minorities are Lithuanians (1.5 per cent), Germans (0.9 per cent) and Armenians (0.9 per cent). Regarding the latter, who are generally regarded as Muslim by their religious affiliation, the largest groups (Tatars and Azeri) constitute about 4,800 and 3,000 members each.[2]

Proximity to Europe and frequent trips of Kaliningraders abroad became a special feature of the exclave during the 1990s and contributed to new European dimensions of self-identification. As a recent survey of 'ethnic', 'civic' and 'local' identifications demonstrates, European affiliation is considerably stronger among the younger groups, aged eighteen to thirty-nine (Melvil and Klemeshev 2005: 38). As compared with the 'natives' of the oblast, respondents who moved to the exclave recently during the post-Soviet period feel themselves less affiliated with the oblast or Russia as a whole. The share of newcomers who identify themselves with Europe is more than twice as high as the same index for 'indigenous' Kaliningraders (ibid.: 42).

The dominant majority of Kaliningrad's population is considered to adhere to the Russian Orthodox Church. However, when referring to religious affiliations during the post-Soviet period in Russia, it is important to consider the so-called 'Orthodox non-believer' paradox demonstrated by public opinion polls. These polls show that the number of people who say that they believe in God is less than the number of those who identify themselves with a traditional denomination. Thus, in the 2000 poll, there were 46.9 per cent believers but 69.5 per cent who considered themselves Orthodox or Muslim. Such a paradox allows one to assume that religious and ethnic identities are mixed; either Orthodoxy or Islam is considered by many as an essential sign of broader ethno-cultural, but not necessarily religious identity: 'If I am Russian, then I am Orthodox; If I am Tatar, I am Muslim' (Mtchedlov

2000). Thus, religious identity in Russia is being defined by ethnicity and culture. As such, religious affiliations are unlikely to provoke conflicts unless supported by stirred ethnic tensions.

However, since the end of the 1980s, the Russian Orthodox Church is being established as the main actor in Kaliningrad's religious field. The efforts of the Church to become the main representative of the 'all-Russian' culture in the oblast have been widely supported by different political actors, from federal to local levels. Moscow, interested in distributing 'loyalty' in a region that has been surrounded by the European Union since 2004, has maintained the symbolic influence of the Orthodox religious institutions. The opening of the Orthodox Cathedral in the central square of Kaliningrad represented the pinnacle of the sixtieth anniversary celebrations in 2006 (Karpenko 2007).

Politically, the increased role of the Church has been in agreement with consolidation of political power around the federal centre in Moscow. Since the 2000s, Kaliningraders have become a target of special measures and activities of the centre which are aimed at strengthening the sense of 'Russianness' among the local population – perceived by the centre as potentially separatist. However, surveys demonstrate that the affiliation to Russia as a whole (their civic affiliation) ranks first for the majority of Kaliningrad's population; it is important for 76.8 per cent of respondents who were asked to rank three choices of possible group affiliation. The affiliation to Kaliningrad (regional affiliation) as well as to different types of settlements like towns, villages, etc. (local affiliation) is important for, respectively, 70.2 per cent and 54.8 per cent of the population. The importance of ethnicity (ethnic affiliation) ranks fourth at 46.6 per cent. For 20.6 per cent of respondents, their affiliation to Europe (European affiliation) is salient, ranking fifth in the given range of choices (Melvil and Klemeshev 2005: 36).

Numerous efforts have been undertaken by the federal centre to impose patriotism on Kalinigraders who are perceived as 'disloyal', which are often met with resistance. This resistance is mainly by the most educated and economically active groups of inhabitants. It becomes apparent in the mockery of some newly erected architectural signs of 'patriotic' identity (e.g. the memorial column on the central square in Kaliningrad, and the monument to the Russian Empress Elisabeth in Baltiysk). Some members of the local press (Kalinin 2007) have articulated challenges to the dominant official discourse of civic identity.

Conclusion

The history of identity-building in Kaliningrad since the dismantlement of the Soviet Union has demonstrated that social identifications and attitudes of the population are not to be considered as being eventually defined by some type of official discourse. Kaliningraders cannot be perceived as a passive audience to any type of ideology. When a discourse of the dominant is meant to suppress and undermine a distinctive sense of regional identity, the local population is likely to demonstrate different forms of resistance. Such resistance is revealed in contending narratives of identity, mockery of official ideology, and local media opposition to the identity politics of the federal centre. These identity issues are being widely discussed within the most educated and socially active groups in Kaliningrad. Quantitative and qualitative social research suggests that Kaliningraders do define themselves in terms of a special 'Europeanised' group in Russia.

Notes

1 Focus groups were conducted in Kaliningrad by the author during March, April and September of 2007.
2 All figures from the official 2002 Census are available on the Internet at www.perepis2002.ru/ct/doc/natcsostav_00.xls (accessed 15 February 2007).

References

Browning, C. S. and P. Joenniemi (2003), 'The Identity of Kaliningrad: Russian, European or a Third Space?' in *The Baltic Sea Region in the European Union: Reflections on Identity, Soft-Security and Marginality*, ed. F. Tassinari, Berlin, Humboldt University: 58–104.
Danilova, E. and V. Yadov (2004), 'Nestabilnaja socialnaja identichnost' kak norma sovremennyh obschestv' ['Unstable social identity as a norm in contemporary societies'], *Sociologicheskie Issledovanija* [*Sociological research*], 10: 27–30.
Dubova, N., N. Lopulenko, and M. Martynova (1998), *The Kaliningrad Region: Contemporary Ethnocultural Situation*, Moscow, Institute of Ethnology and Anthropology, Russian Academy of Sciences, available on the Internet at www.iea.ras.ru/lib/neotl/07112002062703.htm (accessed 25 September 2007).
Gorshkov, M. and N. Tikhonova, eds. (2005), *Rossijskaja identitchnost' v uslovijakh transformatsii: opyt sotsiologitcheskogo analiza* [*Russian identity in the conditions of transformation: an attempt at sociological analysis*], Moscow, Nauka.
Gurov, I. (2004), 'Konfessii v Kaliningrade' ['Confessions in Kaliningrad'], *Baltijskij Almanakh* [*Baltic Almanac*], 5: 30–4.
Hettne, B. (1999a), 'The New Regionalism: A Prologue', in *Globalism and the New Regionalism*, ed. B. Hettne, A. Inotai and O. Sunkel, Basingstoke, Macmillan: xv–xxx.
Hettne, B. (1999b), 'Globalization and the New Regionalism: The Second Great Transformation', in *Globalism and the New Regionalism*, ed. B. Hettne, A. Inotai and O. Sunkel, Basingstoke, Macmillan: 1–24.
Hobsbawm, E. (1992), 'Introduction: Inventing Tradition', in *The Invention of Tradition*, ed. E. Hobsbawm and T. Ranger, Cambridge, Cambridge University Press: 1–14.
Kalinin, V. (2007), 'Rodinu lubit' ['To love the Motherland'], *Kaliningradskaya Pravda*, 31 August 2007.
Karpenko, A. M. (2007), 'Kaliningrad Regional Identity as a Category of Political Practice', in *Regional Cooperation of the EU and Russia in the North-West*, Moscow, Institute of Europe, Russian Academy of Sciences: 123–34.

Lähteenmäki, K. and J. Käkönen (1999), 'Regionalization and its Impact on the Theory of International Relations', in Globalism and the New Regionalism, ed. B. Hettne, A. Inotai and O. Sunkel, Basingstoke, Macmillan: 203–27.

Melvil A. and A. Klemeshev, eds (2005), Problema separatisma v uslovijakh anklavnykh territorij [The separatism issue in the conditions of enclave territories], Kaliningrad, Izd-vo RGU im. I. Kanta, Region sotrudnitchestva [Immanuel Kant Russian State University Press, region of cooperation], 3(46): 33–59.

Mtchedlov, M. (2000), 'Vera Rossii v zerkale statistiki' ['Russia's belief in the mirror of statistics'], Nezavisimaja Gazeta [Independent Gazette], 17 May: 3

Sergounin, A. (2004), 'Regionalizatsija v regione Baltijskogo moria: vosprijatie rossijskih elit' ['Regionalisation in the Baltic sea region: perception by Russian elites'], in Regionalnoe izmerenie rossijsko-baltijskikh otnoshenij [Regional dimension of Russian–Baltic relations], ed. L. Karbeshkin, St Petersburg, Baltijskij Klub: 17–34

Sezneva, O. (2003), 'The Dual History: Politics of the Past in Kaliningrad, Former Koenigsberg', in Composing Urban Histories and the Construction of Civic Identities, ed. J. Czaplicka, B. Ruble and L. Crabtree, Baltimore, Johns Hopkins University Press and Woodrow Wilson Center Press: 58–85.

Sezneva, O. (2007) '"We Have Never Been German": The Economy of Digging in Russian Kaliningrad', in Practising Culture, ed. C. Calhoun and R. Sennet, London and New York, Routlege: 1–22

Tajfel, H. (1978), Differentiation Between Social Groups: Studies in the Social Psychology of Intergroup Relations, London, Academic Press.

van Ham, P. (2000), Identity Beyond the State: The Case of the European Union, Copenhagen, Copenhagen Peace Research Institute (COPRI) Papers, available on the Internet at www.ciaonet.org/wps/vap01 (accessed 12 April 2006).

SILKE SCHIELBERG

8

Kaliningrad in its neighbourhood – regional cooperation with Poland and Lithuania

Introduction

Due to its exclavity, Kaliningrad is dependent on cross-border cooperation (CBC) with its immediate neighbours. In the context of current CBC regimes in Europe, there are differences between cooperation of border regions within the old EU-15, between the EU-15 and the new member states, and at the new external borders of the EU – including border regions between EU member states and regions of countries which will not join the EU in the foreseeable future. The motives and tasks of CBC differ in various categories. CBC between EU regions serves to minimise the barrier effect of national borders and contributes to an ongoing European integration. Since the early 1990s, such cooperation is supported under EU's Interreg initiative. In the course of the development of this cooperation, the Euro-region model has emerged.[1] In contrast, CBC at the external borders of the EU serves to guarantee security and stability reducing the prosperity gap between the EU and neighbouring states through cooperation. Until 2004, this realm was supported by the EU's PHARE-CBC[2] and TACIS-CBC[3] programmes, and then from 2004 to 2006 by the EU's 'neighbourhood programme' (Commission 2003c).

The question, however, is whether the model of CBC between border regions existing within the EU can be transferred to regions at the external borders of the Union (in this case between the Russian region of Kaliningrad and the neighbouring Polish and Lithuanian regions) or whether different approaches are required for the development of CBC in these specific cases. This question has to be answered in light of the EU's new external border separating Kaliningrad from Poland's and Lithuania's adjacent regions. Additionally, socio-economic and institutional asymmetries exist between the oblast and its neighbours. These emerged due to the unequal progress in transformation, which probably will increase because of the EU membership of Poland and Lithuania. The initial situation for the development of CBC in this region therefore differs from the situation within the EU.

This chapter provides, first, a short overview of the development of CBC between Kaliningrad and the neighbouring regions since the dissolution of the Soviet Union. Second, it analyses existing problems of CBC in this particular area. Finally, it tries to answer the question of whether EU objectives and instruments for CBC are adequate for its development at the external borders of the Union. The assessment of CBC is based on sources gathered from the county and city administrations and from NGOs, as well as from a large set of expert interviews conducted in 2004 and 2005 in Kaliningrad, Poland and Lithuania.[4]

The development of CBC between Kaliningrad and the bordering regions in Poland and Lithuania

The analysis of the development of CBC between Kaliningrad and its neighbouring regions is limited to the Polish and Lithuanian regions that directly border the oblast. These are the Polish voivodships Pomorskie and Warmińsko-Mazurskie as well as the Lithuanian counties of Klaipeda, Taurage and Marijampole. Only since the dissolution of the Soviet Union in 1991 has a comprehensive and formalised cooperation existed across these borders. During the Soviet era, Kaliningrad was a militarily closed area and therefore sealed off from its neighbours. Thus, after the dissolution of the Soviet Union, CBC (as developed within the EU) had to be established in these regions almost *sui generis*, mainly because the border between Lithuania and Russia changed from an administrative border to one separating two independent states, with Kaliningrad becoming a Russian exclave.

In light of this, Russia had a vital interest in regulating Kaliningrad's cooperation with Poland and Lithuania. Furthermore, Poland and Lithuania were interested in regulating relations with Kaliningrad on a state level. On 29 July 1991, the governments of the Russian Soviet Federative Socialist Republic (RSFSR) and the Republic of Lithuania signed an agreement on mutual cooperation concerning the oblast (RSFSR–Lithuania Agreement 1991).[5] A similar agreement was signed on 22 May 1992 with the Polish government, in which both sides agreed to support CBC between Kaliningrad and the Polish north-eastern voivodships (Russia–Poland Agreement 1992). These agreements were followed by similar declarations on regional and local levels (between the regional administrations and parliaments, cities and municipalities).[6] They defined, among other things, the motives for such cooperation as well as the fields and the tasks for cooperation. Economic cooperation and infrastructure became priorities, but culture, sciences, tourism and environment were also mentioned. As a result of the agreements between the national governments, joint cooperation councils were established, taking responsibility for the implementation of the agreements and therefore for the arranging of CBC.[7]

Although there were many initiatives from national and regional authorities to institutionalise CBC between Kaliningrad and the neighbouring regions in the early 1990s, the cooperation existed primarily on paper (Hreczuk 2002: 77). One of the main reasons for this was problems in the bilateral relations between Russia and Poland and Russia and Lithuania, which had an impact on CBC between Kaliningrad and the bordering Polish and Lithuanian regions. For example, Polish and Lithuanian efforts regarding NATO membership caused tensions in the relations of both states *vis-à-vis* Russia. However, resentments were not only ascribed to Poland's and Lithuania's orientation to the West, but also to unresolved problems resulting from the Second World War and territorial claims on the Kaliningrad region from nationalistic movements within Poland and Lithuania.[8] This had some impact on regional CBC; for example no meetings of the Polish–Russian Cooperation Council took place between 1996 and 1999. Furthermore, the protectionist politics of Leonid Gorbenko, then Governor of Kaliningrad, contributed to the stagnation of development of cross-border relations between Kaliningrad and its neighbours.

A second main reason for the lack of development of CBC was because regions and municipalities were financially too weak to implement projects on their own. During the 1990s, EU programmes only promoted CBC between regions at the external borders of the EU-15 but not at the borders between future candidate states and their eastern neighbours. It was only at the end of the 1990s that the PHARE-CBC programme, the PHARE programme for the eastern border, and the TACIS-CBC programme were established to support cooperation between Kaliningrad and the bordering Polish and Lithuanian regions. Additionally, due to resettlements and expulsions after the Second World War, there no longer existed an intermediary population in the border regions which could have promoted an existing CBC regime and thus eased mutual resentment. Such an intermediary population is important for the development of CBC, because it functions as a bearer for cultural and social exchange (Krämer 1999: 19). In consequence, anxieties and historical prejudices were an obstacle to the development of CBC.

Once it became clear at the end of the 1990s that Poland and Lithuania would join the EU in the foreseeable future, there were reinforced initiatives from the EU, national governments, and regional and local levels to expand CBC. The EU accepted the challenge at the new external borders in the east with the imminent enlargement and established new support programmes for these borders. For example, since 1999, Poland and Lithuania have had the possibility of implementing small projects with Kaliningrad in line with the Union's CBC programme for the Baltic Sea Region. Moreover, the EU established the PHARE programme for the candidates' eastern borders in 2000, through which it supported not only big national projects with partners from

Kaliningrad but also projects within the framework of a small projects facility. In 2004, in accordance with the European Neighbourhood Policy (ENP), a special Interreg III-A programme for CBC between Kaliningrad, Poland and Lithuania was launched, through which the first joint projects were initiated by the end of 2005.[9]

The prospective accession of Poland and Lithuania to the EU and improved relations between Russia and NATO also contributed to an improvement of bilateral relations between Russia and Poland, and Russia and Lithuania. As a consequence, the cross-border relations between the regions improved. For example, since 1999 the Polish–Russian Cooperation Council has met regularly again. Furthermore, in 1999, a coordination centre for cooperation with the Kaliningrad region was established in Klaipeda, Lithuania. The centre has already implemented several projects jointly with Russian partners.[10] In 2000, the newly established Russian–Lithuanian Cooperation Council agreed on a jointly prepared list of projects for the Northern Dimension initiative of the EU (the so-called Nida initiative). At the same time, Euro-regions were established at the borders between Kaliningrad, Poland and Lithuania. Currently, Kaliningrad and its municipalities are members of the Euro-regions Nemunas, Baltica, Saule, Šešupe and Łyna-Ława.[11] On the one hand this is a result of the lack of initiatives from the national and regional governments, and on the other hand it is due to the fact that EU funding became available for this form of CBC. Nevertheless, irrespective of EU subsidies, the border regions became more active in CBC from the end of the 1990s. This shows that a majority of people, at least in the local and regional administrations, possessed and still possess an interest in CBC with their neighbours. Most of the bordering regions in Poland and Lithuania signed agreements on cooperation with municipalities in the Kaliningrad region only in recent years (Kulesza *et al.* 2004: 33–8).

Making cross-border cooperation work

More than forty Polish and more than ten Lithuanian counties, cities and municipalities cooperate with Russian partners from Kaliningrad. For the most part, the cooperation takes the form of smaller initiatives like participation in city and municipality days as well as sports and cultural events, which could be financed through local resources. The counties and municipalities also cooperate in the social field, exchanging information on construction of local self-government and on issues such as environmental protection and tourism. A good portion of cross-border contacts have an economic context. There are regular fairs and missions organised by enterprises and by the chambers of industry and commerce. During 2005 in Kaliningrad, there were 600 joint ventures involving Polish capital and 680 with Lithuanian capital ('Business cooperation' 2007).

Since 1997, Kaliningrad has had the possibility, alongside regions from Poland and Lithuania, to apply as a partner for complementary projects within Interreg II-C and III-B for the Baltic Sea region (BSR). In these transnational projects, partners from Kaliningrad, Poland and Lithuania are primarily engaged in environmental protection and infrastructure development.[12] However, in most cases the Russian partner 'exists' only on paper. Polish and Lithuanian actors are frequently critical that the project partners from Kaliningrad are not active enough, that they do not apply for funding from the TACIS-CBC programme and that they often do not participate in the meetings of the project partners. This lack of involvement of Russian partners is confirmed by the number of complementary projects within the Interreg III-B projects with participation of the Kaliningrad region: of twenty-nine projects (2000–2006) with partners from Kaliningrad, there were only two TACIS-CBC complementary projects up to 2006. Up to 2005, there were only six TACIS-CBC projects between Kaliningrad and bordering Polish and Lithuanian regions. This was only due to a change in regulations for TACIS applications in 2002 also allowing partners from Poland and Lithuania to apply for TACIS-CBC funding and administer the money.[13]

Similar problems appear in bilateral and trilateral projects within the small projects facility of PHARE and TACIS, which are not linked to the big Interreg projects. They primarily cover the fields of culture, sports, environment and tourism. Other projects promote the exchange of experiences in establishing of local self-government and within the social field. Furthermore, for these small projects, applications are made first and foremost from the Polish and Lithuanian partners and the projects are financed within the PHARE programme and not within TACIS. However, it seems as if cooperation in these small projects is functioning better than before, which is evident in the number of implemented projects: in the framework of the CBC programme for the BSR, there were thirty-four projects with partners from Kaliningrad implemented in Poland (1999–2002) and twenty-two in Lithuania (1999–2001). In the framework of the Polish Eastern Border Programme, seventy-two projects (2000–3) were implemented with partners from Kaliningrad. Nevertheless, even in this realm only a few projects were financed by TACIS; therefore the participation of Russian partners in these projects was limited (Euro-region Annual Report 2001; Association of Communes 2003). That is also the case for the Interreg III-A programme for CBC between Kaliningrad, Poland and Lithuania (2004–6). Until August 2007, 109 projects were implemented in this programme, only twenty-three of them with participation of partners from Kaliningrad and only sixteen financed by TACIS.[14]

It becomes apparent that until the end of the 1990s there were many cross-border initiatives and projects between Kaliningrad and the bordering Polish and Lithuanian regions (bilateral and multi-lateral). Furthermore, in most cases joint projects were initiated by neighbouring regions, municipalities and NGOs, not actors in Kaliningrad. This observation raises questions about the recent discrepancy between intensifying of CBC between Kaliningrad and its neighbours, and the lack of activity by partners from Kaliningrad, despite a clear interest in such cooperation.

Obstacles for cross-border cooperation

It is possible to discern five crucial factors among the obstacles to the development of a comprehensive CBC involving the Kaliningrad region and its neighbours: different 'CBC philosophies' between the EU/Poland and Lithuania on the one hand and the Russian Federation/Kaliningrad on the other; border and visa issues; socio-economic asymmetries; institutional asymmetries; and a lack of communication and mutual trust.

Different approaches to CBC between the EU, Poland and Lithuania and the Russian Federation/Kaliningrad

The EU now treats CBC with Kaliningrad as part of the ENP within its external relations. The EU's aim is to strengthen the stability of new neighbouring states and to secure new external borders, as well as to protect member states against risks spilling over from neighbours. For the EU such risks include illegal migration, cross-border organised crime, cross-border environmental risks and communicable diseases (Commission 2003b: 4). These soft security risks are considered as threats for the Western communities and their standard of living (Bort 2002: 192). CBC is a way of addressing these threats and enhancing EU security. In contrast, the Russian Federation fears a separation of the exclave and therefore the loss of its territorial integrity (Birckenbach and Wellmann 2005: 8). Occasionally, Moscow perceives CBC as an interfering mechanism in its domestic affairs. Nevertheless, Russia is aware of the necessity to develop Kaliningrad with the assistance of CBC in order to reduce the welfare gap between the oblast and its neighbours.

Poland and Lithuania primarily focus on economic cooperation. Yet the improvement of the social situation of the oblast and the development of democracy and civil society structures form important aims within CBC in order to gain stability at their borders from a long term perspective. Actors in Kaliningrad itself – local authorities, at least – favour this economic cooperation, but areas such as environmental protection, the development of democratic structures and support of social initiatives are regarded as secondary.

Border and visa issues

One of the main obstacles for the development of CBC between Kaliningrad and its neighbours is the border itself. Whereas the people of Kaliningrad and the Polish and Lithuanian neighbour regions could cross the borders in the beginning of the 1990s without visas, since 2003 visas for mutual entry have been required. Despite some flexible solutions concerning visas for a transition period (i.e. multiple visas for one year free of charge, simplified application procedures etc.) until the Schengen *acquis* takes effect in Poland and Lithuania, the fact that visas are even necessary to cross the border impedes the development of CBC. Obtaining an international passport and visa takes time and money, and it renders spontaneous visits and meetings near impossible. One reason for limited participation of Kaliningrad partners in the multi-lateral Interreg projects is that they need corresponding Schengen visas for meetings relating to these projects. Furthermore, since June 2007, there has been a new agreement between the EU and Russia that makes visas at the borders between Kaliningrad and its neighbours no longer free of charge (Agreement 2007).

Socio-economic asymmetries

As the processes of political and economic transformation developed faster in Poland and Lithuania than in the Russian Federation (and especially Kaliningrad), a welfare gap exists between Kaliningrad and its neighbouring states. Similarly, funding from the EU has been highly asymmetric, focusing on accession countries rather than neighbouring regions. Furthermore, for much of the time, the PHARE programmes have been lacking compatibility and inter-operability with TACIS. The PHARE-CBC programme made available €180 million per year in 1998 and 1999 and €163 million per year between 2000 and 2003, 10 per cent of the total PHARE budget. In contrast, the TACIS-CBC programme made available €132.5 million from 1996 to 2000 and €30 million per year between 2000 and 2003, 5 per cent of the total TACIS budget. Even the EU's Court of Auditors criticised this unequal distribution of financial resources.[15] Moreover, the programmes PHARE/Interreg (Poland and Lithuania) and TACIS (Russia/Kaliningrad) were administered by three different Directorates General (DGs) within the European Commission.[16] All this has contributed to increasing socio-economic asymmetries at the borders between Kaliningrad and its neighbours and to a deepening of the welfare gap.

One of the results of these asymmetries (and the somewhat significant cross-border price differences) is the widespread semi-legal small border trade and the smuggling of goods like cigarettes and alcohol across the border. It is estimated that in Kaliningrad, 20,000 to 40,000 families depend on this trade/smuggling (Vinokurov 2004: 18). The small scale cross-border trade between the oblast and Poland continues to be the main contact between the populations on both sides of this border.[17] Consequently, the development of CBC beyond this semi-legal and illegal economic activity is hindered by border traders/smugglers crowding border entry points and causing long waits. This situation has changed only slightly with the introduction of visas in 2003.[18]

A further consequence of the welfare gap is that most of the municipalities in Kaliningrad are not able to provide the 20 per cent co-financing required for the implementation of TACIS projects. As a result, complementary projects to PHARE and Interreg barely evolve.

Institutional asymmetries

Both Poland and Lithuania are centrally governed unitary states. Since 1999 and the administrative reform, Poland has had a tripartite administration with sixteen voivodships.[19] The Republic of Lithuania introduced a bipartite local self-government in 1994 and has ten counties and fifty-six municipalities. The self-governmental units of both states receive financial aid from the central state budget and, what is more, can set their own taxes (Constitution of Lithuania 1992: Art. 120 and 121; Chancellery 1998: 18). Until the administrative reform in Poland in 1999, the voivod was responsible for international cooperation on a regional level. The Constitution of 1997 (Constitution of Poland 1997) already allowed local self-government to enter into international cooperation, but since the administrative reform, the parliament of the voivodship has had the right to define the directives of the international cooperation of the voivodship. However, regional agreements with sub-national and local units of foreign states need the approval of the Ministry of Foreign Affairs (Jóskowiak 2003: 160). Lithuanian cities and towns have the right to join international organisations of municipalities (Tauber 2002: 179).

In comparison, the Russian state has a federal structure, and Kaliningrad is one of more than eighty regions subject to the Federation. A problem in Russian federalism is that the distribution of competencies between the central state and the subject regions is not clearly regulated in the Constitution (see chapters 5 and 6 in this volume). Therefore President Yeltsin practised a sort of 'negotiated federalism': each of the subjects negotiated its rights and duties with the federal centre (Russian Federation 1993: Art. 71–3). With the Kaliningrad region such a treaty was signed on 12 January 1996. However, important rights which were granted to other regions, such as budget law, the right to raise taxes and to obtain international and foreign trade relations, were not assigned to the oblast (Schneider 1999: 142). Local self-government was introduced in the Russian Federation in 1993 (Russian Federation 1993: Art. 130–3).[20] According to the Constitution, local self-government is an autonomous unit, but in reality the Russian regional governments are often subordinated to the federal state (Schneider 1999: 166). The mayor is the major political actor on the municipal level with the responsibility for international cooperation. But despite the presence of elected representatives in the Russian regions and municipalities, all important issues, especially concerning international cooperation, are decided in Moscow. This is one of the main obstacles for CBC between Kaliningrad and its neighbours. While the central governments in Poland and Lithuania influence the international relations of their regions as well, regional administrations nevertheless have more decision-making power on important issues, so cooperation is further hampered by the fact that competencies in Polish and Lithuanian regions and in Kaliningrad are often on different levels. What is more, elections for regional parliaments and local administrations take place at different times. This means that the office holders that socialise with one another are constantly changing. Therefore, it is difficult to build up continuity of CBC, not least because personal contacts are very important in this field.

Lack of communication and mutual trust
Some linguistic problems between actors from Kaliningrad and from the Polish voivodships pose a challenge to effective cooperation. Unlike the Soviet era, young Polish people are studying English at school instead of Russian. The older generations learned Russian but most are unable to speak the language well because of lack of practice and a degree of animosity, as it was perceived as the language of the oppressor. The situation is gradually changing though, with schools in bordering Polish regions teaching Russian again, and schools in Kaliningrad teaching Polish. The language issue between Kaliningrad and Lithuania is much less severe, as a majority of Lithuanians speak Russian very well. But again, young Lithuanians prefer to study English rather than Russian. Even in Kaliningrad young people learn English at school, so the future language of CBC could very well be English.

Although there does not seem to be a real problem in communication because of language, a general communication challenge exists between Kaliningrad and its neighbours. Polish and Lithuanian actors complain that partners from Kaliningrad often do not pass on necessary information or material. They assume that one reason for this is a lack of modern communication systems in the oblast.[21] Another explanation they give is often described as a kind of 'Soviet mentality',[22] in which authority and hierarchy continue to have an important figurative role. As a result, people are uncertain when to make their own decisions, actors often remain passive, and when in doubt, they neglect to provide information. While this mentality also exists as a legacy of communism in Poland and Lithuania, it seems to be more pronounced in Kaliningrad and Russia.

The problems of NGOs in the Kaliningrad region consist primarily in the lack of personal and financial resources preventing them from prosecuting their interests towards a broader public. Additionally, they cannot openly express their interests to the local authorities. In interviews conducted by the author, Polish and Lithuanian actors repeatedly found fault with the fact that there is no open society in Kaliningrad. People there are often not aware of their democratic rights. This makes it difficult to have open discussions with partners in Kaliningrad.

Due to problems with communication, mistrust has emerged in CBC relationships. Mutual historical prejudices and stereotypes still exist that have obstructed the development of CBC. Efforts at practical cooperation have resulted in new prejudices; CBC actors from Poland and Lithuania complain that partners from the Kaliningrad region are dependent on Moscow, less active in implementing programmes, and lack a sense of duty, while partners from the oblast complain that Polish and Lithuanian actors do not treat Kaliningrad as an equal partner.

Conclusion and recommendations

This assessment of CBC along Kaliningrad's borders has made clear that the reasons for the difficult development of cross-border relations do not lie in a lack of goodwill by the actors, but in the asymmetric development of the regions and in historical prejudices and anxieties which are difficult to overcome. In Kaliningrad, a lack of competencies within the regional administration to make independent decisions, uncertainty, worries about the future and the still widespread 'Soviet mentality' contribute to a restraint in initiatives for CBC.

In light of the above mentioned obstacles for the development of CBC, particularly the lack of initiative and participation of Russian partners, it becomes clear that the European approach to CBC only conditionally assures success. A specific approach to CBC between regions within the EU and regions in countries which will not join the Union in the foreseeable future is required. Such an approach would need to take into account the specific situation of the Kaliningrad region as an enclave within the EU (separated from its neighbours and mainland Russia by an external border) and the difficult relations between Kaliningrad and the Russian centre. Cooperation at these borders is dominated by socio-economic and institutional asymmetries. The aim of cooperation between Kaliningrad and its neighbours is neither transforming the national border into a border between administrative systems, nor accession to the EU. The goals of cooperation should be, despite increasing asymmetries and the hardening of the border (as an external EU border), to attenuate these tendencies, to converge the border regions, to allow them to develop economically, and to provide confidence on both sides in order to reduce the negative effects of a hardened external border.

As national and EU policies have a strong impact on the development of CBC in this region, the EU and Russia must improve interstate relations and avoid new tensions. Thus the EU, in its policies towards Russia and especially in the approaches and tasks of CBC, should emphasise the development of mutual trust in relations with its neighbours instead of stressing the relevance of security and stability at its external borders. In turn, the Russian Federation should not only acknowledge but also fully respect the sovereignty of Poland and Lithuania so as not to fuel the mistrust these states have of Russian politics (Birckenbach and Wellmann 2005: 18, 35).

In order to mitigate the problems of crossing the border, the EU and Russia should negotiate the abolition of the visa regime from a long term perspective. The Russian Federation has already agreed to a temporary solution for transit regulations to and from Kaliningrad through Lithuania, a compromise that might optimally result in a visa-free regime between the EU and Russia. In the meantime, the Schengen regulations should be applied flexibly for crossing the borders between Poland/Lithuania and Kaliningrad.

To reduce the socio-economic asymmetries between Kaliningrad and its neighbours, the Russian federal government has to further strengthen its engagement with Kaliningrad. The EU should accept that Kaliningrad is a special case and should support it as such to prevent a deepening of the existing welfare gap. A first step was made with the establishment of the new Interreg III-A programme for CBC between Kaliningrad, Poland and Lithuania. Furthermore, the Russian Federation should give its subject regions and municipalities – especially the Kaliningrad oblast – more competencies in relations with foreign regions. Regions need to obtain more autonomy of decision for the formation of CBC. The municipalities need financial assistance from the national budget and the right to set their own taxes in order to finance cross-border projects.

Finally, and most importantly, actors in CBC should consider ways of improving their conditions for cooperation. For their part, it would be wise to articulate their interests in the framework of EU–Russian cooperation. They can counteract differences in mentality and the lack of trust through common activities, meetings, seminars and workshops (e.g. intercultural communication), in which they might be sensitised to the situation of the other. Historical prejudices, which are particularly serious at these borders, could be reduced through communication. Only in a situation of mutual communication and mutual understanding of motives and needs, will it be possible to avoid misunderstandings within CBC and have successful cooperation. This is a reason for even more cultural and youth exchange. The Euro-regions in particular could act as a forum, in which different interests are brought together and existing anxieties and reservations are devitalised.

The development of CBC can only succeed when all actors, not just administrations, participate in cooperation (AEBR 2004: 9). A common internet forum could be set up in order to disseminate information about actors, projects and the legal basis of CBC. Supporting the development of a civil society in the framework of CBC is very important in this regard.

Notes

1   Euro-regions are associations of regional and local administrations and authorities from both sides of the border. According to the definition of the Association of

European Border Regions (AEBR) they are acting as a level of compromise between different structures of administration and different competencies on both sides of the border and serve as a hub for all cross-border relations between citizens, politicians, institutions, the economy, social and cultural partners (AEBR 2000: 9).

2 PHARE: Poland and Hungary: Assistance for Restructuring their Economies. Originally the PHARE-CBC programme was intended to assist the economies of Poland and Hungary, but soon it was extended to other countries in Central and Eastern Europe and since the end of the 1990s, it has aimed at the preparation of the candidates for accession. The programme for CBC has existed since 1994, and since 1998 has been in operation in the border regions with Kaliningrad.

3 The TACIS-CBC programme was introduced in 1991 to support the transformation process in thirteen partner states in Eastern Europe and Central Asia. Since 1996, there has been a CBC programme for the Russian Federation, Ukraine, Belarus and Moldova.

4 Between October 2004 and February 2005 the author visited these locations in the course of her Ph.D. project on 'Regional Cooperation between the Russian oblast Kaliningrad, Poland and Lithuania. An Analysis of the Cross-border Cooperation at the External Borders of an Enlarged EU' at the Schleswig-Holstein Institute for Peace Research on the Kaliningrad region and the bordering regions in Poland and Lithuania. There she conducted forty-seven interviews with staff members of the regional administrations and parliaments, city administrations, Euro-regions and universities as well as with representatives of the business sector and NGOs. The interviews included questions about the institutions and the contents of CBC, about the work of the Euro-regions, the effects of CBC, the relationship between the central government and the regions/municipalities, the effect of the national border, and the obstacles and motivation for CBC.

5 This agreement was renewed with the agreement from 19 June 1999 (Russia–Lithuania Agreement 1999).

6 In 1991, the administration of Kaliningrad signed an agreement with the Polish voivodship Olsztyn, which was followed by similar agreements with the voivodships Gdansk and Elblag (1992). Analogous agreements were signed after the administration reform in Poland of 1999, with the newly-founded voivodships of Warmińsko-Mazurskie (2001) and Pomorskie (2002). Furthermore, the administration of the oblast signed agreements on cooperation with the Lithuanian counties Klaipeda, Taurage and Marijampole (1995). Agreements on parliamentary cooperation have existed since 2002 between the regional Duma in Kaliningrad and the Sejm of the voivodship Warmińsko-Mazurskie as well as with the Sejm of the voivodship Pomorskie. The city of Kaliningrad cooperates with the Polish cities of Olsztyn and Gdansk as well as with the Lithuanian city of Klaipeda since 1993 and with the Polish cities of Elblag and Gdynia since 1994. Furthermore, agreements on cooperation between counties and municipalities were signed, but most of them at the end of the 1990s only.

7 The Polish–Russian Cooperation Council was established in 1994, yet it was not until 2000 that the Lithuanian–Russian Cooperation Council was established as a result of a new agreement between the national governments concerning the cooperation between Lithuanian counties and Kaliningrad in 1999 (Russia–Lithuania Agreement 1999).

8 Unresolved issues in Polish–Russian relations included the 1940 Katyn massacre and the expulsion of a large part of the Polish population after the Second World War. In the fifteen years after the end of the Cold War period, there were territorial claims of the Lithuanian Minor (Paleckis 1993: 27; Wellmann 2003: 282; Schmidt 2003: 170–1) as well as of Polish national movements (Sakson 1993: 39). There have been further

resentments over: Polish authorities expelling Russian diplomats from the Russian embassy in Warsaw in 1999 because of spying; the Lithuanian government rejecting the invitation of Russian authorities to participate in the celebrations marking sixty years since the end of the Second World War in Moscow in 2005; the presidents of Poland and Lithuania not being invited to the celebrations marking 750 years of Kaliningrad/Königsberg, also in 2005.

9   For detailed information about the programme see www.interreg3a.org.

10   Interview with Roma Stubriene, head of the coordination centre in Klaipeda, 3 November 2004.

11   The Euro-region Nemunas was founded in 1997, and its members are municipalities from Russia (Kaliningrad region), Poland, Lithuania, and Belarus (see www.nemunas-euroreg.lt). The Euro-region Baltica was founded in 1998, and its members are municipalities from Russia (Kaliningrad region), Poland, Lithuania, Latvia, Sweden and Denmark (see www.eurobalt.org). The Euro-region Saule was founded in 1999, and its members are municipalities from Russia (Kaliningrad region), Lithuania, Latvia and Sweden (see www.siauliai.aps.lt/saule). The Euro-region Šešupe was founded in 2003, and its members are municipalities from Russia (Kaliningrad region), Poland, Lithuania and Sweden (see www.sesupe.lt). The Euro-region Łyna-Ława was also founded in 2003, and its members from the Kaliningrad region are the municipalities of Bagrationovsk, Gusev, Ozersk and Pravdinsk and the city of Mamonovo; from Poland the members are the municipalities of Bartoszyce, Braniewo, Elblag, Goldap, Gizycko, Ketrzyn, Lidzbark, Olecko, Olsztyn and Wegorzewo (see Modzelewski 2004: 65).

12   See database of the Interreg III-B BSR Programme at www.bsrinterreg.net.

13   Interview with Alla Ivanova, head of the TACIS Local Support Office in Kaliningrad, Kaliningrad, 20 October 2004.

14   See database of the Interreg III-A Programme at www.interreg3a.org.

15   See PHARE Programme and Commission (2003a). For TACIS programme see Court of Auditors (2001); Commission (2001); for TACIS CBC Indicative programmes 2000–3, see http://europa.eu.int/comm/europeaid/projects/tacis/index_en.htm.

16   The PHARE programme is run by the Directorate General (DG) for Enlargement, the Interreg programme by the DG for Regional Policy and the TACIS programme by the DG for External Relations.

17   Interview with Edmund Wojnowski, Professor at the Research Centre Wojciech Ketrzynski in Olsztyn, Olsztyn, 25 October 2004.

18   Own experience of the author at the checkpoint Bagrationovsk (Kaliningrad region) /Bezledy (Poland) in October 2004.

19   Until 1999 self-governed municipalities existed, whereas the self-government of counties and voivodships was introduced in 1999.

20   The Kaliningrad region consists of thirteen regions and three independent cities (Kaliningrad, Sovetsk and Baltijsk).

21   In the Kaliningrad region there is insufficient computer equipment (Internet, email) as well as telephone, fax and paper supply in offices.

22   In reference to a 'mentality', cultural stereotyping is not intended. The idea of a mentality in this context refers to a Soviet and communist legacy that contributed to a particular way of thinking (i.e. those structures, institutions, and people's ideas of duties and obligations while under the Soviet regime).

References

Agreement (2007), 'Agreement Between the European Community and the Russian Federation on the Facilitation of the Issuance of Visas to the Citizens of the European Union and the Russian Federation', *Official Journal of the European Union*, 17 May.

Association of Communes of the Republic of Poland of Euro-region Baltic (2003), *Small Projects Fund in the Baltic Euroregion: Phare Programme – Polish Eastern Border*, Elblag.

Association of European Border Regions, ed. (AEBR 2000), *Practical Guide to Cross-border Cooperation*, 3rd edn, Gronau, European Commission Regional Policy.

Association of European Border Regions, ed. (AEBR 2004), *European Charter of Border and Cross-border Regions*, new version, Gronau, European Commission Regional Policy.

Birckenbach H.-M. and C. Wellmann (2005), 'Managing Asymmetric Interdependence: A Comparative Approach on the Kaliningrad Policies of Core Actors', in *Kaliningrad 2020: Its Future Competitiveness and Role in the Baltic Sea Economic Region*, ed. K. Liuhto, Turku, Pan-European Institute, available on the Internet at www.tse.fi/FI/yksikot/erillislaitokset/pei/Documents/Julkaisut/Liuhto_72005.pdf (accessed 4 May 2008).

Bort, E. (2002), 'Illegal Migration and Cross-border Crime: Challenges at the Eastern Frontier of the European Union', in *Europe Unbound: Enlarging and Reshaping the Boundaries of the European Union*, ed. J. Zielonka, London, Routledge: 191–211.

'Business cooperation of the Kaliningrad Region with Poland and Lithuania' ('Business cooperation' 2007), in *Cross-border Cooperation: Russia and Europe*, (6 March), available on the Internet at www.westrus.ru/eng?part=101 (accessed 4 May 2008).

Chancellery of the Prime Minister of the Republic of Poland (1998), *Effectiveness, Openess, Subsidiarity: A New Poland for New Challenges*, Warsaw, Chancellery of the Prime Minister of the Republic of Poland.

Commission (2001), 'A Guide bringing INTERREG and TACIS together', Brussels, European Commission Regional Policy.

Commission (2003a), 'Report from the Commission. The PHARE Programme Annual Report 2001', Brussels, COM 97 final.

Commission (2003b), 'Wider European Neighbourhood: A New Framework for Relations with our Eastern and Southern Neighbours', Brussels, COM 104 final, available on the Internet at www.europa.eu.int/comm/world/enp/pdf/com03_104_en.pdf (accessed 4 May 2008).

Commission (2003c), 'Paving the Way for a new Neighbourhood Instrument' Brussels, COM 393 final, available on the Internet at www.europa.eu.int/comm/world /enp/pdf/com03_393_en.pdf (accessed 4 May 2008).

Constitution of Lithuania (1992), approved by the citizens of the Republic of Lithuania in the Referendum on 25 October 1992, official translation, Ministry of the Interior, available on the Internet at www.vrm.lt (accessed 4 May 2008).

Constitution of Poland (1997), available on the Internet at www.sejm.gov.pl/prawo/konst /angielski/kon1.htm (accessed 4 May 2008).

Court of Auditors (2001), 'Special Report No. 11/2001 Concerning the Tacis Cross-border Cooperation Programme Together with the Commission's Replies (2001/C 329/01)', *Official Journal of the European Communities*, C 329, 23 November: 1–28.

Euro-region Annual Report (2001), *Fundusz Małych Projektów [Small Project Fund]*, Stowarzyszenie Gmin RP Euroregion Bałtyk [Associations of Polish regions in the Baltic Euro-regions].

Hreczuk, A. (2002), 'Polish–Russian Relations and Kaliningrad', in *Russian Participation in the Baltic Sea Region-Building: A Case Study of Kaliningrad*, ed. P. Holtom and F. Tassinari, Gdansk, Berlin, BaltSeaNet, The Baltic Sea Area Studies: Northern

Dimension of Europe: 68–91.

Jóskowiak, J. (2003), 'Trans-border and Inter-regional Cooperation of Poland at the Threshold of its Membership in the European Union', *Polish Foreign Affairs Digest*, 2(7): 145–76.

Krämer, R. (1999), 'Zwischen Kooperation und Abgrenzung – Die Ostgrenzen der Europäischen Union' ['Between cooperation and isolation: The EU's eastern borders'], *WeltTrends*, 22: 9–26.

Kulesza, E., E. Romanowska and B. Samojłowicz (2004), 'Cooperation by Commune Governments', in *Polish–Russian Cross-Border Cooperation: Report*, ed. E. Romanowska and B. Samojłowicz, Olsztyn, The Borussia Cultural Community: 33–8.

Modzelewski, W. T. (2004), 'Euro-regional Cooperation Between the Borderland Regions of Poland and the Kaliningrad Oblast of the Russian Federation', in *The Framework of Regional Development in Cross-border Areas of North-Eastern Poland and the Kaliningrad Oblast*, ed. T. Palmowski, Gdynia, Pelplin, University of Gdansk: 64–9.

Paleckis, J. (1993), 'Das litauische Resümee' ['The Lithuanian experience'], in *Die Zukunft des Gebietes Kaliningrad (Königsberg). Ergebnis einer internationalen Studiengruppe. Sonderveröffentlichung* [*The future of Kaliningrad. Report by an international study group. Special publication*], ed. BIOst, Köln: BIOst.

RSFSR–Lithuania Agreement (1991), 'Agreement on Cooperation in the Economic and Social-cultural Development of the Kaliningrad Oblast', 29 July.

Russia–Lithuania Agreement (1999), 'Agreement on Long Term Cooperation of the Kaliningrad Oblast of the RF and the Counties of the Republic of Lithuania', 29 June.

Russia–Poland Agreement (1992), 'Agreement on the Cooperation of the Kaliningrad Oblast of the RF and North-Eastern Voivodships of the Republic of Poland', 22 May.

Russian Federation (1993), 'The Constitution of the Russian Federation', available on the Internet at www.constitution.ru/en/10003000–01.htm.

Sakson, A. (1993), 'Das polnische Resümee' ['The Polish experience'], in *Die Zukunft des Gebietes Kaliningrad (Königsberg). Ergebnis einer internationalen Studiengruppe. Sonderveröffentlichung* [*The future of Kaliningrad. Report by an international study group. Special publication*], ed. BIOst, Köln, BIOst.

Schmidt, T. (2003), *Die Außenpolitik der baltischen Staaten. Im Spannungsfeld zwischen Ost und West* [*The foreign policy of the Baltic states in the context of their relations with the East and West*], Wiesbaden, Westdeutscher Verlag.

Schneider, E. (1999), *Das politische System der Russischen Föderation. Eine Einführung* [*The political system of the Russian Federation. An introduction*], Opladen, Wiesbaden, Westdeutscher Verlag.

Tauber, J. (2002), 'Das politische System Litauens' ['The political system of Lithuania'], in *Die politischen Systeme Osteuropas* [*The political systems of Eastern Europe*], ed. W. Ismayr, Opladen, Leske & Budrich: 149–84.

Vinokurov, E. (2004), 'Economic Prospects for Kaliningrad: Between EU Enlargement and Russia's Integration into the World Economy', CEPS Working Document 201, available on the Internet at www.ceps.be.

Wellmann, C. (2003), 'Recognising Borders: Coping with Historically Contested Territory', in *The Kaliningrad Challenge: Options and Recommendations*, ed. H.-M. Birckenbach and C. Wellmann, Münster, Lit Verlag: 273–96.

TOBIAS ETZOLD

9

Regional organisations in the Northern Dimension area and Kaliningrad

Introduction

The Northern Dimension (ND) of the EU was launched in 1997 and has since developed as an initiative to address the challenges and opportunities of north-eastern Europe, in particular its border regions and north-west Russia. From the outset, the Kaliningrad oblast of the Russian Federation (RF) was an issue for action and cooperation. The second Northern Dimension Action Plan (NDAP) stressed the importance of the development of Kaliningrad by establishing the region as a 'cross-cutting theme'.

Regional organisations in north-eastern Europe and other partially sub-regional organisations, initiatives and programmes have contributed considerably to the elaboration and implementation of the Northern Dimension. The major regional organisations include the Council of the Baltic Sea States (CBSS), the Nordic Council of Ministers (NCM), the Arctic Council (AC), the Barents Euro-Arctic Council (BEAC), and the Nordic Council (NC). Several of these regional and sub-regional organisations – especially the CBSS, NCM and NC – have developed activities in Kaliningrad.

The involvement of so many actors in projects or programmes generates both problems and advantages. Among the problems are the duplication of structures, inefficient work, indistinct results and an unclear division of labour and tasks. The main advantages are that activities could complement each other and solve problems more efficiently, comprehensively and with a long term perspective. This, however, requires close and efficient coordination of activities and cooperation between the organisations, which is noticeable in relation to projects in Kaliningrad.

This chapter briefly outlines the main features and characteristics of the Northern Dimension as it pertains to Kaliningrad. It points to potential overlap and coordination problems among regional actors within the ND, as well as the advantages offered by the theoretical perspective known as 'network governance approach'. Furthermore, the chapter identifies the specific measures undertaken by regional organisations that concern Kaliningrad, and analyses their effectiveness and success. Finally, those measures that have been (and could yet be) taken for improving the cooperation and coordination of the activities of different actors in Kaliningrad are analysed.[1]

The Northern Dimension and Kaliningrad

On a Finnish initiative, the plan to develop an EU–Northern Dimension policy emerged in 1997, its main incentive being an increase in attention towards north-eastern Europe. In geographical terms, the ND covers the Baltic Sea region (BSR), north-west Russia, Norway, Iceland and the Barents Euro-Arctic region. The plan sought to address the new and special development challenges in the region which emerged due to significant changes in the 1990s (i.e. the collapse of the Soviet Union, regained independence of the Baltic States, accession of Sweden and Finland to the EU), as well as to address the political, economic, cultural, and scientific opportunities the region has to offer. The principal objective was to provide added value through reinforced coordination and complementarity of activities, initiated by the EU and individual member states, which were directed towards the region and sought to enhance cooperation between the countries of north-eastern Europe (Council 2000: 2). The ND, promoting a partner-oriented approach, established a political framework for cooperation between EU member states, candidate countries (Poland, Estonia, Latvia and Lithuania) and non-member, non-candidate countries (Iceland, Norway and the Russian Federation) (Catellani 2000: 12). It dealt with both internal and external EU policies and offered a common framework for the promotion of policy dialogue and concrete cooperation. Adopted by the European Council in Feira in June of 2000, the first 'Action Plan for the Northern Dimension in the external and cross-border policies, 2001–2003', set out the objectives, areas to be addressed and the means to achieve the goals.[2]

The second Northern Dimension Action Plan of 2004–6 emphasised five broad areas of priority: 1) economy, business and infrastructure; 2) human resources, education, scientific research and health; 3) the environment, nuclear safety and natural resources; 4) cross-border cooperation and regional development; 5) justice and home affairs (Commission 2003). The plan also introduced two 'cross-cutting issues': the Arctic region and the Kaliningrad oblast, marked as regions with specific development needs. Although they had been subjects of cooperation within the first NDAP, marking the Arctic region and Kaliningrad as cross-cutting issues highlighted the specific relevance of these regions. Having identified needs from all five thematic areas, ND activities were to be applied to both cross-cutting issues. The second NDAP stated that 'given its particular geographic situation as a Russian exclave surrounded by the European Union it is however particularly important to enhance dialogue and cooperation between Kaliningrad and neighbouring Northern Dimension partners' (*ibid.*: 13). For example, special attention has been paid to economics in Kaliningrad, with the establishment of an enhanced framework for trade and investment, supporting administrative reform, the promotion of business-to-business links and Small and Medium Enterprise development, the security of energy supply, and the development of regional transport networks. In the oblast, the NDAP also deals with environmental problems such as water and soil pollution, urban waste and chemicals. Furthermore, between Kaliningrad and the neighbouring EU countries, special emphasis was placed on promoting cross-border person-to-person cooperation on economic, social and environmental issues (*ibid.*: 13–14).

After the adoption of a Political Declaration and a Northern Dimension Policy Framework Document, the ND entered a new stage in January 2007. The ND became a common policy of the EU, the Russian Federation, Norway and Iceland, allowing these non-EU states an equally important role in the decision-making and implementation process. The new ND increasingly focuses on north-west Russia and is becoming more instrumental as a regional expression of the four Common Spaces[3] forming the core of a future EU–Russia strategic partnership (Finland Presidency of EU 2006: 3). Cross-border cooperation that enhances regional development and involves civil society and people-to-people contact will continue to be an important cross-cutting theme (*ibid.*). In light of its particular geographical situation, Kaliningrad was again specified as one of the ND priority areas (*ibid.*: 1; Council 2005a: 2).

'Overlapping institutions': regional organisations in the ND area

Originally, the plan was to apply a three-level structure to the ND: EU, regional and sub-regional/local levels. Regional organisations were intended to act as an interface between the EU level – in which the ND policy and objectives were shaped with some impact by external actors – and the sub-regional/local level, where the policy was to be applied (Lannon and van Elsuwege 2004: 25–6). The CBSS, AC and BEAC have been official ND stakeholders since the launch of the first NDAP in 2000, giving them, at least in theory, a role in the ND preparation and implementation process. The NCM became an official partner in 2004. However, it was particularly during the ND's first implementation phase that the status of the regional actors was one of consultancy rather than implementation partners, hampering the realisation of the intended three-level structure (*ibid.*: 28).

Alongside these intergovernmental organisations, parliamentary regional bodies participate in the implementation of the ND, i.e. the Nordic Council and Baltic Sea Parliamentary Conference (BSPC); moreover, international financial institutions, and many partly sub-regional and sub-state organisations of small and medium size, like the Baltic Sea States Sub-regional Co-operation (BSSSC) and the Union of Baltic Cities (UBC), are also involved. While discussing future ND policies at the 2005 ND Ministerial meeting, the foreign ministers praised the efforts carried out by the AC, BEAC, CBSS and NCM (Council 2005b). What is more, the new guidelines for the ND policy mentioned the role of regional bodies positively and called for 'enhancing the synergies of these organisations, maximising the use of the resources available for the region, while avoiding any possible overlapping' (Council 2005a: 2). This last point is of particular importance, as there are still risks of overlap and structure duplication due to the large number of organisations and initiatives with similar thematic and geographical foci.

Though similar on paper, the inputs, the exact geographical scope, the concrete topical foci, and the specific projects of the regional organisations differ to some extent. This is also true of the historical and political background and working structures of the organisations. Therefore, a potential institutional overlap, in some aspects, need not have a negative connotation, especially if the various actors (institutions or individuals) can efficiently cooperate and coordinate their activities. In the theoretical literature, negative overlap implies a duplication of activities and structures, jeopardising efforts more than achieving particular goals (Johansson 2002: 41), while positive overlap is marked by the complementarity of various actors in the same field. The 'network governance approach' could be applied to achieve synergy and 'added value' through inter-institutional cooperation in north-eastern Europe. In this model, several actors at the supranational, national or sub-state level coordinate their policies and resources, 'in order to realise synergies through shared policy and economic projects, and hence jointly create an area of governance' (*ibid.*: 41). Each guided by their own policy interests, the different actors play different roles and undertake different responsibilities, but to some extent cooperate to achieve a common goal (*ibid.*). The ND area has had the potential for applying such a network governance model in practice. Until now it has not been used sufficiently in all areas, although there have been positive indications of its increased application in recent years.

The potential for negative overlap can be identified between the adjacent area policies of the NCM and the general activities of the CBSS, BEAC and AC. All five of the Nordic States are members of these organisations yet the NCM adjacent area policies cover fields for which each of the other organisations were specifically designed. For example, the NCM stresses the importance of cooperation in the Baltic Sea region and its specific problems (NCM 2004a: 2) without explicit or adequate referral to the CBSS in relevant policy documents. Although co-funding of activities between the Councils is a way to interlink activities, the rationale of the Nordic countries in promoting co-funding is questionable because they are active in several organisations that simultaneously fund the same kind of projects (Mariussen *et al.* 2000: 39). In the context of Kaliningrad, it is important to identify the overlap concerning relations with the Russian Federation. The post-Cold War organisations – AC, BEAC and CBSS – were to some extent designed to contribute to a normalisation of relations between Western Europe and the Russian Federation at the regional and sub-regional levels, yet they partially cover similar issue areas and geographical parts of Russia. The Nordic Council of Ministers and the Nordic Council also developed an approach towards Russia through their adjacent areas policies. While cooperation with Russia is discussed at the Councils' meetings, the implementation of concrete projects mainly takes place at a bilateral level, which bears the potential for an additional coordination problem (*ibid.*: 38–9).

Activities of regional organisations in Kaliningrad

Since the second NDAP initiated the cross-cutting region issues, there have been activities in Kaliningrad that pertain to almost all the thematic issue areas of the ND. Of the regional organisations in north-eastern Europe, it has especially been the CBSS, NCM and NC that have frequently discussed Kaliningrad's future as well as developed activities in the oblast.

The CBSS and Kaliningrad

The CBSS comprises eleven member states[4] and the European Commission. It functions as an 'umbrella' organisation for many of the small and sub-regional organisations, initiatives and programmes in the BSR. The CBSS was founded in 1992 with the main objectives of reunifying a divided region, promoting regional cooperation on a wide range of issues, and assisting the avoidance of new divisions between the countries of the region. The Council is mainly active in the fields of economic cooperation, environmental protection, development and promotion of democratic institutions, higher education and culture. From the start, it was willing to take an active role in the ND's implementation and to coordinate the ND activities of various BSR organisations (CBSS Secretariat 2000).

Kaliningrad was an issue of discussion within the CBSS almost from the outset. The specific incentive of the CBSS to get involved in Kaliningrad can be found in its general purpose to avoid the rise of new dividing lines in the BSR and to promote democratic development around the Baltic Sea. In the communiqué of the third Ministerial meeting in Tallinn in May of 1994, the CBSS expressed its support for a request by the Russian government, asking for an extension of the Baltic States' Euro-Faculty to the State

University of Kaliningrad. Furthermore, the increasing interest of Kaliningrad and St Petersburg in sub-regional cooperation was noted. The CBSS expressed its hope that such participation would contribute positively to the economic restructuring and revitalisation process of these regions (CBSS 1994). Within the declaration of the 1999 Ministerial session of Palanga/Lithuania, and in the context of EU enlargement, the Council underlined the importance of enhancing various types of cross-border activities and people-to-people contacts between Kaliningrad and other regions of the RF (CBSS 1999). The communiqué of the 2001 Ministerial meeting in Hamburg expressed the Council's willingness 'to serve as a forum for dialogue, especially promoting projects and issues related to the development of Kaliningrad Oblast' (CBSS 2001). To stress the importance of general Baltic Sea cooperation, the oblast hosted several CBSS meetings at the senior official, working group and ministerial level. The eleventh anniversary Ministerial meeting held in Svetlogorsk in 2002 was a highlight. In the Svetlogorsk Declaration, the CBSS expressed its support for regional measures to promote the development of the oblast, such as the Euro-Faculty project, and tripartite training initiatives in Lithuania, Poland and Russia (CBSS 2002).

One important CBSS project continues to be Euro-Faculty Kaliningrad, launched in 1999 and inaugurated in September 2000. While the Euro-Faculty project for the Baltic States concluded in 2005, Kaliningrad Euro-Faculty continued until the summer of 2007, and there are plans to launch a similar project in Pskov, north-west Russia, based on the positive experiences of Euro-Faculty Kaliningrad. The overall objective of the Euro-Faculty project at the Kaliningrad State University (KSU) Immanuel Kant was to modernise the education of the faculties of economics and law. The project aimed to meet the demands imposed by increasing internationalisation, cross-border trade and contact, and the general need to integrate Kaliningrad more closely in the Baltic Sea region (see chapter 14 in this volume). The CBSS Euro-Faculty assisted the reform of higher legal education by introducing modern teaching methods, retraining young academic staff locally, developing academic courses, and reforming the respective curricula. By 2003, progress had been made in the updating of curricula as well as the libraries, the development of more demanding teaching methods, and foreign language training. These results gave some hope that the positive development can be continued and future sustainable results achieved: thus, the project was extended until 2007.[5] When the project was concluded in July 2007, most of the original objectives had been achieved, and the results seem to be sustainable. Evidence of Euro-Faculty's overall effect can be perceived in the consideration of Russian authorities, in that they now believe that KSU is an 'innovative university' (CBSS 2006b: 5).

The CBSS Working Group on Democratic Institutions (WGDI) dealt with various issues connected to the development of democracy in

Kaliningrad. On a working visit there in May 2006, the WGDI and the Ombudsman of the oblast discussed problems of civil and human rights education, human trafficking, rights of children in custody, the right of freedom of movement and the right to a fair court trial. Furthermore, the WGDI cooperated with Euro-Faculty to hold a mini-seminar on good governance (CBSS 2006c: 16).

The CBSS Working Group for Economic Cooperation (WGEC) has launched plans to establish a business support group in Kaliningrad in order to assist in improving the conditions for economic growth, foreign investment and business promotion. In April of 2005, representatives from the business community and entrepreneurs of the Kaliningrad oblast participated in a special joint session of the Committee of Senior Officials (CBSS-WGEC) that assessed the current economic situation and development prospects in the region. They exchanged views on challenges and opportunities in Kaliningrad and EU countries, and discussed new methods of interaction between their business networks (CBSS 2005a: 11–13). The Business Advisory Council, an autonomous body within the CBSS framework, visited Kaliningrad in March 2005 to establish contacts with the local business community. The CBSS also discussed the reduction of wait times at Kaliningrad's borders to a two-hour maximum (the programme 'Year 2000 – 2 hours'). Finally, the CBSS Taskforce on Communicable Disease Control (2000 to 2004) dealt with the spread of tuberculosis and HIV in Kaliningrad.

The NC and the NCM's adjacent areas policies in Kaliningrad

The Nordic Council of Ministers, established in 1971, is the oldest intergovernmental regional organisation in Northern Europe promoting cooperation between the five Nordic countries and the autonomous regions. The Nordic Council, founded in 1952, serves as an inter-parliamentary forum for the Nordic countries and promotes parliamentary cooperation in various fields. Since the 1990s, following Sweden's and Finland's accession to the EU, the NCM and NC have adjusted their working and organisational structures. It has been particularly the NC that has based its activities on a three-pillar structure: Nordic cooperation, European policies, and cooperation with the adjacent areas (BSR, Baltic States, north-west Russia and Kaliningrad, Barents and Arctic regions). In 2001/02 this structure was amended again; at that time the Council returned to a more issue-oriented rather than geographical-oriented structure.

The main objectives of the adjacent areas policies were to contribute to a secure and stable development in various respects: to strengthen democracy, to broaden common Nordic values to other parts of Northern Europe, to contribute to the development of free market economic systems and to promote sustainable development. The Council implemented specific projects in the fields of democracy and welfare state policies, culture, development of market economy and the sustainable use of resources (Nordisk Råd och Ministerråd 2003). In the framework of its adjacent area policies, the NCM established information offices in the capitals of the three Baltic States (1991) and St Petersburg (1995) and several information points in cities of north-west Russia. These latter have several important functions for north-west Russia. They constitute the local contact points for Nordic sectoral ministerial councils, committees and working groups. They develop networks with national authorities, NGOs and other national and international players. Finally, they serve as the NCM's local observers, identifying trends and opportunities for joint Nordic–Russian cooperation and doing the practical day-to-day work, like organising exchange programmes (NCM 2005b: 113).

During most of the 1990s, the focus of the adjacent areas policies was on the development of the three Baltic States and their preparation for EU accession. After EU enlargement in 2004, the focus shifted towards north-west Russia. The framework programme 2003–5 for the NCM's activities in the adjacent areas emphasised increasing cooperation with north-west Russia and Kaliningrad (NCM 2002: 6). The NCM endorsed 'guidelines' and a specific Russia programme from 2006–8, in order to facilitate future cooperation with Russia's north-west.[6] During this period, funding is to be redirected towards knowledge-building and network programmes, participation in EU/ND partnerships, and cooperation with NGOs (NCM 2005a: 26). In the context of the new adjacent areas policies towards Russia, it could be expected that the NCM will also pay more attention to Kaliningrad than before (although mention of the oblast in NCM documents is still more general than specific). However, the NCM guidelines state that there is significant need for cooperation with Kaliningrad and the development of the oblast will require an increasing commitment by the NCM (NCM 2004b: 4).

Since the end of the 1990s, Kaliningrad has been discussed several times in both the NC and the NCM and has become the issue of several reports and recommendations. The Nordic Council in particular took the initiative to move Kaliningrad onto the Nordic cooperation agenda, proposing measures to become engaged in the oblast more actively and calling on the NCM to establish an information point in Kaliningrad as early as 2000. A committee of the NC dealing with cooperation between its members and adjacent areas, as well as several delegations of parliamentary groups, paid visits to the region in order to obtain a better picture of the situation and judge measures that needed to be undertaken. There was some consensus among Nordic parliamentarians that in order to avoid any further isolation of Kaliningrad in the course of forthcoming EU enlargement, greater efforts were needed to integrate the exclave more closely in the Nordic–Baltic cooperation process. Sven Erik Hovmand, then spokesman of the Danish delegation to the NC, visited Kaliningrad in January of 1999 and stated that unless Nordic countries prevented the increasing isolation of the Kaliningrad and Leningrad oblasts, they would form 'ticking bombs' destabilising the entire region (Hovmand 1999). As the Nordic States would be directly affected by any instability in the BSR, this statement can be interpreted as a clear motive for direct involvement in Kaliningrad by the Nordic countries and institutions. Gun Hellsvik, then Swedish NC President, admitted during her speech to the NC's annual meeting in November 1999 that it was a mistake not to have paid attention to Kaliningrad earlier (Nordic Council 1999).

Perhaps in response to these concerns, the NCM along with the Danish Foreign Ministry and the European Commission organised a conference on 'The Northern Dimension and Kaliningrad Region – European and Regional Integration' in Copenhagen in May of 2000. The aim of the conference was to draw attention to Kaliningrad and to contribute to the elaboration of an ND policy in the region. The conference facilitated the exchange of opinions, information and experiences regarding Kaliningrad, and resulted in the formulation of activities in Kaliningrad for the first NDAP.

After this conference, the opening of an information office in Kaliningrad and organising a donor conference (see below) for Kaliningrad became priorities for the NC's and NCM's Kaliningrad policy. Following their visit to Kaliningrad in 2000, the adjacent areas committee of the NC, and later the civil and consumer rights committee, prepared a report on the democratic development of the oblast. From this report, the NC asked the NCM to take further steps. What is more, the NC agreed to explore the possibilities for democratic development through cooperation between civil organisations and the CBSS Commissioner. The NC also initiated closer parliamentary cooperation in questions of 'good governance' regarding effective administration, functioning institutions and legal reforms (Nordic Council 2002: 1). Finally, the NC report outlined the severe environmental problems and the poor health conditions in the oblast. However, because other regional organisations were already conducting work, the Presidium of the NC decided not to become active in areas like environment and health (*ibid.*: 2).

On the NC's initiative, the NCM launched plans in 2002 to organise a donor conference for Kaliningrad to investigate current activities, jointly identify and prioritise areas of necessity, and then coordinate existing and future projects. This conference should have included those actors active in Kaliningrad (governments, CBSS, EU-TACIS, sub-regions, etc.) and exerted a coordinating framework function for cooperation with Kaliningrad. However, the NCM did not intend to coordinate current funds for Kaliningrad because they perceived that several national governments were already doing this (Nordic Council 2003). Thus, the plans to hold such a conference could not yet be realised, especially as the NCM was of the opinion that it would be unrealistic to organise a conference before an information office was established in Kaliningrad. The NCM believed that a permanent presence as organisational backup was crucial for the purpose of organising a conference (*ibid.*).[7]

After lengthy preparations and negotiations with the Russian Federation, in which it appeared that the Russian authorities were reluctant to give the NCM permission to realise their plans, the NCM opened an information office in Kaliningrad in 2006. Ostensibly, the main task of the office has been to develop, coordinate and implement the policies of the NCM towards Kaliningrad in all relevant policy areas, in close cooperation with local agencies. The information office is also expected to be an important source for information and contacts in the various policy fields for the planning of activities within the region. The exchange and network programmes for civil servants, researchers, artists, politicians and business people are also open to citizens of Kaliningrad (Nordiska Nyheter 2005). Kaliningrad even offers good possibilities for network cooperation. Therefore, due to the exclave's central position in the region and its significant needs, the information office in Kaliningrad could serve as coordination point for all other NCM information offices and points in the Eastern BSR (Ojanen 2004: 38).

Another important focus of Nordic activities towards Kaliningrad is the promotion of cross-border cooperation (CBC; see chapter 8 in this volume). Between 2002 and 2005, the NCM launched a programme on regional cross-border cooperation including training seminars and conferences in Latvia, Kaliningrad, Estonia and Lithuania. The programme was coordinated by the NCM office in Lithuania, and the CBSS was involved as a partner. The main objective was to transfer Nordic CBC experiences to these regions and to prepare the candidate states' border regions for EU membership. As a successor of this programme in 2005, the Baltic Euro-regional Network (BEN) was established. BEN operates under the Baltic Sea Region Interreg III-B programme. It includes thirty-five partners from Belarus, Denmark, Estonia, Latvia, Lithuania, Poland, Russia and Sweden with the NCM office in Lithuania as a lead partner. The CBSS is also actively involved in this network. The Sovietsk municipality (Euro-region Saule, Kaliningrad) and the Kaliningrad Regional Duma participate as partners. The main objective is 'to promote spatial development and territorial integration in the BSR by establishing Euro-regions as competent partners for national authorities and international institutions and by building a permanent network of Euro-regions for continuous capacity-building and sharing of experience' (Baltic Euro-regional Network 2005).[8] The expected result of the project is the establishment of a strong network of Euro-regions active in spatial development within the BSR. This network should develop thorough institutional and strategic planning capacities and BEN expects to contribute to a dialogue between Euro-regions and central authorities, transferring experiences from Nordic–Baltic cooperation to the Russian and Belarussian parts of the participating Euro-regions.[9]

The impact of regional organisations in Kaliningrad

The CBSS was one of the first regional organisations which included Kaliningrad in its agenda. The CBSS might have the potential to upgrade its activities, possibly even taking on an international leading role in Kaliningrad. Compared with the NCM and the EU, the organisation's primary advantage regarding an increased engagement in Kaliningrad is the full membership of the Russian Federation. Through its membership, Russia participates in the CBSS decision-making process and can approve or disapprove measures to be taken for Kaliningrad. For the NCM and the EU, Russia is a cooperative partner, but with limited impact on decision-making. This appeared to be one of the major problems of the ND. Russia felt that the NDAPs were impositions by the EU and that its own involvement in the decision-making and implementation process was limited. Having learned from this experience, the new ND framework documents and implementation process tend to involve Russia more actively and equally, changing Russia's role from one of policy-taker to one of policy-maker (Council 2005b: 1; Heikkilä 2006: 3).

After significant external changes in the region generated by EU and NATO enlargement in 2004, the CBSS is searching for new challenges, functions and tasks. Kaliningrad seems to be a natural field of activity, especially considering that much work remains to be done there. The organisation would theoretically be in a position to exert some sort of leading role and initiate and coordinate international activities concerning Kaliningrad, seeing as they are backed by the member states of the EU-CBSS and the European Commission (also as a CBSS member), and cooperate closely with relevant EU institutions and other regional organisations like the NCM. This leadership role would be in line with the CBSS's willingness to serve as a forum for dialogue and promote projects in Kaliningrad, as expressed in Hamburg in 2001.

While Kaliningrad has certainly been an issue for the CBSS for a long period of time, there seem to be only a few concrete, Kaliningrad-specific projects. The list of priorities of the Icelandic (BSS Presidency 2005–6 and the communiqué of the 2005 ministerial session in Szczecin contain issues of cross-border cooperation, civil security, economic development and the Euro-Faculty, which are of relevance for Kaliningrad (CBSS 2005b; 2005c). But Kaliningrad – including all its current and long-lasting problems and challenges – does not appear on any of the documents as a specific policy priority in itself. In previous documents that have outlined the contributions of the CBSS and other BSR organisations to the NDAPs, only the document on the second NDAP contained comprehensive information detailing the current and future projects and policies pertaining to the oblast (CBSS 2003). The CBSS survey on the ND beyond 2006 mentions Kaliningrad in general terms only. The exception was the Euro-Faculty, identified as the only CBSS partnership project in the social sector, and praised for its success (CBSS 2006a: 12, 17).

On the other hand, the CBSS is active and useful in coordinating the general activities of various BSR sub-regional organisations and initiatives, as well as activities in a specific ND and Kaliningrad context. By listing the projects and activities of several actors' contributions to the NDAPs, the CBSS, and particularly its Secretariat, provides useful overviews on ongoing and concluded work. One possible reason for not stressing Kaliningrad as a priority could be what was earlier identified as an advantage for the CBSS's position towards the oblast. Russia may have had an interest in not involving the CBSS too closely in Kaliningrad.

As for the NCM, the eventual opening of an information office in Kaliningrad certainly provides an opportunity to proceed. However, whether the office can meet the apparent high expectations, and whether it could serve as a coordination junction between the NCM's information offices and points in north-west Russia and the various organisations active in Kaliningrad, remains to be seen. Although involvement of the NC and the NCM in Kaliningrad has increased in recent years, the initial Nordic adjacent area policies lacked practical engagement, with the focus clearly on the Baltic States. With the change of focus, the NCM (backed by the NC) might now have the potential to augment its position in Kaliningrad.

In spite of this, the developments have been slow. The NCM's plans to organise a donor conference in and for Kaliningrad have not yet been realised at all. Most striking is that it took such a long time after the planning stage to establish an information office in Kaliningrad. One can speculate that the delay was due to hesitations within the Russian government – which was the official explanation of the NCM – but another plausible explanation is that the NCM did not push the plans forward decisively enough, and missed opportunities to show clearly what positive effect such an office would have for the oblast. The gap between words and actions is noticeable. In general, NC/NCM efforts and their plans in Kaliningrad are more about forms – how to organise cooperation – than the content of specific thematic projects.

Similar to the CBSS, the NCM and NC had not made Kaliningrad a specific priority within its new adjacent areas policies. Often mentioned only marginally in previous NCM and NC policy documents, more recent documents have stressed the special meaning of Kaliningrad. There could be an important psychological effect in awarding Kaliningrad a special status within general Baltic Sea and Nordic–Baltic cooperation. Instead of just mentioning the oblast among many other regions and issues in the relevant documents, there should be a specific emphasis on the problems and needs of Kaliningrad and the risk of further isolation of the oblast. In addition, the regional organisations could make both their presence in Kaliningrad, as well as their specific contributions to problems and solutions, more obvious and transparent. To this end, the NCM information office could be very useful. By

2007, the office seemed to function well and was well perceived by the public. The people of Kaliningrad show openness and interest in Nordic cooperation and in cooperation with the Nordic countries and institutions (NCM secretariat officials in a conversation with the author in July 2007).

While not thoroughly analysed in this context, organisations such as the BSSSC and the Union of Baltic Cities (UBC) conduct important work in Kaliningrad on the sub-regional and local level. In several cases, activities and projects implemented by sub-regional or local (city) partners look more concrete and closer to the needs of the people. Being networks of sub-regions and cities aimed at BSR cooperation, these organisations include the Kaliningrad oblast and its urban areas as equal partners.

Improved cooperation and coordination

For improving cooperation and coordination of activities between ND actors, several useful measures have been taken in recent years. These include the systematisation of information exchange and general relations, regular meetings between secretariats and presidencies, and joint programmes and reports, as well as co-financing projects (NCM 2003a; 2003b; 2005a). Moreover, increased coordination and mutual knowledge of project activities in Kaliningrad is needed to avoid possible negative overlap and implement projects as efficiently as possible.

It is not only with Kaliningrad (but especially there) that communication and coordination of activities on a systematised basis is required between the CBSS and the NCM, because they are the main regional organisations engaged in the oblast. They have begun to establish routines for information exchange between secretariats and presidencies of both organisations, with a view to improve mutual transparency and synergy (NCM 2003b: 15). Cooperation and joint projects are occurring in the various thematic fields.[10]

As a good example of cooperation and implementation of joint working programmes involving several partners at different levels, the BEN project promotes cross-border cooperation. The NCM office in Vilnius plays the lead role while the CBSS is another important partner for implementation. Because of two partners from Kaliningrad oblast in BEN, the programme might have the potential of affecting some integration of Kaliningrad into the networks of Baltic–Nordic cooperation and BSR sub-regional cooperation.

The European Commission has contributed to better coordination of activities through launching the Northern Dimension Information System (NDIS). The NDIS facilitates regular exchanges of information on initiatives and results within the ND, in order to avoid duplication and overlaps, identify gaps, and share best practices. Further objectives of the NDIS are to increase visibility for ND policies and to facilitate stakeholders' participation in projects, maximising their potential synergy (Commission 2004: 10). The

NDIS website, run by the Commission, contains a great deal of information on projects either covering Kaliningrad among other regions or specifically designed for the oblast.

More generally, the idea of establishing additional coordination steering groups should be handled with care because of the large number of existing institutions. In some cases, a division of labour might be more efficient. Considering the many actors coordinating activities in Kaliningrad, an international steering group with representatives of the EU, CBSS, NCM, parliamentary bodies, sub-regional and sub-state organisations (etc.), might be a sensible approach to improve coordination and cooperation, provided they have a clear incentive not to duplicate existing structures.

With regards to division of labour, the NC and the NCM conveyed a sensible attitude in the previously mentioned 2002 report and the recommendations on Kaliningrad. From the draft report, the presidium of the Nordic Council chose only those proposals with specific Nordic action and which were not already covered by other organisations, in particular the CBSS. This was meant to avoid any duplication of work. Of the measures listed in the draft report, the presidium indicated that the CBSS dealt with the diagnosis and treatment of tuberculosis in Kaliningrad through its Taskforce for Communicable Disease Control, and that the CBSS discussed and handled the reduction of waiting times at Kaliningrad's borders. As all five Nordic States are members of the CBSS, the Nordic institutions need not necessarily become engaged with an issue when other bodies are already active in that particular issue area (Nordic Council 2002: 2–3).

Another useful idea, particularly regarding better organising the cooperation between actors, has been the plan for a donor and coordination conference for Kaliningrad that will assemble all relevant actors with interests and projects. One of the objectives of this conference is an overview of all partners in the oblast and their specific fields of activity, so as to avoid negative overlap and to create synergies and networks. With the opening of the new information office, the chances of holding such a valuable conference might have increased.

Theoretically, the information office not only has the potential to serve as the NCM's local contact and coordination point, but also as a coordination point for networking between national and local authorities, NGOs, and international, regional and sub-regional players. It is difficult to judge at this stage whether it is politically feasible for the office to develop facilitating and coordinating functions for the efforts of various actors and thus also serve as a kind of home base for other regional organisations (like the CBSS) and even the EU. First indications show that the office may be able to do this. If it could develop this function, it would positively underline the recent efforts of both the NCM and the CBSS to more closely cooperate in several fields. An important task for the information office would be to guarantee that those non-governmental organisations and private actors that are active in

Kaliningrad will have access to its infrastructure and relevant information resources.

An example where cooperation, division of labour, joint financing and coordination of projects seems to function well is that of International Financial Institutions within the Northern Dimension Environmental Partnership (NDEP). They contribute significantly to the financing and implementation of projects in the environmental sector in the ND area, including Kaliningrad. The NDEP can be regarded as the most visible branch of the ND delivering concrete results. The NDEP Steering Group, comprised of representatives from four international financial institutions, the European Commission and Russia, could serve as an example of how to set up steering/coordination committees and enhance cooperation between institutions in a specific ND issue area. To some extent, the NDEP demonstrates a realisation of opportunities to create synergies by conducting concrete joint projects.

Conclusions

In Kaliningrad, any international effort is generally welcome and in most cases, projects are implemented with a specific purpose and character. Yet there seems to be a certain lack of coordination between actors, as sometimes these actors appear to have insufficient information about each others' activities. This was a stated reason for organising a donor and coordination conference. The opening of the NCM information office in Kaliningrad offers opportunities for international cooperation and coordination efforts. It is of major importance to continue increasing the transparency of actors involved in the projects, as well as linking these actors closely together. As the Nordic Council stated in its recommendations on democratic development in Kaliningrad, positive overlap is suitable as long as organisations avoid involvement in issues which are already covered by other bodies because it might entail redundancy and duplication of work and structures (Nordic Council 2002). Rather than duplicate the work of other bodies, organisations should support each other's activities.

In Kaliningrad there is considerable potential for positive overlap by creating synergies and network governance. Some examples of this potential include having the CBSS as a coordination body for activities of several different BSR actors, as well as having the NC and the NCM as coordinators of Nordic efforts to enhance cooperation and implementation of projects in Kaliningrad. Other positive projects are the Baltic Euro-regional Network, the NDEP, the cooperation of financial institutions in the implementation of environmental projects, and the opening of the NCM information office.

Notes

1   The findings of this paper are mainly based on the analysis and comparison of policy documents of the EU and regional bodies, in particular the CBSS and the NCM.
2   The main areas addressed within the first NDAP were: infrastructure (including transport, energy and telecommunications), environment and nuclear safety, education, research, training and human resources development, public health and social administration, cross-border cooperation, cross-border trade and investment and the fight against crime, in particular cross-border crime (Council 2000).
3   A Common Economic Space; a Common Space of Freedom, Security and Justice; a Common Space of External Security; and a Common Space on Research and Education, including cultural aspects.
4   Denmark, Estonia, Finland, Germany, Iceland (since 1995), Latvia, Lithuania, Norway, Poland, Russian Federation and Sweden.
5   The project is mainly funded by Denmark, Germany, Norway and Sweden. Denmark acts as a so-called 'lead country' administering the project and reporting to the CBSS Committee of Senior Officials. An expert group monitors the use of the funds and the academic progress. For an overview of Euro-Faculty Kaliningrad, see CBSS 2003: 28–9.
6   As key issues of cooperation these documents list: democratic development, IT cooperation, cross-border cooperation, research and innovation, social and public health issues and environment and sustainable development (NCM 2004b: 4; 2005b).
7   In contrast, the NC regarded an information office in Kaliningrad as a facilitating factor but not as a precondition for organising such a conference. From its point of view, a coordination function could also be exerted by the NCM information office in St Petersburg or in cooperation with regional organisations (Nordic Council 2003).
8   The concrete activities of BEN are divided into four work packages. These packages include the thematic exchange of knowledge and experiences, targeted capacity-building for specific regions, the strengthening of the dialogue between Euro-regions and central authorities, and network durability tools ensuring the smooth flow of activities and guaranteeing the continuity of the network after the project's conclusions (Baltic Euro-regional Network 2005).
9   For an overview of the BEN project see Baltic Euro-regional Network 2005.
10   CBC, Northern eDimension Action Plan (NeDAP), transport, freedom of movement, Baltic Sea Region Energy Cooperation (BASREC), ND Partnership on Public Health and Social Wellbeing and sustainable development in the framework of Baltic 21 (NCM 2005a: 66–8).

References

Baltic Euro-regional Network (2005), *BEN – Baltic Euro-regional Network: Info sheet,* available on the Internet at www.benproject.org/repository/BEN_Infosheet_ENG.pdf.

Catellani, N. (2000), 'Outlining the Northern Dimension: Towards Regional Cooperation in Northern Europe', in *The European Union's Northern Dimension,* ed. N. Catellani and A. Missiroli, Maggio, Labboratorio CeSPI (Centro Studi di Politica Internazionale).

CBSS (1994), 'Tallinn Communiqué from Council of the Baltic Sea States 3rd Ministerial Session', available on the Internet at www.cbss.st/documents/cbsspresidencies /2estonian/dbaFile529.html.

CBSS (1999), 'Palanga Communiqué from Council of the Baltic Sea States 8th Ministerial

Session', available on the Internet at www.cbss.st/documents/cbsspresidencies/7lithuanian/dbaFile465.html.

CBSS (2001), 'Hamburg Communiqué from Council of the Baltic Sea States 10th Ministerial Session', available on the Internet at www.cbss.org/documents/cbsspresidencies/9german/communique/.

CBSS (2002), 'Svetlogorsk Declaration from Council of the Baltic Sea States 11th Ministerial Session', available on the Internet at www.cbss.st/documents/cbsspresidencies/10russian/dbaFile779.html.

CBSS (2003), 'Contribution Towards a NDAP 2004–2006', Stockholm, available on the Internet at www.cbss.st/documents/euamd_baltic_region/eund/contributionsfinal.pdf.

CBSS (2005a), 'Annual Report 2004–2005 – Annex 1: 2004–2005 Annual Report of the Working Group on Economic Cooperation', Stockholm.

CBSS (2005b), 'Szczecin Communiqué from Council of the Baltic Sea States 13th Ministerial Session', available on the Internet at www.cbss.st/documents/cbsspresidencies/13polish/szczecin/communique/.

CBSS (2005c), 'Priorities of the Icelandic Presidency of the CBSS 2005–2006', available on the Internet at www.cbss.st/documents/cbsspresidencies/14icelandic/priorities/.

CBSS (2006a), 'Council of the Baltic Sea States' Survey on the Northern Dimension Beyond 2006: Final Report by CBSS Secretariat Senior Adviser Philipp Schwartz', Stockholm, available on the Internet at www.cbss.st/documents/euand_baltic_region/eund/cbsssurveyonthendbeyond2006finalweb.pdf.

CBSS (2006b), 'Progress report on follow-up to the Chairman's Conclusions from the V Baltic Sea States Summit in Laulasmaa, Estonia on 21 June 2004' [An add-on to the Interim Report presented to the CBSS 13th Ministerial Session in Szczecin, 9–10 June 2005], presented by the Committee of Senior Officials to the VI Baltic Sea States Summit in Reykjavik on 8 June 2006, available on the Internet at www.cbss.st/summits/reykjavik2006/reports/progressreportonlaulasmaasummit.pdf.

CBSS (2006c), 'Annual Report from the Committee of Senior Officials: The 14th Year of the Council's activities 2005–2006', available on the Internet at www.cbss.st/summits/reykjavik2006/ministersdeputies/adoptedcsoannualreport2005–2006.pdf.

CBSS Secretariat (2000), 'Background Paper on '"Northern Dimension": For Discussion on the Role for the CBSS', Stockholm, 17 January.

Commission (2003), 'Commission Working Document: The Second Northern Dimension Action Plan 2004–2006', Brussels, available on the Internet at http://europa.eu.int/comm/external_relations/north_dim/ndap/ap2.pdf.

Commission (2004), 'Commission Staff Working Document: 2004 Annual Progress Report on the Implementation of the Northern Dimension Action Plan', Brussels, available on the Internet at http://europa.eu.int/comm/external_relations /north_dim/doc/rep2004_annual_action_plan_report.pdf.

Council (2000), 'Northern Dimension: Action Plan for the Northern Dimension with External and Cross-border Policies of the European Union 2000–2003', Brussels, available on the Internet at http://europa.eu.int/comm/external_relations/north_dim/ndap/06_00_en.pdf.

Council (2005a), 'Guidelines for the Development of a Political Declaration and a Policy Framework Document for the Northern Dimension Policy from 2007', Brussels, available on the Internet at http://europa.eu.int/comm/external_relations/north_dim/doc/guidelines05.pdf.

Council (2005b), 'Joint Press Release on the IV Northern Dimension Ministerial Meeting, held in Brussels on 21 November 2005', Brussels, available on the Internet at http://europa.eu.int/comm/external_relations/north_dim/doc/press_release_05.pdf.

Finland Presidency of EU (2006), 'Northern Dimension Policy Framework Document', available on the Internet at www.eu2006.fi/news_and_documents/other_documents/vko47/en_GB/1164359527520/.

Heikkilä, M. (2006), 'Europa-Ryssland – viktig fråga i finsk politik' ['Europe–Russia – an important question in Finnish politics'], in *Analysnorden* 26 (April), available on the Internet at www.analysnorden.org/analysorden/artikkel.asp?id=404.

Hovmand, S. E. (1999), 'Kaliningrad ønsker mere nabokontakt. Midtengruppen i Nordisk Råd på vellykket besøg i den russiske enklave' ['Kaliningrad wishes more contact with its neighbours. The Centre group of the Nordic Council on a successful visit to the Russian enclave'], *Politik i Norden*, (February), Copenhagen, available on the Internet at www.norden.org/pin/9902/6.htm.

Johansson, E. (2002), 'Northern Europe – network governance and a possibility for synergy among the EU, NATO, the OSCE and regional organisations', in *Programme on the Northern Dimension of the CFSP – The New North of Europe, Policy Memos*, ed. The Finnish Institute of International Affairs, Helsinki, Final Conference 8 October 2002.

Lannon, E. and P. van Elsuwege (2004), 'The EU's Northern Dimension and the EMP-ENP: Institutional Frameworks and Decision-making Process Compared', Working Paper, Ghent, University of Ghent.

Mariussen, Å, H. Aalbu and M. Brandt (2000), *Regional Organisations in the North*, Stockholm, Nordregio.

NCM (2002), 'Rammeprogram 2003–2005 for Nordisk Ministerråds Aktiviteter i Nærområdene' ['Framework programme 2003–2005 for the Nordic Council of Ministers' activities in the adjacent areas'], Copenhagen, available on the Internet at http://www.norden.org/pub/miljo/naer/sk/ANP2002767.pdf.

NCM (2003a), 'Submission of the Nordic Council of Ministers in Preparation for the new Northern Dimension Action Plan 2004–2006', Copenhagen, available on the Internet at www.norden.org/pub/velfaerd/ europa/sk/2003–725northerndimension.pdf.

NCM (2003b), 'Annex: The Nordic Region – a Region of Co-operation', Copenhagen, available on the Internet at www.norden.org/pub/velfaerd/europa/sk/ 2003–725northerndimension-annex2.pdf.

NCM (2004a), 'Retningslinjer for Nordisk Ministerråds samarbeid med Estland, Latvia og Litauen 2006–2008' ['Guidelines for the Nordic Council of Ministers' cooperation with Estonia, Latvia and Lithuania 2006–2008'], Copenhagen, available on the Internet at www.norden.org/pub/miljo/naer/sk/US2004444.pdf.

NCM (2004b), 'Retningslinjer for Nordisk Ministerrådets samarbeid med Nordvest Russland 2006–2008' ['Guidelines for the Nordic Council of Ministers' cooperation with Northwest Russia 2006–2008'], Copenhagen, available on the Internet at www.norden.org/russland/sk/Riktlinjer_NV_Ry_SK.pdf.

NCM (2005a), 'The Nordic Region in an International Perspective: Nordic Co-operation in a European framework 2005', Copenhagen, available on the Internet at www.norden.org/pub/velfaerd/europa/sk/ANP2005783.pdf.

NCM (2005b), 'Nordiska Ministerrådets Rysslandprogram 2006–08' ['Nordic Council of Ministers' Russia programme 2006–08'], Copenhagen, available on the Internet at www.norden.org/pub/miljo/naer/sk/US2005451.pdf.

Nordic Council (1999), 'Nordiska Rådets Session 1999 Stockholm – Tal 013' ['The Nordic Council's session 1999 Stockholm – Speech 013'] by Gunn Hellsvik, President of the Nordic Council, Swedish Parliament, Stockholm, 8–11 November 1999, available on the Internet at www.norden.org/session99.

Nordic Council (2002), 'Presidietförslag om att stöda demokratiutvecklingen i Kaliningrad' ['Proposal from the presidium to support the democratic development in Kaliningrad'], A 1307/presidiet, Copenhagen, available on the Internet at www.norden.org/nr/2–6–3–foersl/sk/A1307.pdf.

Nordic Council (2003), 'Meddelelse om rekommandasjon 13/2002/presidiet Stöd av demokratiutvecklingen i Kaliningrad' ['Communication on recommendation 13/2002/presidium support for the democratic development in Kaliningrad'], A

1307/presidiet, Copenhagen, available on the Internet at www.norden.org /nr/2–6–4–betaenk/betaenk2004/sk/PDF_D-saker/D_2004_2002_13.pdf.

Nordiska Nyheter (2005) [Nordic News], 'Nordiska ministerrådet öppnar i Kaliningrad' ['The Nordic Council of Ministers opens in Kaliningrad'], available on the Internet at www.norden.org/print/news/news.asp?id=5824.

Nordisk Råd och Ministerråd (2003) [Nordic Council and Nordic Council of Ministers], 'Faktablad: Nordens nærområde – Tolv års erfaring med fruktbart samarbeid' ['Fact sheet: Norden's adjacent areas – Twelve years of experience with successful cooperation'], Copenhagen, available on the Internet at www.norden.org/faktb/sk /naromradena_2003.pdf.

Ojanen, H. (2004), 'Utvärdering av Nordiska ministerådets närområdestrategi: Liten men smart?' ['Evaluation of the Nordic Council of Ministers' adjacent areas strategy: Small but smart?'], Helsinki, Utrikespolitiska institutet Helsingfors [The Finnish Institute of International Affairs Helsinki], available on the Internet at www.norden.org /naromraaden/sk/Evaluering_naer.pdf.

PART III

Empirical evidence: Kaliningrad and policy adaptation *vis-à-vis* the EU

Evgeny Vinokurov

10

Economic policy

Introduction

No Russian region suffered as severe an economic disruption following the dismantlement of the Soviet Union as Kaliningrad, because its location ensured a high level of exposure to the destabilising effects of the post-communist economic transformation. Traditional economic links were broken, and between 1991 and 1998, a 70 per cent reduction in industrial productivity threatened the economic survival of the oblast. However imperfect, the Special Economic Zone (SEZ) established in 1991, and legally anchored in 1996, was a lifesaver.

This region, with a population of less than one million inhabitants, attracted much attention from Russia and the European Union in 2002 and 2003. In 2002, when Kaliningrad found itself at the forefront of EU–Russian negotiations, the EU and Russia both recognised the unique nature of the oblast, the existence of its special problems, and the necessity of applying a special approach to solve them. However, the focus has been on transit regime issues, while a number of more substantial and complicated problems have prevented regional authorities from forming the proper conditions for foreign investment and cross-border trade in Kaliningrad. Aside from more general visa problems, access to the proximate EU market in order to reduce a dangerous over-dependence on the mainland Russian economy is an issue, which will also determine the competitiveness of local enterprises on regional, Russian and foreign markets.

The issue of Kaliningrad's economic development is important not only for the region, but also for the Russian economy and its economic policies in general, as well for EU–Russia relations. The decisions on passenger transit through Lithuania implemented in 2002-3 represent just a fraction of the exclave–mainland communication problem, which in turn is also just one element of the exclave's economic development. Kaliningrad's economic and political transition is still under way and is complicated by conditions of enclavity and exclavity as well as by the need to adjust to external economic and political challenges. Although the great crises of the 1990s have been overcome, exclave-specific problems remain, and Kaliningrad's economic development is still debated despite eight years of continuous growth.

This chapter will discuss the regional and federal economic policy of Kaliningrad, beginning with the domestic context and then analysing the existence and limits of external pressure. For the latter, the primary focus is the EU and its member states as well as their impact on the exclave's economy through trade links and assistance. Does Russia's federal system of governance allow the regional level to autonomously change and adapt to European norms and standards? In the field of economic policy, how can the general mechanisms of adaptation and transfer between 'Europe' and Kaliningrad best be described? To answer these questions, the domestic Russian context is set against an external framework in order to understand which endogenous and exogenous factors are most relevant, so far, in inducing decisive changes in Kaliningrad's economic policy.

The domestic context in Russia

In the economic field, the Russian Constitution of 1993 assigns a number of competencies exclusively to the federal level. Article 71 states that the jurisdiction of the federal government shall include, amongst other things: determining the basic principles of federal policy and federal programmes in the field of the economy; establishment of the legal framework for a single market; financial, monetary, credit and customs regulation; distribution of currency and guidelines for price policy; federal economic services, including federal banks, the federal budget, federal taxes and levies; federal funds for regional development; and foreign trade relations of the Russian Federation. Article 72 of the Constitution describes the joint jurisdiction of the RF and the oblasts, which includes, amongst other things: issues pertaining to the possession, use and management of land, minerals, water and other natural resources; protection of the environment and ecological safety; legislation pertaining to the administration and procedures for labour, family and housing; legislation on mineral and extraction rights; coordination of the international and external economic relations of the regions; and compliance with international treaties of the Russian Federation.

Due to Kaliningrad's location as an enclave in Europe, one of the most pertinent consequences of this particular federal design is that the regional competences in the field of foreign economic and trade policy are strictly limited. In fact, Kaliningrad is not supposed to possess any foreign economic policy of its own and its regional role is limited to two domains: administering the SEZ within the limits prescribed by federal law; and cross-border cooperation. The predominance of the federal level is compounded by recent political developments, in which regional governors are *de facto* appointed by the president, only requiring the regional legislative body to approve the presidential nomination. Vladimir Egorov's term as governor ended in November of 2005, and he was replaced by Georgii Boos, who was 'parachuted' in from Moscow to cement the link between Moscow and Kaliningrad.

Consequently, there are several levels of legislation and strategies, with each level defining the subsequent one. First, there are general federal economic policies and strategies that target Russia altogether and are relevant for all regions. The second level has specific federal policies towards Kaliningrad, particularly through the tools of the SEZ and the Federal Target Programme (FTP). The third is Kaliningrad's regional development strategy, and the fourth level contains the action plans of the regional government, ministries, and municipalities.

Besides looking at the federal structure of the state, a natural question would be whether the regional business community plays an important role as another political actor. As the region is small, there are a number of big businesses and business associations that are highly visible, and manage to transform their size into actual power on the regional level. Such was the case during the regional elections of 2002, when the heads of several businesses supported Governor Egorov, and were rewarded with vice-governorships. Under Governor Boos, the head of the largest regional retail group, *Vester*, has become the head of the regional Duma, whereas the head of the second-largest retail group, *Viktoria*, has been appointed a minister for industry and trade. While the influence of these businesspeople is highly visible on the regional level, where Kaliningrad has much less impact – in Moscow – their influence is much less. The central element of the new federal policy towards Kaliningrad, the new SEZ adopted in January 2006, runs contrary to the interests of the big regional companies that built their businesses on the customs preferences anchored in the previous SEZ.

With the active development of regional business associations, there are two types that have emerged. First, there are a number of industry representations, such as the Association of International Road Carriers (ASMAP) for automobile transportation companies or the association of furniture-makers, which are active in lobbying their cause at the regional level. And as their influence is not strong enough to lobby directly to the Kremlin, they prefer to act through, or in concert with, the regional administration and indirectly via the federal government representatives in the region, its ministries, and the Customs Committee. The second type of business association is that of a 'club'. The most well-established club is the Baltic Business Club, which has provided the venue for meetings between political candidates and potential business supporters, thus following the example set by their Western counterparts.

Altogether, neither legislation nor the concrete political setting provides much room to manoeuvre for Kaliningrad's regional authorities to autonomously change and adapt to European norms and standards in the field of economic policy. Therefore, the economic policy of Kaliningrad is essentially federal, which generally coincides with domestic political developments since 2000. There is an additional factor specific to Kaliningrad: Moscow has a particular interest in keeping tighter federal control over the region because of strategic concerns over separatism. But after acknowledging that Kaliningrad's economic policy is mainly federal policy, there remains the potential for an indirect Europeanisation of Kaliningrad via the Europeanisation of Russian economic policy. This will be touched on later in this chapter in the context of the new SEZ law.

The crucial role of the federal policy: the SEZ and the FTP

The SEZ regime has played the crucial role in Kaliningrad's economic policy as it defined the current economic specialisation of the oblast. Regional industry and trade has re-arranged itself over the last decade to take full advantage of SEZ preferences. The leading industries, food processing and machine building, are to a large extent based on these preferences. If SEZ preferences were removed, it is possible that these industries would not survive. This dates back to the break-up of the Soviet Union and the beginning of the lengthy economic transition period, when Kaliningrad was fully integrated into the Soviet economy. During the early transition period, regional industries underwent a process of fundamental restructuring masked behind the broad definition of sectors. As an industry, machine building was completely changed. The majority of machine production in Kaliningrad during the Soviet era was actually mechanical engineering and production of group 'A' goods (i.e. capital goods) not group 'B' goods (i.e. consumption goods). Only a fraction of the group 'A' manufacturers survived the transition crisis, being replaced by manufacturers of household electronics assembled in Kaliningrad. The food processing industry has also undergone a profound change with fisheries and fish processing in relative decline although remaining significant to the local economy. While food processing relied on domestic sources during the Soviet period, it is now largely based on imported foodstuffs. As a final example, the pulp and paper industry has moved towards producing higher-value goods (i.e. moving from cellulose to paper and paperboard). These examples demonstrate how the regional economy has adapted to new economic conditions while utilising the opportunities provided by the SEZ regime.

The SEZ of Kaliningrad 1996: a springboard to the Russian market

Since 1996, the primary legal document specifying the design of Kaliningrad's SEZ is the Federal Law 'On the special economic zone in Kaliningrad Oblast' (Russian Federal Law 1996). According to this law, the SEZ in Kaliningrad is rather specific and unlike other special economic zones, in that it is a part of the Russian state and its customs territory, but also an unusual type of customs-free zone. As in a typical customs-free zone, there are no import taxes in Kaliningrad (i.e. no customs duties, no VAT on foreign trade transactions, nor excise taxes). What is more, goods deemed to be of local manufacture and exported to the Russian Federation are also exempt from customs duties. In order to enjoy these privileges, locally manufactured products must satisfy the following conditions: for electronics and household appliances 15 per cent value-added; for other goods, 30 per cent value-added. There are some additional criteria for certain manufactured goods (automobiles, tractors, etc.).

The specific design of existing customs privileges has created an incentive to use cheaper imports for manufacturing in order to sell goods on the Russian market. It has provided a powerful impetus towards trade intermediation and the development of industries aimed at this market, with the opportunity to be a convenient springboard for others into Russia not lost on the businesspeople of Kaliningrad. According to the Customs Office, the volume of customs preferences for Kaliningrad-based companies reached 5.1 billion roubles in 2001 (US$170 million). About 80 per cent of the industrial production is shipped to the Russian mainland using the SEZ preferences, and only 20 per cent is either exported or consumed in the region. In 2004, half of the television sets produced in Russia, two thirds of the vacuum cleaners, 16 per cent of canned meat, 37 per cent of canned fish, 11 per cent of fish and marine products, 6 per cent of furniture, 5 per cent of pulp and 2.7 per cent of vodka and other alcoholic beverages were manufactured in Kaliningrad.

The new SEZ regime since 2006

Work on a new federal law for the Kaliningrad SEZ began in 2002, conducted by an expert policy group under the leadership of Igor Shuvalov, Deputy Head of the Presidential Administration. The underlying principles for the improvement of the SEZ regime were the following:

1　Compatibility of the SEZ regime with common international practice (in particular, the WTO rules on the threshold of Russia's WTO accession);
2　Continuity of current and new mechanisms;
3　Change of focus from customs preferences to tax preferences;
4　The maximum removal of administrative barriers.

With regards to the first principle, a number of research and policy-advice projects have been funded by the EU and led by European experts (and others). These projects have fostered the idea that the Kaliningrad SEZ might be incompatible with WTO requirements. Arguably, therefore, EU assistance has indirectly induced changes in the SEZ legislation of 2006.

The new federal law on the SEZ Kaliningrad was adopted in January 2006

(Russian Federal Law 2006). The following is a summary of its core elements. First of all, Kaliningrad remains a customs-free zone; the SEZ is administered by a special authority integrated into the regional Government. The operating time for the new SEZ law is twenty-five years from its adoption. Second, the draft law envisaged a temporary co-existence of two regimes, old and new. The old regime corresponds to the customs preferences of the 1996 law with two changes: companies producing electronics will also have to produce 30 per cent value added to be able to sell their goods to the Russian mainland without taxes and duties; and producers will be obliged to pay export tariffs and duties. The old regime is valid for another ten years (i.e. until 2016), but companies must choose under which of the two regimes they will operate. After the transition period (ten years after the law comes into effect) only the new regime will be valid.

The new regime provides full income tax relief for six years for new companies that invest 150 million roubles (€4.4 million) or more after the new SEZ law has been adopted. During years seven to twelve, the income tax is reduced by 50 per cent. The new regime also provides property tax relief for companies on the same conditions and within the same time frame. To be eligible for the new regime, companies must fulfil several requirements: a minimum of 150 million roubles has to be invested within three years (if the company fails to invest the minimum limit it must pay the taxes in full); a minimum of 70 per cent of the remuneration of labour, 90 per cent of fixed assets, and 70 per cent of actual production must occur within the SEZ; and investment projects cannot be aimed at oil and gas extraction, the production of vodka and liquor, tobacco and tobacco goods, wholesale and retail trade, repair services, or financial services. Furthermore, Russian entry visas will be issued at border crossings for 'representatives of SEZ resident companies, investors, and persons invited to discuss the possibilities of cooperation in the SEZ, based on the application by the regional Government' (Russian Federal Law 2006: Art. 20). While this would seem to simplify the procedure for entering Kaliningrad, the impact will be negligible because it will benefit a very limited group of people.

If the new SEZ regime is not helped by other measures (like intensive export promotion), it will encourage large industrial projects that target the Russian market, likely leaving the export vector unexploited. As the new SEZ law does not support the development of services for smaller business projects and discriminates against the region's small and medium-sized enterprises, it is characteristic of the old industrial paradigm. The law is likely to inhibit the development of modern advanced industries and especially services in Kaliningrad, and effectively promotes a traditional twentieth-century industrial orientation to the detriment of a twenty-first-century service economy. There is a discernible difference between this and the current trends in the regional economic policies of EU states, which strive for advanced post-industrial specialisations.

Federal Target Programme: reproducing the existing costs scheme of economic growth

The first Federal Target Programme for the development of the SEZ Kaliningrad was adopted in 1997 for the time span of 1998-2005. However, this programme was grossly under-funded – the oblast received only 3 per cent of the planned federal financing – and essentially existed only on paper. As the economic situation in Russia improved, a new FTP was approved in 2001, containing various investment projects with a total investment of about US$3 billion over the period 2002–10. The core economic strategy for regional development is to bring the SEZ up to date, accelerate the oblast's socio-economic development, and improve the population's standard of living. This should be achieved by developing trade as well as scientific and technical cooperation with other countries, by creating favourable conditions for foreign investment, technologies and management experience, and finally, by increasing the potential of Russian enterprises and regional exports. According to the FTP, the importance of federal financing for the oblast will gradually increase, counterbalancing the financial support provided by the EU to member states adjacent to Kaliningrad.

The FTP foresees various sources of financing: the federal budget (19.3 per cent of total financing); federal budgetary loans; the regional budget (4.7 per cent); private financing (17.6 per cent); foreign loans (12.5 per cent) as well as other sources. The Programme consists of 113 investment programmes of an extremely diverse nature, from building a deep-water port in Baltiysk to reconstructing stadiums. The Programme puts no emphasis on either import-substituting or export-oriented production which are in the list of Programme measures under the general heading of 'Development of export-oriented and import-substituted manufacturing'. Although the FTP states that 'the core of the planned strategy … is the development of export-oriented sectors and new design of products with an extensive use of the region's hi-tech and industrial potential' (Federal Target Programme 2002: 13), this statement is apparently outside of the real context of the FTP. A total of 9.5 per cent of financing and 28 out of 113 projects are stipulated to be a re-orientation of the region's economic structure towards exports.

The real priorities of the FTP are revealed through the list of the projects where federal financing is envisioned. In fact, the Programme reproduces the existing patterns of economic growth in Kaliningrad; evident in the fuel and power industries which are supposed to attract 47.1 per cent of the total amount of FTP financing. The largest investments in this sector, and for the overall Programme, are made in the construction of a gas-run power station (the TEZ-2, costing RUR 13.1 billion or US$450 million). The construction of this power station furthers the goal of providing power security for the region, but in turn results in the doubling of demand for natural gas in Kaliningrad. This entails not only additional costs for infrastructure development for transportation and storage, but also increased supply dependency.

The FTP does not entail any breakthrough projects nor new ideas that change the economic structure of the region, provide new impulse to its development, or identify its long term specialisation. Development measures for export-oriented and import-substituted production are mostly based on the existing SEZ regime and rely on price competition. However, the Programme does stress the positive results of a potential agreement between Russia and the EU that would guarantee the consistency of SEZ legislation, the application of EU standards across the territory of the SEZ, and special simplified procedures for the movement of people (Federal Target Programme 2002: 7).

The 'Regional Development Strategy'

In 2003, the regional administration published the 'Strategy of social and economic development of Kaliningrad Oblast as a region of cooperation up to the year 2010' (Administration of Kaliningrad 2003). The Strategy emphasises a social mandate and an ambition to increase the living standards and quality of life of the population, with the benchmarks being neighbouring Poland and Lithuania. Although this gap in living standards is not quite as large as assumed by expert data (Samson *et al.* 2002), this remains a difficult target because of the dynamic development of these countries in recent years through the effects of EU enlargement. A secondary but nonetheless important feature of the Strategy is the implementation of principles of sustainable development, balancing economic, social and environmental spheres. A final priority is the future of the oblast as a region of cooperation in which regional, interregional, Russian and international interests will be interlinked.

There are four main components of the Strategy. The first is to ensure the efficient use of natural resources and economic potential to the benefit of national and regional interests. The second is to establish Kaliningrad as a region of cooperation between the Russian Federation, the EU, the Commonwealth of Independent States, other countries of the world and other Russian regions. Third, the region will become the territory where Russia makes contact with Europe, perfecting the mechanisms of integration and interaction between Russia and the EU. The fourth is to maintain Russian military and strategic interests, since Kaliningrad is the base of the Russian Baltic Fleet. As two of the components of the Strategy possess a European dimension, clearly Europe is important in official documentation revealing Kaliningrad's desire to cooperate and integrate with the EU as well as find a place on the EU–Russian economic and trade interface.

An inherent problem of the official Strategy is the gap between the stated goals and actual means used to achieve those goals. The Strategy does not entail any major mechanisms that would explicitly promote Kaliningrad as an open region specialising in high technologies and advanced services. The official Strategy, as well as the FTP in 2002 and the new SEZ law in 2006, have all adopted the conceptual rhetoric of a 'region of cooperation', a 'pilot region', and the export substitution strategy,[1] thereby weakening any concrete liberal content.

The EU's impact on Kaliningrad's economy and economic policy

From 1991 to 2003, direct EU assistance to Kaliningrad was estimated to be over €50 million, with a number of projects related to the economic sphere, primarily supporting regional trade and investment. The EU accelerated its technical assistance to the region after the Kaliningrad transit crisis in 2002–3. €25 million was earmarked for the period 2004–6 under the 'Special Programme for Kaliningrad', a part of the National Indicative Programme for Russia. Here, it was argued that 'requirements for Russia's accession to WTO and the expected evolution of the economic landscape after EU enlargement will question the sustainability of the SEZ system and force a decisive re-orientation on export industry development' (Commission 2003: 31). EU projects covered institution building, energy, transport, enterprise restructuring, management training and the environment. In the economic sphere, the EU promoted innovative small and medium-sized business activities, trade and investment, and the improvement of energy distribution and its efficient use at industrial and municipal levels. Programmes of vocational training were also relevant as a vital part of the economic policy. In addition, of the twelve 'neighbourhood programmes' within Interreg III-A that have been implemented on the EU's eastern border from 2004 to 2006 (see chapter 8 in this book), one of them was a programme with a budget of €8 million for Kaliningrad, Poland and Lithuania.

The impact of EU assistance on Kaliningrad's economic policy has been indirect for an obvious reason: Kaliningrad is an integral part of the Russian Federation making the effect difficult to estimate. The influence is channelled through the following mechanisms:

1 Economic research: A substantial part of the economic research on Kaliningrad's development, trade and investments has been financed by TACIS.[2] TACIS projects have stimulated the elaboration of various development concepts – like the idea that the Kaliningrad SEZ might be incompatible with WTO requirements (see section entitled 'The new SEZ regime since 2006' in this chapter) – which have partially entered the official thinking at both the federal and regional level.

2 Technical assistance: Projects have been implemented in the realms of administration, environmental management, and economic development (including air transportation, port development, etc.). They were funded both through TACIS and by various government funds within the

Baltic Sea area (Denmark, Sweden, and Germany being the most active).
3 Training of officials: Officials from the regional administration,
   Kaliningrad City Hall and other municipalities of the oblast have participated in various vocational training programmes sponsored and
   organised by both the EU and its member states (again Denmark,
   Sweden, and Germany being the most active sponsors). The programme
   themes have included administrative reform, regional development, and
   environmental management.

Indirect evidence of the relative insignificance of the EU on Kaliningrad's
economic policy is demonstrated by an assessment of the consequences of EU
enlargement on Kaliningrad's regional economy (i.e. trade relations, growth,
etc.). After the accession of Poland and Lithuania, the EU became
Kaliningrad's dominant foreign trading partner. Prior to the 2004 EU
enlargement, about 40 per cent of regional foreign trade was with the EU-15,
30 per cent with Poland and Lithuania, and another 5 to 7 per cent with other
EU candidate countries. Since 2004, the enlarged EU accounts for 75 to 80 per
cent of Kaliningrad's foreign trade, approximately equal to the volume of
trade with mainland Russia.

However, empirical evidence from 2004–5 has suggested that the impact
of the enlargement has been modest (Vinokurov 2007: 206–8). Although the
EU eastern enlargement had a one-time impact on Kaliningrad (and will
probably have a more sizeable protracted impact in the long term), none of
the aspects of the EU enlargement became a decisive factor for Kaliningrad's
economic development during the first half of the 2000s, whereas the SEZ
regime formed and dominated the principal economic trends. The SEZ
regime, Russian federal policy and increased consumption in mainland
Russia are also responsible for the growth and composition of Kaliningrad's
trade with the EU. In other words, the positive developments in Kaliningrad
from 2003 to 2005 cannot be attributed to the enlargement *per se*, but rather
to increased production targeting the Russian market because of rapidly
growing consumer demand and the fuller use of opportunities created by the
SEZ regime. Increased exports are explainable by statistical and accounting
methods, not as a reflection of any significant *real* growth. Furthermore, in
terms of the volume and geographical distribution of Kaliningrad's foreign
trade structure, there has been neither positive nor negative change.
Enlargement did not have any apparent short term effect on foreign investment, and the increase of the EU share was simply automatic; the sum total of
previous trade volume with the EU-15 and CEE-10.

The areas of specialisation in the regional economy do not compel businesses to adapt to the requirements of the Single Market, as more than 85 per
cent of SEZ production is shipped to the Russian market. The smaller EU
share is dominated by raw materials, with raw oil making up 67.3 per cent of
these exports in 2004.[3] So there is no compulsion or even indirect-coercive

pressure for Kaliningrad's export-oriented sectors to adapt to the production standards of European partners.

Beyond public economic policy there is also the economic behaviour of private business actors, and how the business community feels about adaptation to 'European' requirements. Interestingly, the dominant and practical orientation towards the Russian market within public policy does not coincide with the ideas of entrepreneurs and business managers when they consider the potential of various markets for Kaliningrad products.

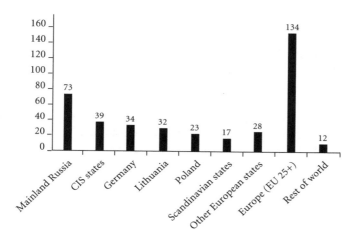

Figure 10.1: What market do you judge to be the most promising for Kaliningrad goods?

Source: Results of the survey within the project 'Development Support of the Kaliningrad Region', 2003.

Twenty-eight per cent of Kaliningrad's business managers consider the Russian market as the most promising (73 out of 258 respondents). However, if all responses given in favour of the European states are summed up (as there was no explicit response option for the EU), 52 per cent (134 respondents) favoured Europe as the most promising destination. While this might be interpreted as a sign of their understanding of the potential importance of EU markets, it is still remarkable that such a large share of Kaliningrad businesspersons and managers regard the EU as potentially the most promising market. While this renders no apparent impact on current regional specialisations, it indicates a widespread understanding of the necessity to change specialisations in the future to adapt to the requirements of the Single Market. And evidence of this understanding can also be found within the regional government and amongst public policy-makers, in a number of official documents and strategies. For example, both the official Regional Development Strategy and the Federal Target Programme put supportive emphasis on the importance of the EU. While the Programme stresses the positive results for Kaliningrad of a potential agreement between Russia and the EU, the Strategy formally aims to establish Kaliningrad as a region of cooperation in the Russia–EU context and as a 'pilot region' of EU–Russia integration.

On the whole, the impact of the EU and its member states on Kaliningrad's economy has been moderate and channelled indirectly (through technical assistance, economic research, and training) and thus been predominantly cognitive. Virtually nothing has been done to adapt to the requirements of the Single Market as far as norms and standards are concerned. Proposals which should have enabled Kaliningrad-based producers to re-orientate their production towards EU markets, like the Centre for EU Norms and Standards (Kiel group 2002), have yet to be put into action. The strength of the Russian domestic framework and the resulting character of the SEZ ensured that neither individual market players nor regional economic policy-makers feel compelled to adapt or orient themselves to Europe (or even interact with any other partner like the United States for that matter). That said, Kaliningrad's enclavity and geographical proximity to the EU has brought about the situation in which the EU and its member states appear to be the only actors, other than Russia itself, which are able to exert any impact on the oblast's economic policy. The only notable exception is the impact of WTO guiding principles on the new SEZ legislation.

Conclusion

Regional authorities in Kaliningrad cannot autonomously change and adapt to European norms and standards in the field of economic policy because neither federal legislation nor the concrete political setting will allow it – Kaliningrad's economic policy is federal policy. It is realised primarily through the Special Economic Zone, supplemented by the Federal Target Programme on Kaliningrad. The SEZ regime has resulted in a one-sided orientation of the regional economy towards the Russian market, and such an economic specialisation provides no compelling reason for 'European' adaptation in Kaliningrad. Although the EU and its member states have exerted indirect influence on Kaliningrad's economic policy, its scope is far inferior to the direct impact of the Russian federal centre. Instead, the EU's influence has been predominantly cognitive and has been channelled through such tools as technical assistance, policy research, and vocational training.

While the Europeanisation of Kaliningrad's economic policy has been limited so far, there has been some influence. First, there was an indirect impact through WTO-related advice concerning the new SEZ law. Second, the official Development Strategy and other official documents have been strongly influenced by the results of EU-funded and led projects (i.e. the necessity of export specialisation, the 'pilot region' concept, a region of cooperation). However, this impact has been more rhetorical than substantial. Third, the cognitive impact through technical assistance, vocational training, and grants and stipends should not be underestimated, even though they require time to materialise in concrete policy decisions. Fourth, there is widespread understanding amongst businesspersons and managers of the potential necessity to adapt to 'European' norms and standards in the long term. Fifth, there has been discernible evidence in official documentation that suggest that policy-makers generally share in this understanding. Finally, Kaliningrad is susceptible to changes through the Europeanised federal economic policy of the Russian Federation.

Notes

1 For a description of the 'region of cooperation' strategy see Khlopeckiy and Fedorov (2000) and Klemeshev, Kozlov and Fedorov (2002); for the 'pilot region' concept see Kiel group (2002) and Birckenbach and Wellmann (2003); for the three-phase transition to export substitution see Samson *et al.* (2000). A comprehensive comparison of these and other development strategies can be found in Vinokurov (2007: chapter 9).
2 Examples include the 'Support for the regional development of Kaliningrad, Russia' in 2003-5 (EUROPEAID/114287/C/SV/RU) and the project that preceded it, entitled 'Promoting trade and investment in Kaliningrad Oblast of Russia'.
3 There is a difference in data for Kaliningrad exports and SEZ exports. The figures for the former are much larger since they include goods produced in other regions but considered by state statistics to be exported from the oblast (North-Western Customs Office 2005: 27).

References

Administration of Kaliningrad (2003), 'Strategiya social'no-ekonomicheskogo razvitiya Kaliningradskoy oblast kak regiona sotrudnichestva na period do 2010 goda' ['The Strategy of the social-economic development of the Kaliningrad oblast as a region of cooperation until 2010'], Kaliningrad, available on the Internet at www.gov.kaliningrad.ru (accessed 15 August 2007).
Birckenbach, H.-M., and C. Wellmann, eds (2003), *The Kaliningrad Challenge: Options and Recommendations*, Münster, Hamburg, London, LIT.
Commission (2003), 'National Indicative Programme: Russian Federation', Brussels, adopted 21 May 2003, available on the Internet at http://ec.europa.eu /comm/external_relations/russia/csp/04-06_en.pdf (accessed 15 August 2007).
Federal Target Programme (2002), 'Federal Target Program of Development of the Kaliningrad Oblast until 2010', available on the Internet at www.programs-gov.ru /cgi-bin/index.cgi?prg=135 (English version at http://kaliningrad-rda.org/en /development/docs.php) (accessed 15 August 2007).
Khlopeckiy, A. and G. Fedorov (2000), *Kaliningradskaya oblast: region sotrudnichestva* [*Kaliningrad oblast: the region of cooperation*], Kaliningrad, Yantarny Skaz.
Kiel international ad-hoc group of experts on Kaliningrad (Kiel group 2002), *Kaliningrad in Focus: Policy Recommendations in the Perspective of Problem-solving*, Kiel, Schleswig-

Holstein Institute for Peace Research, SHIP-Texts 67.

Klemeshev, A., S. Kozlov and G. Fedorov (2002), *Ostrov sotrudnichestva* [*The island of cooperation*], Kaliningrad, Kaliningrad State University Press.

North-Western Customs Office (2005), 'Obshaya kharakteristika vneshney ekonomicheskoy deyatel'nosti Kaliningradskoy oblasti v 4 kvartale 2004 goda i za god v celom. Tamozhenny bulleten' 2004/4' ['General characteristics of the foreign economic activities of the Kaliningrad oblast in the 4th quarter of 2004 and in 2004 in general. Customs Bulletin 2004/4'].

Russian Federal Law (1996), 'On the Special Economic Zone in the Kaliningrad Oblast', FZ 13, *Rossiyskaya gazeta*, 30 January.

Russian Federal Law (2006), 'On the Special Economic Zone in the Kaliningrad Oblast', FZ 16, *Rossiyskaya gazeta*, 19 January, available on the Internet at www.rg.ru/2006 /01/19/kaliningrad-dok.html. (English version at www.gov.kaliningrad.ru/index .php?idpage=584) (accessed 15 August 2007).

Russian Federation (1993), 'The Constitution of the Russian Federation', available on the Internet at www.constitution.ru/en/10003000-01.htm (accessed 15 August 2007).

Samson, I., V. Bilchak and G. Fedorov (2000), *Kaliningrad Region 2010: Potential, Concepts and Prospects*, Grenoble, Kaliningrad, Moscow, Pierre Mendès-France University.

Samson, I., V. Lamande, I. Elisseeva, N. Burova, G. Fedorov (2002), *A New Look at Kaliningrad Region*, available on the Internet at http://web.upmfgrenoble.fr /pepse/IMG/pdf/kalinewlook2.pdf (accessed 15 August 2007).

Vinokurov, E. (2007), *Ekonomicheskaya specializaciya Kaliningradskoy oblasti* [*Economic specialisation of the Kaliningrad oblast*], Kaliningrad, Immanuel Kant Russian State University Press.

Vyacheslav Dykhanov

11

European principles in a Russian context: the transformation of social policy?

Introduction

When compared with other regions of the Russian north-west, the Kaliningrad oblast cannot be deemed successful in terms of its socio-economic development (see Klemeshev and Fedorov 2004; Ministry of Economy 2005). The region's economic decline after the Soviet collapse could not be halted or even reversed by the liberalising reforms of the early 1990s. Regionally specific circumstances, such as small size, exclavity, over-dependence on imports and the failure to adequately convert the Soviet military-industrial complex into civilian industrial structures have created unfavourable conditions for self-sufficiency and growth. The financial crisis of 1998 triggered an economic recovery in Kaliningrad with growth rates above 10 per cent, but did not substantially change the region's social situation.[1] The low employment rates and low incomes are combined with comparatively high prices in an import-dependent exclave, and these have contributed to low standards of living. It is only through a 'grey economy' (contributing from 60 to 95 per cent of the gross regional product), and 'shadow incomes' (equal to 43 per cent of official wages), that socio-economic hardship is not even more widespread (Eliseeva and Burova 2002: 7; Samson *et al.* 2003: 3–4).[2] Nevertheless, the public health situation has deteriorated and the mortality rate increased (see chapter 13 in this volume).

The situation is even more distressing if Kaliningrad is compared to surrounding EU countries. Despite this, Kaliningraders prefer to compare themselves with their neighbours in Poland, Lithuania and even Germany rather than with fellow Russians in the regions of Pskov or Novgorod. Moreover, the Kaliningrad regional authorities have established high expectations with their 'Regional Strategy of Socio-Economic Development for the Period 2002–10', especially in the stated aim of 'sustainable growth in the standards and quality of living for Kaliningrad oblast population [that is] decreasing the gap in the standard of well-being between the oblast and neighbouring countries' (Kaliningrad Regional Administration 2004: 5). The governor of the oblast, Georgii Boos, reconfirmed this strategic goal in his inaugural speech of October 2005, declaring that 'in five years we must catch up with neighbouring countries on the indicator of per capita income'. This priority was included in two new documents on socio-economic development in the region, i.e. the 'Strategy' (covering twenty-five years, see Kaliningrad Regional Administration 2007), and the 'Programme' (covering ten years, see Kaliningrad Regional Administration 2006).

As the idea of 'Europe' is a prominent reference point in the public discourse on living conditions and social standards, to what extent does this play a role in the actual development of social policies and the social situation of Kaliningrad? This chapter will examine the contextual variables in Europe as well as in Kaliningrad's domestic sphere in order to elucidate the influences that have shaped the decisions and developments within social policy in Russia and Kaliningrad.

The Russian social policy model

The shadows of Russia's communist past

The development of social policy in Russia during the 1990s was affected by its communist past, in which a paternalistic Soviet state had secured a high degree of fixed social protection. In contrast, the market economy envisaged by Russia's liberal politicians of the early 1990s proscribed a minor role for the state in social policy. However, the population was not willing to accept a more liberal social policy based on civil initiatives. As a result of the long term Soviet paternalism, it preferred to remain socially passive. Thus, many Russians felt abandoned by the new democratic authorities (see Piirainen 1997: 6–21). In order to lower social tensions within this new and fragile democracy, Russian politicians made promises and expressed preferences to a variety of target social groups. Indeed, social rights were seemingly secured by the Russian Constitution of 1993 and subsequent legislation. But this legislation was not backed by adequate financial resources, which prohibited social policy reforms proposed by the so-called 'old Liberals' (i.e. Egor Gaydar, Anatoliy Chubays, Boris Nemtsov). In a nutshell, social policy legislation during the 1990s was nothing more than declarations of future intent.

Social policy under Putin

After Vladimir Putin's election as head of state in 2000, the conditions and opportunities for fundamental regulatory change began to be realised, including rather unpopular social reforms. First, the strengthening of the federal executive's power and legitimacy expanded their political room for manoeuvre in introducing less pleasant measures. Second, the considerable growth of budget revenues (from US$30 billion in 2000 to more than US$100 billion in 2005) increased the financial resources available for compensatory social measures. Altogether, the wave of social reforms initiated by Putin's 'Mladoliberals' (the 'new Liberals' such as German Gref and Aleksey Kudrin),were aimed at reducing social 'free-riding', encouraging self-development, attracting non-governmental actors to social services and social policy, and introducing competition to so-called 'socially-oriented sectors', such as educational and medical services, and services in culture and sports.

Federalism in the field of social policy

Social policy is embedded in the federal structure and decision-making processes of Russia. Basically, the competences and responsibilities in the field of social policy are distributed between three levels of power: federal, regional and municipal. However, one has to differentiate between various aspects within the sphere of social policy. The main financial source of *social protection* in Russia is the federal government. Regional authorities fulfil most of the actual duties in social protection and labour market regulation, executing federal subventions and providing vulnerable groups with social services. The municipal authorities provide local communities with social services from regional subsidies.

Table 11.1 Distribution of competences of public authorities in social protection

Level of public power	Responsible institutions	Target groups
Federal	Ministry of Social Development and Health Protection, Pension Fund, Fund of Social Insurance	Pensioners; 'social' pensioners (persons with a disability); unemployed persons
Regional	Ministry of Social Policy and Labour	Persons with a disability (in-kind aid, registration, medical expertise); veterans of armed conflicts (World War II, Afghanistan, Chechnya); pregnant women; victims of political repressions; prisoners of fascism; persons diseased by radiation (Chernobyl' etc.), etc.*
Local	Municipal departments (or sections) for social protection of population	Children with a disability; children with diseases (tuberculosis, cancer and other 'social' diseases); provision of meals at school to children from families in need, etc.**

Notes: * These target groups receive financial aid from federal budgetary sources, but the fulfilment of social protection, including additional aid, fringe benefits, social services, etc. are provided by regional authorities.
** The majority of social services for these target groups are subsidised from regional public sources.

In contrast, the distribution of competences in the area of *social–labour relations and labour market regulation* has been less clear and consistent. Since 1 January 2007, the majority of federal competences in social–labour relations and labour market regulation have been delegated to regional authorities, according to Federal Law 199 of 31 December 2005. However, the distribution of responsibilities in this field is constantly changing, and it includes both gaps and overlaps. The distribution of competences does not always look logically consistent, and the efficiency of the whole social policy is reduced, providing the possibility for further changes and transformation in this policy area.

Table 11.2 **Distribution of competences of public authorities in social–labour relations (pre-2007)**

Level of public power	Responsible institutions	Functions and responsibilities
Federal	Ministry of Labour, and its Federal Services of Employment in the regions	Monitoring labour markets; accounting and registering unemployed persons; assisting in employment; vocational training and other activities to lower the level of structural unemployment; social aid to unemployed persons; regulating labour immigration and employing of foreign manpower, etc.
Regional	Ministry of Social Policy and Labour	Regulating social-labour conflicts; assistance in collective bargaining; social adaptation of unemployed: promoting the system of social protection, 'social package' in enterprises; vocational training; implementing measures on creating workplaces; implementing and inspecting the system of labour protection; regulating the system of calculating and paying wages, etc.
Local	Various departments	Different instruments of economic and social policy on creating workplaces

Assessing the Russian model of social policy: its actors and content
Altogether, the whole system of social policy in Russia has yet to be fully shaped with ongoing reforms in structures, processes and content. Nevertheless, it is possible to identify and characterise the current Russian

model of social policy by comparing it to three models in democratic countries: the 'liberal' (e.g. USA), the 'corporatist' (e.g. Germany) and the 'social democratic' (e.g. Sweden) (Esping-Andersen 1990).[3] Arguably, the Russian model is neither liberal nor social democratic: not quite social democratic because the basis of the social-conservative policy followed by the government ensures that liberal taxation is combined with paternalistic relations; not quite liberal because the Constitution maintains that Russia is 'a state with a social market economy', reflecting the concepts of 'socially responsible business', 'social partnership' and 'socially-oriented market'. The Russian social policy model could be deemed corporatist inasmuch as it has been realised through a series of 'corporate' agreements between key actors in this policy realm. This is characterised by the establishment of the Public Chamber in 2005, a corporatist cooperation between the state and business (represented by the Russian Union of Industrialists and Entrepreneurs), and by efforts to make Russian businessmen more 'socially responsible' (but neither through the Soviet system of enforcement nor through the liberal *laissez-faire* policy of equal and fair taxation).

However, characterising the social policy model as corporatist seems somewhat theoretical and artificial when considering the regional level of public power. In Kaliningrad, the main actor in this realm is the regional administration while other potential actors – civil society or business – remain weak. This has persisted from the Soviet paternalistic model of social policy, but it is also characteristic of the general post-Soviet political culture for a variety of reasons. First, public authorities are suspicious and seek to control all players in this realm, scrutinising charities for illegal activity and implementing a complex array of cumbersome procedures to regulate legal activities. Secondly, NGOs are weak, underdeveloped and financially dependent. They have not been able to significantly influence social policy in the oblast, nor are they financially self-reliant, active only through a framework of limited-term donor projects.[4] Finally, charitable activities are not considered the natural nor habitual behaviour of businesspeople, who believe their taxes sufficient to make public authorities responsible for social policy. Businesspeople do not trust public authorities and prefer not to protect their rights publicly within an association, but rather by acting privately through informal agreements with particular public officials and politicians. As a result, businesspeople cannot insist on a public and transparent system of social welfare even if such a system would be in their best interests for public relations. Instead, it is commonplace for businesses to finance concerts of popular singers as part of their public relations activities, paying scant attention to public social welfare projects.

The impact of the Russian social policy model on Kaliningrad

The extent to which this Russian context has had an impact on the social policy of Kaliningrad is exemplified by the following social reforms and initiatives: the 'monetarisation' of social benefits under Federal Law 122 (passed on 21 August 2004, and in force from 1 January 2005); the four 'National Projects' for construction, health protection, education and agriculture; and the social initiatives that followed Putin's address to the Federal Assembly on 10 May 2006 regarding the Russian demographic crisis.

Monetarisation of social policy

The monetarisation of social benefits was widely discussed in Russia and led to public protests in several cities. The primary aim of Federal Law 122 was to limit social 'free-riding' and to encourage Russian welfare recipients to seek self-help and self-sustainability through an optional and competitive system of social benefits. Responsibilities were increasingly delegated to regional administrations from both the municipal, and to a lesser extent, federal levels, so that regional authorities have become the main public actor responsible for social support. However, the law has provided regional authorities with the option to delegate these new responsibilities – and their respective subventions – to municipalities. The regional authorities of Kaliningrad have decided to preserve the *status quo* of the already existing network of local social institutions that otherwise would have been transferred to their level – and surely been more expensive and difficult to manage directly.

The regional administration's decision to preserve the *status quo* has also been applied to other aspects of the law's enforcement, which is just as well because monetarisation policies have been suspended by the federal government. However, the social reforms initiated by Federal Law 122 have resulted in some positive changes for Kaliningrad's social policy: regional social legislation has been partially systematised; municipal and regional social responsibilities and competences have been inventoried and classified; and data management has been improved.

Four 'National Projects'

After unsuccessful monetarisation of social policy, and against the backdrop of increasing criticism about the ideological vagueness of the government and the United Russia party, President Putin announced, in the summer 2005, a new policy of four 'National Projects' regarding construction, health protection, education and agriculture. The ideology of the Projects has been identified by political scientists as a social-conservative one. An immediate setback for the realisation of the Projects was the lack of institutional capabilities within regional administrations, where local political elites often misunderstood them as a federal non-committal campaign and dragged their feet with reforms. Seeing that the Projects required a number of real structural reforms in the area of social policy, Governor Georgii Boos established an *ad hoc* commission composed of experienced public servants to aid the implementation of the National Projects in Kaliningrad; moreover, he super-intends their realisation personally.

Social initiatives following the presidential address on the demographic crisis

One of the central ideas in the presidential address to the Federal Assembly of May 2006 was the necessity of an active demographic policy at the federal level. Prior to Putin's address, Sergei Mironov, Speaker of the upper house of the Duma, had acknowledged as early as 2003 that there was no federal policy on the family (Mironov 2006). As a consequence, Russian regions were encouraged to develop their own regional legislation and social policy pertaining to this area. The result was ten regions elaborating and adopting their own family policy: Kursk, Leningrad, Moscow, Nizhniy Novgorod, Pskov, Sverdlovsk, Tyumen', Velikiy Novgorod, the Vladimir oblast and the federal city of St Petersburg. In November of 2005, Kaliningrad's Minister of Social Policy and Labour, Galina Yankovskaya, was commissioned to develop a family policy. By February of 2006, Governor Boos was developing a draft 'Family Code' for Kaliningrad and after discussions with the regional Duma, he agreed to the idea of developing a draft regional law 'On Family Policy in the Kaliningrad Oblast' by 1 July 2006. More recently, the oblast adopted a regional programme for resettlement to stimulate immigration to the region. Evidently, Kaliningrad's administration has heeded Putin's concerns over a demographic crisis.

Social policy cooperation between Kaliningrad and the EU

European interests and activities

Since the early 1990s, social problems like corruption, crime, drug abuse and HIV infection have been a concern for Russian authorities. Perhaps it has been of even greater concern to Kaliningrad's European neighbours, where some discourses have labelled the oblast a 'black hole'.[5] European partners active in Kaliningrad have also engaged in social policy, funded mainly by TACIS or national donor programmes from Denmark, through the Danish International Development Agency (DANIDA), Sweden, through the Swedish International Development Cooperation Agency (SIDA), or small German and Dutch foundations. Yet until recently, TACIS social policy proj-ects in the oblast had been small – less that €200,000 – when compared with TACIS socio-economic development projects. These latter projects dealt exclusively with economic aspects and indicators, even targeting the labour market, but failed to reckon with the broader social problems of the region. TACIS social policy projects were narrow and addressed urgent specific social problems, such as unemployed veterans, labour market-oriented education, or youth programmes. However, they failed to take a comprehensive approach to social policy and so were unable to influence regional policy-making in this sphere.[6]

Towards a European social policy?

More recently, however, the TACIS project 'Development of a State Social Policy in the Kaliningrad Region (2005–06)' has provided a substantial impetus for the development of a regional social policy. The key partner institutions in this project have been the Kaliningrad Duma (as applicant and beneficiary) and the Finnish National Research and Development Centre for Welfare and Health (STAKES). Other Kaliningrad partners included the regional administration, the Federal Service for Employment, the Federal Migration Service, and Kaliningrad City Hall. Within the framework of this project, four draft laws on regional social policy have been developed: 'On Social Policy in Kaliningrad Oblast'; 'On Human Resource Policy in Kaliningrad Oblast'; 'On Migration Policy on Labour Market in Kaliningrad Oblast'; and 'On Family Policy in Kaliningrad Oblast' (see the previous section entitled 'Social initiatives following the presidential address on the demographic crisis'). All of these draft laws were submitted to their respective Duma committees in June of 2006, with 'On Family Policy in Kaliningrad Oblast' adopted in December of that year. The other three draft laws have been delayed in order to adapt them to the new version of the Regional Migration Programme for 2007–16.

Despite the delay, this legislation has been innovative for Kaliningrad, introducing 'European' conceptions and principles such as 'social inclusion', a 'welfare mix model', 'social partnership', 'subsidiarity' and 'prevention'.[7] Social exclusion is pervasive in Kaliningrad for certain groups: people with neurological, mental, or socially-communicable diseases, children with development delay, former prisoners, homeless people, prostitutes, drug addicts, and alcoholics. Being stigmatised exacerbates their situation and deprives them of opportunities for rehabilitation and social adaptation. A different dimension to social exclusion is the general attitude towards immigrants and visible minorities that is formally non-discriminating but in practice deprives them of opportunities. These forms of social exclusion can be addressed through programmes that better integrate these groups into social life.

Public servants in less-wealthy Russian regions like Kaliningrad often appreciate a 'welfare mix model' for its cost-effectiveness, but it also motivates citizens and NGOs: 1) to become involved in social activities; 2) to be self-helping and self-sustaining; 3) to insist on the protection of human and social rights; 4) to promote and implement social innovations; and 5) to pay attention to the social problems not addressed by authorities.

'Social partnership' is a necessary prerequisite for the successful implementation of an efficient welfare mix model. A system of 'social contracts' implies equal relations between the three main actors of social policy – public authorities, business and civil society. To date, the weakness of Kaliningrad's civil society and the lack of business interest have obstructed such partnerships,[8] but the new draft legislation proposes instruments that will aid in their efficient implementation. The draft legislation establishes two NGO-participatory and inter-departmental commissions, one on family policy and the other on social–labour relations. Moreover, it ensures that NGOs will be equal participants in the tender procedures that are the basis for publicly-financed social policy programmes.

'Subsidiarity' is a useful and efficient instrument for the welfare mix model and the social partnership approach because it distributes competences and responsibilities between social partners. However, it cannot be fully implemented in Kaliningrad because it lacks definition in Russian legislation. It can only be applied in a restricted sense as a guide for certain actors (primarily non-governmental) but not applicable to all relations between federal, regional and municipal authorities.

After a 'fire brigade' approach to social policy in the 1990s that sought to limit the consequences of mismanagement rather than address the causes, regional officials began to support – although not enact – the principle of prophylactic orientation, or 'prevention'. The proposed draft legislation implements this principle in various ways: public authorities must monitor, analyse and forecast social development; a more universal approach is adopted with structural social measures that address not only disadvantaged groups but all parts of society in order to prevent decline; a set of indicators and result-oriented criteria for cost-effectiveness of social expenditures is implemented; and finally, social policy is recognised as a profitable investment in the 'social capital' and future of the region, rather than a political tool to secure votes or social status.

While the draft legislation project led by the Finnish group STAKES has addressed several aspects of social policy, the success of this programme has motivated regional public authorities to develop ideas and a potential agenda for future cooperation. Ideas include the development of a family day-care system, the establishment of a vocational training centre, the promotion of gender education, education on research and methodological tools for regional decision-makers and further institutional and legal consolidation of social partnership relations in Kaliningrad (see TACIS 2006).

Conclusion: regional social policy at the crossroads

In spite of Kaliningrad's dire social situation and the inherent dangers that this has entailed, economic issues related to transportation, transit and energy have dominated EU–Russia discussions about the oblast. The internal integration and compatibility of social standards in the EU have offered

Kaliningrad new opportunities to participate in this integration process by adopting emerging principles of European social policy. However, prior to the reforms of 2005–6, social policy was an under-realised opportunity for cooperation between the EU and Russia.

The results of recent cooperation, in particular with STAKES, might give an important stimulus for keeping Kaliningrad's social policy on the wider EU–Russian agenda of consultations and negotiations about the oblast. The European standards and approaches in social policy are being digested, step by step, by Kaliningrad's political and administrative elites. There is a very close correlation between the amount of support that regional political leadership gives to policy initiatives – whether Russian or European – and their successful implementation. In this light, the fact that the representatives of the regional government promote European ideas, such as 'social inclusion', is encouraging. However, the bottleneck in this process is the insufficient capacity of regional social institutions to implement the already transformed and modernised legislation into a practical and functioning social welfare system. Furthermore, particular NGOs are subject to frequent institutional changes, a problem of which EU–Russia negotiators need to be aware. Besides fulfilling the immediate objectives, social projects should be realised in a way that strengthens NGOs as well as democratic institutions in the oblast.

Missing the opportunity for enhanced cooperation and implementation of the emerging pan-European social model could have dire consequences. New financial opportunities for the Russian authorities, provided by high world prices for crude oil and gas, could potentially lead to a restoration of the paternalistic Soviet model of widespread distribution of social gifts to voters. It is still uncertain which of the two options will be applied in Kaliningrad, so to some extent, it may also depend on the EU's policy towards the oblast.

Notes

1 With recent economic growth there has been a labour shortage, indicated by the low ratio (1:1) of registered unemployed to vacancies in the regional labour market (Komi Republican Committee on Statistics 2006). This ratio is expected to decline even further when the generation born during the 'demographic gap' of the early 1990s enters the labour market.

2 Other social indicators such as 'per capita income', 'living conditions' and 'poverty level' are less illustrative because of the high level of shadow incomes and subjective or politically motivated methods for the calculation of prices and costs.

3 However, these models and those of others (see for example Leibfried 1993) are often arbitrary and remain transitive to a European institutionalised mixed model (Trumm 2005: 72–4).

4 For example, the 'Regional Charitable Public Foundation for Help to the Children Diseased by Epilepsy', one of the most active charitable organisations in Kaliningrad, works only on the basis of irregular external donor financing.

5   Other terms ascribed to the region include an 'island in decay' (Huisman 2002: 9) or 'Russia's hell-hole enclave' (Patten 2001).

6   TACIS projects have been generally criticised for their disregard of local social situations and their lack of a more systematic approach towards existing problems. Other criticisms include that they encourage and support corruption, build 'Potemkin's villages', and instil local citizens with a negative attitude towards the 'wicked demagogy' of Europeans (see Arbatov 2004).

7   While this regional legislation has awaited final ratification, the federal government has introduced a new by-law ('Regulations on Social Standards of Family Well-Being') which reinforces these 'European' principles, and distributes social benefits according to income.

8   For example, regional public authorities, business associations and trade unions formed a three-party commission in order to increase the minimum wage in Kaliningrad. Although they came to an agreement, it was not implemented and the commission has been suspended.

References

Arbatov, N. K., ed. (2004), 'Rossiya i Evrosoyuz: dobrososedstvo bez prava na rodstvo?' ['Russia and the EU: neighbourliness without the right of kinship?'], Moscow, Izdatelstvo Komiteta 'Rossiya v obyedinennoy Evrope' ['Russia in United Europe' Committee Press].

Eliseeva, I. and N. Burova (2002), 'Assessment of the Shadow Economy in Saint Petersburg and Kaliningrad', Report at the RECEP conference, 20–1 September, Moscow, Manuscript.

Esping-Andersen, G. (1990), *The Three Worlds of Welfare Capitalism*, London, Polity Press.

Huisman, S. (2002), 'A New European Union Policy for Kaliningrad', Paris, EU Institute for Security Studies (Occasional Papers 33).

Kaliningrad Regional Administration (2004), 'Strategiya sotsial'no-ekonomicheskogo razvitiya Kaliningradskoy Oblasti kak regiona sotrudnichestva na period do 2010 goda' ['The strategy of social-economic development of the Kaliningrad oblast as a region of cooperation until 2010'], Kaliningrad, Yantarny Skaz.

Kaliningrad Regional Administration (2006), 'Programma sotsial'no-ekonomicheskovo razvitiya Kaliningradskoi oblasti na 2007–2016 gody' ['Programme of the socio-economic development of the Kaliningrad region in the years 2007–2016'], Regional Law of 28 December 2006, available on the Internet at www.gov.kaliningrad .ru/zip/progser2016.zip (accessed 23 November 2007).

Kaliningrad Regional Administration (2007), 'Strategiya sotsial'no-ekonomicheskovo razvitiya Kaliningradskoi oblasti na srednie- i dolgosrochnuyu perspektivu' ['Strategy of the socio-economic development of the Kaliningrad region in the medium- and long-term perspective'], Resolution adopted by the Kaliningrad Regional Administration on 9 March 2007, available on the Internet at www.gov .kaliningrad.ru/zip/stratser.zip (accessed 23 November 2007).

Klemeshev, A. P. and G. Fedorov (2004), *Ot izolirovannojo eksklava – k 'koridory pazvitiya'* [*From an isolated exclave to the 'development corridor'*], Kaliningrad: Izdatel'stvo KGU [Kaliningrad State University Press].

Komi Republican Committee on Statistics (2006), 'Sotsial'no-ekonomicheskie pokazateli Severo-zapadnogo federal'nogo okruga v 1998–2005 gg.' ['Social-economic indicators of the North-West Federal District in 1998–2005'], Syktyvkar.

Leibfried, S. (1993), 'Towards a European Welfare State', in *New Perspectives on the Welfare State in Europe*, ed. C. Jones, London, Routledge.

Ministry of Economy (2005), 'Severo Zapadnyi Federal'nyi Okrug Rossiskoi Federatsii' ['The North-West Federal District of the Russian Federation'], Moscow, Ministry of Economy of the Russian Federation, available on the Internet at www.economy.gov.ru/UnidocFileServlet/FileServlet?unidoc_id=1115380335734&template_id=4 (accessed 15 August 2007).

Mironov, S. (2006), 'Nado spasat' rossiyskuyu semyu' ['It is necessary to save the Russian families'], *Sobesednik*, 11 March: 4.

Patten, C. (2001), 'Russia's Hell-hole Enclave', *The Guardian*, 7 April.

Piirainen, T. (1997), *Towards a New Social Order in Russia: Transforming Structures and Everyday Life*, Aldershot, Brookfield USA, Singapore, Sydney, Dartmouth Publishing Company Ltd.

Samson, I., V. Lamande, I. Elisseeva, N. Burova and G. Fedorov (2003), *A New Look at Kaliningrad Region*, Grenoble, Université Pierre Mendès-France.

TACIS (2006), 'Development of a State Social Policy in the Kaliningrad Region', Final Report by the TACIS Institutional Building Partnership Programme, Key Institutions, 2004/094–569, Kaliningrad.

Trumm, A. (2005), 'The Prospects for the European Social Model in an Enlarged European Union', in *Refining the Social Dimension in an Enlarged EU*, ed. E. Palola and A. Savio, Saarijärvi, Finland STAKES.

GUIDO MÜNTEL

12

Environmental governance in Kaliningrad: lost opportunities

Introduction

As a small Russian exclave, Kaliningrad's development has been dominated by external links and interdependencies with its neighbours in the Baltic Sea region and the European Union. Over the last fifteen years, there have been, on both sides of the border, new security concerns regarding military deployment, trade and transport, as well as environmental issues. Environmental problems are cross-border concerns: Kaliningrad, Lithuania and Poland share the water and fishing resources of the Vistula and Curonian Lagoons and the Nemunas River. Eight other countries within the Baltic Sea ecosystem have the potential to be affected by pollution from Kaliningrad – and, indeed, have been alarmed by environmental developments and decisions in the Russian exclave.[1] Consequently, individual member states and the EU as a whole, along with the Russian Federation and certain international bodies, have recognised the need to focus on environmental issues through cooperation and joint activities.[2] When compared to social or health policy, there is a high level of interaction and cooperation between Kaliningrad and European partners on environmental issues. To what extent do these factors contribute to processes of domestic change as well as adaptation of environmental political structures, processes and policy outputs within the Russian exclave?

This chapter examines environmental governance in Kaliningrad, and the interplay of domestic and external incentives and pressures for its adaptation. However, it concludes by stressing the limitations that exist for Europeanisation of Kaliningrad; post-Soviet political and economic transition and Russian federalism appear to create a rather unfavourable domestic context for significant influence by European partners in the environmental policy area. Another factor is the European approach to policies of assistance, which are partly inadequate and need to be improved.

Kaliningrad's dual environmental challenge

As with many aspects of life in the region, the legacy of the Soviet Union has had a lasting impact on the environmental sphere of Kaliningrad. The region's natural resources were not protected, as environmental concerns were subordinate to Soviet military and industrial planning. Despite political changes, military reductions, declining industrial activity and transfer to a market economy since 1991, the environmental situation has not improved significantly – indeed, the majority of Kaliningraders actually perceive the situation as deteriorating (Welscher 2006). There are a multitude of issues: water consumption is increasing while treatment facilities still date from the Soviet era; industrial air pollution has declined but been substituted by increased automobile emissions; and poor waste management has been the result of a lack of information on aggregate waste, a lack of modern treatment and recycling facilities, and numerous landfills – both legal and illegal – that do not meet sanitary standards. While the immediate effect of these problems on the ecological systems of Kaliningrad and its neighbours is grave indeed, just as alarming is the impact on the public health of the region, observed in increases of environment-related infections and diseases (MPR-UPR 2004; Osipchuk 2004). Altogether, Kaliningrad is the second greatest single polluter in the Baltic Sea area after St Petersburg (see Kropinova 1998; KGU 2002; ERM 2002; Glushkova 2003).

Aside of poor ecological and sanitary conditions, environmental mismanagement and neglect have been a part of the Soviet 'heritage' for Kaliningrad. Due to the enormous size of the Soviet Union, its planners tended to perceive the environment as a near-infinite resource to be exploited, in which pollution was not considered significant. Moreover, due to their anthropocentric perspective, the environment was subordinated to human development and the material needs of a planned economy and communist society. The low salience of environment-related values, attitudes and behaviour was reinforced by a system of governance that obstructed change; Soviet environmental policy was dominated by 'bureaucratic pluralism' and marked by a fragmentation of authority as well as confusion in policy-making and implementation. An environmental movement did exist outside of the state apparatus, but it engaged in only minor and remote activities in education and research. It was not until the late 1980s that the first significant changes in environmental governance occurred, following the Chernobyl disaster and the rise of *glasnost* and *perestroika*. A single State Committee for Environmental Protection was created in 1988, and a greater openness of administrative information was required (officially at least). As the Soviet Union crumbled, environmental movements supplemented their principal agendas with sensitive political goals, and received increased public support (Pryde 1991; Mirovitskaya 1998).

Environmental governance in Kaliningrad and Russia

The necessity and opportunity for change of environmental governance in post-Soviet Russia and Kaliningrad has been evident. At the same time, the processes of transition have called on the Russian government and society to establish a functioning market system, democratic institutions, nation-building and an emerging federal system.

Economic transition

There was the expectation that the transition from a planned to a market economy would have resulted in increased efficiency, as well as environmentally-friendly behaviour by both producers and consumers. On the supply side, it was believed that not only would overall production decline, but producers would also apply resource-efficient technology to their systems in order to minimise costs. On the demand side, it was believed that increased household income and state welfare would allow for more pro-environmental or 'post-material' awareness on the part of individual consumers and political decision-makers.

However, Kaliningrad's economic transition has yet to create, or at least consolidate, a well-functioning and sustainable market economy. During the first years of transition, Kaliningrad experienced a sharp decline in industrial and agricultural output, as the conversion of the military-industrial complex and its related supply industries to the needs of civil production proceeded slowly. Concurrently, the declining production of manufactured goods has increased the need for exploitation and sale of the sparse natural resources – particularly amber and oil – with potentially fearful ecological consequences. It was only in the aftermath of the financial crisis of 1998 that Kaliningrad had an economic regeneration with a growth rate exceeding Western Europe, and even that was based on oil exports and increased domestic demand for regional products.

Kaliningrad's economy remains unstable and hardly self-sustaining, dependent on imports and external developments (Smorodinskaya 2005). The majority of enterprises are still operating according to a 'strategy of survival', with the time horizons involved in planning and investment still limited to months rather than years. In spite of the more recent economic recovery, the general economic decline of the 1990s has had severe social consequences like unemployment and comparatively low wages combined with higher prices for import goods. Altogether, the majority of the region's citizens assess their living standard as 'average' (48 per cent), or even below that (44 per cent) (Klemeshev and Fedorov 2004: 120). As a consequence, environmentally friendly behaviour that would inflict additional costs to individuals is perceived as unaffordable. In fact, there has been a 'browning effect' within the industrial sector; that is an intensification of pollution in which overall emissions have decreased but emissions per production unit have increased. Enterprises lack the financial resources to invest in expensive sustainable technology. Moreover, the slow process of privatisation and the instability of regulations and consumption patterns have a negative influence on environmentally sustainable behaviour (Crotty and Crane 2004: 414; Cherp *et al.* 2003).

Environmental federalism

Political developments in post-Soviet Russia have entailed a seemingly permanent struggle between the federal centre and the regions over resources, influence and responsibilities. Not so for environmental policy, as the Russian Constitution gives joint competence for legislative and executive functions in this field. Yet as a low-profile policy area, Moscow has perceived that environmental policy is not a worthwhile mandate in which to pursue 'genuine' national interests while its implementation is cost intensive. Thus, the federal government has not pushed for control over the regions in environmental policy, allowing this policy area to become increasingly decentralised in spite of the re-centralisation tendencies of President Putin.[3] The resulting system of multi-level governance allows the regions considerable autonomy in decision-making, and hence, establishes a rather conducive background for change and adaptation in Kaliningrad's environmental governance.

However, environmental policy management is still an area of shared responsibility. An indirect consequence is that institutional change at the federal level of environmental management has had repercussions in the regional and municipal arenas. Indeed, federal bodies have undergone frequent organisational restructuring, which is made locally evident when regional branches of federal authorities undergo similar reorganisations. Regional and local authorities are, to some extent, required to accommodate these institutional changes in order to fulfil their responsibilities for supplementary tasks of shared environmental management.

Political structures and processes of environmental management

Federal environmental governance appears to continue the Soviet patterns of administration and development, prolonging institutional instability: government bodies are abolished and re-established; their competences and functions are transferred; and bureaucratic fragmentation of environmental management has persisted. The evidence from the regional level of governance (in particular from Kaliningrad) partly confirms these tendencies, as the regional administration has undergone frequent organisational restructuring comparable to the developments at the federal level.[4] For example, there is still not one regional ministry responsible for the environment; instead there have been governmental divisions concerned with environmental aspects subordinated to various departments, like (until 2005) the 'Department of Energy, Heating, Fuel and the Communal Complex'.

This actually reflects a general lack of interest in environmental protection and policy more than the need to accommodate changing institutional
circumstances at the federal level. When there is a commitment to environmental protection – whether through institutional changes, increased
legislative or administrative activities or the allocation of budgetary resources
– it pertains less to the socio-economic or fiscal situation of the region, and is
more dependent on the personal interest of governing elites, insomuch as
they coincide with changing personnel in the governorship.

Political power in post-Soviet Russia continues to be concentrated in the
executive, at both the federal and regional level (see Ross 2002). One reason
for this has been the traditionally strong role of the head of the executive – as
an institution as well as a person. Another reason has been the high degree of
fragmentation and instability of the political forces representing societal
interests, a problem that Russia has suffered from since the end of the
Communist Party's domination. Where there is some influence of the legislative bodies – Kaliningrad being no exception – it is largely ceremonial or
perfunctory, merely affirming executive policy.

Consequently, only a few actors within the regional parliament or party
system have been able to play any role in the region's environmental governance. Within the party system, a 'green party' is practically absent; although
the Russian Ecological Party 'The Greens' has a regional office in Kaliningrad,
it engages in no observable political activity. This is consistent with post-
Soviet Russia in general – 'green' parties are barely evident in the political
landscape (Yanitsky 2000) – yet electoral support in Kaliningrad for the
Russian Ecological Party 'The Greens' is below even the country-wide
average.[5]

The civil society sector has also had very little influence on environmen-
tal decision-making, with direct political engagement of environmental
NGOs restricted to single groups, compounded by limited channels for advo-
cacy of environmental interests and particular legislative projects. A Regional
Public Chamber with the purpose of consultation with local and regional
NGOs has had a negligible impact on the administration's decision-making.
Direct personal contact with policy-makers has been an alternative lobbying
method for environmental NGOs that has only occasionally led to cooperation on individual legislative projects. Clearly, the degree of openness to
environmental interest groups within the current regional political structure
has been limited indeed.

There are other forms of activism, such as public protest and campaigning that aim at raising awareness of specific environmental problems among
the public and the political elite. The most visible and active group in the
region, 'Ecodefense!', has been the only NGO using such tactics. However,
this has backfired, contributing to a rather negative image of this group
among regional policy-makers, as well as amongst the general public and
other environmental groups. Less provocative environmental NGOs, such as

'The GUIDE Environmental Group', have focused on environmental education and have been better received by politicians. While not as visible as 'Ecodefense!', these NGOs play an important educational role, disseminating environmental information and cultivating environmental values through schools, teacher-training programmes, and communication with bureaucrats in the regional administration.

Environmental NGOs face further obstacles to their influence over both political institutions and general society. The political environment can be characterised as hostile for civil society actors because of state bureaucracy and lack of resources (Yanitsky 1999). Moreover, there is a general lack of public participation and support for them, although there is no lack of environmental awareness amongst the public – 93 per cent of Kaliningraders expressed concerns about environmental problems in their region (Welscher 2006). But individual responsibility and action continues to be missing, whether this means a willingness to pay higher prices or a demonstrable support of environmental movements (see ISSP 1993; 2000).

However, there are changes discernible amongst the young elite and emerging middle class that have been socialised in new political circumstances. In Kaliningrad, the membership of some environmental NGOs has increased substantially over recent years, and public disapproval and protest – although not yet successful – has arisen against certain administrative decisions. For example, the first referendum ever held in the oblast pertained to a decision by local authorities to allow the construction of two oil terminals and storage facilities close to residential areas.[6]

Environmental policy output in Kaliningrad

While the awareness of the public has been increasing, the lack of institutional actors and political will for adequate environmental management has corresponded with a decline in environmentally relevant legislative activities. Many regional laws and administrative decisions include some provisions on the environment, but few could be considered primarily environmental acts. Much of this legislation is declarative, with ambitious targets but little impact. Nevertheless, some of the principles and approaches stipulated therein reflect established 'Western' environmental management principles like sustainable development, provision of information, public participation in decision-making, and the use of economic incentives for environmentally friendly behaviour.

However, a corresponding transposition into specific legislative and administrative directives remains lacking. Nor are the declarative ambitions backed by an appropriate financial commitment for implementation; environmental expenditure has declined since the late 1990s, so that by 2005 it was a mere 0.2 per cent of Kaliningrad's annual budget (approximately €540,000). Yet over the same period, the regional economy experienced unprecedented growth, and other Russian regions actually increased their environmental spending (World Bank 2004: 38–40). In 1998, Kaliningrad had established an environmental fund in which fines for pollution were supposed to generate funds for protection measures, yet in the wake of several changes to the legislation – mainly exemptions for single enterprises – the fund was depleted and scrapped after only three years. Similar financial plans shared the same fate, largely due to the ambiguity between intentions and output.[7]

Moreover, a lack of legislative coherence or systematic environmental policy has been recognised by environmental activists and legislators alike.[8] Even the implementation of the legislation has been inconsistent, as environmental authorities in Russia have made use of their discretionary powers to waive penalties and selectively enforce payment claims (OECD 2003).

Interaction with Europe

Various forms of cooperation have been established between Kaliningrad and European partners. Among the partners involved are state as well as non-state actors, working at local, regional, national and supra-national levels of decision-making, and employing different types of instruments. At the state level, there have been numerous agreements between Russia and either the EU or individual member states, as well as between regional and municipal authorities of Kaliningrad and its neighbours. These agreements have covered a broad range of cooperative areas including environmental aspects. A feature of many of them has been the establishment of consultative mechanisms that directly and exclusively address environmental issues of shared concern. A further feature has been the elaboration of working programmes that outline the specific agenda on environmental cooperation between the partners, including the provision of technical and financial assistance to Kaliningrad, or occasionally even the harmonisation of environmental legislation, norms and standards.

In light of this, cooperation between the EU and Russia is of particular importance, with their Partnership and Cooperation Agreement (PCA) from 1997 providing the legal basis for efforts to develop and strengthen environmental initiatives. The PCA established a sub-committee on 'Energy, Environment and Nuclear Issues' in which representatives from the EU and Russia can exchange their views and positions on relevant issues. This sub-committee supplements the variety of other partnership bodies that have environment-related responsibilities and themes.[9] Another distinctive feature of the PCA was that Russia agreed to adjust its environmental legislation to approximate that of the EU (PCA Art. 55). This intent has been reiterated with the 2005 'Roadmap' (for the creation of four Common Spaces between the EU and Russia) that aims for a convergence of legislation in the sphere of the environment. A practical step in this direction was a TACIS project that investigated the possibilities and limits of adaptation within the Russian legal system.[10]

Since 1991, the TACIS programme has been a major source of financial and technical assistance for Russia and Kaliningrad, with environmental projects ranking second in the total number of TACIS projects in Russia.[11] Approximately €12 million has been allocated to environmental projects in Kaliningrad, which represents almost 25 per cent of overall TACIS assistance to the exclave. What is more, there are other ways in which the EU supports the funding of environmental projects in Russia: through other programmes like 'LIFE: Third Countries Programme',[12] and by promoting the provision of loans to Russia from international and European financial institutions such as the World Bank and the European Investment Bank.

However, the EU is not alone in this respect, and there are many other actors engaged in the improvement of environmental governance in Russia and Kaliningrad. Individual member states from the Baltic Sea region (especially Sweden, Denmark and Germany) provide significant assistance to the oblast, as do international financial institutions like the European Bank for Reconstruction and Development (EBRD) or the Nordic Investment Bank (NIB). Aside from the different forms of consultation and joint decision-making that have been set up at the EU–Russia level, equivalent bodies exist between national, regional and local authorities on each side of Kaliningrad's borders.[13]

A significant part of Kaliningrad's environmental interaction with Western Europe takes place between non-governmental actors. Despite the hostile political tone in Russia – or possibly because of it – NGOs from Kaliningrad and abroad have engaged in a variety of types of cooperation, with securing financial assistance being a priority for all Kaliningrad NGOs, not just the environmental groups. NGOs across Russia predominantly draw on grants from state governments as well as non-state organisations and foundations in Western countries that pursue mutual aims and strategies for the improvement of the environmental situation and/or civil society structures in Russia (see Henry 2001; Powell 2002). Increasingly, however, Russian NGOs are forming single partnerships with groups from European countries that focus on an exchange of experience and supply of resources (not just financially, but also technology or personnel) when engaged in similar or joint projects. Another recent development is the formation of loose 'pools' that are based on personal links between activists, or institutionalised networks of environmental NGOs (like the Coalition Clean Baltic), which concentrate on the exchange of information and access to financial resources.

In terms of financial resources allocated to environmental issues in Kaliningrad, the majority of Western projects have addressed the most urgent problems of pollution or insufficient treatment facilities and have provided modern technical equipment. Yet there have been other projects that have introduced environmental education into schools, that have developed university curricula on environmental management, or that have trained municipal employees of Kaliningrad City in the consideration of environmental aspects in the process of city planning. Financial assistance and legal advice have also been provided to regional policy-makers to develop environment-related legislation based on Western European principles and standards for environmental protection. Regardless of their specific content, these projects generally promote environmental awareness and expertise among present and future political decision-makers, administrative staff and the general public. At the same time, the active involvement of environmental NGOs in these educational projects stimulates and institutionalises cooperation between the public, civil society groups and state actors. Finally, adopting and implementing legislative templates from Western Europe would provide the basis and framework for enhanced legislative and administrative activities regarding environmental management in Kaliningrad.

The limits (and some evidence) of Europeanisation in Kaliningrad

The variety of environment-related programmes and projects pertaining to Kaliningrad metaphorically suggest a 'Europe of many faces' approach. These forms of intense cooperation and integration between the EU (and a broader Europe) and so-called third states, such as Russia, are the cause of adaptation pressures – or Europeanisation – in the latter's domestic institutions, processes and public policies. There are characteristics of a 'European model' of environmental governance that could be transferred, advanced or, at least, encouraged in Kaliningrad. These characteristics include: sustainable development; horizontal integration; high regulatory standards combined with economic incentives and voluntary agreements; growing public awareness and activism; stable and functioning institutions for environmental management; and network governance involving actors from state, business and civil society in the decision-making of environmental policies (see e.g. Lenschow 1999; Weale *et al.* 2000).

The institutional structure for environmental management in Kaliningrad is – at a very basic level – similar to the European model with regards to a system of multi-level governance where responsibilities and competences are shared between several levels of policy-making, ensuring a 'crowded space' with a variety of veto points. However, a clear representation of pro-environmental interests in Kaliningrad is the preserve of a small number of ineffectual actors, mainly environmental NGOs, whereas the environmental governance structure in Europe entails different types of civil society actors (NGOs, parties) working closely with state authorities on environment-related themes. Not only is the institutional setting in Europe more stable and less fragmented, but the interaction and decision-making between various actors in Kaliningrad does not resemble a 'network governance' approach. Exchange and cooperation between Kaliningrad NGOs is limited, and their access to the process of policy-making restricted to informal links with political elites and consultative bodies. Policy outputs in Kaliningrad reflect 'modern' concepts and principles of environmental management although with poor implementation and transposition into specific legislation, while European legislation is highly developed and usually well implemented and integrated into other policy fields.

Therefore, despite visible changes in the environmental governance of Kaliningrad since the end of the Soviet Union, evidence of an adaptation towards a European model of governance is lacking. The limits for Europeanisation of the oblast's environmental governance is mainly – but not solely – imposed by domestic conditions. European influence could provide resources and incentives for change, but the political opportunity structure in Kaliningrad is not receptive to this for a number of reasons. First, the multi-level system of environmental governance creates a high number of veto-points in the processes of decision-making. Second, and more importantly, access to these processes at the regional level is limited for new, pro-environmental actors, like environmental NGOs. It is clearly important that these NGOs receive European assistance to continue their existence and activities, but that has not improved their position *vis-à-vis* the bureaucrats that dominate the domestic institutional setting. Third, the incentive structure during the post-communist transition has been subject to individualistic and short term thinking, and economic cost–benefit analysis. The benefits derived from a healthy environment and the sustainable development of the region are rather indirect and long term, and the influence of this approach on individual and collective decision-making is limited indeed.

Still, European support for Kaliningrad's environmental NGOs – even if only in substantial as opposed to ideational terms – can result in long term albeit indirect political influence. Despite their limited policy-making access, activists already fulfil an important role as 'norm entrepreneurs' through education and awareness-raising. But here exists yet another obstacle. With fluctuations in institutional structure visible to both state and non-state actors, there is a lack of continuity in the personnel involved in cooperation and consultation, again limiting the transfer of ideas between Kaliningrad and Western partners.

The obstacles to the Europeanisation of environmental governance can be observed in the wider Russian context too, with external financial and technical assistance subject to the same shortcomings and inefficiencies seen in Kaliningrad (see Feshbach 1997). While Western partners certainly contribute to environmental protection, the funding is far from sufficient and tends to be concentrated on technical equipment (like for water treatment and waste management). Educational efforts have been comparatively small and comparatively recent, a trend that needs to be reversed in order to have a broader, long term impact on environmental attitudes and behaviour. Besides this shift in funding emphasis, it is essential that donors improve coordination to avoid overlap and improve efficiency.[14] Moreover, in spite of the scarcity of foreign funds, projects often require follow-up, since environmental management is a complex endeavour of interdependent systems that require more than just incomplete, patchwork assistance.

Another obstacle to Europeanisation is the lack of knowledge and sensitivity to local conditions and Russian culture exhibited by foreign consultants, especially when their engagement is short term. Russian partners are often mistrusting and resistant to Westerners' attempts to simply transfer organisational structures, processes and modes of behaviour from their own backgrounds to local settings. This scepticism is confirmed by data showing that only 35 per cent of Kaliningrad residents expect an improvement of the region's environmental situation as a result of the EU accession of its neighbours, Poland and Lithuania (Welscher 2006). However, several of Kaliningrad's European consulting partners have been active on various regional projects for years, thus improving mutual understanding and perception.

The transfer of governance structures and processes – not to mention beliefs and attitudes – between Europe and Kaliningrad has been rather limited. The external incentives derived from international engagement have not resulted in a strong correlation to European norms and modes of environmental governance. The benefits and adaptive pressures of European assistance to Kaliningrad are too limited to significantly alter the incentives and interests of regional decision-makers. As far as environmental governance is concerned, Europeanisation is not nearly as effective a force in Kaliningrad as it is in EU member states ('old' or 'new') or even European third countries like Norway and Switzerland. In spite of the 'many faces' and 'fuzzy borders' of Europe, as well as the numerous forms of interaction between Kaliningrad actors and European partners, adaptive incentives and pressures are not of a similar type nor scale as in the aforementioned cases, because EU membership is not an option. However, there are opportunities for European modes of governance and enhanced integration of Kaliningrad, as it is considered a 'pilot region' for EU–Russian cooperation. Despite its low salience and lack of adaptation, the realm of environmental governance should not be excluded from such prospects. For Kaliningrad's neighbours as well as its own economic performance and general well-being, environmental issues are much too important to be ignored.

Notes

1 An example is the protest by Lithuania (and other Baltic States) against the exploration and exploitation (as of June 2004) of oil fields off the coast of Kaliningrad, a mere six kilometres from Lithuanian maritime territory and twenty kilometres from the Curonian Spit Natural Park, shared by Russia and Lithuania.

2 For examples, see the report of the European Commission (2001) on Kaliningrad, the 2000 'Nida Initiative' between Russia and Lithuania (Wolffsen and Sergounin 2004: 56–7), the Action Plans of the EU's Northern Dimension Policy (Council 2000), or the assessments of the Helsinki Commission on the Protection of the Environment (HELCOM 2000).

3 The 2002 'Federal Law on Environmental Protection' transferred a considerable amount of responsibilities from the federal to regional and local governments.

4 On the contrary, environment-related authorities within the municipal administration of Kaliningrad City have been stable since 1991, when they were first established.

5 In regional elections, 'The Greens' did not participate. In the Kaliningrad election for the federal Duma, they received 0.25 per cent of the vote, even less than the Russia-wide average of 0.42 per cent.

6 Resulting from a public initiative and campaign in 2004–5, a local referendum took place in May of 2005 in the municipality of Svetliy in the Kaliningrad oblast, in which 98 per cent of the voters rejected the plans. However, to be a legally-binding decision, 50 per cent of the registered electorate should have participated, but only 48.5 per cent did so – a shortage of just 333 votes.

7 The projects envisioned in the 'Regional Plan on Activities in Environmental Protection 2000–2001' could only collect and implement 0.25 per cent of the outlined finances.

8 This assessment was taken from interviews conducted by the author in the Kaliningrad region.

9 For examples: the Working Group on Sustainable Development (2001); the Energy Dialogue (2000); or bodies within the Northern Dimension Environmental Partnership (2001).

10 The TACIS project 'Harmonisation of Environmental Standards – Russia' is available on the Internet at www.envharmon.msmu.ru/english.html (accessed 20 January 2005).

11 Total funding for the environment is even higher, although this is difficult to estimate because projects cross policy-areas and different recipient countries include environmental aspects as well (see Commission 2005).

12 As an example, from 2002–5, this programme financed a project between the administrations of Kaliningrad City and the cities of Aalborg (Denmark), Bremerhaven (Germany), and Southampton (United Kingdom). This programme aimed at improving the ability of local authorities in Kaliningrad to develop solutions for environmental problems in the area.

13 Examples include the Russian–Swedish Coordination Committee on Questions of Environmental Protection, the Russian–Polish Council for Cooperation between Russia's Kaliningrad Region and the regions of the Republic of Poland, with its commission on environmental protection, or the Russian–Lithuanian Council for Long-Term Cooperation between Regional and Local Authorities of the Lithuanian Republic and Kaliningrad Oblast, which also meets in a specific commission on environmental protection. Moreover, the Kaliningrad Regional Administration and/or representatives from municipalities in the oblast participate in trans-national Euro-regions (e.g. Baltika, Nemunas, Saule) or the Union of Baltic Cities (UBC).

14 The 'Northern Dimension Environmental Partnership' (NDEP), established in 2001,

is an example for this, coordinating activities of international financial institutions like the European Bank for Reconstruction and Development, the European Investment Bank etc., and national agencies like the Swedish Environmental Protection Agency and the Danish Environmental Protection Agency etc. Three NDEP projects for the Kaliningrad region with budgets of circa €20 million, €50 million and €90 million are in preparation.

References

Cherp, A., I. Kopteva and R. Mnatsakanian (2003), 'Economic Transition and Environmental Sustainability: Effects of Economic Restructuring on Air Pollution in the Russian Federation', *Journal of Environmental Management*, 68(2): 141–51.

Commission (2001), 'The EU and Kaliningrad', Communication from Commission to the Council on 17 January, Brussels, COM 26 final, available on the Internet at http://europa.eu.int/comm/external_relations/north_dim/doc/com2001_0026en01.pdf (accessed 4 May 2008).

Commission (2005), 'EU and Russia. Monthly Newsletter of the Cooperation Programme', *Environment in Focus* (June), Delegation of the European Commission to Russia, available on the Internet at www.eur.ru (accessed 20 January 2005).

Council (2000), 'Northern Dimension: Action Plan for the Northern Dimension with external and cross-border policies of the European Union 2000–2003', Brussels, available on the Internet at http://europa.eu.int/comm/external_relations /north_dim/ndap/06_00_en.pdf (accessed 4 May 2008).

Crotty, J. and A. Crane (2004), 'Transitions in Environmental Risk in a Transitional Economy: Management Capability and Community Trust in Russia', *Journal of Risk Research*, 7(4): 419–29.

ERM (2002), *A Report on the Environment for Kaliningrad, Report for the European Commission*, London, Environmental Resources Management.

Feshbach, M. (1997), 'The Role of External Assistance on Environmental and Health Policies in Russia', in *The International Dimension of Post-Communist Transitions in Russia and the New States of Eurasia*, ed. K. Dawisha, Armonk and London, M. E. Sharpe: 379–97.

Glushkova, L. S. (2003), 'Ekologicheskaya deyatel'nost' kak faktor razvitiya lichnosti' ['Ecological issues as a factor of personal development'], *Ekologya, zdorov'e, razvitie* [*Ecology, health, development*], ed. Tsentr sotsialnoi ekologii KGU [Center for Social Ecology], Kaliningrad, Izdatel'stvo Kaliningradskogo Gosudarst'vennogo Universiteta [Publishing house of Kaliningrad State University]: 10–14.

HELCOM (2000), *Annual Report 1999*, Helsinki, Helsinki Commission on the Protection of the Maritime Environment.

Henry, L. A. (2001), *The Greening of Grassroots Democracy? The Russian Environmental Movement, Foreign Aid, and Democratization*, Berkeley, University of California (Berkeley Program in Soviet and Post Soviet Studies, Working Paper Series, 2001–3).

ISSP (1993), *Environment I*, International Social Survey Programme Köln, Zentralarchiv für Empirische Sozialforschung.

ISSP (2000), *Environment II*, International Social Survey Programme Köln, Zentralarchiv für Empirische Sozialforschung.

KGU, ed. (2002), *Ekologicheskie problemy Kaliningradskoi oblasti i Baltiiskogo Regiona* [*Ecological problems of the Kaliningrad oblast and the Baltic region*], Kaliningrad: Izdatel'stvo Kaliningradskogo Gosudarst'vennogo Universiteta [Publishing house of Kaliningrad State University].

Klemeshev, A. P., and G. M. Fedorov (2004), *Ot izolirovannojo eksklava – k 'koridory pazvitiya'* [*From an isolated exclave to a 'corridor of development'*], Kaliningrad, Izdatel'stvo Kaliningradskogo Gosudarst'vennogo Universiteta [Kaliningrad State University Press].

Kropinova, H. (1998), 'Environmental Issues of the Kaliningrad Region', in *Kaliningrad: The European Amber Region*, ed. P. Joenniemi and J. Prawitz, Aldershot, Ashgate: 96–106.

Lenschow, A. (1999), 'Transformation in European Environmental Governance', in *The Transformation of the Governance in the European Union*, ed. B. Kohler-Koch and R. Eising, London and New York, Routledge: 39–60.

Mirovitskaya, N. (1998), 'The Environmental Movement in the Former Soviet Union', in *Environment and Society in Eastern Europe*, ed. A. Tickle and I. Welsh, Essex, Addison Wesley Longman: 30–66.

MPR-UPR (2004), *Doklad o sostoyanii i ob okhrane okruzhayushchei sredy Kaliningradskoi oblasti v 2003 godu* [*Report on the situation and the protection of the environment of the Kaliningrad oblast in the year 2003*], Kaliningrad, Ministerstvo prirodnykh resursov Rossiiskoi Federatsii/Upravlenie prirodnykh resursov i okhrany okruzhayushchey sredy MPR Rossii po Kaliningradskoi oblasti [Ministry of Natural Resources of the Russian Federation/Department of Natural Resources and Environmental Protection of the Russian Ministry of Natural Resources in the Kaliningrad oblast].

OECD (2003), 'The Use of Economic Instruments for Pollution Control and Natural Resource Management in EECA, Report of the 14th EAP Task Force Meeting', 10–11 February, Tblissi and Paris, Organisation for Economic Co-operation and Development.

Osipchuk, Z. N. (2004), 'Nashi deti obrecheny bolet' ['Our children are doomed to be ill'], *Spectrum* (April).

Partnership and Cooperation Agreement (PCA 1997), available on the Internet at http://ec.europa.eu/external_relations/ceeca/pca/pca_russia.pdf.

Powell, L. (2002), 'Western and Russian Environmental NGOs: A Greener Russia?', in *The Power and Limits of NGOs. A Critical Look at Building Democracy in Eastern Europe and Eurasia*, ed. S. E. Mendelson and J. K. Glenn, New York, Columbia University Press: 126–51.

Pryde, P. R. (1991), *Environmental Management in the Soviet Union*, Cambridge, Cambridge University Press.

Ross, C. (2002), *Federalism and Democratisation in Russia*, Manchester and New York, Manchester University Press: 92–136.

Smorodinskaya, N. (2005), 'Kaliningrad's Economic Growth Problem', in *Russia and the European Union. Prospects for a New Relationship*, ed. O. Antonenko and K. Pinnick, London and New York, Routledge, 263–81.

Weale, A., G. Pridham, M. Cini, D. Konstadakopulos, M. Porter, and B. Flynn (2000), *Environmental Governance in Europe*, Oxford, Oxford University Press.

Welscher, C. (2006), 'Umweltbewusstsein und Umwelthandeln im Kaliningrader Gebiet' ['Environmental awareness and action in the Kaliningrad oblast'], unpublished results of doctoral research, Kaliningrad.

Wolffsen, P. and A. Sergounin (2004), *Kaliningrad: A Russian Exclave or 'Pilot Region'?*, Nizhny Novgorod, Nizhny Novgorod State Linguistic University Press.

World Bank (2004), *Environmental Management in Russia: Status, Directions and Policy Needs*, Washington DC, The World Bank Group.

Yanitsky, O. (1999), 'The Environmental Movement in a Hostile Context. The Case of Russia', *International Sociology*, 14(2): 157–72.

Yanitsky, O. (2000), *Russian Greens in a Risk Society: a Structural Analysis*, Helsinki, Kikimora.

Alexandre Berlin and Greg Mestdag

13

Public health policy: how does Kaliningrad adapt to the EU?

Introduction

Health is a significant component of EU cooperation with Kaliningrad. In the 2001 Communication from the Commission to the Council on the EU and Kaliningrad (Commission 2001), health was mentioned in two sections: the section devoted to issues of mutual interest not directly related to enlargement; and in the annex with background information on the oblast. The Commission's assessment was that the spread of communicable diseases was a serious problem in Russia and particularly in Kaliningrad. Thus, it can be assumed that the EU has a high interest in tackling health problems in the exclave, possibly resulting in a strong engagement with Kaliningrad and Russian authorities on these issues, as well as promoting an adaptation to European norms and standards. However, the question of adaptation to EU norms appeared problematic, since a strong regulatory public health policy in the EU itself has been lacking. Instead, there has been a patchwork of national regulations and standards.

In light of Kaliningrad's health policy: what is the diagnosis, what has been achieved thus far, and what remains urgent? With the growing competency of the EU in the health field, are there now issues directly related to the *acquis communautaire* – and are these issues of strong mutual interest with neighbouring areas in the EU – that deserve urgent attention? This chapter will answer these questions. However, an obstacle is the fact that health information (health status and health structures) specific to Kaliningrad is very scarce in accessible literature or on the Internet. Consequently, there are many gaps in information which complicate analysis and render conclusions and suggestions only tentative.

The health status of the population in Kaliningrad

In terms of health status and health care delivery, Kaliningrad had a similar situation during the Soviet era as other Russian regions. What changes have occurred since the disintegration of the Soviet Union?

Current social data with a potential health impact

During the 1990s, Kaliningrad had 0.6 per cent of the population of the Russian Federation, yet produced only 0.4 per cent of its GDP; the very rapid growth of production in Kaliningrad since 1999 has resulted in it achieving 0.6 per cent of Russian GDP by 2006. On the whole, Kaliningrad's residents have achieved approximately the same level of income as elsewhere on the Russian mainland.

The economic performance in neighbouring Poland (the voivodships Warmińsko-Mazurskie, Pomorskie and Podlaskie) and Lithuania (the counties Klaipeda, Marijampole and Taurage) is below the average of their respective countries, yet direct comparisons of purchasing power show that Kaliningrad remains 10 to 25 per cent lower than these border regions (Samson *et al.* 2002; Samson *et al.* 2004).

The most recent reliable demographic data shows that Kaliningrad continues to experience a significant population decline at twice the Russian average, as well as the ageing of its population.

Universal indicators of health status: life expectancy and infant mortality

Until 1996, life expectancy was the same in Kaliningrad as in Russia: on average, sixty-six years. However, there has been major divergence since then. By 2003, the life expectancy had declined only very slightly for Russia as a whole (65.2 years) while in Kaliningrad it had decreased to 61.7 years – among the lowest in the Russian Federation. The remarkable recent economic performance of Kaliningrad has not yet been reflected in this indicator.

Infant mortality was also similar between Kaliningrad and the rest of Russia before 1996, but much higher than in neighbouring Lithuania and Poland. In Russia as a whole, infant mortality has declined significantly from 17.0 to 11.5 per 1,000 (in 2004), but in Kaliningrad only to 12.7 per 1,000 according to official data (in Lithuania and Poland in the same year, it was 6.7 and 7.2 per 1,000 respectively). However, interviews with health staff in Kaliningrad have indicated that the situation is improving significantly (Druzhinina 2006).

'Self-inflicted' health problems and infectious diseases

These types of health problems, if they are to be solved, require changes in societal and personal attitudes rather than the improvement of health care delivery. The most comprehensive and relatively comparable statistical data has been published by EPI North (EpiNorth 2006), although it must be stressed that usually the data for Russian regions does not cover military personnel and the prison population.[1]

Concerning the population (excluding military personnel and prisoners) with active tuberculosis (TB), there was an increase in Kaliningrad from 25 per 100,000 inhabitants in 1990, to 91 per 100,000 in 2000, and then 134 per 100,000 in 2006 (compared to 30 per 100,000 in 1990 and 80 per 100,000 in 2002 for Russia as a whole, and only 35 per 100,000 in St Petersburg in 2006). It must be stressed that the incidence of TB is still growing in Kaliningrad, while a small downwards trend is observable in Russia. Buhtoyarov, the Vice-Chairman of the Health Committee for Kaliningrad, indicated in 2002 that 'over the last ten years, tuberculosis had spread at a much greater speed than the means to combat it'; in his view, 'this very aggressive social disease was resistant to all drugs currently used and [...] isolation of TB patients was not possible because of the limited number of beds' (NATO 2002). He was never-theless optimistic for the five years to come, mentioning assistance being provided by Germany, Sweden and Norway. Yet his optimistic views have not come to fruition. High incidence of multi-drug resistant TB has been observed among immigrants from Kaliningrad to Germany. Furthermore the incidence of TB in the whole population of neighbouring Lithuania was of only 69 per 100,000 in 2006 (EpiNorth 2006). Of further concern is that active TB among youth (fifteen to seventeen years) tripled from 22.5 cases per 100,000 inhabitants in 2000, to 65 per 100,000 in 2004. This overall epidemi-ological situation needs to be further assessed and analysed with great care.

As of April 2006, there were 3,847 HIV-infected persons registered in the oblast, of which thirty-four were children or adolescents.[2] In the same period, there were 175 AIDS patients, including fifty-four women – a significant percentage that to some extent indicates the nature of the transmission (i.e. heterosexual sex and intravenous drug use). The incidence of HIV in Kaliningrad City is one and a half times the oblast average. Over 1,400 AIDS-related deaths have been registered in the oblast, and the total cumulative number of registered cases of HIV since the start of the epidemic is over 5,500. According to WHO and UNAIDS, 294,000 HIV cases have been registered in Russia while the estimated number of HIV infected persons varies from 450,000 to 1,500,000. A probable and realistic estimate is approximately 900,000 cases. Thus for Kaliningrad, a realistic estimation of cumulative HIV cases is 16,000, with a possible range of 9,000 to 27,000. An estimate for 2006 of the number of persons living with HIV infection was 12,000, with a range from 6,000 to 20,000.

In comparison, the total registered cumulative number of cases of HIV was 10,000 in Poland and 1,000 in Lithuania. In terms of total number of registered cases per 100,000 of the population, there were 30 per 100,000 in each of Lithuania and Poland and 600 per 100,000 in Kaliningrad, a ratio twenty times greater. However, the official statistics of Lithuania should be considered with caution because of poor screening policies (Druzhinina 2006). Nevertheless, even the official data for Kaliningrad demonstrates that in the first six months of 2006, the number of new HIV infections was 250.

According to the data provided by the Kaliningrad Regional AIDS Centre,[3] in the first six months of 2006, 200 AIDS patients died, and the number of patients living with AIDS increased by twenty. It seems that in 2006 about 10 per cent of HIV carriers contracted AIDS (as compared with 1 to 3 per cent in the EU and Poland). A possible explanation is that many of the infected persons are also drug users having difficulties quitting their habits for lack of proper treatment.

Kaliningrad has had a well-equipped and well-staffed regional AIDS centre for the past 10 years, and fighting AIDS in Kaliningrad has been a high priority for the federal government; over the past five years, the centre has received very significant funding both from the federal government and international donors. It provides free testing, promotes primary prevention programmes, and offers some preventive tri-therapy (to prevent the progression of HIV infection to AIDS) for HIV-infected persons, especially pregnant women and children. However, in view of the high cost of tri-therapy – several hundred euros per patient per year even with generic drugs – it is not clear what percentage of the HIV-infected population effectively benefits from this preventive treatment. Galina Perceva, First Deputy Health Minister for Kaliningrad, has stated that only 130 HIV-infected persons have received free treatment (Perceva 2006). It is notable that only Russian citizens are guaranteed free medical treatment under the Russian Constitution, so it is impossible to ascertain what percentage, of even the registered HIV carriers, are not Russian citizens.

The levels of syphilis and gonorrhoea have remained steady but high. In 2006, there were 102 cases of syphilis per 100,000 people, and 48 cases of gonorrhoea per 100,000 in Kaliningrad, as compared to Lithuania which had 10 per 100,000 for syphilis and 12 per 100,000 for gonorrhoea, or even St Petersburg with 46 per 100,000 for syphilis and 38 per 100,000 for gonorrhoea.

Hepatitis among children increased tenfold between 2000 and 2004, reaching 700 cases per 100,000 inhabitants; no explanation could be obtained.

The number of 'registered' drug addicts seems to have remained steady since 2001 (200 per 100,000), although that is twice the 1990 level. Moreover, drug overdose deaths have increased alarmingly: 83 in 2003, 297 in 2004 and 438 in 2005. Needle exchange programmes to reduce the transmission of infectious diseases among injecting drug users started in the 1990s, yet during the mid-2000s they seem to have been terminated, or severely reduced, for lack of funds. Initially, it was a TACIS project that implemented the needle exchange programme, but this was not renewed.

Two major 'self-inflicted' health issues in Kaliningrad are alcoholism and smoking. Recent, reliable and comparable data (with the rest of the Russian Federation and neighbouring Lithuania and Poland) is lacking for both smoking and alcohol health-related problems in Kaliningrad. Pridemore *et al.* (2006) reviewed alcohol-related deaths in the Russian Federation and found that in the year 2000, the overall crude alcohol-related mortality rate per 100,000 of the Russian population was 33.6 (comprising 55.4 for men and 14.7 for women). Kaliningrad had a rate of 64.5 per 100,000, twice the Russian average, and only surpassed by Karelia (with 75.2 per 100,000). The rate for the City of St Petersburg was only 35.5 per 100,000. Pridemore *et al.* (2006) also discovered that for Russia as a whole, alcohol-related deaths peaked in 1995 at 50 per 100,000, decreased to 22 per 100,000 in 1998, and increased again after that to reach 43 per 100,000 in 2002 (the last year for which data was available). They also noted that the highest alcohol-related mortality rate was not among youth, but in the age cohort of forty-five to fifty-four years. As no data could be obtained regarding the impact of alcohol consumption on traffic accidents, one could assume that alcohol is involved in an even greater number of fatalities.

Without specific reliable data on smoking prevalence for Kaliningrad it can only be inferred that the situation is similar to that generally prevailing in Russia. According to the European Tobacco Control Report by WHO/EURO (2007), smoking prevalence for the Russian Federation was 36 per cent of the population (with 61 per cent for men and 15 per cent for women) as compared to 26 per cent in Lithuania and 32 per cent in Poland. A 2006 UNESCO report also indicated a significant increase (from 14 to 18 per cent) in smoking prevalence among youth between 2000 and 2003 (Agranovich *et al.* 2006).

For a profound assessment of the health situation it is also necessary to look at various population groups that are often excluded from both public debate and official statistics (see the comment at the beginning of this section). One of these groups is military personnel, whose number in Kaliningrad is now estimated at around 30,000 (down from over 100,000 during the Soviet era). The impact of the exclusion of this population on health-related statistical figures is difficult to ascertain. For example, while Russian military authorities claim that the level of HIV infection in the military has been reduced in the past few years, the fact that military recruits cannot be tested for HIV for legal reasons results in some uncertainty regarding this assertion (Holachek 2006). Yet according to Torgersen (2007), 'the military population is healthier than the general population, and it is checked regularly with not many infections among them, so the Kaliningrad Rospotrebnadzor means that they do not have serious distortion with regard to these populations'.[4]

There is no statistical data available on the total numbers of the prison population and it seems equally impossible to obtain information on their health status. Thus, an attempt has been made to estimate the size of this population group on the basis of overall Russian data, according to which there are approximately 640 persons in prison per 100,000 inhabitants (as compared with 300 in Lithuania and 210 in Poland). As per Baratov *et al.* (2004), in 2004, there were 418 HIV-positive persons and 398 with TB among approximately 5,000 inmates in the Kaliningrad oblast prison system. This data reinforces EU concerns over the urgency of the EU health project that has taken Kaliningrad's prisons as a key priority. In the most recent TACIS programme about health services in Kaliningrad, specific reference was made to prisons, clearly stressing the importance of the overall health issue among the prison population.

Finally, commercial sex work seems to be very prevalent in Kaliningrad, particularly in the port area of Kaliningrad City, increasing the danger of transmission of diseases.[5]

Health care delivery in Kaliningrad

The most obvious change of the last fifteen years is the geography of the Kaliningrad region, and the possible impact of this on public health in the exclave. The oblast's distance from the centres of medical excellence in the Russian Federation (Moscow and St Petersburg) is approximately 1,000 km. Even the nearest regional Russian administrative centre with significant health facilities, Pskov, is at a distance of approximately 800 km. Conversely, the specialised health centres in Gdansk (Poland), Klaipeda and Kaunas (Lithuania) are only about 100 km from the Kaliningrad border. This should have important implications for the handling of emergency medical cases, especially if medical centres in Kaliningrad are overloaded or do not have appropriate facilities. Yet in spite of this, no systematic arrangements have been made regarding Kaliningraders using specialised medical facilities in neighbouring Lithuania and Poland.

The number of hospitals, hospital beds, and medical personnel has not changed substantially since the dismantling of the Soviet Union, and it remains unclear if the quality of the facilities and personnel has been sufficiently maintained and upgraded. In 2001, there were 9.1 hospital beds per 1,000 inhabitants, compared to 6.3 in Lithuania and a mere 4.1 per 1,000 for the EU-15. Perhaps more significant still, also in 2001, the average hospital stay in Kaliningrad was 13.2 days, compared to 8 in Lithuania and only 7.7 in the EU-15. Health practitioners in Kaliningrad held that the reason that longer hospitalisations continue to occur in the region was caused by the 'many people coming to the hospitals asking for care, but ... suffering from various "extra" problems, i.e.: bad hygiene, infections, malnourishment, etc. Therefore, the hospitalisation can be longer than expected as doctors often must treat surprise problems in patients' (Melishkov 2006). Clearly, this situation is the heritage of the former Soviet-type health care system, as well as an indicator of a less-developed, poorly-funded and low-prestige primary health care service. Even in relative terms, the percentage of GDP spent on health in the Russian Federation is less than 3 per cent, compared with more than 6 per cent in Lithuania and Poland, while at the same time the absolute GDP per capita is much higher in these countries. Thus the amount of money available for health per capita in Kaliningrad is significantly lower than in the neighbouring two countries. With the gradual opening of the oblast's borders and a better informed population, can such a situation be sustained over the long term?

Public health authorities

Well-functioning public health structures are essential for both Kaliningrad's population and its neighbours. As a part of SANIPED (Health and Epidemiological Services), there were well-structured food inspection services, epidemiological disease monitoring and prevention (vaccination) units, and health promotion and disease prevention programmes. It has not been possible to ascertain the current status and efficacy of these entities and programmes.

NGO initiatives in the health field

An overview of the NGOs (local, foreign and international) working in Kaliningrad and the scope of their activities is not available, preventing effective coordination of all responsible and concerned actors – a situation of particular concern for the International Organisation for Migration (Szilard 2007). The local Red Cross does receive some support from the German, Lithuanian and Norwegian Red Cross Societies, and their emphasis is on children, especially 'unregistered inhabitants' and orphans. However, the number of Red Cross centres in Kaliningrad has decreased significantly since 2000.[6]

EU interest and concern for Kaliningrad in terms of health

The European Commission has recognised the need for all levels of Russian government to address the serious health problems in Kaliningrad:

> Public health services in Kaliningrad are close to the Russian average. Diseases such as tuberculosis, diphtheria, measles, and epidemic paratyphoid are widespread. TB is becoming multi-resistant and its prevalence is growing, especially among the inmates of Kaliningrad prisons. Drug use and prostitution have led to the alarming spread of other communicable diseases. For instance, Kaliningrad is among the worst regions in Russia for registered cases of HIV, and by far the most affected area in the Baltic Sea region ... the spread of communicable diseases is a serious problem in Russia and particularly in Kaliningrad. These problems must be tackled at the federal level but preventive action can also be

taken in Kaliningrad itself. TACIS is supporting several initiatives at the local level and in the non-governmental sector to help reform health care delivery systems and to help deal with HIV. In the future, the recommendation of the Task Force on Communicable Diseases Control in the Baltic Sea area will help address the issue of TB and HIV at the regional level. (Commission 2001)

The EU and authorities in Kaliningrad and Russia have been cooperating on health issues for some time. Since 1994, TACIS has financed fifty health-related projects in Russia for a total of €60 million, five of which involved Kaliningrad. The most recent project is being implemented from 2006 until 2008 and has a budget of €3 million. Its overall purpose is to support the federal Ministry of Health in the oblast, improving its health care system and the delivery of health care services. In particular, it aims to develop primary health care services, polyclinics, reproductive health care services, health education and awareness raising programmes (with special emphasis on rural areas), as well as strengthening the prevention and control of communicable diseases among civilian and prison populations. By January of 2008, a call for tender will be aimed at supplying equipment and materials for selected health care facilities in Kaliningrad, enhancing capacity to provide services. The list of materials and equipment to be supplied clearly demonstrates how basic the needs are: anaesthetics, portable X-ray equipment, portable bedside ECG monitors, surgery instruments, gynaecology chairs, infusion pump stations, laboratory equipment (biochemical analysers, urine analysers, heat exsiccators), and ophthalmic equipment (ophthalmoscopes, tonometers and test glasses). Local health professionals expressed some concern that these projects would 'bombard' them with Western expert advice but not provide them with the opportunity to learn first-hand from Western experience.

Specific problems related to EU public health legislation

At the EU level, competencies in the health field have increased only gradually and usually following a public health crisis, like the tainted blood scandals in France and Germany, the Creuzfeld-Jacob outbreak and concerns with avian flu. In terms of legislative possibilities, competencies were added through various revisions of the Treaties. For example, there has been extensive legislation on blood safety, tissue and related components for transplantation; tobacco control; the network for surveillance of infections diseases; a single EU-wide emergency telephone number (112); and food safety. Thus Poland and Lithuania had to adopt legislation in these areas as part of the *acquis communautaire*. Due to geographic isolation from mainland Russia, and without appropriate consultations and arrangements between health officials from Kaliningrad and neighbouring EU countries, there is likely to be a significant impact on the delivery of specialised health services in the oblast, and a divergence of approaches in health care delivery.

In one area, tobacco, there is compatibility between Kaliningrad and EU requirements; cigarettes sold in the oblast must have warning labels as well as indications of tar and nicotine content. In the area of blood safety, as well as organs and tissues for transplantation, Kaliningrad's blood banks seem to have a level of functioning similar to those of its EU neighbours. However it is not yet possible to ascertain if EU requirements in terms of donor selection and blood safety have been implemented, which would be essential for blood exchanges to neighbouring countries (for emergencies or special blood types). It does not seem efficacious to transport blood by air from other parts of the Russian Federation during emergencies. For transplants, it would seem that the oblast's facilities are adequate and that the specialists are well trained. However, this could not be corroborated, and what is more, there is no accessible information on the number and types of transplants, the availability of donors, or if safety procedures are in compliance with EU regulations.

High level health authorities in Kaliningrad have not been aware of any plans to introduce the EU's single emergency telephone number (112). Fully operational in the EU, this number has considerably improved the arrival of emergency services across Europe, especially given the advent of mobile telephones responding to an increasing number of road accidents. As a possible pilot scheme for the Russian Federation, Kaliningrad could introduce this as the emergency response telephone number.

The future

In the realm of health care, regional cooperation and collaboration with Poland and Lithuania continues to be at a very low level. There is one meeting per year between health officials from Kaliningrad and the border voivodships of Poland, and this is generally an exchange of views not to be followed by any concrete action or joint projects. However, meetings between various health specialists have been initiated outside of the public sector, as well as a regular meeting programme between Klaipeda (Lithuania) and Kaliningrad health specialists. Many of the initiatives being considered imply the necessity of closer cooperation between Kaliningrad and its neighbours.

At the EU level, the PHARE programme has clearly identified that Kaliningrad must upgrade its primary health care (particularly in rural areas), prison health and disease prevention programmes in order to have the most rapid impact on the health status of its population. This approach seems to be in line with the 2001 Report of the Centre for European Policy Studies' Task Force, which concluded that in relation to integrating Central and East European countries in the Union, there are two 'technical' arguments for greater EU effort at targeting the health system of candidate countries. The first is reinforced by a growing number of detailed economic studies which argue that investment in human capital, including health, has an impact on economic growth several times larger than that of the EU's preferred vector: infrastructure. The second argument relates more narrowly to the cost-effectiveness of health spending in public budgets, and to public expenditures in the social field caused by failures of the health care system to protect individuals from debilitating conditions making them unfit for work (Hager 2001).

Can the health of the population in Kaliningrad, as an enclave in the EU, benefit from a closer collaboration with neighbouring Poland and Lithuania? Would such collaboration also be of benefit to these countries? While some level of cooperation in the health field already exists in the framework of the Baltic Sea Cooperation (of which Russia is a member), there seems to be a need for a much closer and more intense cooperation at the sub-regional level between Kaliningrad and the neighbouring health administrations.[7] There is a precedent in the model of collaboration and cooperation developed in the framework of the South-Eastern Europe Stability Pact – Health Network, a joint network between all member countries in the Pact which has focused on the close interrelationship between health and economic development.

This type of cooperation could be envisaged between the different levels of administration in Kaliningrad, Lithuania and Poland, or even between border municipalities or universities that might have more freedom of action in the health field (e.g. the planned establishment of a medical school in Kaliningrad would be an excellent occasion for the development of such a network). However, if this collaboration is to develop effectively, the health structures in Kaliningrad must be given some financial autonomy to engage systematically in its activities. The collaboration could take the form of joint projects, led by one entity in each of the three countries or regions and with the participation of the other two. Based on four years of experience with the South-Eastern Europe Stability Pact, possible topics for cooperation include infectious disease monitoring, availability and safety of blood, emergency services and food safety control, as well as health empowerment and public health issues related to commercial sex work. The projects could entail joint training and exchange of staff. Similar approaches could be taken for the other sub-fields, promoting technical cooperation and developing trust at the working level, an essential first step for more formal collaboration at the political level.

A desirable first step would be a meeting between the health authorities of Kaliningrad, Poland and Lithuania, at which the experience gained by the Stability Pact in the field of health could be presented and views exchanged on how such an approach could be applied to the region. For the sub-regional level, the potential of 'The Northern Dimension Partnership in Public Health and Social Well-Being' should not be underestimated. Meanwhile, there should be rapid action in at least one issue: the adoption of the common emergency telephone number 112 (in addition, if necessary, to the national number). This would be of benefit for both Kaliningrad residents travelling through Lithuania and Poland, as well as EU residents travelling through

Kaliningrad, as it should reduce the health services' arrival time in the case of serious emergencies.

Conclusion

Kaliningrad's health situation, far from satisfactory during the Soviet era in spite of a universal health service, has deteriorated. This has been recognised by local and federal health authorities, international institutions, bilateral donors and the European Union. There have been some initial steps to remedy this situation, with a sense of urgency to improve the situation both for the benefit of the local population and economy as well as for the populations of neighbouring countries.

Local health authorities need more autonomous decision-making authority to be able to take advantage of Kaliningrad's geographic location as an exclave of the Russian Federation and also an enclave of the EU. The neighbouring EU countries, Lithuania and Poland, have much higher populations and better health facilities. A closer collaboration between the health structures in Kaliningrad and its neighbours would be of mutual benefit for the health of their respective populations; for example, immediately activating pre-established arrangements for major emergencies or organ transplants. Significant improvements in the health of the population of Kaliningrad could also be achieved at comparably small cost, especially considering the pronounced influence of negative lifestyle factors on health (smoking, alcohol consumption, lack of systematic use of safety belts). Furthermore, a stronger stance *vis-à-vis* infectious diseases would reduce some of the local cross-border problems between the EU and Russia in the region of Kaliningrad. In light of the Stability Pact of countries in south-eastern Europe, implementing a 'Kaliningrad Partnership' approach could be a model for practical cooperation between Russia and the EU, especially because health policy seems to be an accessible starting point for cooperation, requiring a lower cost threshold for agreement.

Notes

1 Interestingly, Kaliningrad is the exception as the local prison population is considered in the data (Torgersen 2007).
2 This data is from unpublished but official 2006 statistics consulted at the Statistical Office of Kaliningrad. It is not clear if this data includes prisoners or military personnel. However, at a press conference on 28 June 2006, Galina Perceva, Kaliningrad First Deputy Minister of Health, mentioned only that close to three thousand Kaliningraders were HIV infected. At the same press conference, Perceva indicated that the present infection rate in Kaliningrad is the lowest among Russian oblasts, without providing any quantitative data (Perceva 2006).
3 From personal meetings with several staff members in 2006.

4   The Kaliningrad *Rospotrebnadzor* is the 'Territorial Directorate of the Federal Service for Surveillance on Consumer Rights Protection and Human Well-being'.
5   From unpublished information based on interviews conducted in March and April of 2006 – sources do not want to be named.
6   From a personal communication with the Kaliningrad Red Cross, 2006.
7   Chief Sanitary Inspectors in Poland and County Physicians in Lithuania.

References

Agranovich, M., N. Korolyova, A. Poletaev, I. Sundiev, I. Seliverstova and A. Fateeva (2006), 'Youth Development Report: Conditions of Russian Youth', UNESCO.

Baratov, R., *et al.* (2004), *Independent Monitoring on the Compliance with Human Rights in the Kaliningrad Oblast*, Kaliningrad, Resource Informational Analytical Centre.

Commission (2001), 'The EU and Kaliningrad', Communication from Commission to the Council on 17 January, Brussels, COM 26 final, Brussels, available on the Internet at http://europa.eu.int/comm/external_relations/north_dim/doc/com2001_0026en01.pdf.

EpiNorth (2006), A Co-operation Project for Communicable Disease Control in Northern Europe, available on the Internet at www.epinorth.org (accessed 6 May 2008).

Hager, W. (2001), 'A European Bargain – Investing in CEEC Health', Brussels, CEPS Task Force Report.

Holachek, J. (2006), 'Russia's Shrinking Population and Russia's Military HIV-AIDS Problem', Occasional Paper, The Atlantic Council of the United States, available on the Internet at www.acus.org/docs/0609–HIV_Russianj_Military-Holachek.pdf.

NATO (2002), 'Civil Dimension of Security', Trip report of the Committee on the Civil Dimension of Security, 22–23 March 2002, International Secretariat, available on the Internet at www.nato-pa.int/archivedpub/trip/av063cc-kaliningrad.asp (accessed 22 November, 2007).

Pridemore, W., A. Sang-Weon and K. Sang-Weon (2006), 'Negative Socioeconomic Changes and Crime in a Transitional Society – Heavy Drinking and Suicide in Russia', *Journal of Drug Issues*, 36(1): 229–47.

Samson, I., V. Lamande, I. Elisseeva, N. Burova, G. Fedorov (2002), *A New Look at the Kaliningrad Region*, available on the Internet at http://web.upmf-greno-ble.fr/pepse/IMG/pdf/kalinewlook2.pdf (accessed 1 October 2005).

Samson, I., V. Lamande and E. Vinokurov (2004), 'Measuring Regional Economic Development in Russia: The Case of the Kaliningrad Oblast', *European Urban and Regional Studies*, 11 (January): 71–81.

WHO/EURO (2007), 'The European Tobacco Control Report 2007', available on the Internet at www.euro.who.int/Document/E89842.pdf (accessed 4 May 2008).

Personal communication and interviews

Druzhinina, Nina Pavlovna (2006), Head doctor of maternity hospital no. 4, Kaliningrad. Interviews during March and April 2006 in Kaliningrad.

Melishkov, Grigorii (2006), Polyclinic no. 6, Kaliningrad. Interviews during March and April 2006 in Kaliningrad.

Perceva, Galina (2006), Kaliningrad First Deputy Minister of Health, press conference in Kaliningrad on 28 June 2006.

Szilard, Istvan (2007), International Organization for Migrations. Interviews during March 2007, Brussels.

Torgersen, Elena (2007), Senior Adviser, Norwegian Institute of Public Health, Oslo. Telephone interviews in September 2007.

For providing valuable information and comments on which this chapter is based, the authors wish to thank the people above as well as various representatives from health-related institutions in Kaliningrad, Brussels, Copenhagen and Oslo, the Immanuel Kant Russian State University Kaliningrad, and the TACIS Information Office in Kaliningrad.

STEFAN GÄNZLE, STEFAN MEISTER AND CONRAD KING

14

Higher education in Kaliningrad

Introduction

Higher education[1] and student mobility was increasingly recognised as an 'EU theme'[2] at a time when the EU was forced to remodel its relations with Central and East European states following the reform movement and gradual dismantlement of the Soviet Union in the late 1980s and early 1990s. Aside of the new programmes fostering education in Central and East European countries (like Tempus), various internal EU educational and mobility programmes – such as Socrates and Erasmus – were made accessible to students from former Communist countries as early as 1998. Consequently, cooperation in the field of higher education was also extended to the newly independent states, with a strong emphasis on Russia as the legal successor of the Soviet Union.

What is at stake, given Kaliningrad's geographic location, is the compatibility of its system of higher education with the remote motherland versus its immediate EU neighbours, in particular Lithuania and Poland. The relationship between these systems offers a test case of the exclave's potential to provide one of Russia's main openings towards Europe in general and the EU in particular. With a view to the EU, we will ask to what extent the European Union has proffered a model or directly influenced the path for transformation of Kaliningrad's higher education system. Therefore, this chapter examines higher education in the Russian exclave of Kaliningrad and the interplay of domestic, federal and external incentives, models and pressures. It will demonstrate that although Moscow only allows for marginal discretion in terms of Kaliningrad's higher educational policy, it seems that a number of actors in higher education have recognised the salience of European models and the need to work closely with partners from the EU.

EU–Russia relations and higher education

Ever since the Partnership and Cooperation Agreement (PCA) between the EU and the Russian Federation was negotiated between 1994 and 1996, higher education has been an important element of bilateral relations. The PCA recommended that cooperation should focus on 'updating higher education and training systems in Russia' and identified several core target goals: student and faculty mobility; executive and journalist training; inter-university cooperation (involving EU member states); and curriculum development, such as European Studies (Partnership and Cooperation Agreement 1997: Art. 63). The Common Strategy on Russia, a new foreign policy instrument initiated by the Treaty of Amsterdam and launched for the first time under the German EU Presidency, reiterated the need for fostering exchange and mobility programmes as well as university cooperation.

Financial assistance to promote cooperation in higher education between the EU and Central and Eastern Europe was allocated through Tempus-TACIS, 'a Community aid scheme for the restructuring of higher education systems in these countries in order to adapt them to the requirements of a market economy' (Commission 2007a). Projects are organised as consortia involving higher education institutions in the EU member states and partner countries, supported by National Contact Points (in EU member states) and National Tempus Offices (in partner countries) that facilitate partner searches (Commission 2007b). The 'Joint European Projects' stream of Tempus has focused on curriculum development, university management and institution building, of which Russia was the highest recipient of projects from 2000 to 2006. From 2002 until 2006, applicants from the Russian Federation received the most individual mobility grants amongst all third country nationalities.[3] The Russian Federation also tends to be amongst the highest recipients of projects pertaining to 'structural and complementary measures': projects that support implementation of Bologna objectives.[4] Clearly, the EU has prioritised the Russian Federation in its higher education assistance schemes, yet Kaliningrad has not been a primary target for these schemes.

Of the 259 Tempus-TACIS education projects that have been directed towards the Russian Federation since 1994, five have involved universities in Kaliningrad. While seemingly a small number, the nature of these projects has addressed some of the specific cross-border concerns of both Kaliningrad and the EU. The first Kaliningrad-specific Tempus-TACIS project was implemented in 1994 and its objectives were to update English language teaching and teacher training at Kaliningrad State University (KSU). Three subsequent projects have focused on raising Kaliningrad's standards of environmental management and education to European levels. Considering Kaliningrad's location, KSU would have seemed an appropriate location for a project in the field of European Studies. Despite this, other Russian universities – as far away as Novosibirsk in southern Siberia – were receiving Tempus-TACIS assistance to implement European Studies programmes as early as 1994. It was not until 2002 that Tempus-TACIS funded a project introducing a European dimension to the curriculum of three faculties at Kaliningrad State University. While relatively late in its inception, this innovative curriculum development initiative has set up a new and substantial cross-faculty Centre for European Studies at KSU (Commission 2007c).

The dearth of EU-funded higher education projects has not been from a lack of receptiveness from within Kaliningrad's universities, which are keen to integrate their higher education programmes with those of their immediate neighbours. Universities in Lithuania have established bilateral exchange agreements or joint projects with universities in Kaliningrad (Fairlie 1999). Other EU member states – particularly the Nordic countries – have also pursued a bilateral agenda in their relationship with the oblast. Furthermore, some member states like Denmark and Sweden have gone further than merely supporting Kaliningrad with a number of projects (including those in higher education); they have also drawn the attention of other EU member states to the specific needs of this Russian exclave on the Baltic coast. Yet the EU has not singled out Kaliningrad as a specific area for cooperation in the field of higher education, instead regarding the Bologna Process as a bridge to all Russian universities.

The Bologna Process was established after the ministers of education from France, Germany, Italy and the United Kingdom met at the Sorbonne in 1998 to discuss the future of higher education in Europe. The following year, the ministers of education from twenty-nine European countries met in Bologna and signed a declaration to establish a European Higher Education Area by 2010. It was an intergovernmental initiative with broad objectives in the realm of higher education, including increased student and academic mobility, as well as improving the compatibility, comparability and competitiveness of higher education institutions across Europe. Forty-six nations (almost all member states of the Council of Europe, the guiding body of the Bologna Process) have since signed the Declaration. Despite the number of new signatory nations that are from outside the EU, the European Commission still has considerable influence over 'Bologna', including having a vote on all Bologna amendments (the only non-state actor accorded such a privilege). With Russia signing the Declaration at the Berlin Conference in 2003, the Bologna Process began to frame bilateral cooperation in higher education. In May of that year, the Common Space of Research and Education, Including Cultural Aspects (as an integral part of the 'Roadmaps' on the Common Spaces in EU–Russia cooperation) was agreed upon at the EU–Russia summit in St Petersburg. This agreement, subsequently signed in Moscow in May of 2005, was clearly geared towards the Bologna Declaration. By signing Bologna, Russia has agreed to fulfil its goals by 2010 and eventually become an effective part of the European Higher Education and Research Areas.

Domestic reforms in the area of higher education in the Russian Federation

At the beginning of the 1990s, the Russian government started to reform its education system fundamentally. The goal was to democratise, humanise and decentralise education, as well as to increase the autonomy of educational institutions. This reform programme was established with the Law on Education in 1992, which was supposed to set the direction of the transformation process. However, in implementing the reforms, the government concentrated on the structural reorganisation of educational institutions, with quality assurance, curricular reform, and improving teaching methods supposedly coming later. It was not until 1996 that a Framework Law on Higher Education (Russian Federal Law 1996) entered into force, at which time universities had already been in the midst of a deep financial crisis for several years. As a result of the political and economic transformation (and near bankruptcy) of the Russian Federation, education expenditures dropped from 9.6 per cent of GDP in 1986, to 3.5 per cent in 1990, and then 2.9 per cent of GDP in 2000 (World Bank 2004).[5] Universities had lost the status of an institution of state priority and were forced to take measures to ensure their own survival. Lecturers began working for multiple institutions as well as earning money through private seminars. Irina Presnyakova of the Russian Academy of Sciences reported that at the start of the 1990s, 'scientific funding dropped ten-fold and scientists were not seen as necessary for society' (Moscow News 2008). To generate more income, universities introduced tuition fees and new courses, as well as renting out rooms, labs and building complexes. Higher education in Russia was becoming a 'quasi-market', without legal or financial regulation (Godfrey 2004: IV).

During this transformation process of the 1990s, the weakening of the central state and the decentralisation of public services allowed university administration to become more autonomous. The formerly centrally-regulated institutions started to interact with their environment independently; with students, with regional administrations and businesses, but also with international institutions (Bain 2003: 47). Under the new conditions, the focus of higher education shifted to regional needs. Institutions started to focus on the regional labour market and especially on the requirements of fee-paying students. For the universities, increased autonomy and a regional orientation created new opportunities for manoeuvrability and self-definition. Regional political administrations started to provide financial resources in an area of federal competence to ensure the survival of their regional universities.[6] At the same time, universities played a stronger role within regional politics and economies, by attracting foreign investment through well-educated specialists and research capacity. This development influenced the interaction between universities, politics and society, as well as affecting the distribution of human resources (Kuebart 2002: 85).

Following the opening of the country and the subsequent increased autonomy of educational institutions, international cooperation shifted from state to university control. With the Law on Education (2005), Russian educational institutions acquired, for the first time, the right to direct interaction with foreign educational institutions, companies and organisations. The Framework Law on Higher and Postgraduate Education created new possibilities in the sphere of higher education (Russian Federal Law 1996): for independent international cooperation; for international economic activities; and to ensure that newly acquired financial resources did not revert to state control. Due to these regulations, foreign relations became an important part of university autonomy, especially as foreign partner universities and international organisations and institutions had financially supported Russian universities during the crisis years. For many of the universities, international cooperation and exchanges became an important non-governmental financial source,[7] and programmes like Tempus-TACIS played an important role in securing the survival of Russian universities. However, critics have noted that during the 1990s, TACIS money was spent primarily on the mobility of administrative and executive staff and less on students and academics. Some changes in methodology and curricula were endorsed by teacher interest; others resulted from student pressure or competition between universities (Eimermacher 2002: 22). Yet overall, international influence has been essential to Russian universities trying to adapt to new social, economic and political standards.

Following the election of Vladimir Putin in 2000, Russian higher education policy was reoriented to play a key role as part of an extensive reform of the Russian state, and its economy in particular. The authors of the 'Concept of modernisation of Russian education up to 2010' (Concept of modernisation 2001) emphasised the need to reform the education system as a reaction to comprehensive global changes that entailed new challenges for the state, society and individuals. The decision to sign the Bologna Declaration in 2003 was an important step in the reform process. The goal of the government was to integrate Russia into the European Higher Education Area and to modernise the Russian university system by means of cooperation with European universities. Along with participation in the Bologna Process, the federal government enacted the 'Federal target programme for the development of education between 2006 and 2010' in December of 2005. In this target programme, the central principles of the reform process were described using the Bologna Declaration as a guideline. As the basis of education policy until 2010, the federal target programme serves as an orientation for all levels of government, including regional and local administrations. A long term objective of the programme is to increase Russia's global competitiveness in education services by cooperating with European universities (Federal target programme 2006).

The federal target programme was critical of the low quality of Russian education, decreased mobility of students and teachers, and the lack of university orientation towards the labour market. It proposed four reforms to overcome these deficiencies. One was to extend cooperation with European states to improve the quality of education and adapt to international quality standards. Another was to introduce comparable degrees as well as standardised and transferable degree descriptions, qualifications (the diploma supplement) and credit equivalency (ECTS). A third was to increase the mobility of students, scientists and university teachers through increased scholarship and loans. The final reform was to expand the export of education services (*ibid.*). Through the adaptation of European quality standards, evaluation criteria and documentation, the export of Russian university services should improve.

Integrating the Bologna Process into a domestic educational reform agenda has influenced both foreign and domestic policy in Russia. Within Russia, this integration has directly affected not only higher education reform, but also the labour market and the public sector (creating independent universities and associations). It helps to bring the Russian higher education system into accord with the requirements of a knowledge-based society and raise the competitiveness of the Russian economy. Furthermore, Bologna has had an indirect impact on government budgets and administrative reform, including limiting the state's regulatory role in education (Pursiainen and Medvedev 2005: 22). The influence on Russia's foreign policy has primarily been related to the dialogue with the EU. In EU–Russia relations, the four Common Spaces are closely linked, so that progress in the most advanced fourth Common Space of Research, Education and Culture can have a positive effect on the other three (*ibid.*: 23). Russia's interests in international cooperation concern questions of mobility – such as the weakening of the visa regimes, especially Schengen – and the recognition of Russian diplomas.[8] These problems play an important role in the Russian dialogue with the EU. At the EU–Russia Summit in London in October of 2005, the EU loosened visa restrictions for people working in certain fields, such as education and science. Cooperation between the EU and Russia in the technological fields should help to transfer technical competence from European States to Russia (Adomeit and Lindner 2005: 16–17). In addition to that, central elements of the Bologna Process and the exchange in higher education in different fields should be supported (Commission 2005). As a consequence, elements of the Bologna Process are integrated into common agreements between Russia and the EU, and Russia uses Bologna for its internal reform process.

The development of higher education in Kaliningrad

Universities in the Kaliningrad region

In the Kaliningrad region, there are eighteen institutions of higher education, both state and private, which also includes seven branch universities from institutions in St Petersburg and Moscow.[9] Two of the eighteen have full status as a university: Kaliningrad State University (KSU)[10] and Kaliningrad State Technical University (KSTU) (Russian Education 2006). Both of these universities are state run; KSTU is subordinated to the state committee for fishing, and KSU is operated by the Ministry of Education. Private universities and branch institutions predominantly offer courses in social sciences, humanities, economics and law and are commercially oriented towards fee-paying students (Klemeshev 2004: 8).

KSU is the largest university in the region, with more than 12,000 students and nearly 600 lecturers.[11] According to the strategy of the university, the internationalisation of KSU and harmonisation of Russian and European education are important components of their education policy. This policy is manifest in KSU participation in EU projects, the Union of European Universities and the Conference of Rectors in the Baltic Sea area. The university also has a European Information Centre, a Centre for Human rights of the Council of Europe, and a language centre for Swedish and English.

Transformation and regionalisation of the regional university system

The dissolution of the Soviet Union and independence of the Baltic States influenced the development of the regional university system. For Kaliningrad – like all other Russian regions – the beginning of the 1990s saw a marked decrease in the public budget for education. Yet it was especially Kaliningrad's isolation from the Russian mainland that hindered traditional communication and cooperation between universities and companies in the Russian Federation and post-Soviet countries. For instance, the former Institute for Fishing (since 1994 KSTU) trained specialists not only for the region, but for all of the Soviet Union. In the early 1990s, the fishing and ship-building industries went into a deep economic crisis and the demand for specialists decreased. As a result, the cooperation with companies in this field decreased not only in post-Soviet countries, but also in Russia. Moreover, between 1990 and 1995, university enrolment was declining in Kaliningrad and across Russia (Klemeshev 2004: 10). According to Andrej Klemeshev, the rector of KSU, the reason for this development was that the focus of education at regional universities did not correspond with the demands of the regional labour market, which increasingly corresponded to a free-market economy (*ibid.*: 8–9). Other reasons for the drop in student enrolment were decreasing mobility of students from other regions and Russia's (and especially Kaliningrad's) difficult economic situation at the time. Since the mid-1990s, student enrolment has increased rapidly as the economy has improved and universities have refocused on the changing needs of regional labour markets.

As higher education in Russia began to transform in the late 1990s, regional universities started to make adjustments to changing regional needs.

Because of growing demand by students and companies, KSU extended specialisations in fields like information technology, tourism, ecology and financial services. The university established a priority in the teaching of foreign languages, increasing the number of lessons as well as using foreign expertise to modernise equipment and pedagogy. The main goal of this policy has been to improve student opportunities in foreign and domestic labour markets, as well as facilitate university integration into the European Higher Education Area by means of increasing mobility for students and lecturers (*ibid.*: 11). For KSU, this new orientation aided by international expertise has been an important step in increasing competitiveness *vis-à-vis* other universities in the region in attracting fee-paying students.

During the Soviet era in Kaliningrad, specialists in agriculture, construction and medicine were provided by universities from other regions, especially the Baltic Union republics. But due to the rupture in traditional cooperation between Soviet higher education institutions, Kaliningrad had to react independently to new situations. For example, an initiative of the regional administration prompted KSU to open a centre for medical education which will evolve into a medical faculty (Pavlova 2006). Thus, universities participate in restructuring the region, and the regional administration influences the orientation of the universities.

Internationalisation through Europeanisation

Due to their physical location, the universities of Kaliningrad have greater possibilities for international cooperation than other Russian regions. There is a high interest amongst neighbouring states in cooperating with the Kaliningrad region because of the differences in social development and soft security risks. Currently, KSU has official agreements with fifty-one universities worldwide, fourteen in Germany and twelve in Poland (Kaliningrad State University 2007b).[12] For a small regional university like KSU, a large number of international cooperation projects can have a huge potential for exchange and reform. But lacking an effective strategy for international relations, the university's limited resources are overtaxed.

KSU is one of twenty-five Russian universities chosen by the federal government to introduce the ECTS system and other elements of the Bologna Process (see Moscow State Institute 2007). But the pro-rector of education, Irina Kuksa, wonders why KSU participates in the Bologna Process in the framework of federal legislation and agreements with the Ministry of Education in the same way as all other Russian universities. In her opinion, KSU should play a special role in this context because of Kaliningrad's geographic and geopolitical location. For universities in Kaliningrad, the pressure to adopt Bologna principles is higher than for all other Russian universities. Due to Kaliningrad's proximity to the EU and high mobility of students and lecturers, the universities must prepare both students and staff for study and work abroad. The greater ease of faculty exchanges with

European universities could ensure that Kaliningrad university lecturers are familiar with new teaching methods and that visiting lecturers from Europe bring new ideas (Kuksa interview 2006).

The main obstacle for full integration of Russian universities into the Bologna Process is its implementation by state authorities. For Moscow, the preservation of national traditions is just as important as mobility and common standards. Russian universities are not allowed to introduce elements of the Bologna Process independently; they can only support the federally-mandated reform process. So even though Bachelors/Masters degrees have existed at KSU since 1992 (they were introduced by the Yeltsin Government as an alternative to the Soviet diploma), Irina Kuksa remains sceptical of a full introduction of a two-cycle degree system because of the strong regulation of the education process by the Russian government. This poses particular problems for students in Kaliningrad: independent Masters Programmes are very rare because of the lack of academic standards and specialists at KSU, and there is little demand for Bachelors degrees on the regional labour market (*ibid.*). Furthermore, there are no possibilities for vocational job training, an important step for Bachelor degree graduates in Europe (Smolin 2005: 51). The differences between the Russian and European education systems are too great for a quick and simple adaptation of Bologna standards. Russian universities need more flexibility and the students more independence for the successful implementation of Bologna reforms.

One of the most important projects for harmonising KSU with European quality standards has been the Euro-Faculty. In March 1993, this project was initiated by the Council of the Baltic Sea States (CBSS). Its goal was to reform higher education in the eastern part of the Baltic Sea region, in the fields of law, economics, public and business administration. While Euro-Faculty centres were opened at universities in Estonia, Latvia and Lithuania in the 1990s, KSU had only established a branch in the faculties of law and economy by September 2000. This project has been financed by the European Commission, the Scandinavian states, Germany, Poland, the Netherlands, Great Britain and the aforementioned host states of Euro-Faculty. Its main element is guest lecturers from European partner universities: they instruct at different levels, initiate research projects, and help to modernise curricula at the host universities (Kaliningrad State University 2007a). The central objective of the Kaliningrad Euro-Faculty is to modernise teaching in economics and law to the point that those faculties are able to respond to international challenges, cross-border trade and the increased integration of the Baltic Sea area. Sustainable change at KSU should be achieved through modernisation of curricula and teaching methods (Progress Report 2002: 68). The main obstacle to these reforms is the lack of flexibility of the curricula and education standards set by the Russian Ministry of Education. For example, introducing new methods and curricula is only possible if the number of lessons is reduced, yet this factor determines lecturers' salaries, resulting in resistance to reform amongst faculty members. A further difficulty is the low level of foreign-language ability amongst students and lecturers in Kaliningrad, a critical aspect for international cooperation. Even though language training has been intensively supported from the beginning of the Euro-Faculty, its improvement remains a long term goal (*ibid.*: 69–71).

Aleksander Salenko, the head of the Euro-Faculty in the Law Department of KSU, describes two main obstacles for the success of the project. First, there needs to be a generational change within university faculties, because of the resistance to reforms by older lecturers and a staunch hierarchy at Russian universities. The second obstacle is the rigid education standards that are fixed from the federal government. The Law Department at KSU received special permission by the Ministry of Education to deviate from the education standards for the purposes of the Euro-Faculty, but for comprehensive adaptation to European norms and standards, Russian universities will need more autonomy (Salenko interview 2006). In turn, Vera Zabotkina, the pro-rector for international relations at KSU, emphasises that the Russian Ministry of Education has accepted all changes of curricula by the Euro-Faculty, so that European standards for university education can be integrated. In light of this, basic courses were reduced from forty to twenty-five hours per week, and more advanced courses were reduced to twenty hours per week (Baltinfo Newsletter 2004: 10–11). In this, it is clear that the new structures of the Euro-Faculty are not directly integrated in the normal study plan at KSU, but exist as a parallel structure. This development is typical for Russian adaptation policies pertaining to European standards: on the one hand, new standards and criteria are partly introduced; on the other hand, important elements of the existing system are preserved. Meanwhile, Moscow continues to pressure regional universities into implementing reforms without creating the necessary preconditions for them.

Conclusion

In the area of higher education, the European Union provides only a few templates. However, further market integration as well as the evolution of the Bologna Process put the EU into a position to shape the internationalisation of higher education. Thus higher education has also developed into an area for cooperation between Russia and the EU. With regards to Kaliningrad, however, both parties have not agreed on the making of a special regime for the oblast; instead they prefer to deal with higher education issues in Kaliningrad rather comprehensively within the context of EU–Russia relations. Today, a multitude of cooperation projects exist in the area of higher education, rendering Kaliningrad into a cooperative test region often by default rather than by design.

The implementation of the Bologna Process (albeit still at an early stage in Russia) seems slow in Kaliningrad, similar to other Russian regions. However, this process has shifted higher education into a more pan-European rather than exclusively EU-driven endeavour. Hence, the Bologna Process appears to be an application of the EU's open method of coordination (from the Lisbon EU Council in 2000) to incorporate non-EU countries into the pursuit of a number goals in educational policy. It is obvious that the Russian government is very much in favour of such an approach, putting Russia on par with the EU and its member states.

Still, a number of problems persist. Implementation problems are generated by institutional path-dependency (personnel, institutional resistance, etc.) and there are no quality control systems ensuring the proper implementation of Bologna objectives, such as curricular reforms. Policy-makers in Russia and Kaliningrad have recognised the need to integrate Kaliningrad into systems of higher education, both federally and regionally (in terms of the Baltic Sea area). While university administrations in Kaliningrad have learned much from EU experience in managing joint programmes, there is still some doubt as to whether these programmes are going to be self-sustainable. Individual projects – such as Euro-Faculty – have provided an important impetus, but they constitute islands of reform in the much larger and rougher seas of Russian higher education.

Hence, only partial adaptation is evident. Resistance *vis-à-vis* European standards prevails because adaptation to and emulation of 'European' and 'Western' standards occurs only in younger segments of university faculties in Kaliningrad. The federal policy in higher education is twofold: while it seeks to restrict regional autonomy, it also attempts to reduce resistance to Bologna on the ground.

Notes

1   In this case, higher education refers to the general and theoretical education provided by tertiary, non-compulsory and degree-granting educational institutions (i.e. universities and colleges).
2   Education was not explicitly alluded to in the Treaty of Rome (1957) thereby implicitly ensuring that it was within the domain of member states. Subsequent treaties have established the EU's role in 'encouraging co-operation between Member States and, if necessary, supporting and supplementing their action, while fully respecting the responsibility of the Member States for the content of their teaching and the organisation of education systems and their cultural and linguistic diversity' (Treaty of Maastricht 1992: Art. 126.1). This policy of a supporting role has been reiterated within Art. 149 of the Treaty of Amsterdam (1997) and Art. III-282 of the Draft Constitutional Treaty (2004).
3   Exceptions: 2nd round 2002, Albania had more. In the later rounds, (1st and 3rd rounds of 2004, 3rd round of 2005, 1st and 2nd rounds of 2006) Egypt had more. Please see http://ec.europa.eu/education/programmes/tempus /stat_en.html.

4 In 2003, the Russian Federation was the target of three out of twelve projects (most); in 2004, Russia was the target of only three out of forty projects; in 2005 (round 1), it was the target of only four out of forty-one projects and for round two of 2005, it was seven of thirty-seven (most).

5 Over this same period, OECD states spent an average of 5.5 per cent of annual GDP on education, with a considerably higher GDP as well (Verbina and Chowdhury 2004: 493).

6 The pro-rector for academic policy at the Moscow State University, Vladimir Mironov, emphasised that good relations with Moscow City Council were decisive in financing electricity and heating costs of the university during the 1990s (Mironov interview 2005).

7 Between 1993 and 1995, more than 200 foreign foundations worked in Russia. In 1996 they financed 9 per cent of the budget of Russian universities (Chvostrostov 2001: 178).

8 Russian degrees are not recognised in the developed world (Smolentseva 2004: 2).

9 Most of the state universities in Russia are under federal control (in 1999 there were 537). Some depend on regional (36) or local administrations (12). As in Soviet times, only some of them are financed by the Ministry of Education, the others by industrial branch ministries (Teichmann 2005: 99).

10 KSU was renamed Russian State University 'Immanuel Kant' in 2005.

11 In 2006, KSU had 12,070 students and 615 teachers (Russian Education 2007).

12 In comparison with KSU, Nizhni Novgorod State University has more than 31,000 Students (in 2005) and a much higher academic and research potential (one of the leading universities in some academic fields), and yet has only twenty-four official international agreements (Nizhni Novgorod State University 2007).

References

Adomeit, H. and R. Lindner (2005), 'Die "Gemeinsamen Räume" Russlands und der EU. Wunschbild und Wirklichkeit' ['The "Common Spaces" between Russia and the EU: Desire and reality'], Berlin: SWP Research Paper 34.

Bain, O. B. (2003), *University Autonomy in the Russian Federation since Perestroika*, London, Routledge Falmer.

Baltinfo Newsletter (2004), 'Euro-Faculty Kaliningrad: Pilot for Higher Education Reform in Russia (Interview with Vera Zabotkina)', *Baltinfo*, May: 10–11.

Blitz, B. K. (2003), 'From Monnet to Delors: Educational Co-operation in the European Union', *Contemporary European History* 12(2): 197–212.

Chvostrostov, A. (2001), 'An Essay on the State of International Cooperation in Russian Universities' in *Russland im Umbruch – Jugend im Aufbruch*, ed. K. Eimermacher and A. Hartmann, Bochum, Lotman Institute for Russian and Soviet Culture.

Commission (2005), 'Roadmap on the Common Space of Research and Education, Including Cultural Aspects', available on the Internet at http://ec.europa.eu /comm/external_relations/russia/summit_05_05/finalroadmaps.pdf#rec (accessed 25 April 2007).

Commission (2007a), 'Funding Programmes in Education and Training', available on the Internet at http://ec.europa.eu/education/programmes/programmes_en.html (accessed 17 July 2007).

Commission (2007b), 'The Tempus Programme: Changes in Higher Education Through People to People Cooperation', available on the Internet at http://ec.europa.eu/tempus (accessed 17 July 2007).

Commission (2007c), 'The Tempus Programme: Description of Tempus Projects (JEPs and SCMs) Financed in the Russian Federation', available on the Internet at http://ec.europa.eu/education/programmes/tempus/countries/projects/russia.pdf (accessed 17 July 2007).

Concept of modernisation (2001), 'Koncepcija modernizacii rossijskogo obrazovanija na period do 2010 g.' ['Concept of modernisation of Russian education up to 2010'], approved on 29 December 2001, available on the Internet at www.hse.ru /science/modern_ed/default.htm (accessed 31 May 2007).

Eimermacher, K. (2002), 'Von Geldern und Menschen: Einsätze, Gewinne und Verluste bei der Förderung von Hochschulen und Wissenschaft in Russland' ['From money and people: Support, benefit and loss in dealing with Russian universities and academia'], in *Vom Sinn und Unsinn westlicher Förderung in Russland* [*Does Western support for Russia make sense*], ed. K. Eimermacher and U. Justus, Bochum, Lotman Institute for Russian and Soviet Culture: 7–32.

Fairlie, L. D. (1999), 'Will the EU use the Northern Dimension to Solve its Kaliningrad Dilemma?', Working Paper 21, Copenhagen, Copenhagen Peace Research Institute.

Federal target programme (2006), 'Federal'naja celevaja programma razvitija obrazovanija na 2006–2010 goda' ['Federal target programme for the development of education between 2006–2010'], approved on 23 December 2005, available on the Internet at www.ed.gov.ru/ntp/fp/fcpro2006/ (accessed 14 December 2006).

Füllsack, M. (2001), 'Bildung als Konsumgut? Folgen der Entstaatlichung des russländischen Bildungswesens' ['Education and consumption: The consequences of the state's retreat from education in Russia'], *Osteuropa*, 51(1): 3–13.

Godfrey, M. (2004), 'Russian Federation, Per Capita Financing of Education: Experiences and Issues', World Bank-Policy Note, September, available on the Internet at http://194.84.38.65/files/esw_files/Edu_PCF_Education_Russia_PN_eng.pdf (accessed 31 May 2007).

Kaliningrad State University (2007a), 'About Euro-Faculty', available on the Internet at http://eurofaculty.albertina.ru/index.phtml?id=127 (accessed 18 January 2007).

Kaliningrad State University (2007b), 'International Relations', available on the Internet at www.albertina.ru/new/index.php?nitem=57 (accessed 17 January 2007).

Klemeshev, A. (2004), 'Vysshee obrazovanie Kaliningradskoj oblasti v usloviajch eksklavnosti' ['Higher education in the Kaliningrad region under conditions of exclave'], *Region sotrudnitchestva, Sfera obrazovanija v Rossii i Evrope v kontekste globalizacii* [*Region of cooperation, education in Russia and Europe in the context of globalization*], ed. Andrej Klemeshev, Kaliningrad, Kaliningrad State University Press, BALTMION, 13(38): 5–15.

Kuebert, F. (2002), 'The European House of Education: Education and Economy – A new Partnership', in *Von der Perestrojka zur Transformation. Berufsausbildung und Hochschulwesen in Russland und Ostmitteleuropa*, ed. O. Anweiler and D. Schulz, Leipzig, University Press: 75–92.

Moscow News (2008), 'Stopping the brain drain', in *Moscow News*, 14, 10 April, available on the Internet at www.mnweekly.ru/national/20080410/55322506.html (accessed 9 May 2008).

Moscow State Institute for International Relations (2007), 'Bologna Process', available on the Internet at http://bologna.mgimo.ru/index.php (accessed 31 May 2007).

Nizhni Novgorod State University (2007) 'International Relations', available on the Internet at www.unn.ru/?main=international&sub=relations (accessed 4 June 2007).

Partnership and Cooperation Agreement (PCA 1997), available on the Internet at http://ec.europa.eu/external_relations/ceeca/pca/pca_russia.pdf (accessed 25 April 2007).

Progress Report (2002), 'Progress Report on the Implementation of the Northern Dimension Action Plan 2000–2003, Excerpt of the "Evaluation of the EuroFaculty Project at

Kaliningrad State University"', Report to the Danish Ministry of Science, Technology and Innovation in Oslo on 4 October 2002, available on the Internet at http://cbss.org/documents/cbsspresidencies/11finnish/cbssprogressreportofndap00-03.pdf (accessed 31 May 2007).

Pursiainen, C. and S. A. Medvedev (2005), 'The Bologna Process, Russia and Globalization' in *The Bologna Process and its Implications for Russia*, ed. C. Pursianinen and S. A. Medvedev, Moscow, Russian European Centre for Economic Policy: 16–26.

Russian Education (2006), Federal Internet Portal, available on the Internet at www.edu.ru/db/cgi-bin/portal/vuzp/vuz_list.php (accessed 24 November 2006).

Russian Education (2007), Federal Internet Portal for Kaliningrad State University Immanuel Kant, available on the Internet at www.edu.ru/db/cgi-bin/portal/vuzp /vuz_inf.php?isn=229 (accessed 31 May 2007).

Russian Federal Law (1996), 'Federalny Zakon "O vysshem i poslevuzovskom professional nom obrazovanii"' ['Federal Law "on Higher and postgraduate education"'], approved on 22 August 1996, available on the Internet at http://edu.park.ru/public /default.asp?WCI=Document&no=35916&print=1 (accessed 5 June 2007).

Smolentseva, A. (2004), 'International Students in Russia', *International Higher Education*, 46, available on the Internet at www.bc.edu/bc_org/avp/soe/cihe/newsletter /News36/text011.htm (accessed 31 May 2007).

Smolin, O. (2005), 'Rossijskie vuzy i Bolonskij process: Vzgljad parlamentarija' ['Russian Universities in the Bologna Process: View from a Parliamentarian'], in *Zwischen Tradition und Moderne, Russische Universitäten als Gestalter des europäischen Hochschulraumes*, ed. Damu, Berlin, Lomonossow Vorlesungen, 3: 49–53.

Teichmann, C. (2005), 'Nachfrageorientierte Hochschulfinanzierung und Effizienz des Mitteleinsatzes im russischen Hochschulwesen' ['Demand-oriented university financing and efficiency in the Russian university system'], in *Bildungspolitik und Bildungsfinanzierung in Russland zwischen Staat und Markt* [*Education and its funding in Russia: The state and the market*], ed. Sonja Steier, Berlin, Waxmann: 89–131.

Treaty of Maastricht (1992), 'Treaty on European Union', *Official Journal of the European Union C191*, Brussels, 29 July.

Verbina, I. and A. Chowdhury (2004), 'What determines public education in Russia?', *The Economics of Transition*, Oxford, Blackwell Publishing, 12(3): 489–508.

World Bank (2004), 'Summary Education Profile: Russia', available on the Internet at http://devdata.worldbank.org/edstats/SummaryEducationProfiles/CountryData /GetShowData.asp?sCtry=RUS,Russia (accessed 13 February 2007).

Interviews (by Stefan Meister)

Kuksa, Irina (2006), Pro-rector for Education at Kaliningrad State University, Kaliningrad, interview on 28 September 2006 in Kaliningrad.

Mironov, Vladimir (2005), Pro-rector for Education Policy and Organisation of Teaching Process, Moscow State University, interview on 26 September 2005 in Moscow.

Pavlova, Alla (2006), Ministry of Education Kaliningrad Region, Head of the Department for Vocational and Continuing Education, interview on 27 September 2006 in Kaliningrad.

Salenko, Aleksander (2006), Head of the Euro-Faculty, Law Faculty at Kaliningrad State University, interview on 16 April 2006 in Kaliningrad.

Alexey Ignatyev, Konstantin Shopin and Pyotr Shopin

15

Integrated management of the EU–Russia common border: the Kaliningrad perspective

Introduction

In the aftermath of the collapse of the Soviet Union, new borders emerged and gradually started to pose a plethora of concerns. Additionally, the EU enlargement in 2004 continues to be perceived in Russia as a potential for creating new dividing lines amongst populations that were accustomed to travelling and trading without restrictions for decades. In some cases, as at the Russian–Polish border in the Kaliningrad region, the much desired trans-frontier cooperation could only develop during the 1990s, before becoming difficult again as a consequence of Poland's EU accession. As part of the preparations for the eastern enlargement, the EU and Russia have made major investments to strengthen the border infrastructure in Russia's western border regions. However, with Russia's southern borders hardly protected (due to limited financial, technical and human resources) and continuously challenged by organised crime, money laundering, drug smuggling and illegal human trafficking, the pressure on Russia's western borders has increased. For the EU, the border regions with western Russia present a challenge due to the risk of an influx of illegal immigrants and cross-border crime.

This elucidates the necessity of developing a consistent policy aimed at the introduction of integrated border management (IBM), i.e. the organisation and supervision of border agencies' activities to meet the common challenge of facilitating the legitimate movement of people and goods, while maintaining secure borders and meeting national legal requirements. This is an important tool fostering trans-frontier cooperation and ensuring sustainable economic and social development of border regions for the EU and Russia. The EU has acquired a great deal of relevant experience in the course of enlargement, which could facilitate the search for suitable solutions during the development of a common EU–Russia border policy.

Many questions still remain open, however. How much time is required to ensure that the whole EU–Russia common border (which is the lengthiest external border for the EU, and one of the lengthiest for Russia) is effective and efficient in accordance with the principles of IBM? Are all of the border regions equally dependent on efficient border procedures in their socio-economic development? Or are there those which should be considered a priority? Will it be possible to avoid some of the mistakes and misconceptions by testing the practical establishment of the IBM approach at specific sections of the border prior to applying the concept to the whole frontier? These are primarily questions about time, priorities and efficiency.

Cooperation at EU–Russia level: moving forward

Expert studies on the EU–Russia border situation (Fairlie and Sergounin 2001; Hobbing 2005; Burkhart 2005) and a series of corresponding initiatives have shown that the problems of border management are very complex and broad in scope, touching on many interdisciplinary areas and interconnected issues. Among those issues are: a backlog and asymmetry in the development of a border infrastructure; a need for re-equipping border-crossing points with new technology; the differences between the technology of controlling persons, vehicles and cargoes that are applied at border-crossing points by the border control and customs services; isolated and incompatible databases on each side of the border and lack of access to them; inconsistency of Russian and EU legislation; lack of coordination of activities of various agencies, resulting in queues at borders and encouraging corruption. Many of these problems are successfully managed in the EU, where enormous experience has been accumulated in developing and implementing an integrated approach to border management, and the elaboration of a common policy has become one of the Union's official aims (Hobbing 2005: 2). For Russia and the EU it seems rather logical to examine and apply this best practice to their common border today. However, a critical question is what would be the best way to do this in practice?

It was obvious from the early stages of EU–Russia collaboration that the principles and approaches employed by the EU in relation to candidate states for accession could not be applied in the case of Russia. That was when the concept of integration through the establishment of four Common Spaces was introduced, allowing the two sides to cooperate extensively on a broad number of issues and to preserve a high degree of political independence in decision-making. The 'Roadmaps' for the four Common Spaces, including the Common Space of Freedom, Security and Justice (CSFSJ) that covers the improvement of border management, were signed by both parties during the EU–Russia summit in Moscow in May of 2005. The CSFSJ outlined the general guidelines and urged both parties to intensify discussions on border management, and to enhance cooperation between respective authorities, as well as to develop collaborative projects to increase efficiency of border management. The intent has been to continue supporting the development of border-crossing points, strengthening the institutional and administrative framework while increasing the capacity of borders and improving border surveillance.

A particular emphasis of this Common Space has been the reform of the Russian judiciary system in relation to border management. With a view to contributing to the concrete implementation of the 'Roadmap', the Justice and Home Affairs Permanent Partnership Council met in 2005 and 2006 and agreed to organise clusters of conferences and seminars, bringing together experts and practitioners on counter-terrorism, cyber-crime, document security and judicial cooperation. There was also agreement on developing greater cooperation between the European Border Agency (FRONTEX)[1] and the Federal Border Security Service of Russia, as well as exploring the possibility of an agreement between the EU Judicial Cooperation Unit (EUROJUST) and the Russian Prosecutor General's Office.[2]

Concerned with issues of Kaliningrad's development in a regional context, the parties promoted a broad agenda for cooperation, ranging from the region's socio-economic development to the common challenges of environmental protection and health issues. Most of the relevant initiatives have been implemented primarily through various joint projects within a number of large-scale cooperation programmes (such as TACIS, Interreg, the Institution Building Partnership Programme, Tempus and the recently launched ENPI Instrument).

A Neighbourhood Programme established by Lithuania, Poland and Kaliningrad as an Interreg III-A project was designed for efficient collaboration between administrations at the level of territories. The programme's scope covered the Lithuanian regions of Klaipeda, Taurage, Alytus and Marijampole (totalling twenty-one local governments) and the voivodships of Pomorskie and Warmińsko-Mazurskie in Poland as well as the entire Kaliningrad region of the Russian Federation. Its primary goal was to stimulate local and regional economic development through cooperation and better communication, thereby removing obstacles to integration and mutual understanding.[3] In 2007 it was replaced by a programme with similar objectives designed to cover the period up until 2013, with an overall budget of €132 million. Notably, Russia's financial contribution to such initiatives is increasing over time,[4] gradually changing its status in these programmes from a mere beneficiary to an equal partner.

Two EU–Russia summits are held every year for consultations on a broad range of issues. From these meetings, the parties have agreed to continue the visa dialogue with a view to examining the conditions for a mutual visa-free travel regime as a long term goal. Work on the CSFSJ already took a significant step forward as negotiations were concluded on the agreements pertaining to visa facilitation and re-admission. The agreements were signed at the EU–Russia Summit on 25 May 2006 in Sochi, Russia, and ratified by both sides in 2007. As a result, visa costs were reduced from €60 to €35 and application procedures were greatly simplified for certain categories of EU and Russian travellers. The meetings will continue to address issues of cooperation on combating terrorism and other forms of trans-national illegal activities (such as money laundering, the drug trade and human trafficking) as well as document security through the introduction of biometric features in a range of identification documents.

Problems persist

While both the EU and Russia seem determined to continue intensive negotiations and to develop further collaboration in the field of border management, the question remains of whether it is yet enough. It has become apparent that the practical introduction of IBM along the entire EU–Russia common border is a task of immense scope, which will take years to achieve. Even minor steps require great efforts from both sides. For instance, experts from the Interdepartmental Working Group on the Issues of the Development of the Kaliningrad Region within the Russian Federation's Presidential Administration have estimated that the establishment of combined – let alone joint – border-crossing points will require amending fifty-eight normative and legal acts in the Russian Federation.

This elucidates another controversial issue of particular concern for both parties. The idea behind the Common Spaces was to start the harmonisation and *rapprochement* of the two systems based on principles of real partnership. However, this process has since acquired a degree of imbalance, as it has been gradually transforming into unilateral influence of the EU over Russia. For instance, this has been somewhat reflected in the EU's repeated calls on Russia to adopt much of its *acquis communautaire*. As international experts (Dewar *et al.* 2005: 22) have pointed out, not only is this unrealistic, but much of it would be irrelevant and even harmful to Russian interests. This approach reflects the concept shared by some circles in Europe, according to which harmonisation of the two systems is essentially a process of the Europeanisation of Russia. At the same time, it would be reasonable to expect the Russian side to consider this an issue of bilateral convergence: Europeanisation of Russia, and simultaneous 'Russianisation' of the EU. Thus, the EU and Russia are clearly willing to put irreconcilable differences and inconsistencies aside, yet both parties rightfully maintain a policy of minimising possible shocks that this process could have on their own development – another argument supporting the view that mutual *rapprochement* at the EU–Russia level will be a long and a complicated process.

Given the above, a logical solution for both parties would be to identify a border section that might be considered a test case where EU best practice could be applied and lessons derived for the benefit of a smoother introduction of IBM for the common border as a whole. Kaliningrad should be the test ground for that.

Why Kaliningrad?

Historical background

Following the end of the Cold War, Kaliningrad underwent a significant transformation from a closed military outpost of the Soviet Union to a Special Economic Zone of the Russian Federation. This marked the changing nature of border management in the region. During the Soviet era, there were no public crossing points on Kaliningrad's border with Poland, while the border between the oblast and Lithuania (then part of the Soviet Union) was a mere line on the Soviet administrative map. At the time, the primary concern for Russian and Polish border authorities was security.

The dismantlement of the Soviet Union caused the situation to change dramatically as the region turned into a Russian exclave; the former administrative border with Lithuania acquired international status and the border with Poland was opened. Kaliningrad's isolation from the mainland and its need for international cooperation with its two neighbour states led to a revision of approaches to border management, as the balance between security and free movement of people, goods and services became vital.

Due to some ambiguity in Moscow's policy towards the regions during the 1990s, the level of freedom in policy-making that the regions exercised varied significantly at different moments in time. The federal government's initial steps in this policy area led to a situation where the division of responsibilities between the centre and the regions was regulated by individual agreements, many of which contradicted the Russian Constitution. This inconsistency was evident in an initiative by one region to grant its parliament the right to declare war and peace; meanwhile the federal government annulled a trade treaty between Kaliningrad and Lithuania on the grounds of its non-compliance with federal legislation (Fairlie and Sergounin 2001: 169).

The new administrative reform launched in 2000 established seven federal districts led by presidential plenipotentiaries entrusted with monitoring the local legislation and coordinating the activities of the regional offices of federal bodies (customs, border security services, security services, etc.). The primary idea behind the reform was to establish a vertical alignment of power, ensuring the alignment of regional and federal legislation as well as reasserting the exclusive authority of the federal centre in the fields of diplomacy, treaty-making, defence and security, definition and protection of state borders, and other relevant matters stipulated by the Russian Constitution.

Border management issues have predominantly been the prerogative of the federal centre, and all border activities are controlled by regional offices of relevant federal structures, such as the Federal Border Security Service, the Customs Service, the Ministry of Foreign Affairs, and the State Inspection for Phytosanitary and Veterinary Control. The main responsibility of regional authorities in this field has been to ensure that appropriate conditions are established that enable an efficient operation of the border.[5] They also provide land plots for border defence purposes and monitor compliance with environmental legislation, informing federal border authorities about the situation in border areas (Russian Federal Law 1993: 23–4).

Thus, international activities of the Russian regions have since been limited to trade, and scientific, ecological, humanitarian and cultural cooperation at the level of regional and local governments of foreign states. Nevertheless, while the regions' manoeuvrability was somewhat narrowed as a result of the reform, they were not prevented from engaging in effective international cooperation and participation in various development projects. Regional authorities were also entitled to elaborate their views and proposals on border management issues and to put them forward to the federal level for consideration.

Building the CBC capacity

For Russian authorities, there are clear indications of a proactive approach towards Kaliningrad's border management issues. Acknowledging the vital importance of cross-border cooperation, Russia eagerly supported the establishment of the Russian–Lithuanian Council on long term cooperation between regional and local authorities of Kaliningrad and the Lithuanian Republic. The Council consists of a number of joint commissions, dealing with issues of transport, joint border and customs control at border checkpoints, education, culture, sports and healthcare. The Russian side is represented by members of the regional government, heads of regional offices of federal bodies, and members of the Russian Ministries of Foreign Affairs and of Economic Development and Trade. A Russian–Polish Council on cooperation between Kaliningrad and Polish regions has also been established. Both structures are similar in nature, and were designed to tackle identical issues with both of Kaliningrad's neighbouring states. It should be noted, however, that an inherent shortcoming of all such bodies involving Russia has been that communities are traditionally underrepresented because NGOs, the Public Chamber ombudsmen or the like are usually excluded.

Russia's Interdepartmental Working Group on Kaliningrad has considered IBM issues at one of its meetings. It proposed an intensification of comprehensive cooperation between Kaliningrad and the EU on issues of improvement of border management, specifically on establishment of joint border-crossing points, enhancement of cooperation of respective agencies and monitoring of their performance. Also, Kaliningrad's regional government sees international cooperation in this field as one of its priorities. After the new governor, Georgii Boos, took office in 2005, a modified government structure was introduced, which included a Ministry for the Development of Territories and Interaction with Local Authorities. Cross-border cooperation issues are within the range of this Ministry's responsibilities, but in the case of border management its authority is confined to elaboration of recommendations only. An important part of the Ministry's work pertains to activities within the Euro-region Baltica, a structure for better cross-border cooperation among countries and regions around the Baltic Sea (see chapter 8 in this volume). It largely focuses on the arrangement of common projects in the spheres of environmental protection, crime prevention, and the improvement of the frontier infrastructure as well as in the social sphere.[6]

The new law on the Special Economic Zone (SEZ) in Kaliningrad, effective since April 2006 and requiring the active participation of the regional government in its administration, contains provisions on the facilitation of permitting foreigners to enter the region. Since the enforcement of the new law, foreigners visiting Kaliningrad have had the opportunity to get a visa at their point of entry to the region, despite a number of difficulties and restrictions that persist. Visitors can only obtain a transit visa or a seventy-two hour tourist visa, and these require a representative of the Ministry of Foreign Affairs to meet them at the point of entry, which is also limited to only three: Khrabrovo airport and the towns of Mamonovo and Bagrationovsk along the Polish border. Yet the new visa requirements ensure that it takes much less time to apply for and obtain such a visa compared with the other types of entry visas obtained from Russian consulates abroad; thus it appears a good solution for those planning a short visit to Kaliningrad. Another change has been the opening of the customs clearance and inspection office in Kaliningrad's Khrabrovo airport on 4 May 2006. This enabled businessmen using air cargo transport to save time on the customs clearance procedures at other custom houses in the region by having such an office right at the airport.

Even though Kaliningrad City is the third-most frequented among all Russian cities regarding consular representation of foreign countries, both the federal and regional authorities provide extensive assistance for establishing further consulates and support the activities of existing ones. In early 2006, permission was granted for the expansion of the Lithuanian consular facilities in Kaliningrad and Sovetsk, a town near the border. In the same year, Sweden opened its consulate and the German Consulate-General became fully operational, both issuing Schengen visas. The opening of a Ukrainian honorary consulate is now in negotiations. At a 2006 meeting with the consular corps represented in Kaliningrad, the governor stressed the importance of such developments for the region and proposed an extension of dialogue by holding such meetings on a regular basis.[7]

Dependence on Russia–EU relations

With limited natural resources and a modest local market that hampers economies of scale for local enterprises, Kaliningrad's economy is highly dependent on foreign trade. The ratio of Kaliningrad's foreign trade (exports plus imports) over its GRP (the so-called coefficient of economic openness) is very high (Dewar *et al.* 2005: 22), exceeding 175 per cent in 2006. This makes the issue of an efficient operation of customs as well as the existence of a well-designed transport infrastructure across the borders vital for the socio-economic development of the region. EU enlargement, accompanied by the revision of legislation in new member states to comply with EU legislation, resulted in some profound changes in cargo and passenger transit across the borders of the oblast. Developments on the border of Russia and Lithuania serve as an example; the introduction of a visa regime by Lithuania led to a crisis in EU–Russia relations, as it put Kaliningrad in an unfavourable position, virtually isolating it from the mainland. The intensive negotiations that followed allowed the parties to reach a compromise, implemented on 1 July 2003. Under the suggested scheme, two types of documents were introduced for transit across Lithuania to and from mainland Russia: the Facilitated Transit Document for cars and buses and the Facilitated Railway Transit Document (Vinokurov 2006). In light of Lithuania's inclusion in the Schengen zone in December 2007, the parties managed to reconcile the use of these documents with Schengen law. However, as these compromises could best be described as last-minute solutions, the negotiation process ensured that Kaliningraders spent an inordinate amount of time mired in a state of uncertainty.

The adoption of the visa facilitation and the re-admission agreements, mutually beneficial for the EU and Russia as a whole, had a negative effect on Kaliningrad. Before these agreements were enforced, Kaliningrad was treated as a special case. Visas for Poland and Lithuania, the most popular destinations among Kaliningrad residents, were issued free of charge to them, and the procedures were so simple that obtaining multiple-entry visas to these countries valid for one year was rather a formality. Moreover, this was done on a reciprocal basis, as Lithuanian and Polish citizens enjoyed a similar favourable treatment when obtaining visas to visit Kaliningrad. The Visa Facilitation Agreement adopted in 2007 contains no special mention of Kaliningrad. Nonetheless, there are indications that the region may become subject of a special approach yet again. Speaking at a press conference on 12 October 2007 in Kaliningrad, Sergey Yastrzhembsky, the Presidential Special Envoy for Development of Relations with the EU, said that Russia and the EU will continue to look for ways to restore the *status quo* for Kaliningrad residents. According to him, Russia may develop bilateral agreements with Poland and Lithuania envisaging special visa processing procedures for Kaliningrad, as a significant area of the region's territory will fall within the EU's 50 km border zone, where eased requirements might be adopted in order to facilitate direct cross-border contacts.[8] Work on the agreements will begin after 1 January 2008, when Poland and Lithuania have become fully-fledged members of the Schengen zone.

Beginning on 1 May 2004, the situation with cargo transit between Kaliningrad and mainland Russia has become more complicated. Cargo transit became subject to the Common Transit Procedure of the EU as well as a number of relevant international conventions. Consequently, the list of control procedures and mandatory documents has been extended, a number of rules and requirements tightened and the amounts of some fees and payments have increased (Zernov and Shopin 2005: 5–7). The conditions of cargo transit of goods between the region and mainland Russia were equated to those of international transit. These changes entailed an increase in prices for consumer goods delivered from mainland Russia as well as an increase in costs for local producers.

These examples demonstrate how traditional approaches to border management are less likely to be successful for the region around Kaliningrad, and sometimes can even be counterproductive. In these particular cases, Russia could be compelled to react by developing alternative passenger and cargo routes – a move that would undoubtedly be against the spirit of cooperation agreed on by Russia and the EU. Thus, with all the existing prerequisites – special geopolitical location, relatively small size and a pilot role determined by Russia's strategy towards the EU – Kaliningrad should be considered as the most likely candidate for the role of a test ground. Russian and EU authorities have seemingly agreed with this assessment, as they have frequently mentioned the region in the context of possible initiatives to improve border management. After all, despite a number of still unresolved problems, the level of cooperation on Kaliningrad issues is unprecedented in the history of bilateral relations between these parties. Speaking at a conference in Kaliningrad on 11 October 2007, EU Commissioner for External Relations and European Neighbourhood Policy, Benita Ferrero-Waldner, called the EU–Russian experience on cross-border cooperation in Kaliningrad a success story.[9]

What could the first steps be?

It is evident that pilot initiatives must be practically implemented in the most efficient way, provided that the whole process is structured in terms of objectives, tasks, activities, time and financial resources, i.e. through development and implementation of projects by competent expert institutions. Thus, our proposal would be to establish the EU–Russia Common Space of Freedom, Security and Justice in Kaliningrad as a 'pilot region' for EU–Russia cooperation, by developing and implementing an IBM project on the Russian–Polish border. This IBM project would create the basis for the practical establishment of joint border-crossing points and introduce a system of public monitoring of border management under the auspices of ombudsmen from both sides of the border.

Conclusion

The issue of managing the EU–Russia common border requires a comprehensive approach because of its complex nature. Although substantial progress has recently been achieved in this field, the overall level of mutual adaptation between the two systems remains low, and still leaves significant room for improvement.

In shaping the core of the EU–Russia CSFSJ, the management of a common border includes two major aspects: philosophical and political dimensions on the one hand, and practical matters on the other. As far as the first aspect is concerned, the question is whether Russia as a whole and the Kaliningrad region in particular should be considered as outsiders regarding European policies in the realm of justice and freedom of movement. With the adoption of the EU–Russia 'Roadmaps', the answer would seem to be no. Declaring the Common Spaces as an objective of cooperation, the parties will have to establish and maintain a common frontier along the perimeter of the current external borders of Russia and the EU, managed similarly and according to the same principles, while the internal common border between the EU and Russia will then be granted a special status. Yet realistically, the stated goal is long term, and a firm determination to attain the goal may not be enough in itself. The next step must be a mechanism of practical cooperation.

The question policy-makers and experts are now facing is: where and how can Russia and the EU acquire experience of joint border management, accord their respective legislation frameworks and gain some practice of collaboration? Kaliningrad has a special role to play in this effort. It is so uniquely positioned that the parties cannot but use the region's border with the EU to learn and test joint border management practices and later apply them to their internal borders (with a special status) as well as to the external border of the EU–Russia common policy space. Preliminary studies have already laid down a solid foundation for successful implementation of such a dedicated IBM project. To make such an initiative efficient, however, the perception of Kaliningrad as a nuisance rather than an opportunity to develop EU–Russia relations via 'test-pilot' solutions should become a thing of the past.

Notes

1 See Council Regulation (EC) 2007/2004 of 26 October 2004 establishing a European agency for the management of operational cooperation at the external borders of the member states of the European Union.

2 See the section on 'EU–Russia Common Spaces' at the European Commission's External Relations website, available on the Internet at http://ec.europa.eu /comm/external_relations/russia/intro/index.htm#comm (accessed 29 December 2007).

3   See the project's website 'Lithuania, Poland and Kaliningrad Region of Russian Federation Neighbourhood Programme', available on the Internet at www.interreg3a .org/interregen/ (accessed 29 December 2007).
4   Russia will allocate €120 million to co-finance such programmes from 2007–13.
5   As part of such activities, the Kaliningrad government developed a regional programme for road network development that has envisaged the funding of roads towards the borders and bypasses around the towns of Sovetsk and Chernyakhovsk.
6   As a result of the annual rotation of the Euro-region presidency, Kaliningrad's Minister for the Development of Territories and Interaction with Local Authorities assumed this position in 2006.
7   See press release of the Kaliningrad Regional Administration, 12 July 2006 (in Russian), available on the Internet at http://gov.kaliningrad.ru/index.php?action =news&nid=1689 (accessed 29 December 2007).
8   See press release of REGNUM News Service, 12 October 2007 (in Russian), available on the Internet at www.regnum.ru/news/898721.html (accessed 29 December 2007).
9   Speech by Benita Ferrero-Waldner, European Commissioner for External Relations and European Neighbourhood at a conference entitled 'Border Cooperation: the Russian Federation, the European Union and Norway', available on the Internet at http://edc.tsu.ru/new/index.php?option=com_content&task=view&id=66&Itemid=28.

References

Burkhart, H. (2005), *Integrated Border Management on the Russian–EU Border: the Kaliningrad Pilot*, Kaliningrad, East–West Institute Policy Brief, available on the Internet at http://kaliningradexpert.org/stuff/pubs/border_eng.pdf (accessed 4 May 2008).

Dewar, S., A. Ignatiev, P. Lindholm, J. Swiecicki, A. Usanov, E. Vinokurov and C. Wellmann (2005), *Support to Transforming Kaliningrad into a Pilot Region of EU–Russia Partnership*, Kaliningrad, available on the Internet at www.ewi.info and http://kaliningradexpert.org/stuff/pubs/pr_au_eng.pdf (accessed 4 May 2008).

Fairlie, L. D. and A. Sergounin (2001), *Are Borders Barriers? EU Enlargement and the Russian Region of Kaliningrad*, Helsinki and Berlin, Ulkopolittinen instituuti & Institut für Europäische Politik.

Hobbing, P. (2005), *Integrated Border Management at the EU Level*, Brussels, CEPS Working Document 227.

Russian Federal Law (1993), 'Zakon "O gosudarstvennoi granitse Rossiyskoi Federatsii"' ['Federal Law "on the state border of the Russian Federation"'].

Vinokurov, E. (2006), 'Kaliningrad Visa and Transit Issues Revisited', CEPS Commentary, available on the Internet at www.ceps.be/Article.php? article_id=531 (accessed 4 May 2008).

Zernov, A. and K. Shopin (2005), *Kaliningrad Transit of Goods: in Need of a Strategic Approach to Problem-Solving*, Kaliningrad, East–West Institute Policy Brief, available on the Internet at www.ewi.info and http://kaliningradexpert.org/stuff/pubs /transit_%20eng.pdf (accessed 4 May 2008).

PART IV

Conclusions

STEFAN GÄNZLE AND GUIDO MÜNTEL

16

Summary: Kaliningrad and Europeanisation 'à la carte'

After the end of the Cold War, the Baltic Sea region developed into a hub for trans-national cooperation involving a wide range of societal and state actors from the sub-regional and regional levels. While access to the Kaliningrad oblast had been restricted for decades, the region has recently become deeply entrenched in a web of close cooperation with its European neighbours. Obviously, Kaliningrad's status as an enclave triggers a number of effects: first, as a small enclave neighbouring two new EU member states, it is compelled to develop various forms of direct cross-border contacts. Second, because of its location at the south-eastern rim of the Baltic Sea, Kaliningrad is embedded in a network of interaction that is considered as the most developed world-wide. Finally, Russia has declared its exclave as serving as a 'pilot region' for cooperation between the EU and Russia – albeit very often rather by default than by design.

The EU has increasingly become the central actor in Kaliningrad's neighbourhood, projecting its own norms and regulatory principles beyond its borders. Throughout the process of enlargement, the EU's norm-shaping power affected post-communist societies and resulted in an unprecedented example of policy export. EU enlargement-driven Europeanisation relies on two institutional logics: the 'logic of consequences' and the 'logic of appropriateness' (March and Olsen 1989: 160–2), which can either work through intergovernmental interactions or through trans-national processes via societal actors in the target state or region. EU conditionality, sanctions and rewards reinforce consequentiality, hence changing the cost–benefit calculations of involved or affected actors within the target state. The impact of such external incentives increases with the size of net benefits as well as the clarity and credibility of EU conditionality. In addition, actors in the target countries and regions may be persuaded to adopt EU rules provided that they consider these rules legitimate and beneficial; and if they identify themselves with the

EU, thus subscribing to the 'logic of appropriateness' (see Schimmelfennig and Sedelmeier 2005: 11–12, 18). The perceived success of Europeanisation in the context of enlargement ultimately triggered the question whether 'Europeanisation beyond Europe' is possible (Schimmelfennig 2007).

In this volume, we have been interested in the extent to which Kaliningrad – its political structures, policy-making processes and policy outputs – became subject to change and adaptation forged by EU models, norms and standards as a result of interaction with 'Europe'. We have built upon the concept of 'Europeanisation' in order to explain domestic change in polity, politics and policy caused by integration in Europe. Europeanisation studies emphasise the interplay of both exogenous and endogenous variables – similarly, we assumed these to be responsible for change and adaptation in Kaliningrad. That is: the types, content and the conduct of interaction between the European and Russian partners; and the domestic constraints imposed by post-Soviet transformation and the autonomy of the Kaliningrad region in the federal system of the Russian Federation. Clearly, we have recognised that the exclave factor is to be considered as highly relevant, reinforcing other variables, such as the degree of cooperation and receptiveness towards foreign ideas and models.

Despite intensive cooperation, Kaliningrad's Europeanisation proceeds only within very narrow margins – the impact of 'Europe' on the governance of this Russian enclave inside Europe is surprisingly modest. Clearly, this overall conclusion has to be examined very carefully, taking into account the results of the policy areas studied in this book: some modest EU impact on Kaliningrad was observed in the fields of economic and education policy. In turn, in the fields of environmental policy, social policy and border management, only a low degree of change and adaptation took place; and there was none to be observed in the area of public health policy. Thus, the results drawn from half of the case studies confirm our hypotheses from the introductory chapter: that is the case in the fields of economic and educational policies as well as public health. However, the other half of cases revealed an outcome different to and – more importantly – below our expectations. With a view to our two main explanatory variables (i.e. the level of international cooperation and the degree of regional autonomy in the respective policy areas), we anticipated a modest or even a high degree of Europeanisation in the fields of social policy, border management and environmental policy, while the effective degree of adaptation in these areas was in fact low. More importantly, the relevance of regional autonomy is by no means a definite determinant. In policy areas with comparatively high regional autonomy, such as social and environmental policy, Europeanisation was, in turn, low. At the same time, other fields with low regional autonomy revealed some modest level of Europeanisation, as seen in economic and educational policy.

Table 16.1 Adapting to European integration? Policy areas in Kaliningrad.

Policy area	Main explanatory framework			EU impact
	International cooperation	Regional autonomy	Expected impact	
Economic policy	high	low	modest	*modest*
Social policy	low	high	modest	low
Environmental policy	high	high	high	low
Public health policy	low	low	none	*none*
Border management	high	low	modest	low
Education policy	high	low	modest	*modest*

Our case selection was built upon a relatively simple model with two explanatory variables, while the more detailed analytical framework stressed the relevance of other exogenous and endogenous variables. The results confirm that the impact of Europe on the structures, processes and policy outputs in Kaliningrad depends on a much greater variety of external and domestic factors that we are going to summarise in the following paragraphs.

The endogenous variables determining the degree of adaptation in Kaliningrad have been centrally framed by Russia's two-decade-long process of economic and political transition. The volatile centre–periphery relationship through the 1990s has been the crux of the Russian federal system determining the autonomy of the 'federal subjects'. However unstable the centre–periphery relationship was, it never developed into a bargaining chip for Kaliningrad. In the 1990s, the exclave was treated as a rather 'normal' oblast. Its status did not spur a more liberal perspective of greater autonomy – rather, on the contrary, ties between Moscow and Kaliningrad have been strengthened for fear of separatism. During Putin's efforts of re-centralisation, Kaliningrad – despite some increased attention given to it in the advent of EU enlargement – was nothing but deprived of its already limited scope for independent domestic and external action.

Even if some autonomy may formally exist allowing authorities some form of external relations, the incentive structure for regional political leaders renders cross-border cooperation a difficult task. Indeed, in the case of policy areas, such as environmental and social policy, which enjoy relative regional autonomy, it does not result in a higher level of Europeanisation (although international cooperation in environmental issues is relatively high). In both cases, weak institutional capacities and lack of interest determine political non-action. Ultimately, re-centralisation combined with the reforms of the party law and of the electoral law generates a national patronage system that severely limits independent action of the regional political leaders, who are accountable to their political patrons rather than to their electorate.

Hence, political openness has decreased, leaving minimal room for societal actors to play a role in decision-making processes. This is particularly evident in the case of environmental and social policies, where NGOs – although existing and active in these fields – have hardly played any role in the development of ideas and policies. Interest groups representing economic interests have been more successful. While their influence used to be informal in previous years, the reinforced patronage system in Russia catapulted economic actors into official positions: some representatives from the small business sector had been elected to the parliament in earlier years, yet only the latest reshuffle in the regional ministerial group and in the legislative in 2005 and 2006 brought representatives from 'big business' into power.

However, although Kaliningrad's business community is now well represented in regional politics, it has not yet been able to transfer its influence to the federal level, where policies, particularly in the economic field (as seen in the case of the Special Economic Zone), are decided. Additionally, the socio-economic decline of the region during the 1990s (occurring simultaneously with the loss of its geopolitical significance) limited the room for manoeuvre possessed by Kaliningrad's political and administrative authorities *vis-à-vis* Moscow with a view to attracting serious attention or even conducting autonomous decision-making. The path of the economic transition process in Russia and Kaliningrad, in various ways, obstructs rather than facilitates Kaliningrad's adaptation to Europe. The region's financial and administrative resources are too scarce to give the authorities leeway to engage in proactive policy initiatives, a result of being entangled in notorious debt crises and credit scandals nearly leading to the bankruptcy of the region.

Given its geographic location, it would have been fair to assume that intense economic links would foster a regulative adaptation. With Kaliningrad's one-sided economic specialisation to meet demands from the mainland, incentives for the business community to adapt to European norms and standards are few. Still, with regards to long-term expectations, regional business elites lean towards the European market, which is seen as more promising for regional trade relations and economic development. But with limited regional autonomy, prospects of regulatory standards adapting to European norms rise and fall with the overall EU–Russian economic integration foreseen in their four Common Spaces project.

This strongly confirms that Kaliningrad finds itself in a triangular relationship with its Russian mainland and its European direct neighbourhood, where the relations between them present the context in which the exclave must find its place. But in order to do so, Kaliningrad would need to enjoy at least some leeway to act autonomously while remaining an entity of the Russian Federation. At the same time, it would be necessary for this region to build on a predictable and advantageous environment in EU–Russia relations. While attention and interaction of the EU and Russia on their enclave/exclave, had grown considerably around the turn of the millennium, the two partners have not managed to turn Kaliningrad into the 'pilot region' of cooperation and integration. The different approaches of both Moscow and Brussels, not only towards each other but towards Kaliningrad, appear to have turned it into a kind of 'plaything' of two wary adversaries rather than into an object of shared concerns and joint efforts of two strategic partners. Hence Kaliningrad seems more a test region often by default rather than by design. While a post-modern Europe seeks to pursue a 'wider mission' to project and implement its own standards of doing things beyond its external borders, it meets the resistance of a modern Russia emphasising sovereignty and equality in mutual relations, prioritising territorial integrity over the exclave's development, and rejecting any unilateral influence or quasi-imperial logic from outside its borders. Thus, the 'window of opportunity' for wide-ranging, thorough cooperation and swift regulatory harmonisation – opened by the promising official declarations at that time – seems to have come to an end.

While Kaliningrad has left the centre of EU–Russia relations, sustainable cross-border cooperation may yet have a considerable impact. The multitude of low-level but intense contacts and interaction between trade partners, non-governmental groups and administrative representatives is a promising avenue. Cooperation in the fields of economy, social policy, environment and education have resulted in some tangible and even growing cognitive change among the elites involved. A note of caution needs to be issued though: even if there is interest and good will between partners, a variety of problems in the implementation often renders it nothing more than cooperation only 'on paper', where such incremental change is slowed down if not completely blocked.

A final relevant variable of exogenous character seems the degree to which the EU possesses and displays a *single* policy model. Here, too, variety prevails across the policy areas analysed: in the EU's most integrated policy areas, such as commercial policy, trade and environment, a single model of policy exists to some extent, and it can serve as a template. It is much less so in the cases with no integrated European policy, such as social policy, higher education or health policy. Here, at best, countries across Europe share some basic principles but display a high variety in the specific structures, processes and contents of policy. What results is a lack of a coherent policy or a single voice, so that Europe can hardly appear as a powerful and norm-shaping actor in its vicinity. But, as the case of higher education demonstrates, Brussels' competence and coherent policy are not necessary conditions either. The attractiveness of a European policy model – as incoherent and based on rather broad principles as it might be – plays an important role. In this regard, higher education enjoys a considerable salience in Europe's relations with Russia and puts it in a governance-shaping position.

It seems that Europe may become a norm-exporter in economic policy, as here the level of integration in the EU is high. For Kaliningrad, however, it is still the Russian market that offers, for the time being, a more attractive alternative. The regional economy of Kaliningrad is closely interlinked with the mainland, be it a consequence of shared currency and language, inherited trade relations that were hardly existent with Western Europe or even Poland, or a shared cultural background with the Russian mainland and remaining prejudices towards the non-Russian neighbourhood.

Pulling these various strings together, one can conclude that a multiplicity of factors are at play, determining the degree of adaptation taking place as a consequence of Kaliningrad's and Russia's cooperation with Europe. The different constellations generated by these independent variables produce a variety of results regarding Europeanisation. We simply conclude that the level of regional autonomy of the Kaliningrad exclave seems equally important as a domestic opportunity structure in the oblast, and in Russia in general, which is open for a competition of different ideas and their supporters. The budgetary constraints and everyday-life challenges of post-Soviet economic transition play the central role in shaping the interests and positions of decision-making elites as well as society. The current state of affairs in overall relations between Russia and Europe, in Moscow, Brussels or the EU member states, appears to matter as much as the conduct, intensity and quality of cross-border cooperation between individual or institutional partners of regional politics, business, or society. And finally, the existence of a policy template and its attractiveness determines Europe's strength of influence beyond its borders.

Direct channels of Russia's, or Moscow's, influence remain much more powerful than indirect channels through which Europeanisation of Kaliningrad occurs. But the differences observed – though in nuances – across the policy fields examined in this book give evidence of a special form of 'partial' and 'deliberative' Europeanisation. Kaliningrad and Russia are far from unilaterally embracing European standards and norms. Instead, political elites seek to choose or facilitate processes of adaptation in areas where it serves their interests most. Moreover, Russia seeks to influence policy-making at the European level to ensure that its concerns are being taken into account. Hence, we are witnessing the making of 'Europeanisation *à la carte*'. With this in mind, Kaliningrad and Russia are in some contrast to other instances of Europeanisation, i.e. the EU member states and applicant countries. Still, our studies confirm the general applicability of the concept of Europeanisation to this Russian exclave, displaying exogenous and endogenous variables that determine the degree of cooperation with, and adaptation to, European models of governance.

References

March, J. G. and J. P. Olsen (1989), *Rediscovering Institutions: The Organizational Basis of Politics*, New York, Free Press.

Schimmelfennig, F. (2007), 'Europeanization beyond Europe', *Living Reviews in European Governance*, 2(1), available on the Internet at www.livingreviews.org/lreg-2007–1 (accessed 23 August 2007).

Schimmelfennig, F. and U. Sedelmeier, eds (2005), *The Europeanization of Central and Eastern Europe*, Ithaca, Cornell University Press.

GABRIELLA MELONI

17

Russia: a case for revising the concept of Europeanisation

Introduction

The European Union's most recent success has been to impose 'the obligations of membership' on candidate countries in exchange for future EU accession, whereby these countries agree to a vast process of legislative transformation aimed at harmonising national laws with the body of EC law (*acquis communautaire*). The result obtained with these countries made it possible to think that the EU's neighbours should also take on 'considerably deeper and broader obligations in aligning with Community legislation', a principle which ultimately inspired the formulation of the European neighbourhood Policy (ENP) launched by the EU Commission in March 2003 (Commission 2003b).

The EU's *acquis* offers a well-established model on which to build functioning markets and to define common (regulatory) standards for industrial products, services, transport, energy, telecommunications networks, etc. The phenomenon that inspired the ENP is impressive. It provides an unprecedented example of policy export, which potentially involves not only candidates for enlargement, but also neighbouring countries in a wide process of Europeanisation. Much of the discussion about whether or not the EU is likely to develop an effective foreign policy is grounded in assessments of its efforts at explicit policy-making. It may, however, be that the external projection of European regimes and value patterns is indeed as powerful a tool, which also can affect the ways in which the Union will acquire influence in a wider global setting.

As Richard Rosecrance (1998) has pointed out, the EU can be seen as a 'new type of international actor' whose integrating power, relying mostly on economic factors, has not produced a 'drifting effect' on the 'balance of power'. As a matter of fact, if the balance of power 'seeks to distribute power centrifugally [the EU has] centripetal effects in economic terms' (*ibid.*: 18).[1] This, for the first time in history, has made it possible for the EU to expand not only with little significant resistance from third powers, but also with the consent of the 'conquered' countries that proved willing to bear the costs connected to legislative approximation. The ENP is nothing other than an extension of a similar strategy to bordering countries, a strategy that – even if apparently sustained by economic considerations – may also have important consequences in the political realm.

In this context, Russia has been a test case for the EU since the mid-1990s, even though it has not been included in the ENP. Since the approval of the Partnership and Cooperation Agreement (PCA), the EU has aimed at exporting the *acquis communautaire* to Russia, using the same tools later applied to ENP countries. If Russia as a whole has been a test case, Kaliningrad has seemingly been predestined to be at the forefront of this process, as it is particularly exposed to EU influence because of its economy, its geographical size and position, and its links with Poland and Lithuania.

The analysis of this process in Russia and Kaliningrad is especially interesting because it could provide useful suggestions about the viability of the model enshrined in the ENP. Such scrutiny would assess the conditions for reproducing the strategy already used with candidate countries, particularly when the 'carrot' of membership – the central facet of the European strategy towards the accession countries in Central and Eastern Europe – is no longer immediately at hand. If membership is not being considered, is the prospect of a 'stake in the Internal Market' (Commission 2003b: 4) a sufficient incentive to embark on the pervasive process of approximation to European rules and standards? If not, what are the alternative models to induce partner countries to adopt at least some elements and principles of the *acquis*? When thinking of the future of the European continent, these questions are of crucial importance despite a gap evident in pertinent literature.

In this chapter, I first consider why Russia should adopt the *acquis communautaire*, emphasising that explanations in purely economic terms are necessary, but not sufficient, to account for the pervasiveness of this process. I describe different models of Europeanisation based on alternative logics of interaction and I demonstrate that conditionality is not the only available instrument to induce legislative approximation. Secondly, I consider how the EU has been trying to 'sell' the *acquis communautaire* to Russia, demonstrating that over time, the EU has used both coercive and persuasive tactics. I argue that since the adoption of the PCA, the EU has promoted a process of socialisation of Russia, setting in motion a mechanism of soft coordination which has some elements recalling the open method of coordination (OMC). Thirdly, I discuss two key notions through which Russia very much defines itself: *sovereignty* and *specialty*. These notions point directly, along different logics of interaction, to the limits of the approach thus far adopted by the EU, emphasising the necessity to revise the patterns of Europeanisation when dealing with a country which is not potentially a new EU member, but still represents the 'other half' of Europe.

Why should Russia adopt the *acquis communautaire?*

The Copenhagen Council of 1993 defined a set of the political, economic and institutional criteria for accession to the EU, emphasising, in particular, the need for including the adoption of the *acquis communautaire.* Hence prospective accession was strictly linked to legislative approximation. However, if membership is not at stake, why should Russia engage in a very costly and pervasive process of legislative approximation?

The economic perspective

The EU justifies legislative approximation with, bluntly put, 'access to the EU kitchen'. This is why an overview of the economic debate is needed in order to understand if there are explanations which can motivate this process from a purely economic point of view. The notion that countries which have increasing volumes of trade should harmonise their law, emerged between the 1980s and 1990s. This was a result of the emphasis given to limiting non-border measures as obstacles to trade, relying on the presumption that differences in national policies become more significant as comparative advantages when trade barriers are low (Pomfret 1997: 214). This issue pertains to the distinction between 'deep' and 'shallow' integration, developed by Lawrence (1996), who advocated for deep integration out of concern for 'fair trade'.

Which policies should be harmonised in order to guarantee fair trade? Pomfret pointed out that 'the simplest equivalence between a tariff and a domestic policy has little relevance' to the analysis of the discrimination in international trade because 'other domestic policies may have equivalent effects to discriminatory trade policies' (Pomfret 1997: 215). In this view, whether the 'spectre of unfairness' can be ignored or must be addressed is a political rather than an economic issue (*ibid.:* 215; Brittan 1995: 763). If every difference in each domestic policy could have discriminatory trade effects, the selection of areas in which approximation is required is not only based on economic grounds, but is somehow also subject to the discretionary judgement of the policy-maker.

With the commitment to adopt the chapters of the *acquis* that are connected to the creation of the single market, Russia would not only abolish residual barriers to the movement of goods, services, persons and capital, but would also engage in a process of positive integration (Tinbergen 1954; Scharpf 1997; 1999). Traditionally, economic theory defines four different steps of integration depending on the depth of the process at stake and on the quality of the links between the parties (i.e. free trade area, customs union, common market, economic and monetary union). The first three steps could be deemed examples of 'negative integration' inasmuch as they aim at the realisation of the so-called 'four freedoms' (free movement of persons, goods, labour and capital). The fourth step – which beyond that provides the conditions for the introduction of common policies in different economic sectors – is a case of 'positive integration' (Tinbergen 1954).[2] If negative integration has a deregulatory or 'market-making' nature, positive integration is an attempt to counteract the unwanted side effects of liberalisation processes through re-regulation at the European level (Scharpf 1999: 45). It is 'market-shaping' because it tries to intervene in the economy and it involves a broader institutional adaptation to a specific European model at the domestic level (*ibid.*). This is exactly what would happen if Russia adopted the *acquis communautaire*, moving it to the fourth level of integration (Meloni 2007a; 2007b).

Russia has been asked to engage in a complex process of legislative approximation which implies not only an economic, but also an important political choice.[3] However, very limited efforts have been devoted to the definition of the economic incentives which the EU is ready to provide in exchange for Russian compliance. The 'Roadmap' for the creation of a Common European Economic Space (CEES) with Russia has been designed to provide a series of rewards essentially in terms of preferential access to the single market. However, from an economic point of view, the offer does not go further than a free trade area 'plus' (Commission 2006), which would be a case of negative integration that would not necessarily require much of an effort in terms of legislative approximation.

Therefore, in view of the engagement of Russia in a process of legislative approximation, I expect that the 'economic discourse' has played a significant role. However, I consider it a necessary (in terms of persuasion), but not sufficient (in terms of motivating reasons) condition to explain why Russia should accept the adoption of an important part of the *acquis communautaire*.

Two different logics of Europeanisation

The tools provided by the concept of Europeanisation can help detect the underlying mechanisms of this process.[4] Almost without exception, Europeanisation scholars have referred to the broad spectrum of theories of the so-called 'new institutionalism' and defined two alternative logics of Europeanisation that explain the decision to engage in a process of legislative approximation (Vink 2004: 4). Following the 'logic of consequentialism' (March and Olsen 1989), the first logic is based on a rationalist-institutionalist perspective that interprets the misfit between European and domestic processes, policies and institutions as an emerging political opportunity structure, which offers some actors additional resources to exert influence in the domestic domain. This implies a cost–benefit approach in which institutions have an impact 'by altering the expectations an actor has about the actions that others are likely to take in response to or simultaneously with his own action' (Hall and Taylor 1996: 939). In contrast to a 'thick' understanding of institutional processes, this 'thin' understanding contends that individuals act strategically to realise their preferences. The second mechanism is based on a sociological-institutionalist perspective which emphasises 'a logic of appropriateness' (March and Olsen 1989) and underlines the importance of processes of persuasion and socialisation as possible mechanisms of Europeanisation. Following this logic, European policies, norms and their attached collective understanding exert adaptational pressures on domestic level processes because they do not resonate well with domestic norms and the collective understanding of those norms. In this perspective, 'change agents' or 'norm entrepreneurs' mobilise in the domestic context and persuade others to redefine their identities (Börzel and Risse 2000).

Subscribing to these two logics, there have been different explanatory models advanced in the literature. In particular, Schimmelfennig and Sedelmeier (2002) have distinguished four different models of Europeanisation. The first two, conditionality and lesson-drawing, have been based on the logic of consequentialism, while the third and fourth, social-learning and model-learning, have been based on the logic of appropriateness (Meloni 2007a).[5] So, if the 'economic discourse' provides a necessary but not sufficient condition in order to justify the decision of Russia to engage in a process of positive integration, the concept of Europeanisation offers additional explanations for the decision to engage in legislative approximation. From the logic of consequentialism, Russia's choice to adopt some core chapters of the *acquis communautaire* may be explained either because of the rewards which the EU attaches to this process (i.e. conditionality)[6] or because adopting the rules is considered useful in order to solve some internal problems (i.e. lesson-drawing). From the logic of appropriateness, Russia may be persuaded to engage in legislative approximation either because it is convinced that the rules under consideration are good as far as they are EU norms (i.e. social-learning) or simply because the norms to adopt are considered good *per se* (i.e. model-learning).

This is extremely interesting in order to conceptualise the ways in which the EU can induce legislative approximation. However, if we exclude a small circle of specialists, conditionality is undoubtedly the only model of Europeanisation which is widely recognised, while the other schemes are generally considered remote and obscure scholastic fantasies. Nonetheless, if without controversy conditionality has been the basic strategy through which the EU has promoted compliance by the national governments of candidate countries (Checkel 2000), the other models of Europeanisation can prove particularly important in promoting legislative approximation in those countries, like Russia, where membership in the EU is not at stake. During enlargement, as a matter of fact, if candidate countries co-owned the project and accepted a system where rewards were strictly connected with the capacity to meet certain conditions, then the weakness of the available set of incentives – in the absence of a common overarching goal in the relationship – would suggest that the alternative tools of Europeanisation were a better method, accepting that it is better to promote a slower co-owned process of convergence between the parties (Meloni 2007a).

How is the EU selling the *acquis communautaire* to Russia?

In this section, I will explain the dynamics of the mechanisms which allow the EU to have an impact on Russia as a developmental relation between instrumental action and norm conforming behaviour. Here, I dismiss the 'either/or' conceptualisation of social reality (which reflects a controversy between radical variants of both rationalism and constructivism), instead adopting a new trend in political science that favours a 'both/and' conceptualisation of social reality. This synthetic model, put forward by March and Olsen, posits that actors enter into new relationships with a view to maximising their own utility, but over time develop identities shaped by shared norms and values as a result of accumulated experience (March and Olsen 1989: 13).

Since the collapse of the Soviet system, the EU has used both coercive and persuasive tactics, trying to exert influence by bargaining over conditions and rewards and by promoting a patient strategy of persuasion. If, on the one hand, the EU has offered institutional ties, technical and financial assistance and finally 'a stake in the Internal Market' in exchange for legal approximation, it has, on the other hand, promoted a process of socialisation that has been sketched out in the ENP.

This strategy dates back to the PCA, which contains an evolutionary clause that explicitly envisages 'the beginning of negotiations on the establishment of a free-trade area [upon] advances in market oriented economic reforms and economic conditions' (Partnership and Cooperation Agreement 1997). To support this process, it defines for the first time the objective of engaging in a process of legislative harmonisation between the parties. Article 55 on legislative cooperation does not impose a clear obligation on the Russian side to approximate its laws to the European ones, but states that 'Russia shall endeavour to ensure that its legislation will be gradually made compatible with that of the Community' (*ibid.*: Art. 55). At the same time, the parties established an institutional framework for a new political dialogue. The EU and Russia made a commitment to hold high-level summits twice a year, one in Moscow and one in the capital of the EU member state holding the rotating Presidency of the European Union. Other high-level bilateral meetings have been scheduled annually, namely between ministers (Cooperation Council), parliamentary representatives (Parliamentary Cooperation Committee) and senior officials from both sides (political directors, or the Cooperation Committee supported by a network of sub-committees dealing with technical issues). This system has since been improved with the creation of a Permanent Partnership Council (PPC) to allow ministers to meet as often as necessary and in a variety of formats to discuss specific issues.[7]

The Common Strategy (CS) on Russia, which was adopted in Cologne in June of 1999, completed the framework already designed by the PCA. The CS was not intended to replace the previous initiatives, but it underlined the need for dialogue and for the development of a programme based on cooperation with Russia across the three pillars of the EU. It has been argued that because the scope of the CS was so broad, it lacked 'any real proposal for concrete action' (Haukkala and Medvedev 2001) and that 'in day-to-day operations of the EU, the impact of the CS has been almost non-existent' (De Spiegelaire 2001). While I recognise the validity of these remarks, I support the argument that the CS succeeded in giving momentum to relations with Russia, and that it was able to emphasise those elements of the PCA which had already proved successful. In particular, the CS proposed to complement the existing PCA-based political fora through the creation of a permanent mechanism for political and security dialogue. The CS also established that every incoming Presidency of the EU should present a work plan for the implementation of the CS, reviewing and evaluating the Union's action on the one hand, and the situation in Russia on the other. These ingredients – not to be underestimated – will be at the basis of the formula of the ENP.

Bilateral institutional contacts established by the PCA also produced many results. The seventh EU–Russia summit held on 17 May 2001 established a joint High Level Group (HLG) within the framework of the PCA to elaborate the concept of the Common European Economic Space. The main task of the HLG was to discuss the core elements which needed to be put in place in order to create the CEES and to form the basis for an EU–Russia medium/long term cooperation strategy. A work plan for the activities of CEES until the end of 2003 was approved in May 2002. The plan covered areas of mutual interest and suggested practical steps to achieve regulatory convergence. Following a targeted approach, the HLG agreed to a list of key issues for work, which reflected the achievements and experience of integration in the EU with the creation of the Single Market.[8]

At the bilateral summit which took place in St Petersburg in May 2003, the EU and Russia included the CEES in a broader project, which entailed the creation of four Common Spaces. Beyond the economic space, there was to be a Common Space of Freedom, Security and Justice, a Common Space of External Security, and a Common Space of Research, Education and Culture. Not long after, at the summit in Rome in November 2003, the parties finally presented a concept paper on the CEES, which definitively concluded the work of the HLG. In this paper, the CEES was defined as 'an open and integrated market between the EU and Russia, based on the implementation of common or compatible rules and regulations, including compatible administrative practices, as a basis for synergies and economies of scale associated with a higher degree of competition in bigger markets' (Commission 2003c: 6). The concept paper established that the CEES will be created progressively and in stages with appropriate interim reviews;[9] it further established that the agreed objectives will be transformed into specific goals and actions by way of Action Plans, as well as addressing potential disagreements among the parties by creating a dispute settlement mechanism based on WTO rules. The Action Plans concerning the four Common Spaces were finally approved during the bilateral meeting which took place in Moscow in May 2005.

The gradual but incremental consolidation of bilateral contacts and the enhancement of a complex system of soft institutional design have provided the partners with an important tool for coordination which has proved critical in order to promote the partnership. This way of managing the relations between the two partners borrows some elements from the open method of coordination. The OMC, which was codified for the first time during the Portuguese Presidency in 2000, was originally applied in the area of employment and then extended to a wider array of other policy areas.[10] The main institutional ingredients of the OMC are common guidelines, national action plans, benchmarking, peer reviews, joint evaluation reports and recommendations (Ferrara *et al.* 2002). These are organised and reiterated over time within relatively structured processes that promote trust and cooperative orientation among participants on the one hand, and learning dynamics on the other. Thus, even in the absence of hard regulation and sanctions, the OMC creates several incentives for compliance and has a strong potential to influence partner states (*ibid.*).[11] The OMC has been applied not only to areas determined by the Portuguese Presidency, but several characteristic elements of the OMC have been used as a tool to manage the EU's relations with Russia and other neighbouring countries.

The institutionalisation of regular meetings between the authorities of the EU and the Russian Federation has provided a framework for discussion and confrontation, which has added new elements of convergence. This is an area where the insights of comparative politics and the new institutionalism explaining organisational behaviour can be combined. The broader argument is that density of interaction facilitates 'policy transfer' across different institutional contexts (Dolowitz and Marsh 2000). Frequent interactions in a dense 'organisational field' can set in motion processes of 'institutional isomorphism' (Di Maggio and Powell 1991) that can account for increasing similarities of regulatory practices (Radaelli 2000). Moreover, in case of expertise-based policy-making, such as the High Level Group within the CEES, professionalisation creates a shared frame of reference which facilitates convergence. National officials are driven by a 'reputation game' with their national counterparts, and they seek to comply with best-practice regulatory standards to maintain their good standing in the professional community (Majone 2000; Eberlein 2003).

Limits to the Europeanisation of Russia

This way of managing relations – to exert influence on partner countries by bargaining over conditions and rewards and also through the promotion of a patient strategy of persuasion – has been further elaborated in the ENP and applied to the relations with all the countries of the so-called 'new neighbourhood'. However, if the ENP is just an extension to other partners of the offer previously made to Russia, why has Russia – initially included in the new main policy instrument towards neighbours – decided not to be in the ENP?

There are two key notions – sovereignty and specialty – through which Russia defines itself, and that can demonstrate the limits of the approach thus far promoted by the EU, be it a logic of consequentialism or a logic of appropriateness. These notions underline the necessity to revise the Europeanisation 'toolkit' when dealing with a country that is not a potential EU member, nor likely to be absorbed into the European constellation in the short to medium term, yet still represents the 'other half' of Europe.

Pertaining to the logic of consequentialism, the notion of sovereignty has to be taken into account when assessing the cost–benefit balance of a state without a stake in EU institutions. Even if the process of legislative approximation is largely perceived as beneficial – from the point of view of the national authorities – the political costs and the economic benefits that are derived from a process of deep integration are barely comparable to one another and do not even pertain to the same scale of values. If we consider the rewards that have been offered by the EU, which are mainly economic, it is evident that any system of conditionality cannot really work. Moreover, if there is a widely accepted yet diffuse interest in promoting cooperation with the EU, there will be a problem with collective action connected to the notion of sovereignty. In fact, the national authorities who would negotiate the agreement are precisely those that must bear the most important cost derived from engagement in a process of deep integration, i.e. a loss of sovereignty.

The notion of specialty must be taken into account when evaluating the appropriateness of how the EU promotes cooperation – and ultimately, rule transfer – with the Russian Federation. Essentially, Russia defines itself as a 'special' European country. It considers it highly inappropriate that it is treated like all the other countries submitted to the same rules; even if its European-ness is fundamentally recognised, Russia has perceived unfair treatment by the EU when the presumed strategic partnership lacks real content. In this framework, the EU's practice is perceived by Russia as unacceptable and, ultimately, exclusionary. Russia has come to support the idea that there is a 'double Europe' and that it embodies an alternative interpretation of the meaning of being European. However, the progress of the dialogue on the creation of the four Common Spaces is a recognition of the fact that as long as Russia is recognised by the EU as an *equal partner* (i.e. equal to the EU, not individual states either in or, worse yet, outside the EU), Russia is ready to engage with the EU and eventually commit important resources to the development of the relationship. If the EU honestly intends to promote a process of integration on a continental scale, a reconsideration of its strategy accounting for these two notions seems particularly urgent. Having Russia participate in the EU's decisions about the future of the European continent is probably the key to overcoming these two main obstacles to Europeanisation of Russia. The possibility of Russia having a say in the 'concert of Europe' will allow, on the one hand, a justification for the partial loss of sovereignty (inasmuch as it would imply a political benefit to counter-balance the political costs connected with deep integration), and on the other, definitely imply the recognition of the special role of Russia on the European continent.

Conclusions

It is unlikely that Russia will ever enter the EU, and allowing Russian partici-pation in EU decision-making remains the main obstacle on the EU side for Russian membership in EU structures – the participation of such a powerful state would radically alter the voting balance in the Union. However, this country represents the 'other half' of Europe, with which the EU must come to terms if it intends to act on a continental scale.

There have been efforts to give content to a presumed strategic part-nership, but the latent disappointment of the Russian side with the effective progress of the relationship elucidates much room for improvement and demonstrates that bilateral relations have yet to be definitively settled. In this chapter, Russia has been revealed as a special case that directly points out the limits of the tools used to conceptualise those processes of policy export which have been thus far promoted by the EU. I have especially emphasised the notions of sovereignty (to be taken into consideration when assessing the interest of Russia in engaging a process of deep integration) and specialty (to be borne in mind when evaluating the appropriateness of the way in which the EU is promoting cooperation with the Russian Federation). Russia requires political compensation to counterbalance the political costs connected to the adoption of a set of laws to which it has not contributed, as well as a recognition of its specialty as the 'other half' of Europe.

For the Russian Federation, the real issue at stake in its relations with the EU is not participation in the EU 'kitchen', but its involvement in EU deci-sion-making *vis-à-vis* the common neighbourhood. In this framework, and concerning the development of a pole of regional integration in the CIS area, devising a more coordinated approach between the EU and Russia is likely to be the test case for a relationship between the two main European neighbours and the key for establishing a real 'strategic partnership' (Meloni *et al.* 2005).

The ENP has not been satisfactory for understanding EU plans for development of its relations with Eastern European countries, while ignoring Russia's enduring role in these regions. The endorsement of a consistent regional approach has been repeatedly indicated as a relevant instrument able to promote the creation of an area of stability and prosperity in the European Union's neighbourhood. Within the 'Wider Europe' initiative of 2003, the Commission stated that 'the EU must act to promote the regional and sub-regional cooperation and integration' (Commission 2003a: 3). More specifically, it acknowledged that 'new initiatives to encourage regional cooperation between Russia and the countries of the Western New Independent States might [be] considered' (*ibid.*: 8). Nonetheless, nothing relevant has been done in this direction.

The re-launch of a dimension of regional integration in the CIS area could allow the EU to engage Russia in a far-reaching dialogue and to give content to the strategic partnership. In this context, regionalism can emerge as an inclusive policy instrument with which to tackle the challenges of the EU's diverse neighbourhood through the promotion of a 'win–win' strategy. On one side, Russia needs the EU in order to ensure partner countries against 'old imperial temptations', while on the other side, the EU needs Russia for its knowledge of the CIS states. Taken together, understanding these needs will allow for more effective stability and prosperity for the entire European continent, a viable prospectus provided that the partners build a relationship of mutual confidence and understanding. Unfortunately, that has not often been the case.

Whether the EU is able to honestly promote such a strategy or whether the Russian Federation is willing to engage in such a process remains to be seen. However, if the partners fail to improve their relations, giving impetus to the agreements already achieved, then bilateral relations – even if still characterised by the post-modern lexicon of dialogue and socialisation – will risk being permeated by (modernist) confrontation. In this framework, Europeanisation will continue to be perceived in Russia as having a subtle quasi-imperial logic, a perspective that EU authorities often fail to understand. The more the EU expands, the more it is evident that Europeanisation means essentially 'EU-isation'. The confrontation with the 'other half' of Europe should induce an agreement on the future governance of the European continent and a reconsideration of the process of Europeanisation. Ultimately, Kaliningrad can still become a real bridge between the two halves of Europe, rather than a space of confrontation as it has been in the past.

Notes

1   Rosecrance argues that 'in the past (again with the Roman exception) a potential aggressor could always be opposed by 60–75 per cent of world power if the other countries united against him. In the future, however, this may no longer be the case. Under these novel conditions, even political and military power might begin to attract, rather than to repel the others [...] In this way, centralised economic power could have the long term effect of creating centralised political power. And the centre would be Europe, a new type of international actor' (Rosecrance 1998: 19).

2   Schematically, from the loosest to the most demanding, the four steps of integration are: a Free Trade Area (FTA); a Customs Union; a Common Market; and an Economic and (eventually) Monetary Union (Tinbergen 1954).

3   The engagement in a far-reaching process of legislative approximation implies not only a political choice, but also important political costs. As Russia has not contributed to the *acquis*, the adoption of its rules and eventual compliance to changes in EU legislation without input would automatically imply a partial loss of sovereignty on the Russian side (Meloni 2007a).

4   Here, I use the definition of Europeanisation proposed by Héritier; 'a process of influence deriving from European decisions and impacting [...] states' policies and political and administrative structures' which may extend from 'a subtle and incremental re-orientation of national policy-making to substantial changes where European policies *crowd out* their national counterparts and modify patterns of political and administrative behaviour' (Héritier 2001).

5   According to the conditionality model, the EU sets its rules as conditions that the recipients have to fulfil in order to receive rewards. By contrast, the lesson-drawing model relies on a voluntary transfer based on a cost–benefit calculation which, by definition, doesn't include direct rewards from the EU, but instead involves benefits that are expected from the adoption of a set of rules considered to be more efficient. The social- and model-learning schemes assume that actors are motivated by internalised, socially constructed identities, values and norms (March and Olsen 1989). The crucial difference between the latter two is that while social-learning assumes that recipients are prone to adopt a rule because they are convinced it is more appropriate to them as it is part of the bulk of the EU's values and norms, model-learning depends more on the perceived legitimacy of the proposed legislation *per se* (Schimmelfennig and Sedelmeier 2002).

6   Rewards might not just be economic; they may range from the promise of technical assistance to the offer of institutional ties.

7   To date, the Permanent Partnership Councils have encompassed the level of Foreign Ministers, Justice and Home Affairs Ministers and Energy Ministers. At the level of senior officials and experts, the exchange within the framework of the Cooperation Committee was supported by a network of sub-committees dealing with technical issues.

8   The work plan identified two stages. In a first stage (until the end of 2002), the EU and Russia had to consider the ultimate objectives of the CEES and, in parallel, prepare the ground to achieve legislative and regulatory convergence, as well as measures to facilitate trade and investment. In a second stage (until October 2003), the HLG had to consider other measures to implement the terms of reference, identify means to achieve common objectives, and propose a time-scale for implementation.

9   The CEES concept has focused on the need to eliminate obstacles and create opportunities in four main areas: cross-border trade of goods; cross-border trade in services; establishment and operation of companies; and movement of persons in relevant fields of economic activity. It covers both horizontal and sectoral targets. A

number of areas for action have been considered for action: standardisation; technical regulation and conformity assessment; customs; audit and accounting; public procurement; competition; financial services; telecommunications; cooperation in space launching; and several branches of industry and agriculture.

10 This new approach was deemed useful for several fields, notably the information society, research and development, enterprise, economic reforms, education, employment and social inclusion (Council 2000).

11 In contrast to the traditional Community method, this approach has been defined as 'soft' and 'national state friendly' (Ferrara *et al.* 2002). It has been indicated as a tool to enhance policy integration, expand policy activities beyond legally limited spheres and speed up European decision-making (Héritier 2003).

References

Börzel, T. A. and T. Risse (2000), *When Europe Hits Home: Europeanisation and Domestic Change*, EIOP online papers, available on the Internet at www.eiop.or.at /eiop/texte/2000–015a.htm (accessed 27 April 2006).

Brittan, L. (1995), 'How to make trade liberalisation popular', *The World Economy*, 18(6): 761–7.

Checkel, J. T. (2000), 'Compliance and Conditionality', ARENA Working Papers 00/18, Oslo.

Commission (2003a), 'Wider Europe Neighbourhood. A New Framework for Relations with our Eastern and Southern Neighbours', Brussels, COM 104 final, available on the Internet at www.europa.eu.int/comm/world/enp/pdf/com03_104_en.pdf (accessed 27 April 2006).

Commission (2003b), 'Paving the Way for a new Neighbourhood Instrument', Brussels, COM 393 final, available on the Internet at www.europa.eu.int/comm /world/enp/pdf/com03_393_en.pdf (accessed 27 April 2006).

Commission (2003c), 'Annex I: The Common European Economic Space (CEES)', *Concept Paper* 13990/03 (Presse 313) 5, Brussels, available on the Internet at http://ec.europa.eu/external_relations/russia/summit11_03/1concl.pdf (accessed 12 December 2007).

Commission (2006), 'Communication from the Commission to the Council and the European Parliament on Strengthening the European Neighbourhood Policy', Brussels, COM 726 final.

Council (2000), 'The On-going Experience of the Open Method of Coordination', Presidency Note No. 9088/00, 13 June.

De Spiegelaire, S. (2001), 'The Implementation of the EU's Common Strategy on Russia', in *The EU Common Strategy on Russia*, Programme on the Northern Dimension of the CFSP no. 11, Helsinki and Berlin, The Finnish Institute of International Affairs and The Institute for European Politics.

Di Maggio, P. and W. W. Powell (1991), 'The Iron Cage Revisited: Institutional Isomorphism and Collective Rationality in Organisational Fields', in *The New Institutionalism in Organisational Analysis*, ed. P. Di Maggio and W. W. Powell, Chicago, University of Chicago Press: 63–82.

Dolowitz, D. P. and D. Marsh (2000), 'Learning from Abroad: the Role in Policy Transfer in Contemporary Policy-making', *Governance*, 13(1): 5–24.

Eberlein, B. (2003), 'Formal and Informal Governance in Single Market Regulation', in *Informal Governance in the European Union*, ed. T. Christiansen and S. Piattoni, Cheltenham, Edwar Elgar: 150–72.

Ferrara, M., M. Matsaganis and S. Sacchi (2002), 'Open Method of Coordination against

Poverty: The New EU "Social Inclusion Process"', *Journal of European Social Policy*, 12(3): 227–39.

Hall, P. and R. Taylor (1996), 'Political Science and the Three New Institutionalisms', *Political Science*, 44(5): 936–57.

Haukkala, H. and S. Medvedev (2001), *The EU Common Strategy on Russia*, Programme on the Northern Dimension of the CFSP 11, Helsinki and Berlin, The Finnish Institute of International Affairs and The Institute for European Politics.

Héritier, A. (2001), 'Differential Europe: National Administrative Responses to Community Policies', in *Europeanisation and Domestic Change*, ed. J. Caporaso, M. Green Cowles and T. Risse, Ithaca, Cornell University Press: 44–59.

Héritier, A. (2003), 'New Modes of Governance in Europe: Increasing Political Efficiency and Policy Effectiveness', in *State Of the European Union* 6, ed. T. Börzel and R. Cichowski, Oxford, Oxford University Press: 105–27.

Lawrence, R. Z. (1996), *Regionalism, Multilateralism and Deeper Integration*, Washington DC, Brookings Institution.

Majone, G. (2000), 'The Credibility Crisis of Community Regulation', *Journal of Common Market Studies*, 38(2): 273–302.

March, J. G. and J. P. Olsen (1989), *Rediscovering Institutions: The Organizational Basis of Politics*, New York, Free Press.

Meloni, G. (2007a), 'Is the Same Toolkit used During Enlargement Still Applicable to the Countries of the New Neighbourhood? A Problem of Mismatching between Objectives and Instruments', in *The European Neighbourhood Policy: a Framework for Modernisation?*, ed. M. Cremona and G. Meloni, EUI Working Paper, available on the Internet at http://cadmus.iue.it/dspace/bitstream/1814/6976/1/LAW-2007-21.pdf (accessed 4 May 2008).

Meloni, G. (2007b), 'Who's my Neighbour?', *European Political Economy Review*, 7 (Summer), available on the Internet at www.ugbs.org/weru/eper/no7/meloni.pdf (accessed 4 May 2008).

Meloni, G., A. Shirov and O. Durand-Lasserve (2005), *Benchmarking the Russian Trade Performance and Competitiveness*, Moscow, Russian European Centre for Economic Policy (RECEP).

Partnership and Cooperation Agreement (PCA 1997), available on the Internet at http://ec.europa.eu/external_relations/ceeca/pca/pca_russia.pdf (accessed 4 May 2008).

Pomfret, R. (1997), *The Economics of Regional Trading Arrangements*, New York, Oxford University Press.

Radaelli C. M. (2000), 'Policy Transfer in the European Union: Institutional Isomorphism as a Source of Legitimacy', *Governance*, 13(1): 757–74.

Rosecrance, R. (1998), 'The European Union: a New Type of International Actor', in *Paradoxes of European Foreign Policy*, ed. J. Zielonka, UK, Kluwer Law International: 15–23.

Scharpf, F. W. (1997), *Balancing Positive and Negative Integration: the Regulatory Options for Europe*, Robert Schuman Centre Policy Papers 97(4), Florence, European University Institute.

Scharpf, F. W. (1999), *Governing in Europe: Effective and Democratic?*, Oxford, Oxford University Press.

Schimmelfennig, F. and U. Sedelmeier (2002), 'The Europeanisation of Eastern Europe: Evaluating the Conditionality Model', Paper for the ECPR workshop on 'European Governance and Enlargement', Turin.

Tinbergen, J. (1954), *International Economic Integration*, Amsterdam, Elsevier.

Vink, M. (2004), 'What is Europeanisation? And Other Questions on a New Research Agenda', *European Political Science*, 1:63–74.

Helmut Hubel

Postscript: Coping with Stalin's legacy and Putin's autocracy – Kaliningrad between post-Soviet Russia and the European Union

Immediately after the Second World War, Soviet leader Joseph Stalin enforced his plan to enlarge Soviet territory by pushing Poland's eastern border westward and compensating Poland for its losses with German territories up to the rivers of Oder and (the western) Neisse. In his calculation these major territorial changes, causing mass migration of millions of Poles and Germans, would guarantee future German–Polish hostility and preserve for the Soviet Union a powerful arbiter's role in Central Europe. It was also Stalin's decision to keep the territory around Königsberg, providing an ice-free strategic outpost for the Soviet military in the Baltic Sea and creating a kind of Soviet western barrier to the newly annexed Baltic States. According to Soviet practices, the oblast was given the name of a leading member of the Bolshevist Party and then President of the USSR.

The European Union, which in May 2004 extended its eastern frontier up to the western borders of the Russian Federation, Belarus and Ukraine, is now faced with the paradoxical situation of a post-Soviet island surrounded by EU territory and confronted with the EU's specific political-economic system, norms and practices. While there has been for centuries a 'European question' for Russia (the debate about her identity and 'proper place in Europe'), the European integration system has recreated and aggravated this problem: how to reconcile today's 'EU-ropean' values and system of governance with (post-Soviet) Russian political traditions and practices?

The EU represents a unique enterprise of constructing a lasting 'peace system' among the European nations, by establishing a new – partly integrated and partly intergovernmental – system of governance. While the integrated elements initially reflect economic rationality, the intergovernmental ones demonstrate the reality that it is still the states which seek to control the process of integration, and that some EU members are determined to preserve at least certain important elements of state sovereignty. These factors have resulted in a highly complex structure, a multi-level decision-making process and ongoing tensions between integrative initiatives and state-centred responses (by at least some members). Primarily because of its evident economic achievements, the Union has attracted many newcomers. Particularly for the new Central and Eastern European member states, the EU promises to increase standards of living and thus to stabilise the sometimes still precarious democratic transformation process.

Kaliningrad confronts both Russia and the EU with Stalin's legacy. During the early 1990s, when Russian political representatives, such as President Yeltsin and his Foreign Minister Andrei Kozyrev, spoke of their desire to incorporate 'Western values' or even to make Russia 'part of the West', there seemed to be good prospects for dealing with the Kaliningrad issue in a truly cooperative or even partly integrative way. Indeed, the EU's aid programmes (like TACIS), and later its neighbourhood policies, offered various possibilities and resources to implement 'a strategic partnership' with the Russian Federation.

Particularly for the enclave of Kaliningrad, such a cooperative approach would have indeed served to deal with many problems left by the Soviet legacy. This concerns not only the issue of transit rights for Kaliningraders to the Russian mainland, but other problems discussed in this book. Despite impressive economic growth over the past years, the region may not be in a position to catch up with adjacent regions in Lithuania and Poland. In a nutshell, and with only a few exceptions, Kaliningrad is forced to integrate much more with mainland Russia than investing in opportunities that might have flowed from its status as a 'pilot region' in EU–Russia relations – as suggested in Russia's 1999 Mid-term Strategy on the European Union.

After eight years of President Putin's rule, this perspective seems to be no longer valid. The difficulties in expanding the Partnership and Cooperation Agreement to embrace the new EU member states are but one proof of that. Although some new EU member states, notably Poland and Lithuania, may have complicated the relationship by pursuing nationalistic rhetoric, the key for the deteriorated situation is clearly Moscow. Determined to restore Russian central power and state control, the successor of President Yeltsin not only abolished the freedom of the press in his country, but also took away most of the newly gained rights and privileges of the Russian regions, including Kaliningrad. Capitalising on Russia's increased and further increasing oil and gas revenues, President Putin and his entourage of *siloviki* in the Kremlin (particularly the representatives of the Secret Service from Putin's St Petersburg years) embarked on a course of re-establishing 'great power' status internationally and an authoritarian system domestically, camouflaged by so-called 'free' elections. It seems that the most important reason for this course of action was the 'Orange Revolution' in Ukraine, toppling a Kremlin-supported government after election fraud. Obviously, the leadership in Moscow interpreted this as a potentially dangerous precedent for Russia, and it hurried to ban 'foreign interference' by bringing NGOs and other independent institutions under its control. Thereby, the Kremlin managed to suffocate the (rather modest) initiatives towards creating a civil society in Russia and re-consolidated state control over all relevant spheres of society.

These domestic changes are reflected in Russian foreign policy. This was a response particularly to NATO's eastern enlargement, which – despite all changes within NATO and the newly established NATO–Russia Cooperative Council – was interpreted as a threat to Russia. President Putin resumed Czarist and Soviet practices: Russia should rather be feared than associated with foreign institutions, not to speak of the EU's values and system of governance. This is exemplified by the recent 'cyber-war' between Estonia and Russia and other cases of Russian political pressure against the Baltic States, demonstrating the aspirations in Moscow towards re-establishing Russia's 'empire'. Another case would be the Russian–Polish disputes, which are simply not about Polish meat or the consequence of nationalist-minded politicians in Warsaw, but rather the consequence of hardened Russian attitudes.

Given these realities, it is no surprise that the contributors to this book, most of them political scientists having worked on either the European Union or the EU–Russia relationship, could not find much evidence of Europeanisation, i.e. effects of the European integration system on Kaliningrad. This is all the more deplorable, since several contributions clearly demonstrate the miserable situation of the enclave's population, particularly the poor health conditions and the economic-social difficulties. The EU's multi-level system of governance, allowing both for integrated efforts and individual or joint national initiatives, could have indeed improved the situation. As demonstrated by the enclave's inclusion in the system of Euro-Faculties and by the considerable investment in terms of finances and personnel, there was (and indeed still is) much good will and initiative on the side of its European neighbours and the EU as a whole. It seems that the major reason for the lack of progress lies in the inability or unwillingness of many Russian partners to deal with their EU counterparts in a productive way. In addition, the re-centralisation of Russian power contributed to stifling most of the initiatives that had remained on the Kaliningrad side. Obviously, with the recurrence of geopolitical thinking and practices in Moscow, this Russian exclave was just too sensitive and important to allow it to succumb to any Western or EU influence.

The proponents of Europeanisation argue that the principles and practices of the Union not only deeply affect and transform the member states, but also its environment. This is indeed the case when the Union can use the instrument of conditionality, i.e. the promise of rewards in return of certain behaviour. In the case of Turkey, seeking full membership in the Union, the effects of the EU's conditionality can be clearly demonstrated (although it is still not clear whether Turkey, despite all adaptations, is capable of meeting the EU's standards concerning human and minority rights, etc.). In the case of Russia, EU membership is out of question, given its size, history, its renewed and widely shared ambition to remain an independent great power and its newly earned energy revenues. Consequently, the EU's capacity to offer rewards has remained very limited.

By dealing with neighbours in its specific multi-level way, the EU indeed projects its values and principles on them. Yet in order to really affect changes, these impulses need recipients and certain 'open' structures. In the case of Putin's Russia, Moscow's re-centralised political will has clearly been used to restrain foreign 'interference', particularly from the EU and its member countries. In this contest between (Russian) geopolitical thinking and (the EU's) soft power, Kaliningrad could not win.

This experience recalls Ernst B. Haas and his expectation in 1958 that a neo-functionalist 'logic of integration' would, 'by necessity' lead to European unification. Later, in the 1960s, Haas had to admit that this logic was not capable of overcoming the political will of certain member states. Indeed, because of this reality the European Union has remained a hybrid system with various opt-ins and opt-outs, rather a semi-confederation than a real union. Being aware of the tensions within the EU, namely between Brussels (i.e. EU institutions) and the most important member states (ruled by Paris, London and Berlin), Putin's Russia repeatedly used bilateral approaches to overcome the EU's multilateralism. Russia's energy policy is just one example, as demonstrated by the project of the Baltic gas pipeline – linking Russia and Germany, bypassing the Baltic States and Poland, and neglecting the EU which lacks a joint energy policy. Thus, when 'high politics' are concerned, it seems that a rather powerful actor like Russia is capable of circumventing EU mechanisms. But even when 'low politics' (like environmental, health and education problems) are concerned, post-Soviet Russia seems to be a special case – as the case studies of this volume demonstrate; the Russian *raison d'état* is overwhelmingly more important than any individual rights for its citizens.

In conclusion, it seems that the EU, in order to project its values and practices, needs distinct conditions – a given partner must demonstrate a genuine interest in cooperation, a receptive political culture and at least basic elements of a civil society. After the chaotic but rather free years of the Yeltsin era, Putin's rule has closed this prospect for Russia for the foreseeable future. The EU's problem of how to deal with this difficult partner is also a problem for NATO and any Western country. The case of Kaliningrad reminds the EU and its member states of their own weaknesses and shortcomings.

Index

Arctic Council (AC) 147, 149–50
Association of International Road
    Carriers (ASMAP) 171

Baltic Sea Parliamentary Conference
    (BSPC) 150
Baltic Sea States Sub-regional Co-
    operation (BSSSC) 150, 159
Barents Euro-Arctic Council (BEAC)
    147, 149–50
Belarus 54, 116, 156, 269,

civil society 3, 5, 71, 75, 78, 100, 125,
    137, 142, 149, 187, 191, 200–3,
    271, 272
    see also Russia
Common European Economic Space
    (CEES) 258, 261–2
Common Spaces 10, 12, 65, 149, 201,
    239, 245, 252, 261–2, 264
    Common Space of Freedom,
        Security and Justice (CSFSJ)
        237–9, 244
    Common Space of Research,
        Education and Culture 43, 224,
        227
Common Strategy of the EU on Russia
    223, 261
Commonwealth of Independent States
    (CIS) 96, 99, 176, 265

constructivism 260
Council of the Baltic Sea States
    (CBSS) 9, 12, 147, 149–61, 230
cross-border cooperation (cbc) 90, 95,
    97–9, 120, 132–42, 148, 156,
    159, 170, 241–4, 251–4

Danish International Development
    Agency (DANIDA) *see*
    Denmark
Denmark 9, 12, 64, 156, 178, 189, 202,
    224
    Danish International Development
        Agency (DANIDA) 189

Estonia 9, 98, 127, 148, 156, 230, 271
European Bank for Reconstruction
    and Development (EBRD)
    78–9, 202
European Neighbourhood Policy
    (ENP) 32, 74–5, 135, 137, 238,
    244, 255–6, 260–1, 263, 265
European Union (EU)
    Commission 7–9, 36, 42, 68, 70–1,
        73–5, 77–8, 138, 151, 155, 157,
        159–61, 209, 215–16, 224, 230,
        244, 255, 265
    Council 8, 10, 78, 148, 209, 232, 257
    Council of Ministers 36
    enlargement 6–8, 10, 11–12, 19, 31,

52, 65, 72, 78, 80, 89, 94–5,
   109, 114, 119, 134, 152, 154,
   157, 176–8, 209, 236–7, 243,
   249–51, 255, 259–60
open method of coordination
   (OMC) 21, 41–2, 232, 256,
   262
Parliament 7, 36, 260
PHARE 132, 134–6, 138–9, 217
relations with Russia 6, 21, 64–6,
   68–9, 79–80, 93–6, 243–4
   High Level Group (HLG) 261–2
   Medium-term strategy of Russia
      towards the EU 96–7, 270
   'pilot region' 1–3, 10, 18, 97,
      114–15, 177, 180, 205, 244,
      249, 252–3, 270
   PPC / Permanent Partnership
      Council 238, 261
   see also Common European
      Economic Space (CEES)
   see also Common Spaces
   see also Common Strategy of the
      EU on Russia
   see also Partnership and
      Cooperation Agreement EU-
      Russia (PCA)
Schengen 80, 94, 138, 142, 227,
   243–4
TACIS 7–8, 12, 77–8, 79, 100, 132,
   134, 136, 138–9, 155, 177–8,
   189–91, 201–2, 212, 214, 216,
   223–4, 226, 238, 270
Tempus 77, 222–4, 226, 238
treaties 216, 223
   see also European Neighbourhood
      Policy (ENP)
   see also Northern Dimension (ND)
Europeanisation 2, 11, 13, 14–19, 31,
   44, 250, 254, 258–60
Euro-region 15, 97, 124, 132, 135, 142,
   242
   Baltic Euro-regional Network
      (BEN) 156, 159, 161
   see also transit

Finland 9, 93, 95, 148, 153
France 60, 216, 224
Free Economic Zone (FEZ) see
   Kaliningrad economy
FRONTEX / European Border Agency
   238
functionalism 73, 79

Germany 9, 11, 35, 60, 64, 116, 117,
   177–8, 183, 187, 202, 211, 216,
   224, 229, 230, 272
governance (as conceptual approach)
   10, 16–17, 20, 32–3, 37–45,
   69–72, 76–7, 148, 150, 203–5

identity 2, 11, 13, 20, 100, 112,
   124–30, 269
incentive structure 16, 103, 204, 251
institutionalism (new) 16, 258, 262

Kaliningrad
   administration (regional) 112–20,
      141–2, 171, 176–8, 187–90,
      198, 199–200, 218, 225, 229,
      238, 242
   Duma (regional) 4, 102, 118, 156,
      171, 189, 190
   economy 6, 64, 113, 117, 119,
      170–2, 177–81
      Free Economic Zone (FEZ) 100,
         112–13
      Special Economic Zone (SEZ)
         6–7, 64–5, 112–15, 117,
         119–20, 169–81, 242

Latvia 8–9, 54, 98, 127, 148, 156, 230
Lithuania 1, 3, 8, 9, 10, 12, 19, 20, 21,
   43, 51, 54–5, 64–5, 77, 116,
   117, 127, 132–42, 148, 152,
   156, 169, 176, 177–9, 183, 195,
   205, 210–19, 222, 224, 230,
   238, 240, 241, 243–4, 270

multi-level governance (MLG) 89,
   92–5, 102–3, 198, 203, 271

non-governmental organisation
(NGO) 5, 12, 16, 118, 133,
136–7, 140, 154, 160, 187,
190–2, 199–200, 202–4, 215,
241, 252–3, 271
Nordic Council (NC) 15, 147, 150–1,
153–6, 158–61
Nordic Council of Ministers (NCM)
147, 149–51, 153–61
Nordic Investment Bank (NIB) 202
North American Free Trade
Agreement (NAFTA) 55
North Atlantic Treaty Organisation
(NATO) 3, 8, 71, 75, 134–5,
157, 271–2
Northern Dimension (ND) 9, 15, 71,
72, 75, 77–9, 147–61
Nida Initiative 77, 135
Northern Dimension Action Plan
(NDAP) 75, 78–9, 147–9, 151,
155, 157–8
Northern Dimension
Environmental Partnership
(NDEP) 78–9, 161
Northern Dimension Information
System (NDIS) 159–60
Northern Dimension Partnership in
Public Health and Social Well-
Being (NDPHS) 218
Northern Dimension Policy
Framework Document 149
Norway 72, 74, 78, 148–9, 205, 211

open method of coordination (OMC)
see European Union
Organisation for Economic
Cooperation and Development
(OECD) 40

Partnership and Cooperation
Agreement EU-Russia (PCA)
10, 21, 43, 74, 78, 201, 223,
256, 260–1
path dependency 20, 74, 232
PHARE *see* European Union
Poland 1, 3, 9, 12, 19–21, 36, 51, 54,

64, 89, 93, 109, 116–17, 127,
132–42, 148, 152, 156, 176–9,
183, 195, 205, 210, 211–19,
222, 229–30, 236, 238, 240,
243–4, 254, 256, 269–70, 272
political opportunity structure 204,
258
post-communism 3, 12, 15, 32, 204,
249
see also transition / transformation

realism 76, 80, 96
regionalism / regionalisation 95, 108,
110, 120, 124–6, 228, 265
Russia
civil society 3, 5, 100, 137, 187, 191,
200–3, 271, 272
Duma 91–2, 99, 101, 114, 189
Federal Target Programme (FTP)
64–6, 113–14, 171, 172, 175–7,
179, 180
federalism 18, 89, 91, 93, 108–20,
139, 185–6, 195, 198
foreign policy 96, 108–9, 223, 271
towards Central and Eastern
Europe 141–2, 271
towards the EU 75–6, 227
see also European Union
relations with Russia
party system 3–5, 199
President 3–5, 10, 90–2, 95–6, 98,
102–3, 109–16, 119–20, 139,
171, 173, 188, 198, 269–71
see also Kaliningrad
Russian Federation (RF) *see* Russia
Russian Soviet Federative Socialist
Republic (RSFSR) 133

Schengen *see* European Union
securitisation 19–20, 68–80
separatism 57, 80, 100–1, 110, 112,
129
soft power 70, 91, 102, 272
sovereignty 56–7, 76, 90, 93, 96, 102,
108–9, 141, 253, 256, 263–4,
270

Soviet Union 1–3, 52, 108–9, 126–30,
        133, 148, 169, 172, 196, 204,
        210, 214, 222, 228, 236, 240,
        269
Special Economic Zone (SEZ) *see*
        Kaliningrad economy
Sweden 9, 12, 64, 148, 153, 156,
        177–8, 187, 189, 202, 211, 224,
        242
    Swedish International Development
        Cooperation Agency (SIDA)
        189
Swedish International Development
        Cooperation Agency (SIDA)
        see Sweden

TACIS *see* European Union
Tempus *see* European Union
transit 6, 8–9, 43, 53, 55, 58–9, 63,
        64–5, 80, 114, 119, 142, 169,

        177, 191, 242–4, 270
FRTD / Facilitated Railway Transit
        Document 9, 243
FTD / Facilitated Transit Document
        9, 243
transition / transformation process 3,
        5, 11, 13, 17, 169, 172, 195,
        197, 204, 251–4

Union of Soviet Socialist Republics
        (USSR), *see* Soviet Union
United States / United States of
        America (US / USA) 60, 96,
        180, 187

World Health Organization (WHO)
        211, 213
World Trade Organization (WTO)
        6–7, 52, 54, 173, 177, 180, 262